Purchasing Power

JEWISH CULTURE AND CONTEXTS

Published in association with the Herbert D. Katz Center for Advanced Judaic Studies of the University of Pennsylvania

David B. Ruderman and Steven Weitzman, Series Editors

Purchasing Power

The Economics of Modern Jewish History

Edited by

Rebecca Kobrin and Adam Teller

PENN

UNIVERSITY OF PENNSYLVANIA PRESS

PHILADELPHIA

Publication of this volume was assisted by a grant from the Martin D. Gruss Endowment Fund of the Herbert D. Katz Center for Advanced Judaic Studies of the University of Pennsylvania.

Published by
University of Pennsylvania Press
Philadelphia, Pennsylvania 19104-4112
www.upenn.edu/pennpress

Printed in the United States of America
on acid-free paper

10 9 8 7 6 5 4 3 2 1

Library of Congress Cataloging-in-Publication Data
Purchasing power (2015)
Purchasing power : the economics of modern Jewish history / edited by Rebecca Kobrin and Adam Teller.
pages cm. — (Jewish culture and contexts)
Includes bibliographical references and index.
ISBN 978-0-8122-4730-5 (alk. paper)
1. Jewish merchants—History. 2. Jews—Economic conditions—History. 3. Jewish capitalists and financiers—History. 4. Jewish businesspeople—History. 5. Jews—Commerce—History. 6. Jews in public life—History. 7. Jewish philanthropists—History. I. Kobrin, Rebecca, editor. II. Teller, Adam, editor. III. Title. IV. Series: Jewish culture and contexts.
DS140.5.P87 2015
330.089'924—dc23

2015006401

Contents

Purchasing Power

Introduction

Purchasing Power: The Economics of Modern Jewish History

Rebecca Kobrin and Adam Teller

It is perhaps no coincidence in our current age of global capitalism, when many comment upon the power of the economy and economic institutions to shape the world, that we are considering anew the larger role of the economy in Jewish history as well as the place of Jews in economic history.[1] In recent decades, the social, and then the cultural, turn in historical research pushed questions concerning Jews' economic activity to the sidelines. This does not mean, however, that economic issues themselves were in any sense marginal in the Jewish historical experience. They most certainly were not. Nor could they have been, since Jews, like all other individuals and groups in human society, had to engage with the economy in one way or another in order to survive.

This last statement, banal as it may be on a superficial level, is important because it points to many of the key questions in Jewish economic history as it is beginning to be understood and practiced today. What was the significance of being Jewish in determining the forms of economic activity undertaken by Jews in different times and places? What were the relative weights of individual and group factors in that process? When did Jewishness abet the formation of commercial alliances and when did it aid in such processes? What might be meant by the use of the term "survival" from an economic lens? Is it to be taken to refer simply to the basic physical needs of Jewish individuals being met, or should it be understood as creating the conditions for the continued existence (and even flourishing) of Jewish society and culture in the often inhospitable conditions of diaspora? Finally, what did "engaging with the economy" mean for Jews and Jewish societies? Did it mean finding a place in an existing economic system, and so being shaped by economic conditions? Perhaps it also meant the ways in which Jews shaped the economy to their own needs and in doing so contributed to processes of economic development and change.

In its engagement with these questions, this volume repositions economics in our understanding of the modern Jewish experience. Historians of the Jews have tirelessly devoted themselves to unraveling the distinctive religious, ideological, cultural, and political threads that came together in modern Jewish life. But in so doing, they have neglected other crucial topics—most notably, the economic circumstances that formed the context for (and even, some would argue, underpinned) this wealth of intellectual, cultural, and political development. As a result, we have yet to see clearly how Jews' economic choices and practices—both real and imagined—shaped not only their place in the global economy but also their historical development as a distinctive group.

To address this shortcoming, the essays collected here highlight the ways in which Jews wielded economic agency, while acknowledging that their independence was limited by the fact that they were continually responding to local conditions—political, social, and economic.[2] Illustrating the ways Jews responded to the different economic circumstances in which they found themselves, this volume also begins the pressing task of bringing our understanding of the economic history of the Jews into line with the subtle but significant rewriting of the history of the global economy that has been ongoing since the 1980s—a rewriting virtually absent from the broader reconsideration of modern Jewish life penned in the same decades.

A central issue connecting all the studies of Jewish economic life in this volume is that of power. At its core, each contribution assesses various aspects of how power relations informed, dovetailed with, and shaped Jews' economic activities in the modern world as well as the ways these activities were perceived. As outsiders in most of the places where they lived in the diaspora, Jews not only found a foothold in society, but frequently went on to strengthen their position by providing key economic services to their neighbors. The Jews' success in identifying economic opportunity and then exploiting it was often the outcome of power struggles either between them and their neighbors or simply within non-Jewish society. Beyond this, wherever possible, their economic activities served as a means for amassing power and influence in the non-Jewish world. This, of course, ran in parallel with the ways in which Jewish economic elites used their financial resources to buttress their position within their own societies. Thus, surfacing vividly throughout the coming pages is the theme of how Jews have amassed, contested, and deployed power through economic means over the last half millennium.

A larger question also hovers over all the discussions as a result of this volume's temporal focus on modernity, which, in the coming pages, is defined as beginning in the early sixteenth century. The question concerns the relationship of the Jews' economic activity to the rise of capitalism. At the turn of the twentieth century, and then again at the turn of the twenty-first, as sociologists, historians, and economic theorists came to the conclusion that Jews benefited particularly from the workings of the capitalist economy, they began to make inquiries as to Jews' role in this historical phenomenon. At issue was not just whether Jews were instrumental in bringing this new economic system into being, but whether there was, as Jonathan Karp has put it pithily, "something characteristically *Jewish* about modern economic life?"[3] Various answers were proposed. Thus, late nineteenth-century scholars tended to argue for an inherent propensity—religious, cultural, or even racial—on the part of Jews for capitalist activity. Late twentieth-century scholars seem to have preferred to focus more on conjunctural factors in developing explanations: Jews were well placed to benefit from the capitalist economy because their historical circumstances had shaped them into a diaspora trading network, a middleman minority group, or an upwardly mobile immigrant society.

In the earlier period, these discussions took a rather radical turn. Under the influence of Karl Marx's 1843 essay *On the Jewish Question*, the German sociologist Werner Sombart published a volume arguing that Jews did not just benefit from capitalism, but were actually responsible for its development.[4] Marx's essay, which ostensibly discussed the issue of Jewish emancipation, had posited that the spirit of Judaism and the spirit of capitalism were essentially one and the same. This led him to argue that what was needed was not the emancipation of the Jews in European society, but the emancipation of European society from Judaism, by which he meant capitalism itself. Sombart recast Marx's somewhat Hegelian argument in the sociological discourse of his day, using both quantitative and qualitative data to show that the capitalist system and approach to economic activity had developed out of Jewish society and that it was the Jews who had introduced it to Europe. In a quite remarkable way, then, Sombart attributed to the Jews and their economic activity the power to reshape the European economy in their own likeness.

The debate over Sombart's theory, his polemic with Max Weber, his later connections with the Nazi Party, and the different Jewish responses to his work have all been extensively discussed in recent scholarly literature, so there is no need to rehearse them here.[5] It is probably sufficient to state that the essentialist underpinnings of his argument—that the key to understanding Jewish economic activity is to be found in some inherent aspect of their religion, culture, or even racial background—are now deeply out of fashion. The chapters in this collection, with one notable exception that looks directly at Sombart, seem, almost consciously, to steer clear of both essentialist explanations of Jewish economic history and the capitalism debate.

In firmly grounding their research in immediate historical contexts, the contributors to this volume begin to bring Jewish history into dialogue with more recent turns in economic history, most notably, that guided by the new institutional economists, who view economic institutions as constitutive of the economic choices which drive development.[6] In a similar way, each author here focuses on the specific local legal, economic and political structures (not to mention the power struggles) that shaped the economic choices made by the Jewish actors in question. This focus also serves to illuminate the complexity and specificity of Jews' economic life at different times and places—phenomena often forgotten or ignored in the search for a unifying grand theory.[7] However, in writing this new kind of Jewish economic history that emphasizes organizational arrangements, modes of governance, social norms, ideological values, and human capital as determinants of the Jews' economic life, the authors are also following a Jewish historiographical tradition, which, though often overshadowed by the Sombart debate, stretches back for over a century. In order, then, to understand the different chapters of this volume in their historiographical context, it is worth giving some thought to the ways in which the history of Jewish economic activity and its relationship to the power wielded (or not) by Jews has been seen in the last hundred years or so. The discussion that follows is far from exhaustive. It merely seeks to survey briefly some of the major themes and personalities shaping the writing of Jewish economic history, beginning in Europe and then moving to the United States. Thereby, we hope to give the reader a clearer understanding of where this volume fits into the sweep of existing research and what its contribution to future scholarship might be.[8]

From the Elite to the Masses: Visions of Jewish Economic History in Europe

From its outset, the field of Jewish history has struggled with the place of economics. In 1818, a year before founding the *Verein für Kultur und Wissenschaft der Juden* (the Society for the Culture and Science of the Jews), the society that would formatively reshape the writing of Jewish history, Leopold Zunz implored his fellow German Jewish intellectuals not to forget economics as they delved into the Jewish past.[9] The sources for such inquiry were plentiful, he maintained, and this aspect of the Jewish past was critical to any understanding of Jewish culture and life. But his plea fell on deaf ears, as those intellectuals who devoted themselves to Wissenschaft des Judentums eschewed economic themes and focused their energies instead on analyzing Judaism or Jews strictly as a religious group.

Zunz's call for the close and serious study of Jewish economic life was not addressed for much of the nineteenth century. Indeed, this avoidance of the economy was a major criticism directed at the pioneering Wissenschaft des Judentums scholars, as eloquently summed up by Ignacy (Yitzhak) Schiper, a Jewish historian from Galicia. Schiper received his doctorate from the University of Vienna but was always a left-leaning academic who was hostile to essentialist theories of Jewish economic activity even before Sombart popularized them.[10] In a now widely quoted observation, Schiper wrote:

> Thanks to them [the nineteenth-century practitioners of Jewish historiography], we possess an impressive picture of the spiritual leaders of Diaspora Jewry. But what is completely lacking is the history of hundreds of thousands of Jews who have left few traces for the future, not of the spiritual riches [of their world] but of their toil and drudgery as well as of their speculative abilities. In short, we know about the Sabbath Jew and his extra [Sabbath] soul. But it is time we got to know the history of the weekday Jews . . . [and] the history of Jewish working life.[11]

This was a clarion call not just for the development of Jewish labor history, but also for a focus on the ways in which Jewish economic activity was shaped by its surroundings. The text served as a kind of manifesto for Schiper and his students from the interwar period, prominent among whom were Emanuel Ringelblum and Raphael Mahler.[12] In his monumental study of Jewish trade on Polish lands from the Middle Ages to the nineteenth century, Schiper paid a great deal of attention to the contexts of his subject, demonstrating the ways in which local conditions affected the developments he was interested in. On the other hand, the highly panoramic nature of his treatment allowed him little room to focus on the kind of detail that sheds light on the economic struggles of the masses. As a result, more often than not, the book makes broad generalizations on the basis of sources relating to the economic elites. This was a problem Ringelblum and Mahler would address in a number of their own studies.

A fine example of this came with Ringelblum's monographic study of the projects for the economic reform of Polish Jewry proposed by enlightened circles within the Polish-Lithuanian Commonwealth in the last decades of the eighteenth century. Using the different memorials penned by the reformers and petitions made by Jews, particularly during the period of the Four Year's Sejm (1788–1792), as a starting point, Ringelblum succeeded in giving a group portrait of the poorest strata of Polish Jewry. His particular focus was on those working in the sectors into which the reformers wanted to move them, most prominently manufacturing. As a result, the study as a whole has a somewhat unbalanced feel, especially given that the vast majority of Polish Jews, who made their living from trade, are somewhat marginal in his discussion. However, Ringelblum's perspective did allow him to shed light on some of the darker recesses of Jewish economic activity, which had previously evaded the scholarly eye. A similar approach was espoused by Raphael Mahler in his demographic studies based on the 1764–1765 census of Polish Jews, the last of which he was able to publish only after the Holocaust in 1958, when he was settled in Israel. Though these by no means ignored Jews engaged in trade, they laid strong emphasis on the minority of Jews who made their living from craftsmanship and other "productive" activities.[13]

What is striking about all the studies written by this group of socialist historians and their students (similar ones were penned by their contemporaries in the Soviet Union)[14] is the focus on Jews' economic life as a factor largely internal to Jewish society. To the extent that they looked at the larger picture, these studies tended to portray Jewish economic actors as largely powerless, suffering from economic and political forces much greater than themselves. Though such a view is not without basis, it is far from representing a full picture of Jews' economic activity, which—especially in the field of trade—played a dominant role in the Polish economy for long periods of time.[15] This is not to say that these historians were shying away from the question of whether Jews wielded economic power. They were not. Rather, they were simply reframing the issue in socialist terms: Jews were to be viewed as a powerful force in history not because their activities led to the development of capitalism, but rather because they (or, at least, the most important of them) formed a crucial part of the emerging proletarian forces, which would eventually challenge the rising bourgeoisie. Their power came not from their own activity, but from their position within the economy.

The pioneering studies of these Polish Jewish scholars and the students they were training were cut short by the Holocaust, in which, among all the terrible losses, a whole generation of Jewish scholars was murdered. One of the few survivors was Mahler, who had spent the war years in the West.[16] Mahler continued to write in his prewar vein, but found himself isolated after he moved to Israel in 1950. There he came into conflict with the "Jerusalem School," which was much more interested in the Jews' cultural and political history than with their economic life in the diaspora.

The apotheosis of Mahler's approach came with the publication in 1958 of his brilliant, but highly controversial, Marxist interpretation of the struggle between Hasidism and the Haskalah in the nineteenth century.[17] Despite its remarkable insights into the economic and social conditions of life in eastern Europe and the wealth of detail and rich source base it provided, his class-based treatment of the conflict was greeted with contempt by the Israeli historical establishment.[18] The less orthodox Marxist (though still socialist) approaches to the economic and class aspects of early Hasidism propounded by Ben Zion Dinur and Chone Shmeruk were received much more positively, though they too did not spawn further research.[19]

The study of Jewish economic history fared little better in the West. The intensive critique of Jewish economic activity as the basis for Jewish power that had formed one of the mainstays of the anti-Semitic propaganda leading up to the Holocaust made examining these issues a highly charged business. This became evident in the early 1950s when there was a small burst of interest in the court Jews of central Europe. Having formed a central plank in Sombart's theory, their economic role had been dismissed by Max Weber, who described them contemptuously as "pariah capitalists"—rapacious bankers whose outsider status in society meant that they were powerless to affect its economic development.[20] In 1950, Selma Stern returned to these figures, using many of the same materials as Sombart, but recasting them to show just how much the court Jews had formed an integral part of the baroque milieu of the absolutist court. In her reading, the court Jews were no more pariahs than were the absolute monarchs themselves. On the contrary, through their economic and political efforts not only did the modern state develop, but the foundations were laid for the Jews' successful integration into it.[21]

Stern's treatment of the court Jews was hailed by Jewish historians, but two other works published in the next few years made the issue too hot to handle. The first of these was Hannah Arendt's influential *The Origins of Totalitarianism*, first published in 1951. In the book's opening section, Arendt picked up on Stern's positive evaluation of the court Jews' political role in the development of the modern nation state, but cast it as the first stage in an arc of development that would eventually lead to Nazi anti-Semitism and the extermination of European Jewry.[22] To be sure, neither Stern nor Arendt argued that one could construct a direct line from court Jews to Nazi anti-Semitic portrayals of the Jewish economy, but following Arendt's critique, Jewish economic practices and strategies must have seemed tainted topics, best avoided.

That situation became considerably more complicated with the publication in 1953 of the first volume of Heinrich Schnee's six-volume study, *Die Hoffinanz und der moderne Staat: Geschichte und System der Hoffaktoren an deutschen Fürstenhöfen im Zeitalter des Absolutismus* (Court Finance and the Modern State: The History and Structure of the Court Jews at the German Courts in the Age of Absolutism). Though based on a wide range of primary sources, Schee's work was tainted by a clear anti-Semitic bias.[23] As the Jewish historian Bernard Weinryb wrote in his review, "Schnee denies Sombart's thesis about the big role of the court Jews in the creation of the absolutist state, depicting them as "only helpers" . . . [but] his statements and, still more, his implication gives a picture of an all-powerful group." In conclusion, Weinryb wrote, "This reviewer wishes he could be more certain that the racial ideology of the author did not influence his selection of the documents, and thus be assured that the factual parts of the book have a scientific value."[24] This seems to have convinced the Jewish historical establishment in the West that the topic was simply too difficult and fraught with problems.[25] It was not until the 1985 epochal study of Jonathan Israel, himself an outsider among scholars specializing in Jewish history, that the court Jews—and Jewish economic history in general—once again became an acceptable topic for historical research.[26]

Between Historians and Economists: The Study of Jewish Economic History in the United States

The study of Jewish history took quite a different turn in the United States, though its initial steps were hesitant. Those were taken by another Jewish historian, born and educated in central and east-central Europe, though by then living and working in the United States: Salo Wittmayer Baron.[27]

Appointed the Nathan L. Miller Professor of Jewish History at Columbia University in 1929, Baron became the leading scholar of Jewish history in the interwar period in America. While he did not share the Jerusalem School's view of Jewish life in the diaspora as decadent, his scholarly inquiries, along with those of the students he trained, focused more on the religious, cultural, and political aspects of the Jewish past than its economic features. As his biographer, Robert Liberles, noted, "considering how important the place of economic history was in the *Society and Religious History of the Jews* [Baron's monumental 1937 work], it is strange how brief and ineffective was his relevant discussion [of economic factors]."[28] To be sure, Baron did not totally erase the economic dimensions of the Jewish past. Instead, he posited a *metaphysical sympathy* between Jews and capitalism. But his summoning of "sympathy" to describe the relationship should not obscure how highly critical he was of capitalism and the changes it wrought on Jews as individuals and as a community. In his 1942 article on "Modern Capitalism and the Jewish Fate,"[29] he tried to reframe Sombart's work by asking not how the Jews had influenced the rise of capitalism, but what capitalism had brought the Jews. Echoing themes he had laid out in his seminal 1928 article, "Ghetto and Emancipation," Baron emphasized his view that neither emancipation nor the spread of capitalism could be considered positive developments in modern Jewish history.[30] In fact, Baron tended to avoid close analysis of Jews' role in the economic sphere, perhaps because he saw how the intensive critique of Jewish economic activity as the basis for Jewish power had formed one of the mainstays of anti-Semitic propaganda during the Nazi era. Favoring instead the study of the rationalist and elitist elements in Jewish history and directing his students along similar paths, Baron steered the study of Jewish history in the United States away from contemplating Jews' economic activities.

The topic was saved from total obscurity by a group of leading economists who turned their attention to Jews' place in the economy. This effort was spearheaded by Simon Kuznets, a leading economist, who won the Nobel Prize for his research on the relationship between economic and social structure and the processes of development.[31] While most remember Kuznets for his pioneering work on economic development (he created the system to accurately measure gross national product) and on the relationship between economic growth and inequality, few in the realm of economics appreciate how his theories were influenced by his research of Jewish economic activity.[32] As E. Glen Weyl has argued, it was his appreciation of persistent economic inequality in the history of eastern European Jewish life that shaped Kuznets's theories on income inequality and the development of economies.[33] Indeed, his early days spent as a student and an active socialist (and loyal Bund member) in Kharkov may not have led him to embrace Marxism, but they did clearly lead him to "a fascination with the relative distribution of income . . . [and] the question of whether an improved relative distribution (meaning a movement to household income equality) was compatible with general economic growth."[34]

Kuznets's groundbreaking work questioned the "normalization" of Jewish economic life and the connection between group identity and economics.[35] The Jews' concentration in particular economic sectors despite rapid modernization and secularization, he argued, provided a structural bulwark against the total loss of collective identity. Similarly, Arcadius Kahan, a University of Chicago economist, collected data in the 1970s related to Jewish labor in the United States in order to understand the encounter of Jews with the American economy. His enormously influential research on East European Jewish immigrants and the United States labor market before 1914 transformed how scholars thought about this group, migration, and the factors shaping immigrant mobility in early twentieth-century America. In further research, he devoted himself to unpacking other dramatic chapters in modern Jewish history, conveying the "poetry of the epic," as historian Jonathan Frankel has aptly summed it up, "through the terminology of mathematics."[36]

For both Kuznets and Kahan, the starting point of their interest seems to have been the Jewish immigrant experience—a personal experience for both as each had moved from eastern Europe to the United States. This tended to direct their attention away from issues of economic power wielded by Jews and the ways their activities might have shaped the economy. Kuznets's and Kahan's were essentially histories of accommodation. On the other hand, it was these economists' emphasis on noneconomic factors such as institutions and culture that led other social scientists to speak more readily about Jews in the context of economic theory. This new focus was expanded upon in the work of economist Barry Chiswick on Jewish occupational mobility in the United States.[37]

Furthermore, this shift to using the economic experiences of Jews to explore larger economic theories can be seen in the embrace of middleman-minority theory to explain Jewish economic behavior. Building on the theoretical work of Edna Bonacich and Walter Zenner, it became fashionable to examine Jews as model "middle men" in the economy, with scholars using Jews' minority status to explain their economic activity. Basically, middleman-minority studies posit the existence of various immigrant (or "sojourner") societies, which concentrate their economic activities in various economic niches situated between those of the elite and the masses. Often the minorities are forced into high-risk, low-prestige professions, which do not demand great capital investment, by the unwillingness of other groups to take them on. However, by utilizing specific middleman-minority strategies such as ethnic solidarity, personal thrift, and entrepreneurialism, they are able to succeed in achieving high levels of economic success.[38] This does not, however, bring them significant social advancement. Rather, their success often arouses hostility and even violence from members of the larger society.

But even while social scientists (writing as historians) devoted their energies to placing Jews in the landscape of the American economy, the long shadow cast by Baron on the study of Jewish history encouraged few historians of the Jewish experience to delve into economic research. Among those in the United States perhaps best positioned to do so, then, the study of Jewish economic life continued to languish, perhaps still a victim of the reluctance to touch upon issues that many believed brought on hatred and anti-Semitism in Europe. Instead, as Eli Lederhendler points out, culture and identity garnered the lion's share of these historians' attention. Trained primarily to unpack texts from the Jewish past, they also lacked the requisite economic and statistical competence to continue the work of the social scientists.[39]

By the 1990s, even those economists who had previously exhibited interest in the case of the Jews abandoned their research of Jewish economic life in the United States.[40] While the fraught qualities of the subject may have contributed to this shift, also to blame were the ways in which knowledge came to be organized and produced in the American academy. Within the discipline of economics, economic history has tended to rank low in prestige, and few of the scholars who engage in it are concerned with Jewish history. Ethnic studies, too, stopped seeing Jews as a minority or outsider of central concern. As they became more integrated into American society and less threatened, Jews also became less interesting.[41] Paradoxically, then, it might be argued that it was American Jewry's very success in amassing enough economic power to improve its social status that rendered it marginal in much social scientific research. It was only with the end of the Cold War, the rise of globalization, and the apparent victory of capitalism as an economic system, that renewed the asking of questions about Jewish economic activity began to be asked.

The Beginnings of an Economic Turn in Jewish History

The first sign of an impending change came as early as 1986, when Jonathan Israel published his epochal volume, *European Jewry in the Age of Mercantilism*.[42] Because Israel was not primarily a historian of the Jews, he was able to write a study that brilliantly presented the Jews' experience in the accepted discourse of European history. He thus evaded many of the approaches and conceptualizations common among Jewish historians, but unfamiliar and off-putting to others. He also avoided the so-called cultural turn that was then beginning to sweep Jewish history. In fact, his book was, in many ways, a rather old-fashioned study of the ways in which the Jews of early modern Europe interacted with the states in which they lived. However, this approach encouraged him to integrate economic issues deeply into his narrative and to do so without all the concerns about anti-Semitism, which seemed so to bother his contemporaries. His conclusions were quite startling: he pointed to the significant roles that Jews played in the economies of the countries in which they lived and even posited the existence of a separate and vibrant "Jewish economy" existing alongside (or inside) the European one, with the court Jews playing a crucial role in it. Although it was the European context that shaped Jewish social and economic life for Israel, rather than the other way around, his study nonetheless laid great emphasis on Jewish agency, presenting the Jews as major players in the story he told. So, for all its old-fashioned approach, Israel's book seemed to open up new and exciting vistas for Jewish historical research.

Still, it would be some fifteen years before the gauntlet that Israel threw down would be picked up in serious fashion. This was done by Derek Penslar in his 2001 study, *Shylock's Children: Economics and Jewish Identity in Modern Europe.*[43] Focusing largely on the attitudes towards economic activity expressed by European Jews from the eighteenth to the twentieth century, it was highly innovative in, among other things, its development of a concept of "Jewish Political Economy." This allowed Penslar to integrate into a single narrative both visions of the Jews' role in the market and attitudes towards social and philanthropic issues within the Jewish community.

Yet, remarkably, though the discussions of "the Jewish Question" in Europe at the heart of the study might be seen as eventually leading to the Holocaust, the book's tone was upbeat. Penslar demonstrated how, despite all the external pressures, the image of the economically successful Jew could be a source of pride in Jewish society, and described with no little admiration the forms of social organization that European Jewry set up to deal with the social issues that faced it. His reason for doing so was perhaps explained in the conclusion to the book: "Although today's Jews are still haunted by many specters from the past, Shylock's ghost is not among them. Jews continue to have grave, even existential problems, but for the vast majority of world Jewry, the 'Jewish Question' as it was understood throughout modern European history has ceased to exist."[44] Despite everything then, the Jews would seem to have won out. For Penslar, their economic history, at least, is a story with a happy ending.

In this way, *Shylock's Children* took the fear out of studying Jewish economic activity and so opened up again the issue of Jews and capitalism. Milton Friedman, economic adviser to Ronald Reagan, had argued that the Jews had contributed greatly to the rise of capitalism in the United States—a view widely espoused in free market circles. By the first decade of the twenty-first century, conditions were ripe to examine this point of view more critically. A number of different approaches were taken. Jonathan Karp examined the ways in which thinking about Jewish economic activity had influenced European political thought, and vice versa, from the seventeenth to the nineteenth century. His study covered the period often called "the transition to capitalism" and ended more or less with Marx's composition of "On the Jewish Question."[45] Fundamental to his project was examining the development of a political and economic vocabulary to describe Jews' commercial activities, which would influence thinking about them in later periods. In many ways, Jerry Muller picked up where Karp had left off, focusing on economic thought after Marx. His intellectual starting point seems to have been the unabashed acceptance of the idea that Jews historically had enjoyed "disproportionate economic success" and played a key role in the development of capitalism. It was the way this success was viewed by ideologues of different stripes, Jewish and non-Jewish, that Muller was interested in uncovering.[46]

Other studies have tried to examine the connections between Jews and American capitalism in a more empirical fashion. Eli Lederhendler returned to the Jewish immigrant experience in order to explode the idea that Jews had any innate penchant for the capitalist economy. His study argued that the Jews' success was born entirely of their accommodation to the American economy of the turn of the twentieth century.[47] This idea was also central to the volume *Chosen Capital: The Jewish Encounter with American Capitalism*, a collection of studies edited by Rebecca Kobrin. Two major themes of the book are the ways in which American capitalism acted to reshape Jewish life in America and the ways in which Jewish economic activity affected the development of capitalism there. Thus, though the debate in all these studies on the Jews' relations with capitalism has ranged far beyond the ideas of Sombart, the fundamental importance of the issues he raised remains unquestioned.[48]

Other new approaches have moved thinking about Jewish economic activity in some quite different directions. Gideon Reuveni and Sarah Wobick-Segev's collection of essays on various aspects of how Jews produced, marketed, and consumed goods in the modern era tantalizingly suggests the types of insights to be gained from "putting the economy back on the agenda of Jewish studies."[49] Of particular interest is the focus of several essays Jewish economic activity in imperial and transnational contests. Through such an approach, the importance of the state as the determining framework for economic activity, including that of the Jews, is downplayed. The center of concern becomes the trading network itself, which consists of businessmen living and acting in a range of environments. The diasporic nature of Jewish history has lent itself to the creation of such networks, which have begun to attract a great deal of attention and new studies. Here, too, Jonathan Israel has been extremely influential with his massive 2002 study, *Diasporas within a Diaspora: Jews, Crypto-Jews, and the World Maritime Empires, 1540–1740*, which has effectively opened the field of network studies to Jewish historians.[50] Though much of his study is not overtly concerned with economic issues, scholars in his wake have begun to some of the basic spadework he did not pursue.[51] The early modern Sephardic/New Christian network that developed in the wake of the Spanish and Portuguese expulsions on which these studies focus clearly lends itself to this kind of study.

Sara Abrevaya-Stein's research has revealed a different kind of network, based mostly on the activities of the Ashkenazic immigrant diaspora, which came into being following the great exodus from tsarist Russia in the 1880s. Connecting farmers and merchants in South Africa, the trading emporia of London and Paris, and the workers in the Garment District of New York, her book situates the economic network involved in the manufacture and sale of Ostrich feathers as a fashion accessory in a modern and clearly capitalist framework.[52] Nonetheless, Abrevaya-Stein eschews the question of a possible grand relationship between Jews and capitalism, focusing instead on the conjunction of factors that led to the brief flourishing of this Jewish niche. Her interest lies much more in the ties of business and culture that connected the different parts of this far-flung network in its heyday.

The nature of this kind of business network has also attracted the interest of economists. Prominent among them is Avner Greif. Interested in medieval Jewish practices in long-distance trade, he expanded his perspective in 2006 to a comparison with those of the Genoese international merchants in order to develop of theory of how such trans-regional mercantile networks functioned. Focusing on such issues as trust relations, risk management, and contract enforcement, his study relies heavily on game theory and combines classical historical narrative with the abstract tools of model-building used in economic research.[53] While his methods, particularly in the field of history, and many of his conclusions remain controversial, this work may be seen in some ways as a continuation of the theoretical interventions made by economists such as Kuznets and Kahan nearly half a century earlier.[54]

Greif is a leading figure in a relatively new field of economic research known as "the new institutional economic theory." Championed by the Nobel-prize winning economist Douglass North, among others, this school has demonstrated that classical economics—with its assumption of the individual's ability to make rational and free choices in the market—does not take into account the fact that in most cases the individual is unable to make totally rational and free choices.[55] The ability to engage in economic activity is circumscribed by the existence in any society of a variety of economic institutions. These are understood to range from the legal and constitutional structure of the state, which determines property rights and contractual relations, to various social attitudes and ideologies, which determine how economic activity is perceived and pursued.

This theory, therefore, portrays the choices of economic actors as being largely culturally determined. In order to follow processes of economic development, it is important to map out the economic institutions in any society and examine how they changed over time. Such an approach can prove highly congenial to social and cultural historians, who can use the tools of their trade to analyze those institutions that shaped the economic activity in which they are interested. Jewish historians, too, have begun to pick up on this idea and use it to some effect. Perhaps the first to do so was Adam Teller in a Hebrew-language study of Jewish economic activity on a magnate's estate in eighteenth century Lithuania.[56] In mapping out the various institutions that allowed the estate economy to function, he was able to identify the central roles played by the Jews in marketing and exchange, and to show how these roles brought Jewish society on the estates money, power, and influence. He further determined that employing the Jews in these functions was part of a conscious economic policy on the part of the magnate family anxious to boost its cash income. This allowed the family—and the other magnate families who adopted a similar policy—to form the closed oligarchic elite that dominated Polish-Lithuanian society throughout the eighteenth century.

A second study to adopt this theoretical approach was that of Francesca Trivellato, published in 2009.[57] Its focus is on the role of Jewish merchants in trans-regional trade, and the transcultural connections that this brought in its wake. The book focuses on a single Sephardic trading house, centered in the Mediterranean port of Livorno, and examines the mercantile network that it constructed throughout the Mediterranean world and the Ottoman Empire and reaching as far as Goa. On the basis of her very extensive research into business correspondence, Trivellato was able to return to many of the issues raised by Greif—networks of trust, risk management, and contract enforcement. However, her emphasis on the cross-cultural nature of the trade allowed her to ask some deeper questions concerning the Jewish aspect of this mercantile network as well as the reasons for its success (and ultimate failure). Her conclusions are highly surprising: though heavily Jewish, the network brought many non-Jews—Christians, Moslems, and even Hindus—into its orbit. Dismissing any shared ethnicity or religion as the basis for the network's internal cohesion, she posits instead a shared trans-regional mercantile culture that tied the disparate merchants together. For her, then, its successes and failures cannot be ascribed to elements of Jewish culture or religion, but are to be sought in the exigencies of early modern trade.

Although the new institutional economic historians have focused much of their interest on the rise of the West (by which they mean, the rise of the capitalist system), neither Teller nor Trivellato falls into that teleological trap. Both emphasize the immediate context of the cases they study—the feudal economy of eastern Europe and the mercantile culture of the early modern Mediterranean—and feel no need to squeeze their findings into a predetermined view of capitalist development.

Today, then, the return to Jewish economic history has brought ever more contextualized studies, whose authors have demonstrated little interest in the grand theories (of capitalism or socialism). There also seems to be a cautious form of openness to approaches and theories developed in the field of economics—certainly more than was seen in the 1960s and 1970s, for example.[58] A major shift seems to have been that the nervousness over a possible anti-Semitic backlash, caused by research into the history of Jewish economic strategies and the power they have sometimes brought, is considerably less influential. In its place, scholars are beginning to submit the anti-Jewish discourses around money and power to critical examination, and, through processes of contextualization, to defang them. As a result of all this, there has been a very strong swing away from the kind of essentialist views that find the causes of Jews' economic choices in their religion or culture. Instead, conjunctions of factors are seen as being of primary importance—sometimes to the point of denying any significance to the Jewishness of the subjects under discussion. Whether or not this last is seen as an extreme stance, the development of the field as a whole does seem to have opened the way to freer discussions of Jewish economic activity and its broader implications, including the questions of Jews acquiring and wielding power.

* * *

It is against this historiographical background that the chapters in this volume have been written. The editors' goal was to bring together a group of essays, which, for all their differences of historical perspective, would engage in the critical examination of the nexus between economic activity and the practice of power—both real and imagined—in Jewish history. To ensure at least a minimum of cohesion, the decision was made to limit the discussions to the modern period, understood as beginning in about 1500. Though many important insights from earlier periods are thus missing, the editors hope that the trade-off in assembling a group of essays that can enter into a much closer dialogue with each other is worthwhile.

The volume is divided into two major sections: the first examines forms of Jewish empowerment involving networks of exchange and the creation of economic niches; the second considers the Jewish exercise of power in the international arena through the deployment of economic resources, particularly in the realm of philanthropy. Its final chapter acts a thematic and methodological afterword to the volume, dealing with the economic representation and self-representation of Jews in historical research.

Part I, on "Networks and Niches," opens with Bernard Cooperman's examination of Jewish moneylenders in early modern Rome, which serves as a case study of the connections between money and power in Jewish history. Drawing on *responsa* (rabbinic legal decisions), notarial acts, judicial decisions, and loan receipts from Rome's rich archives, he shows how the city's Jewish bankers' service of papal economic needs led to the creation of a Jewish banking cartel. In a world of cutthroat competition, the members of the cartel proved adept at maneuvering between the different jurisdictions within which they worked and created a trade association whose power exceeded that of the local community—and even that of the rabbi. Cooperman goes on to show the limits of this success, demonstrating that, even though the bankers managed to break into the communal leadership, changing economic conditions and competition within Jewish society put an end to the cartel and the power of its members.

While Cooperman is interested at looking at the power struggles between Jewish bankers within Jewish society, Carsten Wilke's paper focuses on power relations between Jewish (in this case, crypto-Jewish) businessmen and the state. To fill its empty coffers, seventeenth-century Spain established a monopoly on the sale of tobacco, which it entrusted to "Portuguese New Christians" who had been increasingly excluded from fiscal administration in the capital, Madrid, as a result of intensive Inquisitional activity. It did so because the far-flung economic network of the New Christians centered in Bayonne improved the supply of cheap tobacco to Spain and allowed profits to rise. For their part, the Portuguese looked to this trade, which they quickly turned into a Jewish niche, not only as a means of personal enrichment, but as a way of protecting family members who acted as agents in the hostile atmosphere of Madrid. Though this was not always possible, Wilke concludes that, in the seventeenth century at least, "the tobacco economy saved both partners—an empire in straits and an impoverished segment of the Jewish diaspora."

Cornelia Aust's chapter continues the exploration of the sources of Jewish economic power, but does so through the analysis of a failed partnership.

Examining the Ashkenazic Jewish economic networks which covered eighteenth-century Europe from Amsterdam to Warsaw, she focuses on the sources (and limits) of trust as the major factor in economic success. She, too, draws a picture of Jewish businessmen navigating among different poles of authority and power—the business community, Jewish and non-Jewish, the Jewish community (particularly its courts), and the state. She concludes that ethnic and religious solidarity could not necessarily underpin the kind of trustworthy, and thus creditworthy, reputation that successful businessmen needed. The creation of trading networks that included non-Jews and enjoyed the support of the state were no less important. Once these broke down, even the most far-flung ethnic network could not help the unfortunate Jewish merchant—or his partners.

Glenn Dynner examines the issue of Jewish economic power through a different lens entirely—that is, in terms of the way it was perceived by non-Jewish authorities, in his case, the tsarist regime in Congress Poland during the first half of the nineteenth century. On the basis of openly stated fears that Jews would take over the urban economy entirely, the tsarist authorities instituted a policy of residential segregation for Jews throughout the kingdom—a move largely supported by the Jews' Christian competitors in the towns. In his examination of the consequences of this legislation and the various responses to it within Jewish and non-Jewish society in Poland, Dynner shows that though it led to a great pauperization of Polish Jewry, it did not lead to their economic marginalization as they struggled to find alternative forms of income or to evade segregation. Avoiding essentialist terms, Dynner attributes this economic vibrancy to a number of reasons such as Jews' lobbying and litigiousness, along with their high rates of literacy, urbanization, and female workforce participation. Taken together, these facts enabled Jews to remain economic competitive and adapt to their new circumstances.

An interesting parallel, or even counterpoint, to this story of pauperization and degradation can be found in Adam Mendelsohn's study of two Anglo-Jewish merchants, both called Moses, who made their fortunes in colonial commerce. Both made their living from selling secondhand clothes, an occupation identified with the poorer economic strata. However, by breaking into the British colonial trade with these items, they soon became enormously wealthy. Mendelsohn stresses that it was not simply the opportunities opened by the British colonial economy that allowed them to escape the poverty trap. Equally important was their adopting more modern business structures and their role in creating far-flung ethnic networks. For Mendelsohn, perhaps the most important aspect of the networks was that they were willing to provide credit to these second-class Jewish entrepreneurs, whom other banks treated with suspicion. Once their fortunes were made, both families tried to buttress their place in British society and avoid further discrimination by changing their names, though this seems to have proved futile since one English observer noted that they "could change their names but not their noses."

Jonathan Karp's essay on Jewish entrepreneurs in the popular music business in the mid-twentieth century United States and United Kingdom takes the arguments developed in the previous chapters a step further. He not only examines the reasons for the success of this Jewish niche, but also shows how their economic strategies actually shaped the world of popular music, giving them a form of cultural power and influence well beyond their numbers. He points to very successful networking (which even crossed generations) as well as a socio-economic positioning between disadvantaged groups or classes and the music market as keys to their success. Particularly interesting is that he discovers these trends in the very different economic settings of the two sides of the Atlantic. This would seem to suggest that the broader context alone does not provide a sufficient explanation for these Jews' economic success. Two separate groups of businessmen in quite different environments seem to have been able to identify similar economic opportunities and exploit them to very great effect, and this raises the question how and why this could come to be.

In all, then, the chapters in Part I explore the ways in which Jewish economic actors were able to amass economic power and influence in different times and places in the modern world. They map out the changing roles of the state and the Jewish community both as determining factors in Jewish economic activity and as centers of power and influence that Jewish businessmen sought to control. The interplay of economics and power is not seen as unidirectional—Jewish failures are treated alongside successes—and there is certainly no sense of all roads leading to Rome, in the sense of the Jews' involvement in (or penchant for) capitalism. Nonetheless, a number of chapters seem to be beginning—hesitantly and without even openly admitting it—to raise the question of whether Jews' economic choices are entirely determined by a variety of situational factors, or whether deeper causes are also at play.

The chapters in Part II, on "Philanthropy, Money, and the Deployment of Power," move the discussion away from the amassing of economic power in order to examine how this power was used. Derek Penslar has argued that the "application of Jewish power" in the modern period (at least prior to the establishment of the state of Israel) was primarily economic in nature and was expressed chiefly through Jewish philanthropic organizations.[59] Following this insight, the chapters here examine the ways in which Jewish philanthropic activity and fundraising efforts worked in the international arena. Though this use of economic power served primarily to achieve Jewish philanthropic goals, its deployment across borders could sometimes give it geopolitical significance well beyond the fate of the Jews involved. On those occasions, Jewish philanthropic activity can be seen—on some level, at least—to be shaping the world around it, in addition to the benefiting the disadvantaged Jews who were its object.

Part II opens with Abigail Green's study of the development of modern transnational Jewish philanthropy in what she calls the "Jewish International." This was, according to her, "a cluster of voluntary transnational organizations and representations crystalizing around international issues." These were largely based in the powerful states of western and central Europe, and so were often working—and even serving—larger imperial interests. Green points to the power of the press and mass subscription fundraising as being means by which a small, elite group of philanthropists was able to mobilize much broader strata of Jewish society to contribute to its activities and created an international basis of support. This mobilization could be in the service of specifically Jewish causes, such as supporting the poor Jews of the Land of Israel, as well as to support those Jewish causes with great international significance, such as the Damascus Blood Libel of 1840. In 1860, the "Jewish International" even marshaled resources on behalf of the Christians of Syria. Though not always successful in achieving its goals of forcing autocratic regimes, such as Russia, Romania, or Persia, to alleviate the Jews' suffering, the ability of the "Jewish International" to speak for a wide Jewish constituency from whom it collected the money it needed to fund its various activities made it a force not to be ignored on the international stage in the later nineteenth century.

In his chapter on the financing of Israel's War of Independence, Derek Penslar argues that it was precisely the activity of transnational Jewish philanthropic organizations that made this a unique event in twentieth-century history. Although other anticolonial movements, which are examined in some detail here in the first comparative study of its kind, had tried to mobilize funds from distant diasporas, they had never really amounted to anything significant. In 1948, on the other hand, it was the success of the Jewish organizations, largely in the United States, that provided the Yishuv and the fledgling state with the tens of millions of dollars it desperately needed to purchase arms. Without ignoring fundraising efforts made elsewhere, such as Canada and western Europe, Penslar focuses attention on two Jewish fundraising networks, which were particularly active. The first was the Sonneborn group, a group of financiers, businessmen, and lawyers, who organized the more-or-less clandestine purchase of arms and materiel for the Haganah and had it smuggled across the ocean. The second was the United Palestine Appeal, which was supported by the broad masses of American Jewry. These last were persuaded to donate as much as 2.5 percent of their total disposal income to the Yishuv—a huge amount by any account. Motivated by a desire to improve their self-image, to help fellow Jews still reeling from the effects of the Holocaust, and to protect the poor Jews of the Land of Israel, these American Jews wielded their economic power in such a way as to change the entire course of twentieth-century history.

Not only did Jewish philanthropic organizations help Israel win the War of Independence; they also deployed innovative programs to help rebuild Jewish communities in Europe, as can be seen through the example of Antwerp. As Veerle Vanden Daelen argues, the Belgian government's interest in reestablishing Antwerp as a center for the diamond trade coincided with the goal of various Jewish philanthropic organizations to resettle Jews still in Europe. The huge wealth deployed by the transnational Jewish diamond business, which was largely Orthodox in nature, played a crucial role in these efforts. Many strange bedfellows and new types of coalitions came together as Jewish diamond dealers from around the world, Jewish philanthropists, and local officials remade the city of Antwerp into a place that an Orthodox Jewish population would feel comfortable calling home and one where they would thus develop their business operations. More than this, however, these efforts played a crucial role in reestablishing Antwerp as a major European diamond center following World War II. As she argues, the "orthodox diamond diaspora . . . succeeded, via its religious, political and economical networks and connections, in shaping, throughout the twentieth century, both the specifically Jewish history and more general history of a major Western European port city." Once again, it would seem that transnational Jewish philanthropy was not just relieving Jewish distress, but actually reshaping the world in which the Jews lived.

As a counterpoint to the somewhat triumphalist approach to the issue of transnational Jewish philanthropy in the modern age represented in the chapters thus far, this volume includes Jonathan Dekel-Chen's sobering account of the Cold War campaign on behalf of Soviet Jewry in the mid-twentieth century. Despite the movement's very high-profile activities, Dekel-Chen concludes that it failed in its crucial goals: it did not persuade successive American presidents to make the issue a platform of U.S. foreign policy; it was not able to bring significant economic pressure to bear on the Soviet Union; and it did not force the Soviet Union to change its emigration policy. Even the involvement of a sovereign state, Israel, in the arena proved ineffective: it failed either to displace the previously existing transnational philanthropic organizations or to have a significant effect on the plight of Soviet Jewry. Here then was a case of international Jewish philanthropy proving unable to translate Jewish economic power and political influence into any tangible achievements. When all this is put into the context of the survey of Jewish transnational philanthropic and diplomatic activity with which Dekel-Chen ends his chapter, the reader is left to wonder whether this failure was the exception or the rule.

Particularly interesting is the way in which the authors here treat with approval an issue that has played a major role in modern anti-Semitic discourse. This is the idea of a transnational network of wealthy Jews manipulating the international arena, which is perhaps best known from the infamous "Protocols of the Elders of Zion," but existed well before their publication. Contemporary scholarship, far from trying to prove the canard wrong or sweep the matter under the carpet, would seem to be willing quite openly to acknowledge the Jews' move from amassing economic power to wielding it, as best they could, in both local and trans-regional environments. In an interesting fashion, this would seem to move the discussion full-circle. The successes, however limited, of various Jewish bodies not only to amass great economic power, but also to exploit it on the world stage clearly came in the age of capitalism, not before. This returns us to the question of the relations between capitalism and Jewish economic activity—an issue that has been on the academic agenda for over a century and a half without any satisfactory form of resolution.

It is no coincidence, then, that the volume concludes with Adam Sutcliffe's study of Werner Sombart's classic 1911 work, *The Jews and Modern Capitalism*.[60] Though Sombart's proto-racist approach and his later adherence to the

Nazi Party (not to mention his many factual errors) have led to the work being largely discredited, Sutcliffe's analysis situates it comfortably within the social scientific discourse of fin-de-siècle Germany concerning the history and nature of capitalism. Though perhaps outdated, this scholarship is by no means discredited—a situation that suggests perhaps that Sombart's book, too, is worth another look despite the distaste it arouses. The rather positive reception that his book received in Jewish academic circles in the pre-Holocaust period, described by Sutcliffe in the second section of his chapter, strengthens this impression. In fact, as Sutcliffe points out, the critical rereading of Sombart has begun to happen in recent years in the work of scholars such as Jonathan Israel and Natalie Davis. Suttcliffe embraces this move, seeing in it a return to the field of Jewish economic history as a trans-historical endeavor. He goes on to argue that comparative studies would lose their essential meaningfulness, without some recognition of the persistent overrepresentation of Jews in commerce—the phenomenon at the heart of Sombart's analysis, despite its flaws. He concludes: "The road toward a more ambitious, integrated, frank, and challenging approach to Jewish economic history is signaled by a return to big questions about the relationships between commerce, culture and power across the broad sweep of Jewish history" (see p. 257).

Taken together, the essays collected here represent an attempt to refocus the attention of Jewish historical scholarship on Sutcliffe's "big questions." The method has been the careful contextual study of the historian rather than the broad modeling of the social scientist. Nonetheless, we firmly believe that these microhistories of Jewish economic activity mark just the beginning of a new field in which scholars devote themselves to seeing more clearly how modern Jews have penetrated, lived within, and shaped different the economic contexts in which they functioned, and how, in turn, these contexts have influenced and affected Jews individually and collectively. Indeed, it is our hope that these studies will not stand alone for long, but rather will encourage further scholarship on the various relationships between money and power in Jewish history that we have raised here. The study of culture and identity, so popular in recent decades, has proved an extremely valuable and enlightening (and, in some senses, also comfortable) approach to understanding the complexities of Jewish history. Perhaps the time has now come to return to the much harder—not to say harsher—issues of the material bases for Jewish life, and the ways in which Jews have exploited them in their search for wealth and power in the worlds they inhabited. Our understanding of the Jewish past will be immeasurably enriched in the effort.

PART I

Networks and Niches: The Creation of Jewish Economic Power

Chapter 1

Licenses, Cartels, and Kehila: Jewish Moneylending and the Struggle Against Restraint of Trade in Early Modern Rome

Bernard Dov Cooperman

On Saturday evening, October 7, 1542, three men appeared before the *keri'a*, the Jewish community council of Rome, with what seems at first a puzzling set of demands. Speaking in the name of the community membership (*murshim mi-tsad ha-kahal*), Moses da Cammeo, Joseph Babbo, and Solomon Lancian demanded that the council either abolish moneylending in Rome or else end the bankers' restrictive monopoly, thus opening up the business to every Jew. If neither of these demands were met, the plaintiffs insisted that the issue be brought before a rabbinic court.[1]

How are we to understand this moment? Clearly the plaintiffs did not oppose moneylending per se. On the contrary, they themselves wanted to engage in it in order "to earn their livelihood like every other [Jewish] householder in Rome." But then, why ask that moneylending be abolished? Perhaps they were bothered by the licensing system that restricted moneylending to only a few Jews. But bankers were licensed by the papal authorities. What was the point of demanding that the Jewish communal council cancel or open up the trade? Again, if the issue was one of equity and justice, matters appropriate for a rabbinic court, why bring it before the community's lay governing body in the first place? In this study I will argue that the plaintiffs were in effect trying to sue the *keri'a*. They objected not to the licenses issued by the papal *camerlengo* (chamberlain), but to the way these licenses had been recognized by, and become integral to the fabric of, Jewsh communal governance. Careful study of the history of Jewish moneylending in Rome shows that there was an intimate connection between licensed moneylending and the structure of the communal council. To the plaintiffs, restriction of competition was not only unfair but also Jewishly illegitimate because it had overwhelmed the council itself. Money and politics had become hopelessly entangled; the *keri'a* had become an agency of the moneylenders. The plaintiffs assumed that a rabbinic court would agree with them—in other words, that halakhic logic precluded the public institutionalization of economic privilege.

We realize intuitively that money and politics are intertwined, that institutions of governance are everywhere shaped by powerful financial pressures, and that accommodations are demanded and regularly received by those who can afford them. But although wealth and power are everywhere interrelated, their ties are articulated differently in each society according to the specificity of local law and custom. In this respect Jewish moneylending did not differ from any other financial sector; it was incorporated into, and defended by, an institutionalized system of law and administration. As Antonio, the fictional merchant of Venice put it, the city was bound to enforce even Shylock's bloody demand because to "deny the course of law . . . [would] much impeach the justice of the state."[2] In real life as much as in Shakespearean drama, Jewish moneylenders relied on and sought to manipulate the law in order to defend and promote their business. In the circumstances that I will be examining—those in Rome during the second quarter of the sixteenth century—the Jewish moneylenders operated within two separate legal systems: that of the city administration, headed by papally appointed officials, and that of the Jewish community, directed by its own elected representatives. The Jewish *banchieri* of Rome built their businesses at the crossroads of these two systems, answered to both, and tried to use both to their advantage. This chapter is an exploration of the complicated nature of that effort, and of the considerable opposition to it. If this case study is not yet a history of Jewish moneylending in Rome, much less of the relation between wealth and communal power—there are still far too many unstudied documents for that—it will, I hope, point out one of the directions in which a fuller analysis might proceed.

Jewish moneylending is well documented. Scores of articles—most, but not all, local treatments—have described the licensing and day-to-day operation of Jewish banks all over medieval and early modern Italy.[3] But Rome, because of the exceptional history of its Jewish community, provides us with an opportunity to explore financial and political aspects of the banking business not seen elsewhere. In many towns of central Italy, a *condotta* or privilege to a moneylender was typically the foundational document of the local community. So long as the license lasted, a limited number of Jews were able to settle in the town under the more or less fictional claim that they were part of the banker's extended household. In such communities, and even in larger cities, such as Bologna, where banking and settlement rights were not so closely tied, the special status of the loan bankers inevitably gave them enhanced political power over their fellows. Either they were themselves the communal leaders, or they could claim immunity from communal demands.[4]

In Rome the situation was different. Its Jewish community had existed since Republican times, and the oft-repeated medieval charters were not linked to moneylending.[5] When papal authorities licensed Jewish moneylending in the city in 1521, the bankers quickly laid claim to both economic monopoly and privileged political status within the *already-existing* community structures. These claims were at first accepted and then vigorously opposed by other members of the community. The documentary evidence generated by that struggle gives us an unprecedented picture of the close interrelations between business and politics as lawsuits and litigants made their way through the multiple legal systems governing Rome's Jews at the time.

It is the chance survival of three different types of documentation that allows us to analyze this struggle in some depth. First, there is a copy of what has been called the constitution of the Roman Jewish community, prepared for papal ratification in 1524.[6] Second, there are the legal briefs (responsa) of Rabbi Isaac de Lattes, a Provençal active in Rome in precisely these years who left an autograph manuscript filled with opinions he wrote "in the heat of battle."[7] Finally, there are the wonderfully detailed records of Jewish notaries, carefully prepared legal documents meant as permanent evidence of everything from real estate transactions to marriage agreements, contracts, claims, debts, and partnerships formed and dissolved—in other words, of the many aspects of daily life that did, or some day might, come up for litigation.[8] What is unusual about these documents, and in particular the first two categories, is that they preserve the names of the parties. Thus the historian can, so to speak, triangulate to properly pinpoint events and draw a realistic picture of Jewish finance in preghetto Rome. We can begin to see the complex ways in which Jewish businessmen and the Jewish community as a whole carefully negotiated their way through the multiple jurisdictions and multiple systems of law that governed their fates.

Jewish Bankers in Rome

Jewish *banchieri*, whom Roman urban statute had outlawed in the 1360s, began to reappear in the city toward the end of the fifteenth century.[9] Typical were Isaac and Abraham da Siena, sons of the well-known banker Jacob di Consiglio, who held lending licenses in Marino, a small town near Rome. From there, they offered credit, whether legally or surreptitiously, to the urban population through Jewish agents in the city.[10] Gradually, at least some of these Jewish lenders were able to negotiate individual licenses to operate openly in Rome.[11] By 1521 Roman authorities had decided that it was time to regularize this trade. On September 14 a papal *motuproprio* gave the *camerlengo* authority over "changing, renewing, and confirming" existing licenses.[12] As we might expect, the papal decision was motivated by a combination of practical and religious goals. Consolidating the licensing of the Jewish banks meant more efficient taxation and control of this part of the money trade.[13] It definitely allowed the government to negotiate a much lower rate of interest; in return for their new licenses, the bankers had to agree to charge only half of what they had been allowed previously.[14] At the same time the banks were part of the city's response both to the needs of the local poor and to increasing demands for credit from the many pilgrims, students and clerics, ambassadorial retinues, and government functionaries flooding into Rome in those years. Up to twenty banks were now licensed to offer the pawn-secured, consumer and small-business loans in which Jews specialized.

What is most significant for the present study is that the limited set of twenty licenses effectively created a closed cartel and allowed the bankers both to keep out competitors and to control individuals within their own circle.[15] Every six months the bankers elected two of their number to serve as representatives to the outside authorities. Their primary task, of course, was to negotiate license renewals and fees. Presumably they also worked out any legal formulas needed to ensure that Jews' loan records were enforceable in courts, and they thrashed out the day-to-day regulations about how, for example, the banks would be run and how pawned objects would be protected from mold, vermin, and other threats.[16] But these men, referred to as *deputati* and *fattori* in Italian and as *brurim* and *parnasim* in Hebrew, had an equally important role within the cartel.[17] There were twenty individual bank licenses, each of which could be, and often was, shared by a number of partners, active or silent, limited or general.[18] Friction was inevitable, and the two officials were "to rule and judge about matters of the Jewish banks as they see fit. Whatever they rule shall be considered of standing and binding [*yihye lahem ma'amad ve-kiyum*]."[19] Their authority was ratified (or at least recognized) by the *camerlengo*, as can be seen in the license renewal of 1534, which spelled out not only the twenty individual bankers but also their leadership by name: "Concerning the amount lent, the pledges and their condition, the term of deposit and restitution of pledges, as well as all other matters relevant to this trade, full faith shall be given to the written records of the said Jews so long as these are confirmed by their leaders [*superiori*] whom they shall elect every six months, currently Maestro Dattylo, *physico* and Angelo de Benafria."[20] Most important, these were the only people with jurisdiction over the bankers' affairs. Already in their very first Roman license, the bankers negotiated a provision explicitly exempting them from sanctions such as excommunication issued "by any or every rabbi [Jewish teacher, *magister*]."[21] This was not, I hasten to stress, an anticlerical statement. In the language of the time, it was a claim to exclusive jurisdiction. At least in their businesses, the bankers wanted to govern themselves.

Even though this sort of autonomy for bankers harkened back to well-established precedent, it was already something of an archaism that would be increasingly challenged over the course of the sixteenth century. For reasons linked as much to the emergence of centralizing territorial states as to changing policies toward Jews, there was a sharp decline in the number of small-town Jewish communities where bankers had once dominated. In the larger cities, expanding Jewries were led by a range of Jewish merchants: international traders, grain dealers, and local retailers. These communities insisted on more formal structures and procedures, investing governing authority in elected committees rather than privileged individuals.[22] Even in places like Bologna where bankers continued to be licensed, they found themselves fighting a rearguard action against communal taxation and control.[23]

In Rome, the bankers' claims to monopoly and to immunity from rabbinic control are especially striking. As mentioned earlier, the newly chartered banking cartel of 1521 was superimposed on a large and long-established community, but this community seems to have lacked a crucial power of municipal self-government: the right to exclude strangers. In many areas European Jews had developed what was called a *hezkat yishuv*, that is, a recognized right to keep nonresident Jews from joining the community and competing for an existing government-granted business license. It must be stressed that the Jewish *hezkat yishuv* depended in theory and in fact on the government license; in the absence of an existing license, at least in Italy, Jewish law seems not to have recognized an exclusionary right.[24] Rome's papal government seems not to have recognized this right or had not previously granted the type of exclusive licenses on which the Jewish claim could be built. As I have suggested elsewhere, it was this structural weakness that, from the later decades of the fifteenth century, allowed the inflow of relatively large groups of Jewish immigrants into Rome, immigrants sufficiently numerous to form liturgical or ethnic subcommunities with synagogues and other communal institutions separate from those of the Italiani majority.[25] By the early sixteenth century these *oltramontani*—that is, Ashkenazic, French, Provençal, and Iberian immigrants—had developed a composite institutionalized identity of their own and demanded representation on the community council or *keri'a*.[26] Documents preserved in the city's notarial archive give us a sense of the gradual and somewhat cumbersome stages through which power was reallocated and governing institutions were reshaped more equitably. By 1505 the *oltramontani* had managed to secure a papal decree that guaranteed them at least one of the seats on the community's executive board of three *factors*.[27] This did not erase the distinction between the two communal units. Rather, it defined a working relationship in a federated "Università of [Italiani] and *oltramontani* or foreign Jews all living within the beautiful city of Rome."[28] Although the outside government presumably treated Roman Jewry as a single unit, from an internal and organizational perspective it remained a federation of rival groups—at least ten[29] separate Jewish synagogal associations and two overarching political units—each with separate memberships, properties, and shares in the common responsibilities.[30] In 1521 the papal authorities had complicated matters even further. They had recognized yet another form of Jewish organization: a trade association with substantial self-regulatory powers, as well as the right to exclude rivals. The bankers apparently felt that they were therefore entitled to a special status within the community structure.

By October 14, 1524, the community had agreed to their demands.[31] Roman Jews moved to draw up a new series of organizational rules that would accommodate the bankers and guarantee them a role in communal governance. Daniel da Pisa, leader of one of the wealthiest Jewish families of the day and himself well connected at the papal court, was asked to draft a set of bylaws (*capitoli*)—in effect, a constitution. Da Pisa brought experience and prestige to the process. Equally important, neither he nor his family held a banking license at the time, and so da Pisa likely appeared an objective arbitrator to all the parties.[32] The bankers and representatives of the rest of the community met in da Pisa's home to elect a drafting committee. By December 12, 1524, Pope Clement VII had ratified the *capitoli*.[33]

The Bankers and the New Constitution

It has long been argued that the new constitution was meant to address the problem of ethnic tension within the community. This was the position of Attilio Milano in his lengthy study published more than seventy-five years ago.[34] Indeed, it is clear that the deliberations and final structures carefully took ethnicity into account. But, as I have mentioned, a working relation between Italiani and *oltramontani* had already been formalized several decades earlier, and the arrangements of 1524 made little change in this regard. Close examination suggests that the most important innovation of 1524 was to expand the community council from twenty to sixty members.[35] This unwieldy number was dictated by the need to give a seat to every one of the twenty bankers while still allowing the rest of the community a two-thirds majority on the council.

The link between the bankers' license and the constitution of 1524 is clear, I believe, in the earliest known copy of that document, currently held in Harvard University's Houghton Library. This manuscript identifies the participants in the initial discussions both by name and by subcommunity and thus allows a better sense of the dynamics of the meeting.[36] Before drafting the new *capitoli*, Daniel da Pisa met separately with three different classes of Roman Jews—first with the *banchieri*[37] and then with the *artieri* and the *mediocri*. Each group was asked to select four representatives to the drafting committee that would write the constitution, to swear to abide by the new constitution, and to obey any rules issued by the new government.[38] The distinction between *artieri* and *mediocri* is not completely clear. One authoritative historical dictionary associates the term *artieri* with wool-cloth merchants or, more generally, those who employed craftsmen, adding that the term suggests status above that of an artisan but below that of someone who, like a banker, lived on invested capital.[39] In the later manuscript of the *capitoli* (the one published by Milano) the two groups are described in greater detail, but unfortunately the terminologies as reported are somewhat confusing and even contradictory, and it is not clear whether this is because the scribe of that manuscript no longer understood the terminology of an earlier era or because Milano's transcriptions and paraphrases are inexact.[40] In any case, the difference between the two groups was clearly relative. All were taxpayers in the Jewish community,[41] although *artieri* paid more than *mediocri*. Moreover, the distinction was apparently long established in the Roman community, since the *capitoli* had no need to define the two terms or distinguish between them. These were not rigid professional designations. Jacobbe Abuachar (Milano: Abucar), for example, represented the middle group, while Angelo di Cialone (Milano: Celloni) spoke for the third group, but both were physicians to be addressed as "M[agnific]o."[42] In the listing of the eventual council of sixty, representatives of the two groups were simply lumped together.[43]

The bankers, however, were another matter. These men were not elected; their role in the constitutional process and their eventual seats on the sixty-member council came to them because each held a papal license to lend money at interest in Rome. In other words, there was a causal link between exclusive privilege in an economic sector and the exercise of communal power, that is, between monopoly and jurisdiction, a relationship that exactly mirrors the development of European urban autonomy and government generally. The new Roman constitution—the earliest, or close to the earliest, Jewish communal constitution in Italy—acknowledged and guaranteed the special position of the bankers in communal governance.

Claims Against the Cartel

Although monopolistic privilege may have lent the cartel power and status within the community, it could not completely shield the bankers from fierce competitive forces. There were rivalries even among the twenty licensees. The bankers insisted on holding their licenses individually even though they paid the annual license fee collectively (*in solidum*). In 1534, for example, the *capitoli* were "granted and renewed" to each of twenty specific individuals listed by name rather than to an association or guild of bankers. The renewal insisted that "in no way shall anyone else be allowed to lend at interest or against pawns in Rome except for the above-mentioned twenty Jews," but it also specified that "should any of the above-mentioned Jews want to give up the right and privilege granted by the present *capitoli*, he can do so in favor of anyone he sees fit."[44] The bankers also had the right to take in partners. In 1536, for example, twenty-eight or more individuals had a vote in electing the cartel's representatives even though there were still only twenty licenses. Although the papal administration had to be informed of any such partnership, neither the cartel nor the community had any power of oversight or veto.[45] Controlling their personal title to these lucrative licenses was always paramount in the minds of the bankers.

We get a sense of the competitive atmosphere through careful consideration of a rabbinic responsum or legal brief by Rabbi Isaac de Lattes, a scholar active in Rome at the end of the 1530s and in the early 1540s.[46] The case, brought on Monday, February 24 (6 Adar II), 1539,[47] involved David da Sicilia, son of one of the original twenty license holders. Da Sicilia claimed that the cartel had illegally taken his inherited license from him, that he had the right to operate a bank in Rome, and that all profits made from the bank in the intervening years should revert to him. The cartel was represented by its *parnasim* or elected leaders, Mordechai ben Yo'av da Benafri and Isaac ben Jacob Goios[o].[48] De Lattes, here identified as "the Provençal medical doctor," was chosen as arbitrator for the cartel.[49] In his decision the rabbi rejected da Sicilia's claim, noting that the latter had formally ceded his right to participate in the monopoly in a signed document (פוליסה) held by the twenty. De Lattes transcribed the original Italian text carefully into his own Hebrew response, stressing that the plaintiff had acknowledged the document before the arbitrators and the court: "fe me cõfesso haver liberato e cõcesso el mio loco et ca' et prometo mai p[er] nullo te[m]po godere ne far godere il supra dicto loco anzi lo renu[n]zo da mo et cedolo ali dicti vintj."[50] As might be expected from the bankers' representative on the court, de Lattes made such a strong case on behalf of his clients that it is hard to understand da Sicilia's bringing the suit in the first place. Should we assume that the plaintiff was simply an unusually and unreasonably litigious individual?[51]

Whatever David's personality, the issue was apparently not nearly as straightforward as de Lattes argued. For one thing, David da Sicilia's representative (Rabbi Baruch ben Yo'av) must have made an equally strong case on behalf of his client since, on Sunday, March 9 (19 Adar II), the two rabbis were forced to declare themselves at a deadlock and selected a third arbitrator, a Rabbi Ishmael (Laudadio), to join their board and break the tie.[52] All in all, the case, which was supposed to be decided within ten days, dragged on for two months.[53] On Monday, March 24 (5 Nisan), 1539, David's brother,

Gershom (Italian: Pellegrino; Latin: Peregrinus), appeared before a notary to cede his portion in the family's claim to the banking license, and to authorize David to act unilaterally in the matter, whether in Jewish or non-Jewish courts.[54] Although such a document might suggest that the family was continuing the suit, it seems to me more likely that it was intended to clear the way for a settlement; the bankers wanted to be sure that any arrangement they made with David would not be challenged later by his brother.[55] A month later, the case was finally settled. On Tuesday, April 22, David and his brother admitted in a painstakingly detailed document and before two separate sets of witnesses that the release held by the bankers had indeed been written by David, and they swore never to contest it.[56] Two days later, on Thursday, April 24, there was a last entry: a Rabbi Yo'av ha-Rofe (the doctor) issued his own legal decision (*psak din*) in the matter. The notary was ordered to record that the bankers were to pay David 5.5 scudi (that is, 55 giulii). But, Rabbi Yo'av was quick to add, this was not to be considered repayment of a debt. Rather, it was merely an act of goodwill. Such an unusual notarized rabbinic ruling that intentionally steps outside the framework of the halakhically required makes more sense when we realize that Yo'av ha-Rofe is identical with the Maestro Dattylo "il fisico" whom we have already encountered as elected leader of the bankers' cartel in April 1534, and who would again be one of its *parnasim* in October 1540.[57] In other words, the *psak din* was actually a peace offering (or a payoff) from the bankers. The reader will probably not be surprised to learn that after such lengthy litigation, David rejected this token.[58] Still, it would seem that there had been at least some merit and some weight to David da Sicilia's case.

What do we know about the litigant? The da Sicilia family was likely among those who left Sicily during the mass expulsion of 1492, settling first in the Kingdom of Naples and then slowly making their way northward into one or another of the small towns of the Papal States—in this case, to the town of Tivoli, a few miles north-northeast of Rome.[59] By 1521 David's father, now known as Sabbetai da Tivoli, was in Rome, where he acquired one of the original twenty Jewish banking licenses. As Sabbatuccio di Tivoli, he is listed fourth among the Italiani bankers who shaped the communal constitution of 1524.[60] Three years later, in 1527, the city underwent the looting and pillaging by imperial mercenaries that would shock contemporaries and be remembered by historians as the Sack of Rome. It is not surprising that wealthy Jews were a frequent target of the depredations. Well known is the case of the banker, physician, and papal favorite Joseph Sarfati, who died horribly of an infection he contracted after escaping from four *latrones* (thieves) who had invaded and pillaged his home, imprisoning him in order to extort a large ransom.[61] A Magister Raphael Astronomus of Mirandola, one of the original licensees of 1521, likewise fled the city and managed to get to Naples, where he died.[62] This is likely also what happened to Sabbatuccio da Tivoli and his family. When, on June 17, 1531, David Sabbatutii, now described as "a Roman banker in Naples," was given a two-month safe-conduct and moratorium on his debts so that he might return to Rome and "settle his affairs," the concession stated explicitly that he had fled to Naples during the Sack of Rome.[63]

With this in mind, we can now try to reconstruct David's claim. Back in Rome, he quickly found that recovering his license and restoring his family business would not be easy. Once order had been restored in Rome, the papal *camerlengo* had unilaterally assigned the licenses of absent bankers to other candidates who now had a vested interest in pushing their own claims. David turned to the court of the papal vicar to bring suit against Salamone da Pisa, one of the wealthiest of the bankers, but da Pisa was able to obtain a papal ruling (March 5, 1535) declaring that the case fell exclusively within the jurisdiction of the papal chamberlain—that is, the very office that had transferred the license.[64] Apparently the vicar did nevertheless issue some sort of ruling on the case, but it likely went against David since he tried to hide it. Ten days later (March 15, 1535) David was ordered to hand over the verdict and a papal *rescritto* concerning the matter.[65] Four years later, as we have seen, David tried to revive the case, this time in rabbinical court.

For the bankers, David da Sicilia's suit was no trivial matter. More was at stake than one disgruntled litigant. They were willing to invest much time and effort battling his claim because to do otherwise was to open the door to other heirs who could demand the return of their parents' licenses from current owners. In the short term, the bankers' efforts paid off. Over the coming years David da Sicilia was caught up more than once in unsavory financial schemes, but he did not compete again for a banking license.[66] Yet, in winning the battle the bankers were already beginning to lose the war. More litigation quickly followed. On Tuesday, July 1, 1539, the cartel gathered in the city's largest synagogue, the Scuola del Tempio, to choose two representatives for the suit being brought by Giuseppe di Isaaco Zarfati over various matters, including his right to a license.[67] A week later, on July 8, 1539, the bankers empowered two other representatives to act on their behalf against "the twelve people who have risen up—and indeed all people who may rise up—to incite and quarrel with us and to infringe on our territory"—that is, to try to compete against the monopoly. To hire the *defensori* and *procuratori* required for the trial would not be cheap, but the bankers authorized their representatives "to spend money [from the funds that were levied for this purpose] as they see fit."[68] David da Sicilia had paved the way. On February 13, 1540, when Joseph Sarfati's daughters demanded restoration of their father's license before Christian arbitrators, the cartel chose, or was forced, to agree to a twenty-first license.[69] Similarly, Angelo (Mordechai) da Mirandola was allowed to resume his late father's business license in 1548.[70] Perhaps the bankers decided that it was too expensive to fight the increasing flood of litigation. Instead, they agreed to dilute their monopoly. On at least two other occasions, individuals who had given up banking licenses were able to negotiate special licenses, once in 1543 and again in 1551.[71]

Whose Jurisdiction?

The complicated, multiyear lawsuit of David da Sicilia highlights an important aspect of the banking business in Rome—how it functioned under, and between, the various legal jurisdictions. Historians have often assumed that premodern Jews were committed to legal autonomy for their community and that on principle they avoided gentile courts (*erka'ot shel goyim*) for suits against coreligionists.[72] This is, one suspects, a naive view of how businessmen operated in the real world. When Gershom da Sicilia empowered his brother to pursue the case in Jewish or gentile courts, this was not an aberration. As the legal historian Asher Gulack notes, early modern Jewish powers of attorney, or what might more properly be called assignments of claim (*shtarei harsha'a*) to third parties, quite regularly empowered the assignee to sue in a non-Jewish court.[73] And the Hebrew notarial records of Rome demonstrate that, in that city at least, resorting to non-Jewish courts was not limited to instances of collection from distant debtors. Roman Jews regularly dragged their fellows before non-Jewish courts for all manner of things if they thought that it was to their advantage. For example, on the page immediately following the da Sicilia case, the notary recorded that Salamone Corcos refused to be judged before a rabbinical court, insisting that he would respond to a suit from Moise Levi ibn Abi Shabbat only before a non-Jewish court.[74] On Sunday, February 27, 1541, a disagreement over real estate likewise turned on the question of which court would hear the case. The wealthy moneylender Joseph d'Arignano refused to have the case judged according to *dine yisra'el*, that is, according to Jewish law. The plaintiff brought the disagreement before the communal council, and the *parnasim* (who now included Yo'av "the doctor") had a notarized statement drawn up attesting that they had heard the refusal. By the next day they were able to convince d'Arignano and his family to agree to have the case heard before Roman rabbis, "who would rule according to the halakha [*al pi din tora*]" with an eight-day window for appeal.[75] We cannot assume, however, that communal officials would always insist on a Jewish venue. On June 15, 1539, Solomon and Isaac Zarfati had the community messenger Moise Levello testify before the notary that he had been repeatedly hired by the two bankers to approach the communal *fattori* (*memunim*) to have a tax matter settled in a rabbinic court. This time it was the *fattori* who had refused.[76]

How and why did Jews choose to bring their cases before a specific court? The answer is not always clear. People do not seem to have hesitated to have their business affairs known outside the community nor to have even personal and family troubles adjudicated by non-Jews.[77] All we can assume is that in civil matters where they had a choice, Jews sought out either the Jewish or the non-Jewish venue where they thought they had the best chance of winning. Within each legal universe Jewish litigants picked the most promising legal system, the most accessible bureaucratic official, or, in the case of arbitration, the system of customary norms or the principles of equity that seemed most sympathetic to their cause. What was necessary was for both sides to agree to the rules of the game in advance. To document their decision, they turned to a Jewish notary, a keeper of public record who, through formulaic writing and careful inscription of date, place, and witnesses, made it clear which option had been chosen. The Hebrew text might dictate that only non-Jewish systems of arbitration or law would apply, or litigants might agree to use Jewish arbitrators but to give them a relatively free hand to decide "according to [Jewish] law, an approximation of the law, or their own personal views." And in some cases, such as that of David da Sicilia in 1539, the notary would specify that judgement had to be rendered "according to Jewish law or an approximation of the law" (*beyn din hen karov la-din*), a phrasing that on this occasion was taken to mean that halakhic norms of procedure would apply. The multiplicity of legal systems is highlighted by the frequent (and, to the modern reader, ironic) addendum to many of these Hebrew notarial documents that they were to be considered as binding "as if drawn up by a Christian public notary."[78]

It seems that the bankers, suspended as they were between multiple law systems, became particularly adept at manipulating the differing legal norms to their own best advantage. The responsa issued by Rabbi de Lattes include several striking examples. As I have mentioned, loan shops were often conducted as partnerships, with an active partner who ran the day-to-day business and a silent partner, an investor who owned the license and provided a percentage, or even all, of the capital. On two occasions we hear that when such a working arrangement came to an end, the silent partner sent his teenage son to settle accounts. The active partner, suspecting a legalistic trap, refused to settle on the grounds that a receipt signed by a boy under twenty, while binding under Jewish law, could not be enforced in a non-Jewish court of law. It is hard to believe that the silent partners had not been aware of this legal norm and had chosen their teenage messengers unintentionally.[79] Indeed, it may be that age played a part in da Sicilia's case as well. Did David sign away his rights before reaching majority and try to have his waiver invalidated in the vicar's court on that ground? His unwillingness to produce what he considered an illegitimate document would now make sense. But the argument would not work in the Jewish court, and the waiver was judged binding.[80]

Clearly, in regard to banking licenses, the expected venue was a non-Jewish court—more specifically, the court of the papal *camerlengo*. Recall that when David da Sicilia first sued, he turned to a non-Jewish court, in that case, the court of the Roman vicar since he was appealing a decision made by the *camerlengo*. His attempt was rejected specifically on the grounds of jurisdiction. A few weeks later, on July 1, 1539, Giuseppe di Isaaco Zarfati insisted that his case be heard by Christian arbitrators and "according to the laws of the gentiles" despite the fact that David Ram, one of the most prominent of the bankers, specifically begged him to bring his case before a Jewish rabbi.[81] In fact, all the instances of litigation over bank licenses that I have discussed—the two suits in July 1539, the suit brought by the heirs of Joseph Sarfati in 1540, and the suit by Angelo da Mirandola in 1548—were heard by non-Jewish adjudicators, whether in formal trials (as in the case of July 8, 1539, where *defensori* and *procuratori* had to be hired) or in arbitration (as in the Sarfati case).

Obviously, then, when David turned to the rabbinic court in 1539, he did so only because his first efforts had failed. David had prepared himself well for his second trial. In the intervening years he had been studying rabbinic law to the extent that, starting at least from 1538, he was considered competent to serve as an arbiter in disputes between Jews. True, at the time of his trial in 1539, David was still a *haver*—that is, on some level a tyro.[82] Indeed, in the very first case in which he was chosen as an arbitrator (May 9, 1538), he was quickly disqualified specifically on the grounds that the *compromesso* or arbitration agreement had insisted that the case be tried according to Jewish law with two rabbis; since David da Sicilia was a *haver* and did not yet have the title "rabbi" (*she-eino musmakh be-shem rabi*), he could not yet issue a *psak din*.[83] But now he tried to turn his training to advantage in a Jewish court.[84] Yet, one question remains. What did David da Sicilia expect to gain by suing before a rabbinic court in a matter that pertained only to a government-licensed franchise and regarding which halakha had no standing? To answer that question, we have to put this case in a broader context.

An End to the Cartel?

Jurisdiction was not the only concern of the bankers. The business climate was changing around them, and despite their efforts, they would not be able to maintain their exclusive cartel much longer. For one thing, the Jewish pawnshops were beginning to face competition from *monti di pietà*, church-sponsored free-loan societies under the protection and supervision of the Franciscan order. Originating in the fifteenth century, such *monti* had become more viable from a business point of view after 1515, when Pope Leo X officially allowed them to charge at least a limited rate of interest in order to cover expenses.[85] Rome finally had its own *monte* from Holy Wednesday, April 2, 1539, possibly in response to increasing Spanish influence over the religio-political climate in the papal city.[86] At first, the Roman Monte di Pietà seems to have been a quite limited operation, aimed only at the poorest residents of the city and encumbered with relatively inflexible standards on when and how it might extend credit. Indeed, Jewish loan banking would continue to be licensed in Rome until October 1682. Still, the Monte presented an alternative to Jewish moneylending that from the start challenged the Jews' freedom of operation and claim to high interest rates.[87] The Franciscans' preaching in support of the Monte also carried with it a threat of physical danger. It has been suggested that their sermons, as well as an elaborate performance of a passion play on Good Friday (April 4), 1539, led to an outburst of street violence against Rome's Jews. Even though the city police and Pope Paul III responded quickly to put down the riot and punish the perpetrators, at least some of the bankers must have wondered how long their controversial livelihood would continue.[88]

But the main threat to the cartel seems to have come not from the outside, but from within the Jewish community itself. I have already mentioned the increasing litigation the bankers faced from those who demanded reinstatement of their licenses. Other Jews simply tried to evade the licensing procedure altogether, offering cheap loans without the proper license. Both the government and the bankers, of course, had a stake in trying to stop this black market in credit,[89] but they could not quash the spreading resentment of the very idea of a business monopoly within the Roman Jewish community. By the fall of 1540, matters reached a crisis point. A public meeting was called on Sunday, October 3. In the Scuola del Tempio, the bankers came face-to-face with all of Rome's Jewish organized communities, as well as the *fattori* of the combined communal council. The bankers asked the notary to speak on their behalf—that is, to present their case—but at least ten of them attended in person, including the current *parnasim* of the cartel, Yo'av "the doctor" and David Ram. Although we do not have all the details of what was said, it is clear that matters did not go well for the cartel. They were forced to give up their closed monopoly. Moreover, they would agreed to contribute two hundred scudi annually to fund a free-loan program for the Jewish poor. Whether this was a response to real needs (and possibly real social tensions) within the Roman Jewish community or merely a token concession by the bankers to buy off their rivals, we unfortunately cannot know. But it is interesting that this new charity was modeled after the new Christian Monte di Pietà: clients would still have to deposit pledges, although they would not pay interest on their loans.[90] It would seem that the balance of power between community and cartel had clearly shifted.

Of course, the bankers did not give up without a fight. They did manage to win important concessions. Moneylending would not become a free-for-all. Only Roman residents could take part. New moneylenders could not simultaneously engage in any other form of trade under pain of excommunication. Each new lender would also have to contribute at least two scudi to each tax levy. Even more important, the bankers were able to impose substantive limits on the new banks—limits that may have been left unsaid at the meeting since they were not spelled out in the notarized minutes. Perhaps in a separate arrangement with the papal chamberlain, then, the bankers ensured that the number of additional licenses would be limited to twenty, and the new lenders would be allowed to charge only half as much interest as their more established counterparts. The cartel members must have congratulated themselves on managing to co-opt twenty of their opponents by offering them only a pale shadow of the established licenses. Whether or not people at the meeting knew it, the cartel was not yet dead. It had only been grudgingly expanded to include some quite weak competitors.[91]

The tensions between the *banchieri* and the rest of the community continued to grow. On May 22, 1541, the "Twenty of the *keri'a*" met with representatives of the bankers who "engage in exchange" (*she-osim ha-hiluf*) in the Catalan-Aragonese synagogue. The bankers were facing some sort of legal case with non-Jews and wanted the *keri'a* to take on the matter as one concerning the entire community. The matter was given over to arbitration; Obadiah and Abraham represented the *keri'a*, and Joseph Sarfati and Moses ben Isaac the money changers. They were to decide the matter before the upcoming festival of Pentecost (that is, in slightly less than two weeks), and if they could not agree, they were to call in a third party to break the tie. The notarial entry ends with a statement whose import is not completely clear: "The principle that emerges is that the community [*kahal*] does not wish to assume responsibility for the case, but rather to rule, negotiate, and insist to the people who want to engage in exchange that they will have to pay." Whether that last statement was the final resolution of the case or simply a clarification of the Twenty's position, two things are clear. First, even though the bankers had automatic seats on a sixty-member council, some form of twenty-member council had reemerged, at least to negotiate with the bankers. Second, at least by 1541 there were clearly substantial voices within the community that sought to distance communal governance from the bankers' cartel.[92]

And now, at last, I return to the document with which I began. The three men who appeared before the *keri'a* on October 7, 1542, were speaking in the name of a broad coalition. The notary described the three as *yehide ha-kahal* (communal notables), possibly an indication of some special status.[93] But he also identified them as the *murshim mi-tsad ha-kahal*, a legal phrase that indicates they were delegated representatives. They demanded an end to the council's support of the monopoly.

The issue was obviously serious. David Ram immediately rose to announce that he had been appointed delegate by the twenty established old lenders and was willing to go to rabbinical court. For their part, the new lenders asked for a day to discuss the matter among themselves. The next day they met in the Scuola del Tempio and appointed their own three representatives for a trial to be conducted "according to the Law, in approximation of the Law, or by way of a compromise." But they were very worried about being used as sacrificial goats to the general anger. They wanted to be sure that all parties in a trial would be equally exposed. They insisted, therefore, on seeing clear evidence that David Ram had been legally delegated and that all of his group would abide by any decision he signed. In addition, the entire twenty-one-member communal council had to be physically present to elect the community's representative.[94] The new lenders argued, not unreasonably, that should they default on the agreement they had signed with the *camerlengo*, they would be exposed to a fine of 1,000 scudi. They did not want to expose themselves to such a risk without being sure that everyone else was equally committed.[95]

Rivalry, Regulation and Jewish Agency in Premodern times

The story here comes to an abrupt end. So far, no documentary evidence of that rabbinic trial has come to light. It is clear that the cartels did manage to survive; they continue to be mentioned in papal documents, although the rates they could charge declined.[96] The many responsa, notarial acts, judicial decisions, and thousands of loan receipts that await the historian's attention in Rome's rich archives will undoubtedly yield further insights to the dedicated researcher. But already the curtain has been lifted on the fierce, even cutthroat, business competition between Roman Jewish bankers. Economic rivalry affected everything within the community, from personal interactions to communal structures and law systems. Even halakha did not function in ethereal intellectual isolation. Living in the interstices among legal systems, Jews had learned to wend their way carefully between rival jurisdictions. And communal leadership did not automatically enjoy communal support. In matters of economic importance, attempts to create de facto institutional realities were challenged both by individuals and by larger groups within the community. Powerful people could not simply override well-established patterns of economic organization. Calls for justice could not be ignored, and even the wealthy had to respond to the mechanisms of social consensus.

Historians have usually understood regulations and restrictions on Jewish moneylending as motivated by the church's religious teachings. But we have seen that Jewish moneylending, like any other government-licensed business, created profit and endured loss at the intersection between opportuntiy and regulation, and that regulation itself could be a source of profit. Licenses implied monopoly, and monopoly was worth defending. From the cases examined here, we see, moreover, that regulation itself did not come merely from the outside authorities. The Jewish community had its own internal interest groups and fiscal principles that led to various types of regulation.

We should not be surprised that the competing moneylenders of Rome were actively engaged in negotiating their economic fate. In this they demonstrate to us that Jewish historical agency was not limited to the organized collectivity or to internal religious matters. These individual Jews chose the arenas and strategies of their actions in accordance with their own perceived self-interest. When it suited them, Roman Jews turned to Roman courts by choice, without thereby abandoning internal institutions as venues for brokering social tension and economic competition. Jewish historians have long portrayed Jewish modernization as the replacement of communal and halakhic control by the state. From the perspective of the documents, however, modernization might be better seen as putting an effective end to the freedom of choice that early modern Jewish businessmen had enjoyed—the freedom to maneuver among multiple jurisdictions.

Chapter 2

Contraband for the Catholic King: Jews of the French Pyrenees in the Tobacco Trade and Spanish State Finance

Carsten L. Wilke

On a winter day in 1672, a French merchant and a Spanish cavalry captain strolled across Madrid's most fashionable square, the Puerta del Sol. When they passed the *estanco*, the booth of the royal tobacco monopoly, the soldier approached the salesman and, with a ghastly friendliness, greeted him: "*Adiós judío*," "hi, Jew." The Frenchman was astonished. Was there, at the central spot of the capital, under the watchful eyes of the Inquisition, a barely disguised Jew selling His Catholic Majesty's leaves and snuff? The soldier explained to him that this was indeed the case. He had once met the same tobacconist in Bayonne, France, coming from the local synagogue. The Frenchman went to alert the Holy Office.[1]

A coincidence had revealed to him the fact that much of the tobacco monopoly and other royal tax incomes all over Castile were leased to Portuguese crypto-Jews based in France. Other contemporaries were better informed about this open secret; and many of them found it scandalalous. Francisco de Torrejoncillo, the bilious Franciscan author of a 1674 anti-Jewish booklet, blended the pipe and the pyre into a horrifying comparison. "Having sold so much smoke during their lifetime, those Jews vanish like smoke, as they will all have to die in smoke. They crave for honors, ranks, and offices, so as to fumigate the world's poor children and to choke them with their smoke."[2] Brother Francisco, this Judeo-phobic antismoker, offers an early version of the phenomenon that Sander Gilman has described as the "strange but powerful association of Jews . . . with smoking tobacco."[3] Furthermore, Torrejoncillo exemplifies the slow shift of anti-Judaic obsession from the stereotype of the greedy usurer to that of the ambitious parvenu, the state-supported inventor of banking and taxing schemes.[4]

In focusing on the Jewish-administered tobacco monopoly as an unlikely cooperation between state and contrabandists, I will give a multilayered description of a trans-Pyrenean commercial system and assess its surprising impact on Jewish geography, society, and culture. An intersection of seemingly contradictory economic and religious interests, this system has to be approached simultaneously from various perspectives that in Jewish as well as Iberian historiography have usually been isolated from one another. Beginning with an overview of the European background of colonial expansion, revolution in consumer culture, and innovation in public finance, I will then consider the critical conjunction in the 1650s of the peak of Inquisitional persecution, the military and fiscal straits of the Spanish monarchy, the demographic pressure and mental flexibility that made New Christians migrate back to Spain, and the concomitant emergence of a border economy in the Basque country that sustained Sephardi life in early modern France. Next, I will document the concrete ways in which the tobacco economy was organized by interconnected family networks, and finally, I will look at the cultural strategies that succeeded, even under such difficult conditions, in bridging geographical space as well as political and religious cleavages.

Administrating Tobacco Monopolies

During the rapid seventeenth-century expansion across geographic and social space, tobacco consumerism and the money economy came to be linked together, as well as being tied to the economic policies of the time. When the exotic plant turned into an article of mass consumption in the 1640s, it immediately became the object and tool of major fiscal innovations.[5] Jewish trade networks were prominent in the elaboration of these administrative and commercial schemes because of the three assets that in certain historical circumstances enabled Jews to handle complex commodity chains: their readiness to discover and exploit economic niches, their transnational networks created by recent migration and cultural flexibility, and their previous experience in similar areas.[6] A recent study by Mary Norton shows that Portuguese New Christians had been involved in the Spanish tobacco monopoly since its very beginnings. Antonio de Soria, a Portuguese tax collector in Murcia, prided himself for having conceived and designed in 1636 that ingenious system for retailing vice and reaping cash for the state from it.[7] He and his migrant community had manned the monopoly with a complex pyramidal order of central, provincial, and local administrators, alongside individual salesmen and wholesale merchants importing the plant from the colonies.[8] Henceforth the New Christians' presence in the monopoly would have its ups and downs, but it remained permanent for eighty-nine years until 1725, when the king, during a devastating Inquisitional persecution, prohibited any further lease of tobacco incomes to "the Jews."[9] Monopoly organization was first centered in a chief tax farmer in Madrid; from 1701 onwards, it was directly governed by the royal treasury; and in 1887, it was entrusted to an incorporated state enterprise. When European Union laws finally suppressed the monopoly in 1995, the royal tobacco booth on the Puerta del Sol had been in place for 359 years.[10]

In short, Antonio de Soria's business idea became one of the most successful in European history. Subsequently, in 1674, the French monarchy created its own monopolized tobacco production and distribution system.[11] Other European governments followed suit, some of them relying likewise on the help of New Christian or Jewish continental networks. One such network was headed by the Lopes Pereira family, who were present in the European tobacco business from 1653 to 1747. The founder, Francisco, born in Mogadouro, Portugal, leased the tobacco monopoly for Granada and later for all of Castile; his son Manuel held the same position in Portugal, based on his English connections; and the grandson Diego finally introduced the monopoly to the Austrian Empire and was ennobled for this contribution with the title of Baron d'Aguilar.[12]

On the basis of similar cases in some German and Italian states, a historian in Sombart's Germany tried to define the financial adventurism of "Jewish moneymen" as a recurrent element in the organization of the early European tobacco monopolies.[13] Stretching the point even farther, a recent scholar claimed that all these tobacco monopolies formed a "European Jewish commercial system."[14] Against exaggerations of this kind, it is important to keep in mind that nowhere in Europe was the impact of Jewish (or rather, crypto-Jewish) tobacconists as powerful, as penetrating, and as constant as it was in Castile. The extent and persistence of their participation in financial policy recalls the fortune of a more notorious Jewish-administered taxation system in the feudal liquor monopoly of early modern Poland.[15] But unlike the Polish "political economy of vodka," the Spanish case implied an obvious paradox. Why did a country at war, which violently persecuted anything Jewish, entrust an important royal institution to Jews in disguise who operated from enemy territory? Why did Jews flock into this business sector at a time when it was not only incompatible with any regular Jewish religious practice, but also a most dangerous way of gaining a livelihood? The fact that Antonio de Soria had provided the initial spark does not, of course, give a sufficient answer to these questions. We have to look at the circumstances that, two decades after the invention of the scheme, prompted its major expansion.

The Turn of the 1650s

During most of the seventeenth century, the Spanish government contracted financial services from competing bankers belonging to three groups reputed to be loyal to Spain: the Italians, Portuguese, and Castilians. The Portuguese had started their activity in Castilian state finance in the sixteenth century with the organization of the slave trade in the Indies; in 1627, they began to supply armies[16] and then shifted quite naturally to fiscal administration, because the treasury often repaid military loans with future tax incomes.[17] This group was constituted exclusively by New Christians (to such an extent that Castilians of Jewish origin tended to join the Portuguese), but few of its initial members had any link to the Jewish religion and diaspora.[18] Crypto-Jewish newcomers gained a larger share in the financial services of the Portuguese after the state bankruptcy of 1647.[19] Spanish leaders were heavily predisposed against leasing taxes to them, given their suspected Judaism, their contraband practices,[20] and the insecurity in which they lived. Indeed the Spanish Inquisition carried out the most important anti-Jewish persecution of its entire history during the years 1651–1656.[21] In reporting the flight of two hundred suspects on June 29, 1654, the Madrid chronicler Jerónimo Barrionuevo added that "no one gives credit to Portuguese anymore, because they may go bankrupt from one day to the next and emigrate in order to escape from the Inquisition."[22] Surprisingly, however, quantitative research has shown that the financial services of the Portuguese were still more reliable than those of competing merchant corporations.[23] According to a 1654 report by the Council of Finance, they were the only merchants who had the intelligence, the experience, the information (*noticia*), and the credit necessary to implement the complex financial logistics of the monopolies.[24] More precisely, they were often the only party who dared to bid for leases. Defending its financial interests, the Crown obtained on September 7, 1654 an agreement (*concordia*) with the Inquisition, which exempted from confiscation all capital invested in the state treasury. As a result, state incomes administered by a convicted heretic had to be returned to the latter's relatives and associates, and in consequence the New Christian business network resisted even the heavy blows subsequently directed against its chief executives.[25] One year later, Barrionuevo observed that "no tobacco seller remains in Madrid whom the Inquisition has not captured. In recent days, it apprehended two entire families, parents and children; and many others have fled to France." But it was never long before a new tenant reopened the booth on the Puerta del Sol. Barrionuevo was left with the impression that "these people sprout like mushrooms."[26]

For the New Christians, running the Spanish tobacco monopoly meant not only that they had to maintain a centralized financial network and a manpower-intensive retailing system. It also meant that they periodically had to replace their arrested or emigrated agents. The high tide of recruitment fell in the years of 1656–1659, when Antonio de Soria's long-time rival, Diego Gómez de Salazar (1606–1670), a Castilian New Christian from Ciudad Rodrigo, was chief administrator of the tobacco monopoly for the whole kingdom, which he developed into an extremely complex administrative pyramid. Madrid alone had no less than eighteen tobacco administrators, mainly Portuguese, with their respective districts and outlets. Even after Gómez de Salazar's arrest by the Inquisition, his firm continued its activity, thanks to the 1654 *concordia*, and many of his Portuguese collaborators all over Castile stayed in place.[27]

The triangle formed by the Crown, the Inquisition, and the crypto-Jews henceforth lost its "impossible" character.[28] Still, the alliance the monarchy struck with the hunted heretics must seem incomprehensible unless we remember the desperate state of the Spanish treasury in Gómez de Salazar's time. While King Philip IV tried to wage war on three fronts, against France, Portugal, and England,[29] the silver fleets were lost to English attacks in 1656 as well as in 1657, and enemy offensives penetrated Spanish territory from various sides, including the Low Countries, Italy, Extremadura, and the Caribbean. The silver supply from the other groups of Crown bankers, Italians and Castilians, had in the meantime fallen almost to zero.[30] In this disastrous situation, the Hispanic monarchy had no other choice than to mount a huge fiscal offensive.[31] Castilian consumer taxes skyrocketed; they would attain an historical peak in 1658.[32] But since the taxing of basic foodstuffs always kindled the fire of rebellion, it was increasingly supplemented by luxury and vice taxes levied on sugar, pepper, cocoa, playing cards, and, most important of all, tobacco. With all his customary sources of money dried up, the Catholic king took a gamble on Jews and tobacco, though neither of the two up until then had demonstrated any exceptional financial performance. Compared to the 3,471 million *maravedís* that the Crown derived in 1658 from its three major indirect taxes (*alcabala*, *millones*, *cientos*),[33] the 62 million that Gómez de Salazar contributed per annum from his tobacco monopoly seems almost negligible.[34] But the Crown monopoly, which had the effect of raising the consumer prices of tobacco by 250 percent,[35] was to increase in value almost five times in the course of the following two decades, and eventually succeeded in making up for the dwindling supplies of silver from the Indies.[36] From the 1660s onward, the Spanish treasury extracted more hard currency from the lungs of its subjects than from all of its American mines, and in the beginning of the eighteenth century, monies from tobacco taxes made up about a quarter of its net income.[37]

If the Crown's dependence on Jewish taxmen can reasonably be explained by a lack of alternatives, it is more difficult to understand the tobacconists' interest. Their economic culture of secret Jewishness existed under a form of state protection, but at a daily risk. Several among Gómez de Salazar's successors as chief administrators of the tobacco monopoly ended up like him in the dungeons of the Inquisition. The same destiny awaited many of the sub-lessees. Salazar's administrators of the Granada *estanco*, the above-mentioned Francisco Lopes Pereira and Francisco Rodrigues Lopes, both enjoyed brief terms of office, in 1653–1658 and 1658–1661 respectively, before the Inquisition hauled them in.

A still more pernicious danger to this economic network emerged from within, whenever some well-placed member of the group turned informer, either in a sudden attack of Catholic enthusiasm or for more selfish reasons. Joseph Garcia de Leão from Lisbon, after long travels across the Jewish diaspora and a juridical conflict in Amsterdam, denounced New Christians to the Inquisition in order to exact hush money from those he spared. For some time in 1661–1662, he and a number of accomplices maintained a Mafia-like structure inside the Portuguese merchant community of Madrid, the magnate of which, Simão da Fonseca Pina, apparently silenced Joseph by ceding him a lucrative position in the Málaga salt tax administration.[38]

Furthermore, state tobacco administration needed a far-flung trade and contraband network abroad. For the Crown, the monopoly had been from the outset a means of reaping benefits from a contraband trade that it was unable to repress because its own colonial monopolies made it so lucrative.[39] In 1627, Portuguese contraband merchants of Bayonne still exported sizeable quantities of the Venezuelan "Barinas" brand of tobacco to the Netherlands;[40] two decades later, most of the illegal trade across the Pyrenees flowed in the opposite direction. The Spanish tobacco monopoly had control over the imports of the plant and thus allowed its administrators to engage in a kind of legalized fraud: they could replace the expensive tobacco from Venezuela and Cuba by the cheaper sorts from Brazil or Virginia, purchased from the Portuguese or the British enemy, and sell them at the same prices. The same was true for salt, pepper, and other monopolized commodities.[41] The important Madrid merchant Fernando Montesinos, who traded with his Jewish brother in Amsterdam, extensively used his position in different monopolies in the early 1650s to bring in grain and salt imports from France that would otherwise have been illegal.[42] Portuguese merchants endeavored to control these supply chains by placing them in the hands of their own relatives and agents, many of whom were members of Jewish communities abroad.

In this context, the Spanish business adventures faced a complication from a religious point of view. Whereas non-baptized Jewish businessmen and diplomats could receive special permits to enter the Iberian territories,[43] most Portuguese Jews of the time were baptized in their youth and had to cross the Pyrenees as counterfeit Catholics. As Yosef Kaplan has shown, the main Portuguese Jewish communities of the mid-seventeenth century imposed a penitence ceremony on members who came back from business trips to Spain and Portugal; these men were furthermore excluded from honorary offices for two to four years following their return.[44] Even in a society obsessed with reputation, this sanction was too benign to act as a deterrent against such travels. It did, however, allow the expression of a symbolic disapproval and ultimately became a kind of rite of passage marking the border between Jewish and Christian spaces. The ritual was introduced in Amsterdam by a community board ordinance of June 16, 1644, and was followed by similar regulations in Livorno on March 28, 1655, and in Hamburg on December 23, 1657. The respective community boards defined the forbidden destinations in neutral terms as "a country belonging to Spain or Portugal" (Amsterdam), as "the lands of the West where it is forbidden for Jews to dwell" (Livorno), or simply as "Spain and Portugal" (Hamburg). Only in the solemn formula recited in the synagogue were these destinations rhetorically demonized, as penitents had to ask for forgiveness for "the evil act that I did in going to a land of idolatry."[45] In Amsterdam, the sanction remained in place for a century and was applied eighty-five times; however, two thirds of those instances occurred during the first fifteen years. The peak of the phenomenon, with five cases per year, is recorded in 1656–1659.[46]

These measures were aimed at otherwise loyal community members, with the threat of exclusion from synagogue honors being precisely the main penalty involved. We have no reason to suppose that travelers from Amsterdam to Spain were as a rule dissenters from Judaism. On the contrary, when unmasked by the Inquisition on their journey, some displayed a militant Jewish stance and became celebrated martyrs. In 1655, Abraham Nunes Bernal and his nephew Isaac d'Almeida Bernal, circumcised in Amsterdam, and subsequently agents for the Bayonne magnate Diogo Rodrigues Cardoso, died at the stake in Cordova and Santiago proclaiming their Jewish faith until their last moments. In 1665, again in Cordova, Abraham Athias, Jacob Rodrigues Caceres, and Raquel Nunes Fernandes met the same fate.[47] Thanks to a poem Daniel Levi de Barrios published in their honor, they are commemorated in the prayer book of the Sephardi Synagogue of Amsterdam until the present day. Paradoxically, the same liturgy would have treated them as evildoers, had they been fortunate enough to avoid arrest and to find their way back home.

The historian can arrive at a more nuanced idea about the religious profiles of the travelers by researching some of the Inquisitional interrogations held with the scores of traders and taxmen who had the bad luck to be identified. Most interrogations with Portuguese coming from the north were clustered between the years 1658 and 1662—that is, a few years after the peak of persecution inside the Spanish capital.[48] As to the motivations of their return, the interrogations of the arrested traders furnish a wealth of information on the evolution of their religious convictions and doubts. David Graizbord's pioneering study of these conversion and re-conversion stories uncovered the long-overlooked fact that New Christian emigration from Spain had a significant reverse flow. The Inquisitional material leads him to conclude that "habitual returnees were chiefly economic refugees who dissented from certain normative social and religious patterns" of Jewish life. In Graizbord's view, travel to Spain seems to be explicable only in terms of religious doubt and deviance.[49]

The Inquisitional records are precious sources for almost every aspect of seventeenth-century history, but it seems doubtful that they can be relied upon in terms of their central documented concern, the spiritual biographies of the defendants.[50] Whereas the prisoners predictably presented their emigration to France as a result of unlucky circumstances,[51] they insisted upon the deep spiritual significance of their return, claiming that they had never felt at home in the Jewish religion and that they had increasingly longed to return to the bosom of the Church. António Rodrigues da Mezquita, the protagonist of Graizbord's study, a tradesman on the mule track between Bayonne and Madrid, evokes before the Inquisitors three successive religious crises that allegedly alienated him from Judaism and gradually brought him back to committed feelings for the Catholic religion by 1664, the year his business went bankrupt and he presented himself to the Inquisition in order to abjure his apostasy and receive the permission to settle in Spain again.[52] Even informers of his kind, who volunteered to denounce persons from their former religious milieu, cannot be safely classified as apostates from Judaism. In fact, they often followed a transparent strategy of setting their records straight with the Holy Office before taking up new positions in tax administration. As an informer wrote from Bordeaux in 1661, "they do it for convenience, in order to be safely able to rob the world; they refrain from indicating any accomplice among the many they have in Spain; in exchange they charge many Jews of France, alongside some good Catholics in Spain as well as in France."[53] Many of the preserved trial records illustrate exactly this pattern.[54]

In reality, Jewish travelers had sufficient sentimental, cultural, family, and above all commercial motivations to bring them back to Spain; and their return voyages do not automatically furnish evidence of a religious crisis.[55] In spite of painful memories, the Hispanic countries remained from the Sephardic perspective an essential pole of self-identification and were never set apart, let alone demonized, as coherently as they were in Protestant propaganda.[56] This powerful nostalgia was not directed to a merely mythic homeland. Contemporary Spain still exerted an extraordinary attraction that could counterbalance its manifold dangers. In spite of the xenophobic frenzy expressed in Spanish religious and political literature, and in spite of the permanent and successful anti-Jewish propaganda organized by the Inquisition, Portuguese New Christians seem to have encountered little verbal or physical aggressions from average Spaniards, who left the monopoly of religious violence to the Inquisition.[57] In general, Spaniards proved to be willing partners in trading, partying, and even courting; and New Christians wishing to intermarry normally found a family free of blood purity prejudices. A crypto-Jewish tobacco merchant coined the aphorism that the Iberian Peninsula was the best place on earth to pursue reputation and prosperity, if only that "stepfather" called Inquisition did not spoil the picture.[58] Expecting a greater degree of resentment, many readers have been bewildered by Benedict Spinoza's positive judgment on Spanish tolerance expressed in the third chapter of his *Theological-Political Treatise*. Indeed, the philosopher took an almost touristic perspective when, three years after his exclusion from the Amsterdam synagogue, he told a Spanish captain in a private conversation "that he had never seen Spain, but would like to see it."[59] The graphic terms "lands of idolatry" or "lands of Inquisition" opposing Spain and Portugal to the rest of Europe occur less insistently in the sources than in modern secondary literature, which has evidently been influenced by Black Legend traditions and Cold War experiences.[60] It is time to go beyond this dichotomist mapping and realize that in the perception of seventeenth-century Portuguese Jews, the Pyrenees were no Iron Curtain, and Spain was as much a travel destination as any other European country would have been.

This conclusion is even more valid for the Portuguese communities of southwestern France. Since the turn of the seventeenth century, several hundred Portuguese merchant families lived in semi-clandestine Jewish communities in the border region around Bayonne. As the burghers of this port city did not admit foreign competition, the immigrants settled in the suburb of Saint-Esprit-lès-Bayonne and in the country towns of Peyrehorade and Labastide-Clairence, protected by a lineage of regional nobles and military governors, the Counts (later Dukes) of Gramont. An illegitimate son of King Henry IV with his mistress Diane d'Andouins, Count Antoine, Antonin de Gramont (1572–1644), was simultaneously an independent-minded lord of Bidache castle and a defender of royal interests in his function as governor of Navarre and Béarn. For his protection of Portuguese crypto-Jews and their lucrative commerce, he repeatedly risked confrontations with the clergy and municipal authorities of Bayonne.[61] His son and successor, Duke Antoine de Gramont (1604–1678), one of Prime Minister Mazarin's closest agents, even tried to shield Portuguese Jewish assets in Spain against the Inquisition.[62] In 1637, there were one hundred Judaizing families in Saint-Esprit and in

Peyrehorade;[63] by 1655, the number had risen to three hundred. Whereas the Peyrehorade community seems to have attained its zenith in the 1670s,[64] that of Saint-Esprit continued to grow steadily well into the eighteenth century.[65]

Why did most of the Portuguese Jewish population of France cluster near the southwestern tip of the kingdom? Committed to the idea of a one-way emigration of New Christians from Christianity to Judaism, I. S. Révah believed that this huge border settlement was necessary as a "stopover" (*escale*) for helping Iberian refugees on to Amsterdam.[66] More recently, Jonathan Israel identified contraband as a more convincing reason for the geographical clustering.[67] The Portuguese of Saint-Esprit and Peyrehorade found their economic mainstay in a kind of border commerce that the Spanish jurist José Pellicer, in a polemical booklet that he directed in 1640 against Jewish smugglers, summarized in the formula "to bring linen and to take wool."[68] During the 1650s, various French linen fabrics were brought to Madrid across the Pyrenees,[69] some of them destined for the huge Hispano-American markets. The traders also dealt in nontextile commodities. For example, in 1641, Joseph Sanches, based in Peyrehorade after a sojourn as a Jew in Livorno, loaded his mule with pepper, sold the spice to a Madrid grocer, and smuggled the silver money back home.[70] Others invested their Spanish profits in chocolate or saffron.[71]

Jonathan Israel has stressed the importance of the Hispano-Dutch embargo of 1621 for the development of this border commerce.[72] However, Anne Zink's exhaustive analysis of the Bayonne notary deeds has found evidence of a fluctuating presence of Portuguese merchants, which the military events cannot sufficiently explain. During the Hispano-Anglo-Dutch war years of 1626–1630, the overall value of Bayonne's trade peaked,[73] but Portuguese participation remained negligible. Only in 1658 did it edge sharply upward, with the number of attested business transactions involving local Portuguese suddenly rising fivefold.[74] Mass immigration is also responsible for the construction fever that seized the crypto-Jewish villages in that same year.[75] According to Zink's explanation, the consolidation of Jewish settlement in the Bayonne region was due not so much to wartime smuggling as to the economic recovery that followed the Peace of the Pyrenees.[76] But this hypothesis also runs into a chronological difficulty. The spectacular rise in the drawing up of notary deeds took place two years before the peace, at a time when the Spanish embargo was being maintained more rigidly than ever.[77] As Zink herself noted, Jewish commerce in Saint-Esprit largely escaped the impact of the military events because it was not concentrated in a particular sector of foreign trade. Though the exchange between the Portuguese diaspora and the

Iberian countries remained their mainstay, Saint-Esprit Jews also tried their hand at many occupations inside the regional economy, such as cod fishing and the distribution of textiles in the countryside.[78]

The line of argument from international politics evidently leads to contradictory conclusions: it points to the commercial benefits of smuggling whenever there is war and to those of free trade whenever there is peace. In Jonathan Israel's view, when the Spanish war embargo against the Netherlands was abolished in 1647 and the ensuing fifteen years assured a "trading boom," Portuguese Jews and New Christians again played "a major, and in the view of Spanish officials, the leading role."[79] According to more recent studies, however, this legal trade, as well as contraband French, Portuguese, and British goods, was "practically monopolized by the Dutch."[80] The Portuguese share in the volume of trade actually declined, aside from the merchandise that their administration of monopolies and customs allowed them to import.[81] In sum, factors such as tobacco consumption and the state of Castilian finances seem to explain the sudden expansion of Jewish border trade during the fateful 1650s far better than the sequence of war and peace.

We are now in a position to reconstruct the actual chain of events. The diaspora of Portuguese New Christians lived through critical moments and a major readjustment in the middle of the 1650s. The Inquisitional crackdown in Spain peaked in 1654; the expulsion of the Jewish community of Dutch Brazil during the same year by the victorious Portuguese kingdom exerted an additional demographic pressure upon the Portuguese Jewish settlements. Almost at the same time, new opportunities were offered by Castilian fiscal policy. The result was a considerable reflux from the Jewish diaspora into Spain and, two years later, the sizeable rise in Portuguese economic activity in the villages on the French border. During these years, the Portuguese became prominent in the Spanish tobacco monopoly not only in spite of the constant Inquisitional persecutions, but also, in a way, because of them. Emigration and overpopulation permitted and, indeed, forced the crypto-Judaic families to engage in financial ventures involving uncertain gains and huge risks, which deterred other merchant groups.[82] In brief, the decisive factor in the Pyrenean border economy was neither a religious crisis nor the alternation of war and peace, but demographic pressure from the pool of unemployed and impoverished, yet well-trained refugees that the Portuguese diaspora had to offer.

The most striking fact about this border economy is its strongly counterintuitive impact at the religious level. The community of Saint-Esprit not only grew numerically during the heyday of the Franco-Spanish tobacco economy; it also witnessed the consolidation of publicly recognized Jewish life.[83] Around 1653, a medical doctor from Amsterdam, Manuel, alias Isaac de Avila, became the suburb's first rabbi. The community rented for him a big building on the margins of the built area, which served as a synagogue. Congregants called the place *escuela* in Spanish, or *medras* in Hebrew.[84] Through his sermons, Doctor Avila gained the support of the community majority. He stayed in Saint-Esprit until the end of his life, which lasted for at least two more decades,[85] though he had to overcome the stern condemnation of the Dutch rabbinical authorities, the resistance of the more lukewarm members of the community, and the initially unfavorable political conditions.[86] Only in 1656 did the Duke of Gramont obtain a royal charter prohibiting investigations into the private life of the Portuguese immigrants.[87] The congregation, later named Nefutsot Yehudah (Judah's Dispersion), had already acquired a cemetery in 1654; and in 1657, more than four hundred males underwent circumcision by a visiting circumciser from Amsterdam. Others were circumcised by Doctor Avila. From this moment, biblical names and Hebrew dates began appearing on the tombstones of the men (the women had adopted them a few years earlier). After 1665, the parish records did not register Portuguese births, apart from those of illegitimate children. In 1666, a Spanish cleric confirmed that precautions of secrecy had been abandoned.[88] Border economy seems to provide an explanation for this otherwise surprising turn to normative Judaism accomplished by one of the crypto-Jewish communities of France.

The Cross-Border Business Networks

The antagonistic military, financial, and religious policies of France and Spain should have made the Pyrenean border a sharper divide than ever. However, Portuguese merchants employed sophisticated techniques in communication, transport, and social organization in order to make this border porous for themselves. "Due to the union and brotherhood they have among themselves," Pellicer wrote, "everybody lives in the place of his dispersion as if he was still the lord of his home."[89] The Saint-Esprit base allowed for a partial emigration that did not require the sacrificing of business relations in Spain and could be reversed at any moment. New Christians crossed the Pyrenees on their temporary escape from the Inquisition, but also from bankruptcy, as did the Madrid banker Salvador Vaz Martins in 1649 and the tax farmer

Gonçalo Vaz da Paiva in 1656. The latter underwent circumcision in Saint-Esprit, and then returned to Spain to occupy a new administrative position.[90] Of three Miranda brothers, all of them royal agents, the first stayed in Madrid even after his condemnation by the Inquisition, the second went to Bordeaux but returned temporarily, and the third remained in hiding for a year and a half in Navarre, from where he could recover outstanding debts and still cross the French border in case of emergency.[91]

Dividing one's nuclear family was an even more common way of bridging space. While a man held functions in Spanish tax administration, he expatriated his wife and children to the French side of the border, since Inquisitors tended to torture women in order to obtain information against the family head. In 1641, an arrested mailman wrote down a long list of "women of Peyrehorade, who have husbands or sons in Spain."[92] The female overpopulation in the Pyrenean villages is evident from a massive participation of local girls in the Amsterdam-based dowry lottery, Dotar: between 1620 and 1665, this Jewish charitable society received almost seventy applications from girls of the villages Peyrehorade and Labastide-Clairence and about thirty more from the cities of Bayonne and Bordeaux.[93] Once New Christian traders had sent their womenfolk to France, it was much easier to secrete commercial gains beyond the reach of the Holy Office. After 1654, a tobacco administrator had two safe places for his capital: the Spanish state treasury and his wife's home in the French Jewish border colonies. The task was to transfer the silver coins from one account to the other. "They keep here only the naked persons, but their money is in the enemy's coffers," wrote Pellicer. He believed them to carry, with the help of ordinary mule drivers, six thousand doubloons every week to Saint-Esprit and Bordeaux.[94]

Most of the Jews in southwestern France traveled regularly to Spain. The direct road to Madrid led from Bayonne through the usual border crossing near Saint-Étienne-de-Baïgorry into Pamplona,[95] then via Tafalla, Agreda, Almazán, Padilla, and Alcalá[96] over a distance of 230 miles, corresponding to a bit more than one week's journey.[97] Some cautious traders covered only the forty-six miles from Bayonne to Pamplona to sell their merchandise. Even so, custom officers at the border of Navarre and Castile were on the smugglers' payroll, since the border stations were administered by the tax collector Simão da Fonseca Pina,[98] and as a result, most of the border commerce extended straight into the Spanish heartland. Segovia, the hub of the Castilian wool trade, and Zaragoza are mentioned in 1652 as being among the major destinations of the Portuguese contrabandists based in Bordeaux.[99]

According to a 1671 source, the smaller wool fair at Soria in Northern Castile had become a favorite place for the Portuguese of Saint-Esprit to discreetly acquire their merchandise.[100] However, the majority of the border traders, who sought better prices, accomplished by themselves the entire journey to the capital or even ventured as far south as Seville.[101]

In order to do so, border traders counted upon a network of gentile helpers. In the Spanish cities, certain lodging houses, run mostly by discreet Castilian widows, specialized in sheltering crypto-Jewish smugglers from France.[102] Besides the Puerta del Sol and rural fairs, the inns served as the main meeting places for itinerant merchants.[103] One stopover east of the Franco-Spanish trade route was the small ducal town of Pastrana in central Castile, whose feudal lords were as notorious as the Gramonts for sheltering crypto-Jews and crypto-Muslims. The homes of the local Portuguese were said to be "always open to Jews who come from France to Spain, no matter whether they have presented themselves to the Inquisition or not." Jews and Muslims could rely upon each other in that town; "they do not harm one another."[104] Assistance came also from the muleteers, most of them of Basque or Morisco origin, who were experienced in the avoidance of legal barriers.[105] Some Portuguese had entered their circles and specialized as escape agents (*pasadores*); one of these, Vicente da Costa, who was based in Antwerp, was said to have traveled into Spain three times in 1634.[106] Based in Madrid, the Portuguese muleteer Francisco Fernandes and his partner, called "Diego the Basque," organized risky escapes for Portuguese businessmen, supplying them disguises, mounts, and escorts to France.[107] In war times, the Portuguese family networks had their own messengers. Thus, in 1641, Joseph Sanches traveled with packs of letters between Diego Gómez de Salazar in Madrid and his clients in Saint-Esprit.[108] Twenty years later, in times of peace, Salazar relied on the newly organized French mail service, with Daniel Gomes' servant carrying their business letters daily to the Bayonne dispatch station.[109]

The transregional network structure of the Portuguese Jewish diaspora colonies, first analyzed by Gérard Nahon in a classical article on the relations between the French and Dutch centers,[110] extended deep into Spanish territory. Crypto-Jewish traders on both sides of the Pyrenees formed, indeed, a single community.[111] Saint-Esprit, the westernmost Jewish suburb of the early modern period, was no less a suburb of Madrid than it was a suburb of Bayonne. Like the twin cities of Hamburg and Altona, Warsaw and its suburb Praga, or Vienna and the Moravian border town of Nikolsburg, the Spanish metropolis and the French village of Saint-Esprit formed two poles of a single commercial system, which compensated the Jews for their exclusion from the urban centers. There was an steady flow of people, goods, and news between the Madrid business quarter and the meeting places across the border, including "the Elm" of Saint-Esprit (a tree surrounded by benches near the well on the village square) or the "Medusa Bench" of Bordeaux (a well in the center of the Portuguese quarter, Le Mirail). According to Inquisitional documents, in these places of exile "the observant Jews hold gatherings as the people of Madrid do in the Vallecas or on the Puerta del Sol."[112]

Saint-Esprit and Madrid, two closely interlinked spaces, were distinguished by season, life cycle, gender, sociability, religious practice, and culture in ways that made them almost as corresponding as the commercial exchange of wool for linen and cocoa for tobacco. Francisco Vaz Isidro usually went twice a year from Bordeaux to Madrid and stayed there for several months.[113] Jorge de Figueroa, a linen seller based in Spain, declared that he did the reverse trip almost yearly, and once (in 1656) he stayed for four months among the French Jews.[114] Jerónimo Gomes traveled thirty times on the Bayonne-Madrid route.[115] Two brothers in Saint-Esprit, António Lopes and Gaspar Lopes Paez, went to Spain "every day" according to an informer's impression.[116] The seasonal rhythm that governed the travels of a young salesman during the 1650s is well reconstructed from the testimony of Francisco Rodrigues Idanha, of the third generation of a Portuguese traders' family established in Ciudad Real.[117] On his mother's death in 1648, his father sent his sister to Saint-Esprit in anticipation of coming events—and correctly as it turned out, since he was arrested twice by the Inquisition in the following years. The three sons escaped temporarily, joining their sister on the other side of the border, where they received some degree of Jewish instruction. When the father was released for the second time and emigrated to Saint-Esprit in June 1656, Francisco's turn had come to take up the border trade. Aged twenty-four, he left Saint-Esprit right after the Jewish Day of Atonement to visit his brother at Ciudad Real. They liquidated assets and came back across the border in May 1657. When Yom Kippur was over, Francisco headed for Madrid, but came back to Saint-Esprit almost immediately in November. In January 1658, he married Isabel Soares in a dual religious ceremony celebrated first before the rabbi and then before the parish priest. He stayed with her until Passover and then left for a long trip to Madrid and Valladolid, from where he came back in time for the High Holidays. He was back in Madrid in November and worked there until March, when he returned to Saint-Esprit for a one-month Passover vacation. During his 1659 business season, he traveled extensively to Zaragoza and Valencia, but as a matter of course, he was back to Saint-Esprit for the Jewish New Year. He spent six weeks with his family and departed for Madrid again. This time, he ran into the trap of the Inquisition.[118]

Work in the tax business followed this rhythm of seasonal migration, though it obviously demanded longer stays in Spain. Francisco Rodrigues Lopes, who kept his house, wife, and children in Peyrehorade, sometimes remained absent for one or two years, working as a tax collector and tobacconist for the Spanish Crown. Each time his wife urged him to come back, he would obey, stay with her until his savings were spent, and then go south again. This lifestyle was widespread among his kin. In 1661, when he was arrested, he was an administrator of the tobacco monopoly in Granada, his two brothers occupied the same position in Burgos and in Zafra, his uncle did so in Medina del Campo, his cousin did so in Arévalo, and so on. In order to offer merchandise for a variety of tastes and purses, Francisco Rodrigues Lopes also needed to travel frequently inside Spain, buying legal Cuban tobacco in Seville as well as contraband tobacco in Madrid, Málaga, and Burgos.[119]

The Franco-Spanish tobacco economy structured biographical time and diaspora space in a parallel way. According to the ideal tripartite itinerary, male youths earned their experience in the border trade between France and Spain, then in their maturity obtained a tobacco administration post in Spain, and finally retired with their fortune in France, if not elsewhere in the Jewish diaspora. Crypto-Jewish taxmen and traders used to justify their religious flexibility on the pretext that it was a temporary practice, kept up only for the purposes of gathering fortunes for emigration. However, flexibility had long been habitual among many. The Madrid tobacco administrator Manuel da Silva, alias Joseph Cordovero, arrived in 1649 in the Venetian ghetto, only to send his freshly circumcised son back to care for his business in Spain.[120] A self-sufficient Jewish economy did not exist anywhere, least of all in the communities north of the Spanish border. The few male members who stayed there permanently depended no less on the tobacco system than the cross-border commuters did. Already in 1641, Peyrehorade had three tobacco mill owners, who, as it was rumored, worked mainly for the contraband export to Spain.[121] The roasting, cutting, and perfuming of tobacco was the task of several elderly and pious community members, among them Daniel Gomes, the one-time spiritual leader of the Saint-Esprit community,[122] and a young Italian Jew, Ishaque Barah, who sometimes read the scriptures in Hebrew at clandestine religious gatherings.[123]

For Jews from southern France, as well as Italy and Amsterdam,[124] to be continuously drawn into tax collectors' Spanish networks was in no way deviant. On the contrary, moving from the Jewish into the Christian environment was inseparably connected with the practices of endogamous family alliance, heritage, and succession; it was a career path that had to be built with much labor, patience, and care for one's relations and religious reputation. Martim Gonçalves, who had lost his first wife and fortune in the Jewish community of Recife in Dutch Brazil, spent five years in the border trade between Madrid and his mother's home in Saint-Esprit, until he had sufficient capital to marry a niece and to obtain, in 1659, a tobacconist's post in Granada. His wife, of course, stayed in Saint-Esprit. His success attracted a widowed brother-in-law from a Turkish Jewish community.[125]

The stool pigeon Joseph Garcia de Leão accurately summarized the underlying network structure of these transnational family businesses. "The Jews of Amsterdam, Bordeaux, and Livorno are better informed about the [crypto-]Jews of Spain than the latter are among themselves, due to their correspondence and mutual communication, and because most of them have lived in Spain and know what is going on here."[126] Andrês Nunes Belmonte, an informer for the Inquisition among the Jews of Amsterdam,[127] was able to reconstruct entire family histories from the business correspondence of his fellow Jews. His account of the Portuguese family Nunes Mercado, baroque in its complexity, shows how fiscal positions, money, and women were maintained inside the family though its members moved between Spain, France, and the Netherlands, driven as they were by the push factor of peril and economic failure and the pull factor of monopoly and marriage.

Henrique Nunes, a rich taxman who died in 1648 in the provincial Castilian town of Llerena, ruled on his deathbed that his children be sent to his brother-in-law Jorge Nunes in Amsterdam. This vow was fulfilled. In turn, his nephew João from Peyrehorade took possession of the estate and established himself in Madrid, where he married a cousin called Ana, but died shortly afterwards. At that point, his brother Manuel traveled from Peyrehorade and slept with Ana, thus becoming her levir according to Jewish law. With the woman and the family fortune in his hands, Manuel made a career as a silk taxman in Granada. When the Inquisition arrested him in 1652, his pregnant levirate wife and his mother-in-law both rushed off to Peyrehorade. A cousin, Jorge Nunes II, looked after the silk tax business in their absence until he ran into debt in 1658, at which point he, too, escaped to Peyrehorade, where he opened a gambling house. Manuel lost his mind in prison before he could confess anything, and when he died, the Inquisition had to relinquish his property. His legal heirs were his Amsterdam cousins, whose tutor Jorge Nunes I had died in the meantime. Jorge Nunes II of Peyrehorade promptly took over his Dutch uncle's identity, claimed the money from the Granada Inquisition, brought his wife back to Spain, and settled there. They lived happily for nine years until he wound up in an Inquisition cell in 1670.[128]

The long waiting list in the Nunes Mercado family shows that positions in the Spanish tax and tobacco administration were not for dropouts of Jewish society, but on the contrary for men well qualified in the eyes of their families in terms of commercial diligence, Jewish loyalty, and, most important, consanguinity. The dynamics of these business enterprises can be gleaned from an extremely rich but still untapped source—namely, the miscellaneous papers of the Inquisition, where I found a huge collection of business letters, including the entire archives of Francisco Lopes Capadose and Diego Gómez de Salazar, the chief administrators of the salt and the tobacco monopoly, respectively, the former arrested in 1653, the latter in 1659.[129] To give an example taken at random from the archives, a client named here "Juan Negrete" recalls to Capadose their earlier "good friendship and correspondence" and then apologizes: "If I didn't serve your business as much as I wished, the reason is not a lack of good will, but that I am at the end of my rope. The time is terrible, and the Hebrews are derelict, and you have pleased not to heed my advice. Jacob asks for permission to go to Madrid and I desire infinitely that you make a deal with him."[130] The author of this letter dares a risky allusion to his Jewishness when he urges his protector to support a young family member's business trip into Spain.

The New Christian tax business, with its annexes of tobacco trade and tobacco processing, was based on kinship bonds and thus called for endogamy—normally among members of the same extended family, so that family property could be kept together, and in other cases with other crypto-Jewish families of good repute.[131] This dynastic link between economic activities is illustrated in 1658 by the marriage of Gaspar da Paiva, an experienced tobacco contrabandist on the Bayonne-Bilboa route, with Ana Maria, daughter of the administrator of the Castilian tobacco monopoly, Diego Gómez de Salazar, the magnate whom we have already met several times. Paiva was the orphan son of a Bayonne lady from the Portuguese province, but people in Amsterdam said that as "a good chap of Jewish blood, God-fearing," he was worth each one of the 10,000 ducats Salazar had spent on the dowry.[132]

The architecture of crypto-Jewish business operation in seventeenth-century Spain was based on a series of inherently hierarchic patronage relations rather than on associations between equals.[133] When "Negrete" describes his patron-client relation with the powerful Capadose in terms of "friendship and correspondence," the phrase is hollow. In seventeenth-century Spain, taxmen and contrabandists were vertically organized, in contrast to the circles of eighteenth-century Sephardic merchants, or at least to the idea of these circles put forth by Francesca Trivellato, who insists that a code of reciprocity and mutuality crossed ethnic borders and was manifest in the rhetoric of "friendship, love, and affection" between associates.[134]

As to its horizontal structure, economic activity within the Portuguese nation is fairly well represented in terms of the three levels of cooperation that Trivellato has found among the Livorno tradesmen. As a rule, general partnership was reserved to the next of kin; correspondence was practiced inside the ethnic pool of other Portuguese Jewish families; agency on behalf of another with a power of attorney was the closest form of interaction outgroup partners could get to. All three types of interaction, including the "weak ties" on the interethnic level, were equally important for the economy of the Portuguese Jews, who "attached a very flexible form of agency to a very traditional business model."[135] This should be kept in mind when we study the peculiar type of agent employed by the tobacco traders of the Portuguese nation. Already in the 1650s, the Jews of Bordeaux and Bayonne maintained an Old Christian Castilian in Madrid, Antonio Anaya, whom they praised as "a very good man." Acting as as a straw person for most of them, Anaya signed all kinds of transactions in Spain, distributed property belonging to imprisoned New Christians, and even mutilated and falsified account books before Inquisitional agents could lay hands on them.[136] In the 1670s, hardly any of the big Portuguese merchant families of Madrid could do without such a Castilian agent, who would take care of their businesses in case of danger.[137]

New Christians were convinced that they needed an exceptionally "good man" such as Anaya to work as an agent for their "nation" without being ethnically part of it. Financial correspondence in any case coincided with intermarriage and thus with shared religious loyalties.

Contraband and Culture

Many contemporaries believed that this complex network of commercial and kinship ties was held together by only a symbolic and religious glue. "It is impossible to dissolve the knot which unites commerce and religion among these people," concluded Pellicer.[138] However, the markers of ethnic and religious identity were far less obvious and easier to manipulate for seventeenth-century New Christians than they would be for Jews of the eighteenth century. Participation in the border commerce required in most cases a controlled performance of features associated with two different religions and three national cultures, and most of the contrabandists could behave as if they belonged to any of these. For instance, on weekdays, the Portuguese of Saint-Esprit ate the dishes cooked by their French maids, whereas for the holidays, they prepared their own Iberian classics, chicken with olives being the favorite choice.[139] In their dress, they readily adopted French fashion. The French-style sleeveless vest had some religious connotations, because it made the customary changing of shirts on Friday more obvious.[140] They also wore their hair long as was fashionable in France, and after the Peace of the Pyrenees, they also started wearing wigs.[141] When crossing the border into Spain, while some Jewish traders were not afraid to appear in French clothes,[142] others took care to don their foreign attire which risked betraying their identity. In his pamphlet, José Pellicer alerted his compatriots to the fact that "there walk among us countless people who have arrived from the synagogues of Amsterdam and Italy, and it is impossible to recognize them or to keep them out . . . because they look Spanish in language and costume and nobody cares about knowing their true identity."[143]

The regular wandering in a land which outlawed Judaism might be expected to relax Jewish religious discipline. Surprisingly, however, the union of border commerce and state finance, though it implied systematic border-crossing, risk-taking, and religious duplicity, strengthened a common religious identity. There was a complementary relationship between the increasingly developed Jewish religious ritual in France and the dissimulation practiced in Spain. The more French Jewish practice became regularized, the more Spanish crypto-Judaism could be reduced to secret "declarations" among its adherents—that is, to a meta-ritual practice of talking about Judaism instead of actually practicing it.[144] Thus, for example, on a business trip across the border, three Portuguese tobacconists from Cordoba had to switch from upholding devout Catholic ritual to listening to the anti-Catholic polemic of their host in Saint-Esprit, Diogo Rodrigues Cardoso, who gave them a "bad talk on the cult of saints, images, and the crucifix, saying that he would not place his faith in a piece of wood or stone."[145] Even persons with little education were fond of engaging in theological controversy.[146]

As in many border cultures, the condition of living a double life produced a coded language used in conversations and correspondence.[147] Correspondents from Saint-Esprit and other Jewish communities sent their letters to Spain unsigned or under false names, the sender being recognizable only by his handwriting. His religion could be secretly inferred from the "Laus Deo" or some similar formula that appeared at the top of the letters instead of the usual cross.[148] Among themselves, the tobacco traders knew to decipher even the slightest nonverbal indications of cultural liminality as a possible sign of Jewishness. This can be concluded from a revealing anecdote which the Inquisitors extracted from Francisco López Villanueva, an itinerant Pyrenean trader of mixed Hispano-Portuguese ancestry. In 1644, when he visited Salamanca during the bullfight festival, he took part in a fencing contest held before the event. After the contest, he was approached by a Portuguese who introduced himself as Gaspar de Velasco, administrator of the royal tobacco monopoly for Salamanca, Zamora, and Ávila. The man had observed that Francisco fenced in the French style, and Francisco confirmed that he had indeed visited the neighboring kingdom. The next day, Velasco called on Francisco at his boarding-house. The two men, complete strangers, suddenly revealed to each other their common faith in the Judaic religion as confidently "as if they had grown up together during all of their lives, with the frankness of close friends." When asked by the Inquisitors to explain this spontaneous fraternization, Francisco presumed that from the point of view of his interlocutor, a Portuguese who had traveled between Spain and France could not be other than a secret Jew.[149]

López Villanueva's skill with weaponry—he had even tried to enlist in the French army in his youth—was at not exceptional among the traders transporting valuables on unsafe mountain roads. The traveling merchants and taxmen also imitated the notoriously libertine lifestyle of Spanish soldiers. Many of them, who in any case did not see their wives more than twice a year, had paramours in Spain. At sixty, Francisco López Villanueva had a Portuguese-Jewish cousin-wife in France and several children with a Basque woman in a border village, but shared his bed and board in Pastrana with his maidservant, a girl of gypsy background.[150] Another former soldier, Gaspar Vinagre, who acted as a preacher in the crypto-Jewish gatherings of Saint-Esprit, married a Portuguese Jewish woman before the local rabbi, though he already had a Christian wife in Spain. He furthermore patronized a famous Madrid courtesan during his visits there.[151]

The mass circumcisions of 1657, which became the key element in the religious normalization process in Saint-Esprit,[152] had the obvious result of preventing too close encounters of traders with women in Spain, where the covenantal sign could horrify even hard-boiled professional prostitutes.[153] Circumcision allowed for a great measure of secrecy while setting limits to it. The cases in which young men were expected to be circumcised before being allowed to cross the border[154] give the best example of the correlation between mobility and the turn to religious discipline. To be sure, surgical intervention did not render these merchants better behaved, but they now sought their adventures outside the realm of the Inquisition. In the 1660s, some twenty illegitimate births of Portuguese fathers and French mothers appear in the Saint Esprit parish register, which had had no record of such cases before. In 1663, Jerónimo Rodrigues baptized illegitimate children he had from two different Frenchwomen.[155] Their adventures, which in some cases evolved into marriages, supposedly allowed them to exert a greater degree of self-restraint when touring Spain.

Besides language, national symbolism, and sexual activity, consumer behavior also played a role in the identity of this French-Portuguese group, which thrived on the increasingly global exchange of goods, as well as identities.[156] Tobacco and playing cards were not only objects of Spanish state monopolies and of a commercial and cultural exchange across the Pyrenees in which Jews played an important role; consumption of these two items was also the main pretext for social gatherings of a crypto-Judaic character. Pipes and cards were offered to clients at the Portuguese gambling houses of Saint-Esprit, the patrons of which would retire to a room on the first floor for clandestine prayer meetings.[157] For those who led strained undercover lives in Spain, tobacco served as a palliative drug and even as a painkiller when smuggled into torture chambers. The poet Antonio Enríquez Gómez, a dropout of the Portuguese merchant colony of Rouen, who lived in Seville under a false identity, was visited in 1661 by his brother, who alerted him that the Inquisition was on his heels and that his wife back in France feared for his life. The poet "fell silent, and then took out a bit of snuff."[158]

The legal marginality of their economic pursuits, their typical blend of cultural and linguistic features, and their composite religious tradition give the Bayonne-Madrid trading networks some features akin to present-day "contraband cultures." But the newly developing tobacco business of the seventeenth century was not simply a niche economy into which even persecuted outsiders could penetrate. Due to a persistent link between contraband and early modern state finance, the crypto-Jewish border economy had a clear role in the establishment of political order.

Views among historians diverge strongly on whether the financial stratagems of the Portuguese were the cause of Spain's economic crisis or whether they were its only possible remedy. Some (mainly Spanish) authors have imputed the decline of the monarchy to its excessive reliance upon the parasitical agents of global finance;[159] others (mainly foreigners) have blamed it on an overdeveloped state apparatus, whose obsession with economic protectionism as well as racial and religious purity blocked the salutary initiatives undertaken by cosmopolitan and unprejudiced bankers.[160] Both conflicting views on capitalism are far too schematic to account for the ambiguous situation of the 1650s, when the interests of the Castilian state and of Portuguese Jewish contraband networks seem to be linked. It is difficult to assess the effect of this unlikely arrangement, but I would surmise that without it, Saint-Esprit would not have become Jewish nor would Badajoz remain Spanish during the war year of 1657.[161] The tobacco economy saved both partners: an empire in straits and an impoverished segment of the Jewish diaspora.

At the same time, the cooperation or "symbiosis"[162] between the government and crypto-Jewish businessmen was extremely costly for both sides. For the monarchy, huge sums were lost due to the precarious position of its bankers, and for most Portuguese, insertion into royal finance did not result in the security they hoped for. A condition of crisis and pressure pushed both sides to make uncomfortable choices, to throw religious principles overboard, and to look for unusual political, social, and economic allies. This explains "the ambivalent, confused, contradictory and at the same time pragmatic policy of Spain," as Yosef Kaplan succinctly wrote.[163] The same observation applies to the Franco-Portuguese traders, who did not disdain to support the country that persecuted them against the one that protected them, who served royal interests while hiding in anachronistic noble estates, who worked in Spain as Catholics, but raised their families in France as Jews, who thrived on duplicity, but enforced at the same moment a normative Jewish identity on community life.

Castilian tobacco policy and Jewish family strategy mainly reacted to short-term constraints. On both sides, the "symbiosis" was an immediate remedy to acute misery, yet it had a lasting impact on both the growth of state administration and Jewish community building.[164] Beyond the Pyrenees, the tax farmers' cultural economy brought about the definitive takeoff for Sephardi normative Judaism in France. In some way, this new Jewish life anticipated the modern separation between domestic Jewishness and public conformism, though the domestic and the public sphere were in this case separated by a trifling 230 miles. The Franco-Spanish diaspora structured space and lifetimes according to a sophisticated conjunction of illegal and public economy, of synagogue and church attendance, of women's and men's residences, of distribution and production of wealth, of a private and a public realm. With its ambiguous contraband culture, Madrid's trans-Pyrenean suburbs offer a striking example of how economic specialization breaks down religious identities and how by the same token it can create them anew.

Chapter 3

Daily Business or an Affair of Consequence? Credit, Reputation, and Bankruptcy Among Jewish Merchants in Eighteenth-Century Central Europe

Cornelia Aust

Commercial success of ethnic minorities is, more often than not, directly and automatically linked to ethnic solidarity and the apparent existence of higher levels of trust among members of the same distinct ethnic or religious group. David Landes has examined the importance of family and kinship as bases for economic activity and, not uncommonly, entrepreneurial success in the modern period.[1] This relationship appears to have been even more applicable to the early modern period. The belief in ethnic solidarity is based primarily on two classical works on "trade diasporas," an expression coined by Abner Cohen in 1971.[2] Cohen and Philip Curtin were highly influential in creating a historical scenario in which trade diasporas were generally equated with trust networks based on kinship and ethnic or religious belonging. More recently, scholars of commercial networks based on ethnic and/or religious communities have criticized this model and sought to describe the mechanisms underlying the creation of mutual trust among commercial traders of the same ethnic and/or religious background and with other merchants of dissimilar backgrounds. Francesca Trivellato, for example, speaks of "networks of mercantile trust" that were not necessarily ethnically or religiously homogenous.[3] Sebouh David Aslanian describes social capital generated within social networks as a "key factor . . . to generate and maintain trust, trustworthiness, and uniform norms," in this case among early modern Armenian Julfan merchants.[4]

Based on these insights, trust can be defined as the belief in the positive outcome of future business undertakings with a specific and regular business partner. It is based on the assumption that repeated business transactions with a particular business partner create an atmosphere in which meaningful economic and even social consequences will occur if a business partner's expectations are not matched. Commercial networks are defined here as regular connections and repeated commercial interactions among multiple individuals. In speaking of Jewish commercial networks, it is important to emphasize that such networks were rarely limited exclusively to Jewish merchants. Non-Jewish merchants, clients, and sometimes state officials were often regularly involved. A merchant's position within a network was defined by the distribution of different resources—that is, by the merchant's access to commodities, capital, and knowledge. Commercial networks always had a dynamic character and were exposed to developments arising from political events, bankruptcy of individual merchants, strife among merchants, and evolving familial, political, and economic constellations.[5] These repeated interactions entailed not only familiarity between merchants but also that business misconduct carried potentially serious consequences both for the concrete commercial connections and for a business person's reputation. Thus, the functioning of trust and sanctions within the network, and in this case the wider Jewish society, was a crucial issue for commercial networks.

The failure or disruption of large commercial networks in the early modern period has been rightly ascribed to broader economic and political developments such as the decline of particular cities and the downfall of empires.[6] Less attention has been paid to the temporary disruptions of commercial connections that evolved from conflict between business partners, for example, and from commonplace merchant insolvencies and bankruptcies. Such disruptions, though they did not cause larger commercial networks to shift significantly or fail, could have long-term consequences for the individual merchants involved. Examining these smaller disturbances can add to our understanding of how trust was created and maintained, especially when looking at trust at the moment when it was put into question or even broken. Although kinship and ethnic ties among business partners could strengthen trust, they were hardly insurance against disruptions caused by external circumstances or the behavior of business partners.

This raises the question of how trust was built and maintained, and, more importantly, what happened when commercial networks fell apart. Was disruption of business connections among Jewish merchants a normal part of regular business or did such disruption carry far-reaching consequences for a merchant's future business life and reputation? How did various institutions—family, Jewish communal bodies, courts, or other state institutions—intervene in cases of economic failure? And how did Jewish merchants overcome such disruptions?

Using examples of Jewish commercial activities in central Europe during the second half of the eighteenth century, I will explore the question of the disruption of such networks. Phenomena such as bankruptcy were, then as now, common components of economic life. This raises the central question of how different kinds of conflict among regular trading partners and the disruption of commercial networks impacted individual merchants, their families, and their wider commercial networks. I will argue that business behavior—especially a merchant's reputation not just among fellow merchants but also with state authorities—was crucial to the ways in which merchants weathered disruptions in their business connections.

Bankruptcy and Other Inconveniences

Disruption of commercial networks could take different forms, from termination of a business partnership to cases of bankruptcy that ended in lengthy trials. Termination of business partnerships was a common occurrence and could be triggered by numerous factors, ranging from the death of a business partner to a shift in the geographic area of trade or to a change in merchandise. In some cases, disagreement among business partners was the underlying factor but did lead to prolonged strife or legal repercussions. Bankruptcy, although a common phenomenon in the world of commerce, was probably the most drastic form of disruption to any commercial network. It is important to remember, however, that bankruptcy was not something easily measurable but rather a situation brought about by creditors who demanded return of their assets. Thus, it "is a legal, rather than an economic category."[7]

Although some division between *Falliment*, or insolvency due to outside circumstances, and bankruptcy due to negligence or fraud existed already in the sixteenth century, more normative processes of dealing with business failure developed throughout the early modern period, as did sharper (at least theoretically) distinctions between different categories of business failure.[8] By the eighteenth century, courts across Europe distinguished between (criminal) bankruptcy and business failure due to ill fate.[9] The late eighteenth-century economic encyclopedia of Johann Georg Krünitz makes similarly fine distinctions and emphasizes that a *Falliment* is first merely a lack of presence of the merchant in the marketplace or bourse or a shortage of credit; it is the demands of the merchant's creditors that turns it into a bankruptcy. Here Krünitz distinguishes three categories of financial failure: inability to repay creditors due to one's own fault or unethical intentions; misfortunes that prevent one from being able to completely satisfy one's creditors; and temporary inability to pay creditors due to misfortunes, but with capacity to do so in the future. The first condition precipitates a merchant's disgrace and loss of credit, whereas the second warrants pity. The third case affords prolonged payment that allows for reestablishment of credit and trust, as does the second if the merchant can reconcile terms with his creditors and start anew.[10]

These distinctions and the corresponding legal measures had become well established in western Europe by the late seventeenth century. The markets of central Europe, however, lagged behind in this regard as well as with other legislation, as the example of Leipzig shows. In 1682, in a concerted effort to increase the attractiveness of the Leipzig fairs for international merchants, the city established a commercial court (the first in a German city) to relieve the overburdened city court. At the same time, the city introduced regulations regarding the trade in bills of exchange. Such regulations had existed much earlier in Frankfurt/Main (1578), Hamburg (1601), and Nuremberg (1621), and had been introduced a few years before in Riga (1671) and Breslau (1672). It was not until the early eighteenth century that exchange regulations were introduced into general state laws in Prussia (1724) and Russia (1729).[11] So as to facilitate the trade in bills of exchange, the Leipzig regulations of 1682 also allowed for usage of endorsement, the option to transfer a bill of exchange from one merchant to another before the bill was due.[12] The simultaneous introduction of the joint liability rule ensured that merchants enjoyed a higher level of legal security in cases of default.[13]

However, it would be several decades before the city of Leipzig also introduced new bankruptcy measures that reflected the previously noted distinctions of different kinds of bankruptcy and *Falliment*. In an attempt at stronger oversight and regulation, Leipzig issued new bankruptcy laws in 1724, following the bankruptcy and escape of a major Christian wholesale merchant. As they did elsewhere in Europe, these regulations distinguished between insolvency stemming from theft or natural disaster and intentional or criminal bankruptcy, which implied moral corruption as well. In the first case, merchants could announce insolvency and submit their account books to the Leipzig commercial court. Bankruptcy, however, constituted a crime that was to be punished. Fraud of bills of exchange and escape received the harshest penalties and, according to contemporary pamphlets and weeklies, also entailed social death.[14] Though merchants, including Jewish merchants, were generally not reticent in taking each other to court, the ensuing lawsuits were usually not only lengthy and expensive but also potentially devastating to a merchant's reputation.

In practice, however, it was often difficult to distinguish between misfortune-based insolvency and criminal bankruptcy and to determine a merchant's exact role in his downfall. Especially in bankruptcies evolving from larger economic crises—such as the crises in Amsterdam in 1763 and 1773, or the widespread collapse of banking houses in Warsaw in 1793—it was, and remains, difficult to judge the responsibility of individual merchants or bankers for their bankruptcy or the extent to which they had been ensnared within the wider economic maelstrom. In other cases the downfall of merchants or bankers resulted from risky but illegal business deals or outright fraud.

Voltaire and Other Rascals

In 1753, Gotthold Ephraim Lessing published the following epigram:

> Tell me Muses, which God assisted the poet,
> And pointed him directly to this indirect rascalry?
> . . . .
> But let us leave you, brave God, out of it,
> To cut to the chase and grasp the reason,
> Why the Jew
> Did not succeed with his deceit?
> The answer in a nutshell would be
> Mr. V** was a greater rascal than he.[15]

Mr. V** was none other than Voltaire; "the Jew" was Abraham Hirschel, a Saxon Court Jew who had moved to Berlin a few years earlier and had recently caused Voltaire great distress and a lawsuit following their shady business deals.[16] These had nearly cost the philosopher the support and admiration of Friedrich II. Besides Lessing, the Prussian king and the court had realized that Voltaire, despite distrusting Hirschel, had indeed tried to benefit from the latter's illegal speculations with Saxon state bonds. The affair, however, presumably damaged Hirschel's reputation far more seriously.

This episode points to at least three issues that were crucial in the making and breaking of eighteenth-century business deals. Though Hirschel's dealings with Voltaire were probably not regular or long-term, the affair points to the importance of trust as well as personal responsibility in business transactions. Moreover, since various bills of exchange and claims regarding their falsehood were involved, the matter also suggests the possibilities and dangers that ensued from wide circulation of endorsable bills of exchange. Finally, the significant attention this affair drew from the wider public underscores the importance of both communication and increasingly available information to the future reputation of those involved.

Abraham Hirschel was part of a far-reaching central European business network of Court Jews and other wealthy Jewish merchants and bankers. He was the son of Hirschel Abraham, from Posen (Poznań), who in 1743 became a court factor of August III, Elector of Saxony and King of Poland. His son received the same privilege in 1751, even though he and his father were living in Berlin, where they held Prussian privileges and where Abraham Hirschel traded in jewels. They continued business with Poland, where Abraham's brother Moses Hirschel resided; an uncle, Zacharias Abraham, constituted one of their connections to Hamburg. Abraham Hirschel remained well connected with Saxony, regularly traveling to the Leipzig fair and maintaining ties with the highest echelons of the Saxon state administration. His father had links to Amsterdam—via his representatives, the brothers and merchant-bankers Benjamin and Samuel Symons—which were crucial for any business utilizing bills of exchange in central and east-central Europe at the time.[17] Thus, the family's commercial connections covered geographical nodes essential for a central European commercial network. Saxony was crucial as a connection to Poland at this time, given that the Saxon electors ruled as Polish kings and the fair in Leipzig was a commercial hub between East and West. Prussia, and especially Berlin, was on the rise as a new commercial center; this was supported financially by credit from Amsterdam, which was usually transmitted via Hamburg.[18]

The family's representatives in Amsterdam, Benjamin and Samuel Symons, attempted to extend their own commercial connections eastward from the mid-eighteenth century onward. A nephew, Isaac Symons, moved to Berlin; his brother Simon Symons moved to Frankfurt/Oder in the late 1750s and married the daughter of one of the city's most affluent textile merchants.[19] Simon Symons' new brother-in-law, Levin Pincus Schlesinger, became his business partner, and together they moved to Warsaw in 1765 as court factors of the Polish king.[20] When Simon Symons' wife died, he married a sister of Schlesinger's wife from Amsterdam; thus their business relationship, as well as their connections to Amsterdam, were further strengthened by family ties.[21] The Symons family's connections now reached from Amsterdam to Frankfurt/Oder—including ties to Hamburg, Berlin, and Leipzig—and from there into Poland; they also intersected with the family of Abraham Hirschel in Berlin, in what became extremely complicated relations.

The conflict in question emerged after Hirschel offered Voltaire Saxon state bonds that had lost much of their value but that Saxony had agreed to honor according to their original 1745 value. This meant that trade with these bonds became illegal thereafter, and so Friedrich II (whose guest Voltaire was) feared Saxony would resign from the agreement if more bonds entered circulation. After Friedrich II realized Voltaire's intention to illegally buy such bonds, the philosopher sought to stop the deal; however, he had already issued a bill of exchange for over 10,000 Reichsthaler to Hirschel. The bill was protested in Paris, while Voltaire tried to cover his wrongdoings by claiming the money was for purchase of jewels and fur. After a failed attempt to settle out of court, Voltaire sued Hirschel over additional bills of exchange and alleged debts. The fact that Hirschel was never punished indicates that neither the court nor the king believed Voltaire was completely innocent in the affair.[22]

In the end, no clear moral winner or exoneration was determined, though Voltaire claimed otherwise. Nevertheless, the case had severe implications for Hirschel's reputation. Throughout the trial, he had complained that its only rationale was for the "damage of his credit." He argued that it was his competitor in the jewel trade, Veitel Ephraim, who had not only offered Voltaire a better deal in regard to the state bonds but also tried to ruin him (Hirschel). According to Hirschel, "the illegal and highly criminal procedure of Monsieur Voltaire against me, intends nothing else than the degradation of my credit and thus (maybe in favor of the local *Schutzjude* Ephraim) the intended complete ruination of myself and my family."[23] Hirschel's non-Jewish lawyer argued that even though his client was a Jew, "he is nevertheless an honest man, well-known as jeweler at court and in the whole city."[24]

Despite the ambiguous outcome of the trial, Hirschel attracted near constant troubles in the years to come. It would seem safe to assume this was influenced not just by his personal business behavior but also by the fact that his strife with Voltaire had been widely publicized in the contemporary press.[25]

Though more normative processes of handling bankruptcies had evolved over the early modern period and now distinguished between misfortune, on the one hand, and irresponsible or even criminal conduct, on the other, the notion of personal responsibility remained central to the future creditworthiness of a merchant and his family. Moreover, the maintenance of credit was dependent not only on the individual merchant and his business behavior, but on his interactions with various other formal and informal institutions—namely, the family, the Jewish community, and the state or state institutions. The example of Abraham Hirschel, even beyond the incident with Voltaire, demonstrates the interplay between these different institutions in the building and losing of credit.

Establishing Trustworthiness

A glance at autobiographical accounts of seventeenth- and eighteenth-century Jewish merchants like Glikl bas Leib (1646–1724), Aron Izaak (1730–1816), and Ber of Bolechov (1723–1805) can give some insight into how individuals sought to create an impression of reliable credit and trustworthiness with regard not only to themselves but also to their family members. Though these texts were not intended for publication and thus not for a wider audience, they point to a strong need to present a picture of good family credit. In their writings, each author made a marked effort to establish his or her own trustworthiness and that of family members. In her attempt to portray herself and members of her family as trustworthy merchants, Glikl regularly emphasized that they were "well respected among Jews and non-Jews."[26] This hints at the importance of business connections with Christian merchants and the mutual trust necessary on both sides. Her narrative is built on the notion of respect and honor, or what is usually described as trust by historians. Most obvious in this regard is Glikl's constant usage of the combination of *oysher un koved* (riches and honor). As Natalie Zemon Davis has noted, honor (*koved*) is a central category in Glikl's narrative.[27] The phrase *oysher un koved* is used primarily to describe honesty and integrity in business, and thus, the basis for trust. All three narratives emphasized the importance of honest business behavior toward all partners, regardless of any particular partner's religion.

Aaron Izaak, in describing his family after the death of his father and their struggles for economic survival, stressed the honesty of his older brother, Abraham: "My brother Abraham was very frugal and very honest, because he wanted to move forward."[28] Aaron noted that his father had sent Abraham to the Leipzig fair, telling him that he usually paid cash there, but that if it became necessary to ask for credit, none of the merchants would deny him, as everybody knew his father.[29] Ber of Bolechov made similar attempts, especially in praising his father as a highly skilled and experienced merchant who earned his living "very abundantly and in great honor [*be-kavod gadol*]." He depicted his father as being highly respected and honored wherever he went, among "Jews and the uncircumcised in the land of Poland and in the land of Hungary."[30] Recalling a situation in which his father had run out of money, Ber of Bolechov emphasized that his business partners in general, and Polish nobles in particular, trusted him and so extended him credit.[31]

The desire to establish trust and creditworthiness extended to the whole family, even if there was no reason for praise. Ber of Bolechov repeatedly referred to disputes among himself, his brother Ariyeh, and his brother's wife, and recounted at great length his brother's attempt to establish his own wine-trading business without their father's support. Despite the criticism of his brother, Ber never described him as dishonest or untrustworthy; it was only a lack of experience in the wine trade that led to his brother's failure and eventual return to their father's supervision.[32] The establishment of trust and good reputation was, even in personal writings, of crucial importance in a time when credit, bills of exchange, and money were of unstable value.[33]

Glikl's narrative is even more outstanding in this respect and is characterized by her attempts to underline the righteousness and honest business behavior of her children, including the less successful ones. Her son Löb married into a family from Berlin, where he was then supposed to establish new business connections. However, in trading as well as in money-lending, he was defrauded by business partners and even by his in-laws. The latter case offers an example of when familial ties did not automatically create stable and successful business relations. Glikl was forced to spend significant sums to save her son, but finally defended him: "He had over all a good reputation among Jews and non-Jews, and it was well known, that he lost what was his, because wicked and reckless ones—may their names be blotted out—defrauded him, and—for our many sins—he was too good and he believed in everybody."[34]

Although contemporaries often perceived the ties between merchants of the same ethnic background—in this case Ashkenazi Jews—to be stronger than those with fellow merchants of different backgrounds, Glikl had more than one story to tell about dishonest Jewish business partners and trustworthy Christian ones. Her narrative and those of Ber of Bolechov and Aaron Izaak warn against simplistic conclusions regarding close-knit ethnic networks based on implicit trust and reliability.[35] Both Ber and Glikl mentioned Jewish business partners who betrayed them or behaved dishonestly. Though the narratives reference legal institutions—Glikl even presented the decision of a city court as proof of her son's honesty and trustworthiness—formal institutions hardly diminished the importance of personal trust.

Unfortunately, we do not have similar documents for most merchants of the period; in many cases, not even business correspondence remains. In the case of Abraham Hirschel, we can learn more about his family relations only from court proceedings. Whether partially or entirely because of the Voltaire incident, Abraham Hirschel's family connections became extremely complicated by the early 1750s, and were probably a major reason for his economic downfall. His father died in 1751, leaving Abraham the head of the family and responsible for his five younger siblings, including two sisters for whom marriages needed to be arranged. Things were not going well in this respect, either. After a proposed match for one sister, Friderica, in Hamburg fell through due to the bankruptcy of the future father-in-law, the seventeen-year-old Isaac Symons, a nephew of their late father's representatives in Amsterdam, appeared to be a fine solution. Symons had moved to Berlin in 1753, where he traded in jewels and other goods with the financial backing of his father, Berend Symons.[36] These plans did not work out because in 1754, Berend Symons filed action against his son, accusing him of embezzling his money. The elder Symons alleged that the Hirschel family had seduced his son into this misconduct, and thus strictly opposed his son's marriage to Friderica.

According to Abraham Hirschel, two of Isaac Symons' uncles, Benjamin and Samuel Symons, who regularly traveled to the Leipzig fairs, met Hirschel there and sought to pursuade him to prevent the planned wedding.[37] Whether the resistance against the wedding was related to Abraham Hirschel's already dubious reputation following the Voltaire case is difficult to say. The complicated familial circumstances, however, clearly contributed not only to his own further economic difficulties and legal disputes but also to those of Isaac Symons.

The Role of the Jewish Community

The opposition to the marriage between Friderica Hirschel and Isaac Symons and thus to the latter's commercial dealings with Abraham Hirschel came not only from family members. The Berlin Jewish community, under the elder Veitel Ephraim (who, as noted earlier, was a business competitor of Hirschel), rejected the marriage, claiming that Isaac Symons had entered Berlin without official permission and, moreover, could not prove the necessary financial assets for marriage due to his father's legal claims. In Prussia, the Jewish community had to ensure compliance with the strict marriage regulations of the state. Eventually, in 1755, Isaac Symons and Friderica married, most likely in Mecklenburg.

Beyond this, communal institutions did not become directly involved in the conflicts between, on the one hand, Abraham Hirschel and his brother-in-law Isaac Symons and, on the other, their business partners and the rest of the Symons family. According to Jewish law, taking a fellow Jew to a non-Jewish court or threatening him with arrest by non-Jewish authorities was strictly forbidden and regarded as a sin. However, such appeals to non-Jewish courts, even when the dispute in question involved only Jews, was not uncommon in early modern Europe, as Moshe Rosman and others have shown.[38] Although communal cohesion has rightly been described as one of the distinctive features of the early modern period in Jewish history,[39] it was accompanied by growing laicization of communal authority and the emergence of a strong lay leadership, the latter consisting mostly of members of the Jewish mercantile elite. The influence and power of rabbinic authorities declined, and with it, one can assume, that of the *batei din*, the rabbinical courts. One could argue that the reason for these developments was the inability of the mercantile elite to resolve their conflicts within the inherited communal structures coupled with state regulations that strongly limited the power of Jewish courts beyond family matters. In Prussia, such cases could only be taken to a non-Jewish court—the Prussian Supreme Court (*Kammergericht*) in Berlin, in this case—as the General Codes of 1730 and 1750 had stripped Jewish courts of the power to judge cases except in ceremonial matters.[40]

This does not mean, however, that cases were no longer brought before the *beit din*. In 1765, for example, a case involving two Jewish merchants who disagreed about the state of their partnership and the related division of financial losses that one of them had incurred was adjudicated by the communal *beit din*; afterward, however, one of the merchants turned to the Berlin city court and withdrew his acceptance of the *beit din*'s decision.[41]

In the case of Abraham Hirschel and Isaac Symons, there may have been additional reasons why their case was taken straight to Prussian courts. Berend Symons, being from Amsterdam, may not have trusted the *beit din* in Berlin to find a satisfying resolution or to have the means to enforce a ruling regarding the assets he claimed his son and his son's brother-in-law had embezzled. Abraham Hirschel and Isaac Symons had even less reason to trust the communal court. After all, it had been Veitel Ephraim, royal jeweler and head of the Jewish community, who had intervened against the marriage between Friderica Hirschel and Isaac Symons, and the Hirschel family still blamed him for their subsequent misfortune. Apparently, Abraham Hirschel and Veitel Ephraim had been adversaries for a number of years, and Ephraim had once reported Hirschel to the authorities for shaving his beard.[42] That Hirschel's and Symons' adversaries did not take them to the *beit din* was also likely due to the lack of legal measures in the hands of the community. After all, Veitel Ephraim took even small issues to the non-Jewish court. During the disputes between Isaac Symons and his wife, Friderica, and their relatives in Amsterdam, Veitel Ephraim turned to the court to complain about the married couple's written and oral slander against him. Eventually, the court fined Isaac and Friderica. However, it was also decided that Veitel Ephraim was behaving no better in calling Symons an imposter and other "crude insults," and so the court penalized him as well.

Thus, the influence of the Jewish community was rather ambiguous. At least in central European states like Prussia, the legal measures of the communal *beit din* were severely limited. Even if the Jewish court was asked for arbitration, it had no legal means to implement judgments and punishments. Nevertheless, communal elders had the power to exert social pressure on individuals and to spread rumors.

Formal Institutions

Formal institutions such as more sophisticated commercial law, commercial courts, and police forces increasingly complemented, but did not replace, personal trust.[43] Although "sophisticated financial instruments such as double-entry bookkeeping, bills of exchange, bank to bank transfers, and insurance were all in use"[44] from the late Middle Ages onward, as Gunnar Dahl observes, communication between different locals remained slow, legal support was not always available, and international law was still underdeveloped or nonexistent. For example, Israel Jacob, a velvet and silk merchant from Flatow in West Prussia, turned (in vain, it would turn out) to the Prussian authorities for legal support in 1788 because he had been unable to collect his debts at the fairs where he met his debtors. Legally, he was allowed to take them to court only in their hometowns, and this led him to complain that collection of debts had become impossible for him.[45] Similarly, Prussian Jewish merchants regularly turned to the Prussian authorities and especially to the Prussian ambassador in Warsaw for support in legal issues related to their commercial activities. Their letters express deep mistrust of the Polish legal system and the possibilities it offered them to advance cases on their own.[46]

Bills of exchange were the most important means to overcome state borders and different legal systems and to enable trans-regional and long-distance trade. However, they also constituted a potential source of fraud. By the eighteenth century, bills of exchange had developed into a sophisticated instrument for raising credit. The practice of endorsement made the bills transferable and negotiable, and thus more flexible. Eventually, the joint liability rule, widely accepted by the eighteenth century, provided a somewhat higher degree of security for trans-regional transactions. Each endorser attested, with his signature, to his shared responsibility in case of the drawer's default.[47]

The phenomenon of rejected and thus protested bills of exchange is usually regarded as having been connected to disruption of business partnerships and closely linked to bankruptcy. It is regarded as a sign of illiquidity or at least an indication of serious financial problems on the part of either the drawer or payer of the bill. However, protested bills of exchange were not always an indication of economic difficulties. To refuse a bill of exchange before its due date was often a technical measure; in many cases the letter of advice from the bill's issuer was still missing.[48] Only in few cases did a drawer's unreliability or a payer's illiquidity lead to rejection of payment for a bill of exchange.

The repeated inability to pay (or rumors suggesting it) could eventually lead to bankruptcy or *Falliment* if multiple creditors began to demand payments at the same time. Often, however, creditors had no interest in forcing a debtor into bankruptcy if they saw any chance that he might be able to stabilize his financial situation and to return to business.[49] Moreover, there were various measures to avert bankruptcy at least temporarily. In cases of Jewish merchants who had close ties to local rulers and served, for example, as court suppliers, a moratorium provided a form of temporary protection. A moratorium allowed merchants to continue their business and to collect their debts while being protected against legal actions from their own creditors. In the 1770s, the last Polish king, Stanisław August Poniatowski, for example, regularly issued moratoria for his Jewish suppliers, such as the Prussian army supplier Wolfgang Heymann and the previously mentioned banker and jewel merchant Simon Symons from Amsterdam and his business partner, Levin Pincus Schlesinger from Frankfurt/Oder.[50]

Once the state framework crumbled, as did the Polish-Lithuanian Commonwealth, this option was no longer viable. This was the case with the Jewish merchant and army supplier Hirsch Markiewicz, from Mszczonów, who did business in Warsaw and was apparently one of the most important army suppliers of his time.[51] He went bankrupt eventually, after he was suddenly forced, in 1790, to satisfy all his creditors at once. This development was evidently not entirely his fault, however. Since Markiewicz had close business relations with the Polish nobleman Adam Poniński, it was clear to Markiewicz's creditors that the Jewish merchant would not remain unharmed, especially when Poniński was accused of espionage for Russia and arrested by the Four-Year Sejm. Thus, in this case it was not necessarily Markiewicz's lack of funds that precipitated his downfall, but rather the withdrawal of all his creditors at once. When creditors began to withdraw their money, the Polish government created a commission, and various newspapers in Poland, Hamburg, and Leipzig called for all of Markiewicz's creditors to register.[52] Though the Polish state took some action at this point, it became even more powerless a few years later, when, during the second partition of Poland, in 1793, all major Christian banking houses went bankrupt. The disaster emerged as a combination of a general downturn of the European economy, including the bankruptcies of several English and Dutch banks, and the political turmoil in Poland that led to the disappearance of the Polish state. This historical shift also shows the powerful effects of rumors on the financial market. When rumors spread in 1793 that the banking house of Tepper was experiencing financial difficulties due to unreturned loans by the Polish government, the bank's creditors began arriving in Warsaw to withdraw their capital. The bank's subsequent failure came as a shock and took down other Warsaw banks as well.[53]

Returning to Prussia and the Hirschel family—the case shows that involvement in various court trials and a poor reputation were poisonous for the continuation of business, regardless of the individual's financial situation. Already in 1754 (before the familial quarrels), Abraham Hirschel's credit was low. When he applied to establish a textile manufactory in Prussia together with his five siblings and another Jewish business associate, the plan was rejected by Prussian officials. They justified their decision by noting the high costs of such an enterprise, and remarked that "Abraham Hirschel from general hearsay has more wind than funds and credit."[54]

Shortly thereafter, the quarrels with the Symons family from Amsterdam began. What followed was a nearly impenetrable web of mutual accusations, requests for arrest, flights, and slander. Both Abraham Hirschel and Isaac Symons became involved in numerous lawsuits at the commercial court in Leipzig and at the High Court (*Kammergericht*) in Berlin. As mentioned previously, in 1754 Berend Symons in Amsterdam filed action against his son, accusing him of embezzling his money. The case dragged on until 1758, especially after Isaac Symons and Hirschel's sister Friderica married in 1755, without the required permission from the Prussian state. In another case, Israel Pincus, a former partner of Abraham Hirschel, claimed debts from Isaac Symons and Friderica but was himself accused of falsifying bills of exchange and bribing witnesses. In 1755, Benjamin and Samuel Symons entered the scene, filing action against Hirschel due to bill debts; according to Hirschel, they had threatened to do so earlier. Eventually, even Friderica, Isaac Symons' wife, became involved in a criminal lawsuit of her own, after she sought to regain bills of exchange that she and her husband claimed to have been forged by Israel Pincus. Apparently, some of these had been issued to the wife of the deceased General von Dockum. Friderica had asked a young servant of the widow to return the bills of exchange, offering her an attractive reward for her cooperation; the servant, however, was far too overeager and attempted, unsuccessfully, to murder her mistress.[55]

Without going into extended detail about the assorted lawsuits, it suffices to say that they shed light on various issues crucial to the disruption of networks. Such issues include flight and the issuance of moratoria, as well as the complications brought about by the wide circulation of bills of exchange. Ultimately, however, it was the fear of losing credit and reputation that was of utmost importance to the merchants involved.

In 1755, when Isaac Symons and Friderica Hirschel married outside Prussia, Abraham Hirschel had already left for Saxony, due to the ongoing court cases and financial demands against him in Prussia. Hirschel, however, emphasized vehemently that he had not fled Berlin and that his departure was widely known. He claimed that his leaving was just a matter of avoiding being ensnared in Berlin by his dogged enemy Veitel Ephraim and being unable to travel to Leipzig for business as a result.[56] It was crucial for Hirschel to make this point, as flight in avoidance of debt payments or bankruptcy procedures was considered among the worst crimes a merchant could commit. Nevertheless, Hirschel later stated, in a subsequent document, that he had been forced to flee from Prussia, as an arrest there would have cost him his credit and name; thus, according to him, he had had to leave his house (and everything inside) behind.

Hirschel's close relations with the Saxon authorities apparently provided him safety for the moment. He resided in Pförten, an estate acquired in the 1740s by the famous Saxon Count Brühl, and there attempted to set up a mulberry and saffron plantation for manufactories established by Brühl.[57] He also seemed temporarily safe from his creditors, since, unlike the Prussian government, the Saxon officials were unwilling to pursue his adversaries' demands. Already in 1755, Benjamin and Samuel Symons transferred their claim against Abraham Hirschel (amounting to around 4,000 Reichsthaler) to the authorities in Dresden, demanding either payment or the arrest of Hirschel. Saxon officials, however, refused to arrest Hirschel, claiming that an arrest for unpaid debts from bills of exchange would be highly unusual and that this was, after all, "a common animosity among Jews doing business among themselves."[58]

Eventually, however, Hirschel wished to return to Prussia and to reestablish his business there. To do so, he sought to receive a moratorium from the Prussian king that would allow him to return with no danger of being arrested or pursued by creditors. In arguing for this, he emphasized not only that he had left Prussia simply for business, but also that the regulations regarding the trade in bills of exchange were especially strict and closely surveyed in Leipzig, and thus that his travels to Saxony alone should be proof of his innocence.[59] One of the reports in the government files supports his return under a moratorium, arguing that it had not yet been proven that Hirschel falsified bills of exchange and that his adversary Isaac Pincus had provided untrustworthy witnesses. In the end, however, the officials decided that Hirschel's having fled because of debts deprived him of the right to ask for clemency, much less for safe conduct. The dilemma faced by Abraham Hirschel was stark: an arrest in Prussia would have prevented him from attempting to sort out his business affairs; yet his earlier flight, though it had afforded him some agency to settle his claims and quarrels from afar, was now considered by the Prussian officials a reason against issuing a moratorium. Thus, concerning failure of individual merchants, one can conclude that open lawsuits, accusations of misconduct, rumors about falsified bills of exchange, and general untrustworthiness effectively eliminated any chance for a merchant, Jewish or not, to receive a state moratorium or other such support to put his finances in order and to start anew.

Reestablishing Credit—A Difficult Business

The details of these lawsuits and the arguments proffered by the different parties allow for insight into the role of the state, defense strategies, and how Jewish merchants employed networks of relatives, Jewish business partners, and officials to forward their cases. However, the issue of credit and reputation appears to be of greatest importance, at least to those involved in multiple court cases and under pressure from multiple sides. The preservation of their reputation was clearly the most important objective for Abraham Hirschel and his family, who apparently were still suffering from the damage done by the widely publicized Voltaire incident. Already in 1754, when Berend Symons filed action against his son Isaac Symons, Hirschel's mother, the widow of Hirschel Abraham, complained in a letter to the Prussian king that the attempted arrest of Symons and the appearance of five or six soldiers at their house "nearly brought the death" to her and her family and that she feared "the complete downfall in their business and credit." Everybody, she claimed, would believe that the presence of these officials was related to family debts. She also stated that Ephraim, who she claimed was the family's fiercest adversary, was spreading the information widely.[60] Her complaint points to the central issues in losing one's reputation and credit: besides lengthy court cases, one would also likely have to cope with the presence of state officials and soldiers as well as widespread rumors and information that could easily damage a merchant's credit.

During his ongoing legal battles, Abraham Hirschel himself complained repeatedly that his earlier trial with Voltaire, though it had been settled years before, was now being brought up incessantly. Regarding his trial with the Symons brothers, he said, “My whole weal and woe rests on the fast conclusion of this important trial, because it is this trial that costs me my honor, credit, good name and all of my assets.” The Symons brothers, he explained, “try to stain my name with the most hideous color of a bankrupt.”[61] Eventually, the trials concluded, though not with the intended outcome for anybody of the Hirschel family. Abraham Hirschel was sentenced to four years of prison labor, and Isaac Symons to three; Friderica Hirschel received three years’ imprisonment; and it was resolved that, after serving their sentences, each would be expelled from Prussia.[62]

Thanks to their close connections to the Saxon state administration, Isaac Symons and Abraham Hirschel moved to Dresden with their families after being released from Prussian imprisonment. The question remains as to how their trials and imprisonment influenced their subsequent economic futures. In Symons’ case, although he probably did not continue business on the scale that his relatives in Amsterdam did, he fared relatively well: in 1770, he received a privilege as court factor in Dresden; he traded in jewels and bills of exchange; and he and his wife had a live-in servant. He described his financial situation as being not especially great though also not particularly bad. He was evaluated by the Jewish court factor Bondi, the elders of the Dresden Jewish community, and the non-Jewish authorities as an honest man and was recommended for a renewed privilege in 1775.[63] Thus, it appears that the legal dispute with his father and even his time in prison did not irreparably damage his reputation, and he was able to continue his former trade in jewels and bills of exchange.

The situation of Abraham Hirschel and his family, in contrast, was hopeless. In 1763, he lived in Dresden with his wife, their four children (ages five to fifteen), and a sister. The city records list him as trading in jewels, but the officials attested to his poor financial situation and his “generally very bad reputation” and recommended his expulsion. Twelve years later, the records note his widow and four children but list no income or assets. Later that year, two of the children are listed as orphans living on communal charity.[64] Thus, Abraham Hirschel’s economic difficulties and presumably his business behavior damaged not only him but also his family in the years to come; it lowered or completely blocked their chances of finding marital matches and left his children in poverty. After his prison term, Isaac Symons was usually described as an honest man, whereas after Abraham Hirschel’s, his poor reputation was brought up routinely and not only prevented him from successfully returning to business, but also negatively influenced the economic prospects of his children.

Conclusion

Trust among merchants, Jewish or not, is often discussed in terms of the building of commercial networks and the flow of goods and money within those networks and their extensions. One should not forget, however, that the disruption of commercial networks, the shift of commercial connections, the incurring of debts, and the legal disputes over transactions were part and parcel of commercial life. They were anticipated and did not necessarily lead to commercial failure for a merchant; nor did temporary situations of illiquidity permanently end a merchant's business.

Trust and thus the existence of credit and reputation were crucial in any business operation. Jewish merchants relied heavily—and probably more heavily than their non-Jewish fellow merchants—on kinship and ethnic and/or religious connections. Yet these were not guarantees that business would proceed smoothly. In a world of ever more complicated and developing transregional connections via bills of exchange, yet absent fully adequate legal means of enforcing payments, the importance of trust and reputation remained crucial. The case of the Symons and Hirschel families shows the limitations and fragility of such network structures; likewise, it also hints at an opposing factor, as both sides employed specific groups of close business partners in Amsterdam, Dresden, Halle, and Berlin to successfully pursue lawsuits against their opponents.

The study of bankruptcy and business failure demonstrates the limits of trust based on kinship and ethnicity and confirms that such connections cannot automatically be equated with trust. Trust needs to be built and maintained, and it functions only in interaction with formal institutions, be they the Jewish community, commercial courts, or regulations of the trade with bills of exchange. In general, issues of trust and reputation did not differ significantly in commercial networks and connections involving mainly Jewish or mainly Christian merchants. More comparative research remains necessary to determine if there were major differences in how different commercial networks (of Jewish and Christian merchants, respectively) overcame disruptions.

One of the most important differences likely evolved from the different and often inferior legal status of Jews. This would have been the case especially in German states, where commercial failure and poverty—not just criminal bankruptcy—could lead to expulsion. In court, however, as far as can be ascertained from the example of Abraham Hirschel and Isaac Symons and their adversaries, Jewish merchants were not treated differently. This reminds us not to regard the Jewish economic past, and especially Jewish commercial undertakings, simply as successfully operative networks based mostly on trust created through kinship connections and shared religion or ethnicity. Moreover, it underscores that state regulations or interventions were not the sole factors that could cause economic difficulties, and that, at least partly, the economic behavior of individual merchants was of crucial importance.

Chapter 4

Jewish Quarters: The Economics of Segregation in the Kingdom of Poland

Glenn Dynner

Contrary to popular belief, Polish Jewry was not confined to ghettos, at least not before the Nazi occupation. Nevertheless, after the partitions of Poland, when an autonomous "Poland" was allowed to tentatively reemerge as the Duchy of Warsaw (1807–1814) under Napoleonic auspices and then as the Congress Kingdom of Poland (1815–1918) under tsarist rule, Jews were officially barred from living and working on choice streets in many towns and cities, beginning with the capital, Warsaw. If these residential restrictions did not warrant the description of "ghettoes," nor compare in scale to the Pale of Settlement in the tsarist empire proper, their timing was certainly inauspicious, for they were imposed at a time when formal ghettoes were finally being dismantled across western and central Europe.[1]

Why, we must wonder, was the Jews' presence on select Polish streets and thoroughfares now deemed so threatening, and how were residential restrictions justified at such a late date? Officials of the Duchy of Warsaw and its successor state, the Kingdom of Poland, may have been beholden to absolutist monarchs, but they also saw themselves as enlightened and opposed to medieval corporatism. This chapter argues that Jewish residential restrictions derived chiefly from the misplaced conviction that Polish Jewry's economic might, reinforced by its sheer numbers, had to be contained in the interest of "fairness" to urban Christians. The latter were considered helpless when pitted against the multitudes of allegedly clannish, collusive Jews who congregated in towns and cities as central as Warsaw—where Jews had only recently been readmitted. If areas where Jews could live and work were restricted, officials reasoned, then decent Christian inhabitants would at least have a fighting chance.[2] Nor did officials consider the current situation good for Jews, who by crowding into urban centers, isolating themselves by means of language and dress, and engaging in trade and lease-holding were, it was felt, denying themselves the moral benefits of pursuing agriculture and crafts. The architects of the new residential policies apparently hoped that by offering exemptions from these residential restrictions to Jews they considered desirable—that is, Jews who were acculturated, productive, and wealthy—the rest would be moved to cast off their own antisocial tendencies and strive to join their more civilized coreligionists.

In practice, residential restrictions did little to alleviate fears about Jewish economic might and separatism. On the one hand, some wealthier urban Jews indeed obtained special permission to live, work, and compete with Christians on choice streets, yet their acculturation hardly made them less competitive. On the other hand, officials miscalculated the values and priorities of the great majority of urban Jews, who proved willing to shun the lucrative opportunity to live and work on choice streets in order to maintain their traditional way of life. As a result, the new residential policies merely succeeded in sifting wealthy and acculturated Jews out of Jewish neighborhoods while leaving behind a more proudly tradition-oriented and traditionalist-led Jewish populace.

Polish Jewish Residential Restrictions

Polish Jewish settlement had always been formally controlled in certain locales. Medieval privileges for Christian townspeople, known as *de non tolerandis Judaeis*, theoretically precluded Jewish residence in at least ninety towns, including Warsaw (from 1527).[3] In addition, distinctly Jewish areas of settlement existed in a handful of other towns, some of which were conceived during the towns' initial planning phases (e.g., Zamość and Przysucha). Some Jewish quarters were walled in (Kalisz and Sandomierz); others (Piotrków Trybunalski and Poznań) had originated as separate Jewish towns or, in the case of royal towns (Radom, Rawa Mazowiecka, and Lublin), as Jewish settlements on royal administrators' (*starosta*) lands.[4] Yet Jews and

Christians usually lived relatively interspersed in most towns and cities in the Polish-Lithuanian Commonwealth, particularly those who could afford to live in houses surrounding the market square (*rynek*).[5] Moreover, most restrictions and formal distinctions had effectively lapsed by the end of the eighteenth century, the period of the partitions. The partitioning powers, Prussia, Russia, and Austria, initially upheld the status quo.[6]

This attitude of benign neglect would begin to change in 1809, after the creation of the autonomous Napoleonic Polish entity known as the Duchy of Warsaw. Jewish residence in the capital city, Warsaw, which had just been legalized during the brief period of Prussian dominion, in 1802, was now to be strictly controlled. An 1809 decree had labeled a handful of Warsaw streets, portions of streets, and areas like the Old City "restricted" (*exymowany*), meaning off limits to Jewish residences and businesses, citing the "indecent state of affairs" resulting from so many Jews living on principal or narrow streets; accompanying dangers like conflagrations, epidemics, lack of cleanliness, lawlessness, and disorder; and, finally, the allegedly sordid nature of the economic activities in which Jews typically engaged, such as trade and tavern-keeping.[7]

The 1809 restrictions were apparently not well enforced. In 1812, Ignacy Sobolewski (1770–1846), the minister of police, complained that despite the 1809 decree, Jews had continued to pour unrestricted into the capital, clogging up and defacing the most beautiful streets and depriving Christian residents of their share of profits. As a solution, he proposed moving all but the most acculturated members of the Warsaw Jewish community to the relatively deserted northwestern-most section of the city and surrounding it with sturdy walls.[8] Sobolweski's plan, which advocated outright ghettoization, was not put into effect. However, the next year, in 1813, Frederick August, the Duke of Warsaw, issued a decree that, while claiming to be merely a fulfillment of the 1809 decree, resembled Sobolewski's plan in important ways. The 1809 decree had ruled out only a few neighborhoods; now, the majority of Jews were indeed to be confined to the northwestern section of the city, which Frederick August euphemistically designated a "Jewish City." Although no walls were to be constructed, the rest of Warsaw was to be effectively off limits. Those Jews with the means to do so could purchase empty lots or knock down wooden structures and build stone ones, but only within the Jewish City (the 1809 decree had allowed such practices even on restricted streets).[9] As one historian has noted, this clever, if draconian, policy effectively enlisted Jewish wealth and initiative to build up a desolate section of the city while at the same time thwarting unwanted Jewish expansion in more economically developed sectors.[10]

Frederick August's 1809 and (even more so) 1813 decrees might seem to warrant the description of ghettoization. But both contained something novel: Jewish families who possessed at least 60,000 zlotys, eliminated their beards and other distinguishing Jewish markers, enrolled their children in Polish schools, and fit a desired professional profile (factory owners, large-scale merchants, doctors, artists) were eligible for exemption from residential restrictions. The policy thus rewarded acculturated Jews by allowing them to reside on restricted streets while penalizing the rest for fidelity to traditional Jewish sartorial and educational norms. At the same time, the wealth requirement signaled a strong fiscal concern that, true to the dictates of cameralism, often trumped other considerations. Twenty-two Jewish families had obtained exemptions in Warsaw by the time the Duchy was dissolved in 1815.[11]

Jewish residential restrictions reflected a more general change of heart by Napoleon, who, through his subsidiary, Frederick August, had already suspended citizenship, political rights, and hereditary rights to real estate for Jews for a period of ten years, after which it was hoped that Jewish acculturation in the Duchy of Warsaw would have caught up with the rest of Europe. Soon, inhabitants of additional towns, beginning with Wschowa, Płock, Maków, and Przasysz, came forward with requests to set up their own Jewish quarters consisting of a few designated streets, which they justified by pointing to the 1809 Warsaw decree.[12] Their repeated invocations of the 1809 decree have created much confusion among scholars, since what they were really requesting was the creation of additional "Jewish Cities" along the lines of Fredrick's 1813 decree, not the zones of restricted streets decreed in 1809. At the same time, they, too, proposed exemptions for acculturated and wealthy Jews.[13]

When much of the Duchy of Warsaw came under tsarist control in 1815 (the tsar was technically "king" of the new Kingdom of Poland), its residential policy was adopted and expanded, proving to be one of Napoleon's most enduring legacies in the region. The interethnic jostling began almost immediately. Christian residents approached the tsar's Polish viceroy, Józef Zajączek, with a demand to re-implement the segregation policy in Warsaw, while Jewish mercantile elites approached the tsar's chief Russian representative in Poland, Imperial Commissioner Nicholas Novosiltsov.[14] The latter brushed aside Zajączek's fears about arousing "Christian ill will" and managed to suspend the residential decree for the next six years.[15]

In 1821, however, the Christian townspeople, helped by recommendations made by the Committee on Towns (1815–1816) and Interior Minister Mostowski (1816–1818), prevailed.[16] Tsar Alexander, as king of Poland, announced that there would be a reversion back to the 1809 "restricted streets" policy, which, it is important to remember, had never actually been enforced.[17] Apparently unaware of the 1813 "Jewish City" decree, Alexander prohibited Jews from living or working on the streets and areas mentioned in 1809 and added several new restricted streets to the list. The result was an enlarged version of the inverse ghetto that had been intended back in 1809: a horseshoe shaped zone of streets open to Jewish settlement and businesses in the remainder of the city, referred to as a Jewish quarter (*rewir*).[18] In addition, the tsar required nonresident Jews who wished to do business in Warsaw to pay a sojourner's tax (*billet*) and an escort fee (*geleitzoll*), both in force during the prior Duchy of Warsaw period.

Unlike his predecessors, Tsar Alexander rigorously enforced the residential decree. Expulsions from homes and businesses on Warsaw's restricted streets proceeded apace in 1824, causing a ripple of panic throughout Jewish Warsaw. Although Jews could in theory move to any street in the city not deemed excluded, many were indeed impelled to move to the northwestern section, Frederick's "Jewish City," which contained more available space. Without any formalized Jewish city, however, portions could be usurped by the government at any time. For example, the construction of the notorious Alexander Citadel in the wake of the Poles' 1830–1831 uprising against the tsar entailed the destruction of 136 Jewish-owned houses, although the Warsaw municipal government eventually permitted expelled Jews to rent unused wooden barracks. The Warsaw municipality continually encroached upon eastern portions of the Jewish quarter, causing it to migrate westward and southward. Warsaw's Jewish quarter shrank and shifted.[19]

At the same time, exemptions for acculturated and wealthy Jews on the basis of the 1809 decree continued to be extended: by 1836, 124 Warsaw Jewish families had obtained exemptions; and an additional seven families did so by 1842.[20] Those families were to enjoy the benefits of living and working on streets that were more desirable from an economic perspective. But this aspect did not tend to inspire their coreligionists. As mentioned earlier, enticing wealthy and acculturated Jews out of heavily Jewish neighborhoods inadvertently reduced their influence over the Jewish masses, who remained in increasingly tradition-accented and traditionalist-led enclaves.

After the reintroduction of residential restrictions in Warsaw in 1821, Jewish quarters were established or reinstated in thirty additional towns and cities in the Kingdom of Poland at a rate of about three per year.[21] In addition, Jewish quarters identified by the term "compass" (*obręb*) were established or reinstated in twenty-four towns possessing *de non tolerandis Judaeis* privileges.[22] Other Jewish quarters were planned but never enforced.[23] These figures yield a grand total of fifty-five operative Jewish quarters among the kingdom's 456 towns.[24] The towns with restrictions tended to be larger and more economically vital, which may explain why roughly half of the kingdom's Jewish population resided in Jewish quarters by 1833, the year in which the creation of further Jewish quarters was formally halted.[25]

As in Warsaw, expulsions of even wealthy Jews who refused to bow to the regime's acculturation imperatives continued apace. According to Privy Councilor Turkul', Jews who owned the finest houses around the market squares of certain towns yet refused to visibly acculturate were expelled to Jewish quarters before local officials could find Christian buyers for their homes, sometimes causing their ruin (many had their wealth tied up in their homes).[26] Yet expulsions probably occurred less frequently in smaller towns, where the economic effects would have been more drastic.[27]

A year after the suspension of further Jewish quarters in 1833, existing Jewish quarters received an additional Jewish influx when, in an effort to curtail smuggling (most smugglers were believed to be Jews), Jewish settlement was banned in 111 towns along the Prussian and Austrian borders. Jews were also expelled from state mining towns in an attempt to undercut the black market in base and precious metals. Most refugees had little choice but to gravitate towards one of the kingdom's fifty-five Jewish quarters, which, despite their overcrowded conditions, seemed to promise the most economic opportunity.[28]

Jewish Responses

Raphael Mahler paints an exceedingly bleak picture of conditions in Jewish quarters, based on the portrayals of three sympathetic Polish nobles from the 1830s and 1840s. According to the first observer, Jakub Klimontowicz, three-fourths of the Jewish population in cities were "without a means of [steady] livelihood and sustain themselves by questionable kinds of small trade and by acting as middlemen." According to the second observer, Antoni Ostrowski, a visitor to a Jewish quarter beheld "a picture of human deterioration, shocking poverty, all black, sad, gloomy. Lacking everything, dirty,

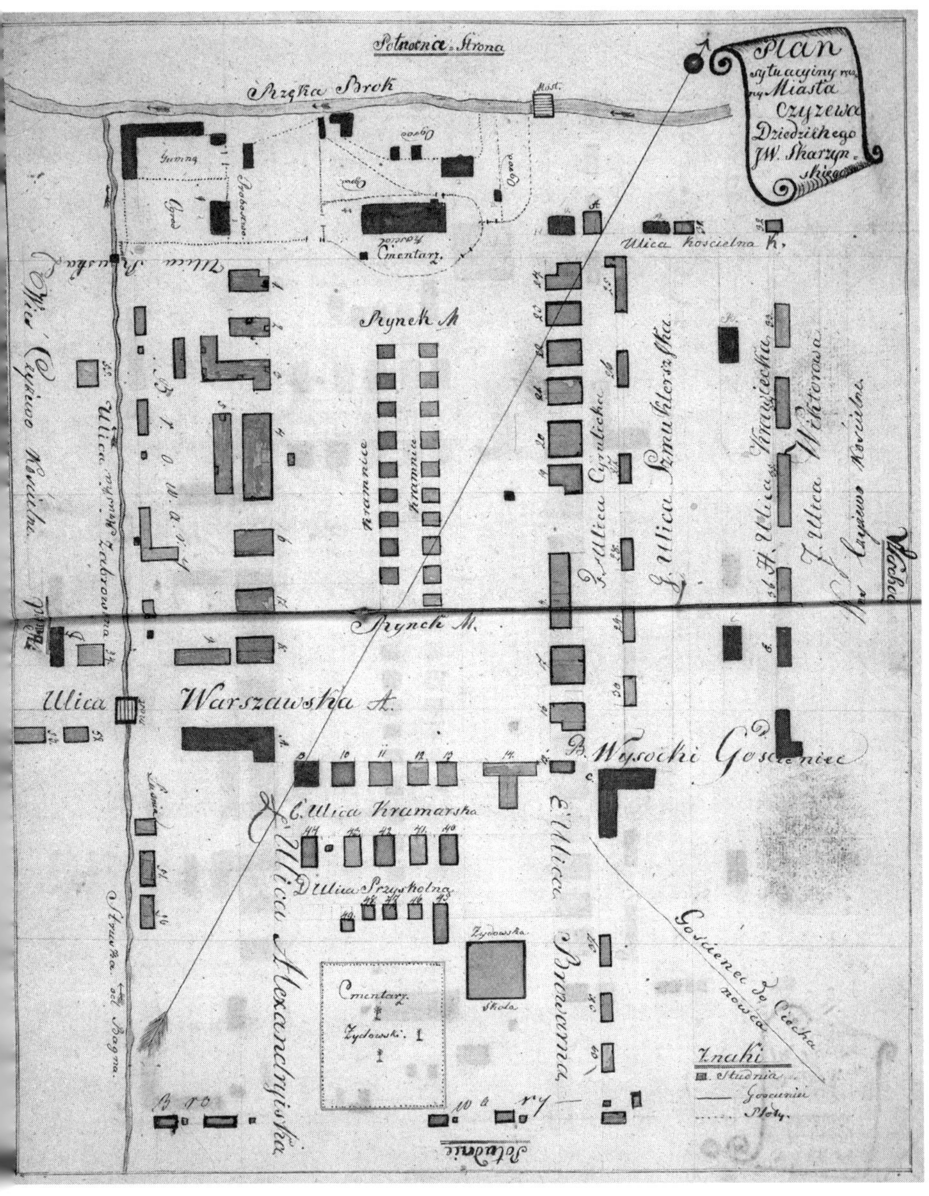

Figure 4.1 Map of the Jewish quarter (*rewir*) in Czyżew. AGAD, Kartografika z innych Oddziałów, nr 82 (formerly KRSW, nr 4125, k. 206).

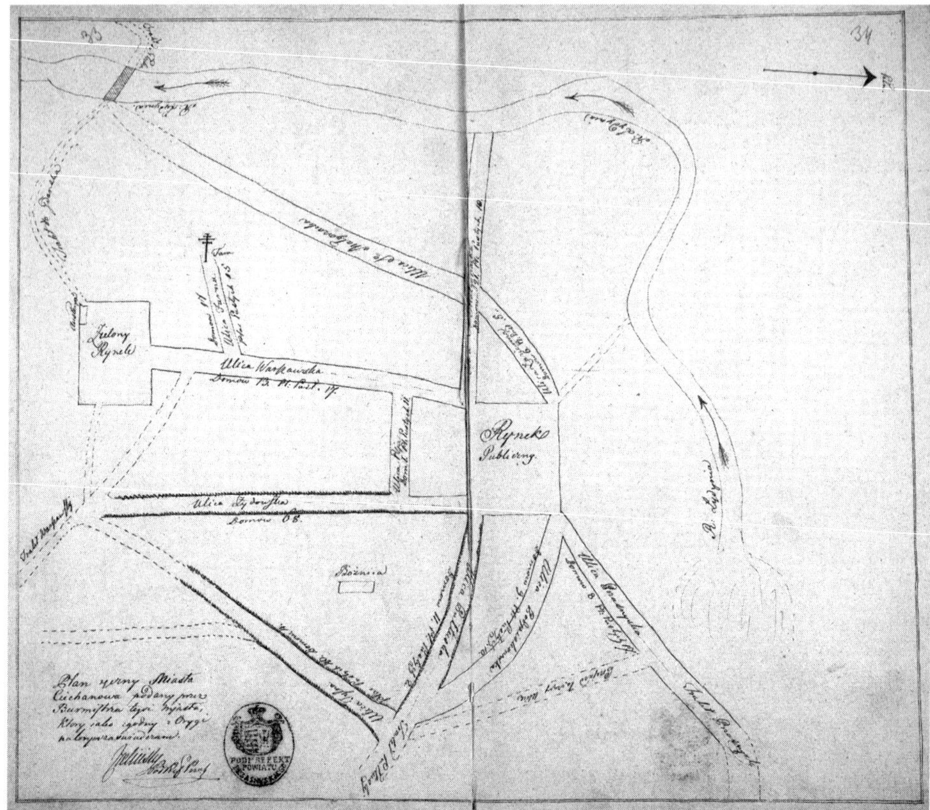

Figure 4.2 Map of the Jewish quarter (*rewir*) in Ciechanów. AGAD, Zbiór Kartograficzny, nr 349-15.

naked in part or altogether, the children cry." A third, anonymous author, who has been identified as Józef Gołuchowski, proclaimed that "there is no wretched race under the sun such as the poor Jewish people who dwell in our towns. . . . With the minor exception of a few with greater means, there dwell in one small room which is stricken with a plague-ridden miasma, over a dozen Jews, begrimed, half-naked, who lie down at night in actual layers one over the other in hammocks, engaged in an almost incessant struggle with hunger, illness, and all too often even with death."[29]

Yet those portrayals seem to represent worst-case scenarios. There was no out-migration approaching anything like that which would occur in the

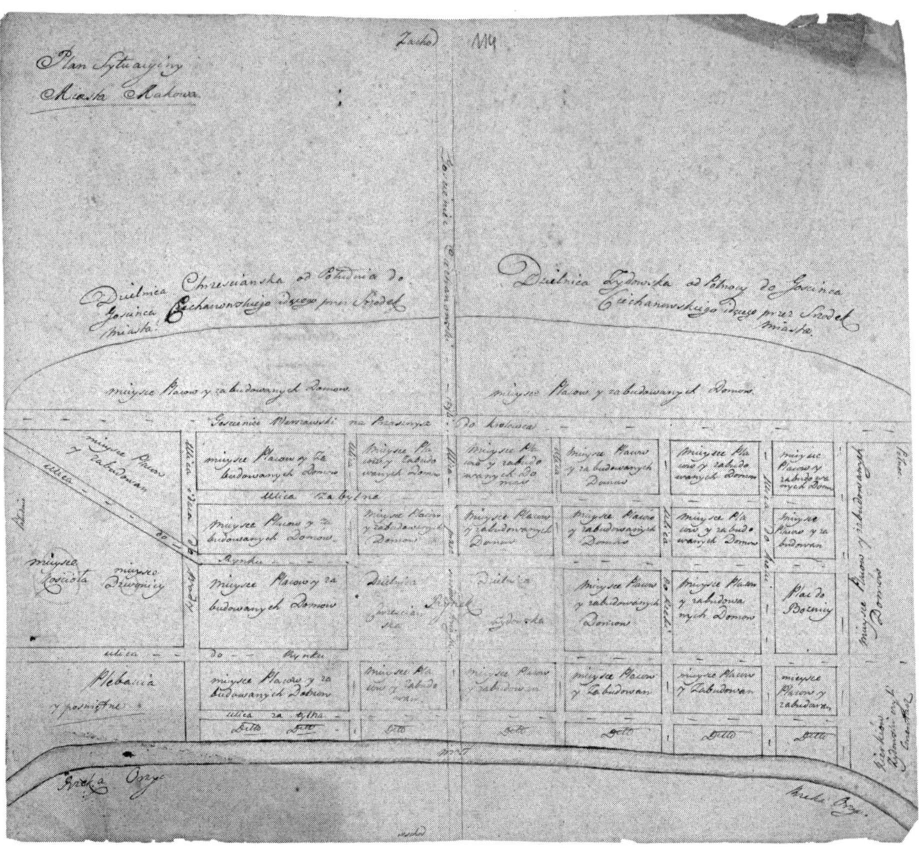

Figure 4.3 Map of the Jewish quarter (*rewir*) in Maków Mazowiecki. AGAD, KRSW, nr 4394, k. 114. See eastern portion of map.

1880s, a period of truly widespread economic crisis.[30] Instead, a large improvised economy composed of petty side-pursuits, however precarious, seems to have enabled most Jews to get by. In fact, a government survey of Jewish occupations in the Kingdom of Poland in 1843, based on about one-quarter of the Jewish population (106,514), found only 1 percent completely unemployed but labeled another 25 percent "day laborers," a probable euphemism for the improvised occupations mentioned by Klimontowicz. Among the other large categories, a full 28 percent were involved in crafts, 11.3 percent in trade, and 9.7 percent in legal, registered tavern-keeping.[31]

At the other end of the interpretive spectrum, Bina Garncarska-Kadary argues that residential restrictions proved advantageous, at least in the case of Warsaw Jews. The now heavily Jewish northwestern part of Warsaw may have been unattractive from the perspective of residential real estate, but it proved very attractive to factory builders, who began flocking there to purchase the cheap, Jewish-owned land and to hire workers from among the Jewish poor. This process was accelerated when Leopold Kronenberg, the railroad baron of Jewish descent, unified railroad lines on both banks of the Vistula River in such a way that (intentionally or not) caused the major line to traverse northwestern Warsaw and the heavily Jewish Praga suburb. Thanks to residential restrictions, apparently, the Jews of Warsaw wound up with front row seats to the East European industrial revolution.[32]

This latter view seems equally selective.[33] Archival sources actually point to a widespread desire among Jews to escape Jewish quarters, albeit without having to shed their visible cultural distinctions. Of course, some petitioners really had begun to dress like Polish townspeople, attain literacy in Polish, and enroll their children in public schools—in other words, becoming the type of Jew that the government was trying to engineer through its exemption policy.[34] Among them were Jewish army veterans who pointed out that they could not very well go back to living among Jews after so many years of military service among civilized fellow Poles.[35] But since eviction and resettlement could in principle be evaded, almost every Jew with a story seemed to try his or her luck.

After the failed 1830 Polish uprising against the tsar, petitions flowed in torrentially, since many Jews felt they deserved to be rewarded for their neutrality or loyalty and compensated for damages to their homes and businesses incurred during fighting. Their petitions tested and challenged Polish officials' sense of priorities, since in the aftermath of insurrection officials worried most of all about the loyalty of the population and replenishing the state's depleted treasury. Certain Jewish petitioners spoke to fiscal concerns alone, with some success. Ludwik Libas' house at 966 Targowicy Street contained a lace-making factory, which had collapsed in 1830 as a result of the uprising. Now, having revived it, he was to be expelled and forcibly relocated to Warsztatów Street, where his factory would never succeed, he claimed. Ludwik warned officials that he would have to leave the kingdom and set up a new enterprise abroad, to the detriment of the local economy. "I did not take a cent from the Regime nor ever abuse the care of the Regime, which rarely refuses to help increase the numbers of factories," he argued.[36] Although he made no claims to being acculturated, officials agreed that economic reconstruction must take precedence and annulled Ludwik's expulsion order.

A great number of Jews seeking permission to retain their homes and businesses on restricted streets were working women. This was likely due to their less conspicuous traditional dress, in addition to the higher incidence of working women in Jewish society relative to the general society. Many were widows who hoped that their desperate familial situation would sway officials.[37] Some were even involved in the Jewish liquor trade, the bane of social reformers and tsarist officials alike, but managed to obtain exemptions by demonstrating their affluence and acculturation.[38]

Most appeals were denied, occasionally with absurd results. For example, officials denied Esther Zweygebaum's request for a permit to trade on excluded streets on the grounds that her husband refused to shave his beard or change his traditional attire. Yet they allowed her bearded husband to retain his own permit.[39] Certain Jews, upon learning of an 1848 ban on taverns that lay within fifty feet of a church, actually attempted to have their Christian competitors expelled.[40] One woman, Perla Mirla Lewin, who already had permission to live on a restricted street herself, made so bold as to question the logic of all residential restrictions. Perla asserted that prime areas in Warsaw had remained nearly empty a decade after the banishment of Jewish merchants, and dared to add that "in this enlightened time it is unconscionable to so forcibly restrict the use of such a significant portion of the city," particularly in the case of a population as loyal as the Jews. Officials remained unmoved.[41]

Some of the most fascinating exemption requests are those that transcended interethnic rivalries. A female Christian named Elżbieta Zalawka testified that her Jewish neighbor Malka Brodman had been falsely accused of sharing her permit with another Jew by her trade rival's husband, a "quarrelsome" Christian cook of "poor character" named Jan Szrupiński, who was already embroiled in a court case with a Christian neighbor. Szrupiński had gotten his friends, also of "poor character," to bear false witness against Brodman. When Brodman had been expelled, they had pressured her, with curses and abuse, to sell her furniture to them on the cheap. Since two other Christian witnesses had confirmed this account, officials were initially persuaded. But as the investigation progressed, officials were shocked to discover that Brodman was living, working, and producing children with a Jewish man out of wedlock according to her own admission. Next, they discovered that the two were, in fact, married after all. Why had this woman "falsely claimed to be a whore," officials wondered? Apparently, she had been sharing her permit with her husband all along, as Szrupiński had claimed, but had tried to disassociate herself from him during the investigation. Her expulsion was indignantly upheld.[42]

Elżbieta Zalawka may have been defending Malka Brodman on moral grounds. But it is also possible that Brodman was a good-paying tenant whom Zalawka did not want to lose. In fact, several Christian landlords petitioned officials on their Jewish tenants' behalf. Józef Kowicki complained that he had rented part of his house to a Jew, who had run a tavern in it. After the Jew's eviction, he had tried to run the bar himself, but the customers had been frightened away, and his profits had suffered.[43] An army major named Połbrecht, who owned a house on Franciscan Street with a storefront bordering one of the excluded streets, explained that since Jews ran the store around the corner on a permitted street, Christians were simply too intimidated by the prospect of competing with Jews to even consider renting his store. Połbrecht was suffering such losses that he could not even pay his property taxes, surely a concern of the regime, and requested permission to rent the store to Jews once more.[44] During the 1830 uprising, Adam Charczewski implored the revolutionary regime to allow Zelik Lipszyc, a Jew from Praga whose store had been burned down, to rent his house on the restricted Rynek Nowego Miasta. Most Christians were too poor to rent it, Charczewski claimed, and he could no longer pay his taxes or contribute to revolutionary soldiers stationed in Warsaw. Lipszyc, though a Jew, was clean and well-liked, he promised.[45]

A declining nobleman named Rudzki, who sought permission on behalf of a Jew to rent one of his houses, which lay too close to the Alexander Citadel, appealed to class solidarity: "I beg the Government Commission to consider the poor state of property owners, a class to which both the Government and I, myself, belong, and further [consider] that it is impossible to rent out this residence at but the lowest price, and [consider] the tax increases. . . . If you refuse, I will not be able to pay my taxes and satisfy my most desperate needs."[46] Though the motivation for such Christian petitioners was clearly financial, their actions are somewhat unexpected in a context of tense interethnic rivalry.

A less savory reminder of the limits of ethnic solidarity is found in cases where Jews informed against fellow Jews. Hersz Aleksander Haybuszowicz informed authorities that Szmul Hersz Lantsztain had received permission to live in a house on a restricted street as a result of his separation from his wife Sura (actually named Szyndel) But he had remained with her there trading in iron products and "had become uncivilized, walking around with a beard like a typical Jew." Haybuszowicz demanded his coreligionist's expulsion. However, authorities determined that Lantsztain's wife had herself received permission to trade in iron on the restricted street in 1825, that she in fact lived at a different address, and that her estranged husband lived with his mother on a permitted street.[47]

Jewish communal bodies, in contrast to individual Jews, protested segregation rarely, and usually only immediately before or after a political transformation. Following the demise of the Napoleonic Duchy of Warsaw, as mentioned briefly above, a delegation of several wealthy Jewish merchants requested Novosiltsov's help in delaying the implementation of residential restrictions in Warsaw. This was only one of several delegations to Novosiltsov, usually aimed at preventing expulsions of Jewish tavern-keepers from the countryside (Nowosiltsov effected an indefinite delay).[48] In the case of residential restrictions, it will be recalled that Novosiltsov managed a six-year delay. Ettinger, Cohn, and Neuding approached him in Berlin on October 25, 1815, arguing that Warsaw Jews would be able to escape their miserable economic condition only if they could enter any profession and purchase a house or shop on any street in the city, and proclaimed that "religion does not determine the measure of a man."[49] On March 3, 1816, Ettinger, Cohn, and Neuding, now joined by Moses Furstenberg and Jacob Epstein, presented Novosiltsov with another, more detailed petition about residential segregation. They complained that the Jews of Warsaw had been given only six weeks to transport their businesses from excluded streets and reestablish them, thereby exposing them to considerable losses of profits and clientele, and again asked him to use his influence to delay the impending expulsion.[50] But this was to be the last formal protest against residential restrictions by Jewish communal leaders for four decades.

One reason for Jewish communal leaders' reticence may be that the exemption policy benefitted precisely those who were best positioned to evade the policy—that is, prominent, wealthy Jews who could obtain permission to reside on restricted streets. Even the influential Hasidic patrons Berek and Temerel Sonenberg-Bergson won permission to reside on a restricted street in Warsaw, which included a remarkable permission for Berek to retain his beard and traditional markings (Ettinger was less successful in this regard).[51] Rare was the Jewish resident who obtained a personal exemption but continued to fight for the rest of Warsaw Jewry, as Perla Mirli Lewin had done.

Nor did the rabbinical leadership seem to so much mind Jewish quarters, which provided for better communal control and religious scrutiny. The presence of Jewish quarters did not apparently affect choices of towns for Hasidic courts, either.[52] Even maskilim occasionally approved of them. Elazar Tahlgrin insisted that restricted streets constituted an appropriate punishment for Hasidic flamboyance, meaning their distinctive dress, loud prayers, immersions, shouts, and singing: "They forgot all the sorrows that we endured because of such behavior. And why were we banished from the streets of our city? Only because of the ugly deeds we dared to do in the presence of the nations, lacking proper conduct [*derekh eretz*]. They should open their eyes and observe the decree of the Saxon King and Duke of Warsaw [Frederick August, in 1809]."[53] On Sabbaths and festivals, Tahlgrin lamented, Hasidim were not ashamed to walk around wrapped in a *tallit* (ritual garment) on any street of the city, "even where no Jews live." During the Sanctification of the Moon, they did not shrink from "making themselves look like hoodlums and maniacs, with loud shouts in public streets." They also left windows open during public prayer, exposing themselves to ridicule by "thousands of passers-by, Jews and non-Jews alike." Nor were Warsaw Jewry's "ugly deeds" confined to ostentatious piety. Jews were failing to respect their own synagogues and study houses, spitting on the floors and even urinating on the walls outside in full public view. Religious leaders were, furthermore, turning a blind eye to acts of theft against non-Jews, rationalizing that it was strictly a police matter.[54] Jews had brought residential restrictions upon themselves, Tahlgrin concluded bitterly.

A more radical integrationist, Jan Glucksberg, did decry the debilitating effects of residential segregation on Jews, but only anonymously in French (in 1829) and Polish (in 1831), languages that were inaccessible to most Polish Jews: "The results of this decree are so harmful that Israelites have been deprived of their last funds. Driven from place to place, they lead a practically nomadic existence and lose both their savings and their furniture; so that they can engage neither in trade, nor agriculture, nor crafts. Their destiny becomes uncertain, and of necessity they become a burden to the state and sometimes become dangerous criminals."[55] Glucksberg demanded exemptions not only for wealthy Jews but for army veterans, graduates of the modern Rabbinical School, artisans, and small factory owners.[56] But it was only in 1856, as debates over peasant and Jewish rights gained currency in official circles, that Jewish communal leaders finally stepped forward with a lengthy protest against Jewish quarters.[57] Six years later, in 1862, the progressive Jewish periodical *Jutrzenka* announced the official cancellation of Jewish residential restrictions in the kingdom, but with surprisingly little fanfare.[58] Nor was there any mass rush out of Jewish quarters. In Warsaw, according to one historian, "the largest and most principle concentration [of Jews] remained on the territory of the old ghetto" long after the abolition of residential restrictions, thus testifying to the success of Jewish accommodation.[59]

Why Residential Restrictions?

The tsarist regime and its supporters attempted to justify the segregationist policy throughout this period with a regularity that suggests a degree of moral discomfort. Some officials invoked aesthetic considerations, bemoaning the numerous Jewish hats and beards on Warsaw's main thoroughfares.[60] But fears about Jewish economic power surfaced most frequently. Restricting areas where Jews could live and work would level the playing field for Christian merchants and, paradoxical as it may seem to us, ultimately unify and homogenize the kingdom by drawing Jews out of their economic niches and residential enclaves.

Polish reformers were already fanning fears of the "danger of the total domination of trade and industry by the Jews" during the first years of the Kingdom of Poland.[61] Once residential restrictions were implemented, most fell silent, but some attempted to defend them. Benjamin Radzyn, for example, claimed that the lifting of prohibitions for one excluded street in Warsaw had resulted in fierce competition between dozens of people in a single residence, and that competition had sharply diminished when the street was re-restricted. No further proof was needed.[62] Polish officials supplied similar justifications. The commissioner of Mazowia, for example, explained the purpose of Jewish quarters as not only to cleanse the main streets of Jewish slovenliness and lure Jews out of the liquor trade by means of exemptions, but also "to give Christians an opportunity to make profits and become more industrious."[63] Residential restrictions were, according to others, a humane alternative to the outright expulsion of these cunning, aggressive traders.[64]

Complaints about Jewish urban overpopulation increased towards the mid-century. So many Jews had swarmed into the city, officials worried, that they had overwhelmed their Christian rivals and caused their enterprises to collapse despite residential restrictions. According to an 1845 report, the government had established Jewish agriculture colonies but, because of their disgust for farming, Jews had continued to flock to towns. That year, according the report, a full 450,027 Jews out of a total of 524,776 Jews in the kingdom lived in towns, almost attaining the size of the urban Christian population.[65] The remaining rural Jews avoided real agriculture and engaged in "speculative" enterprises like cattle ranching, in cottage industries, and, until its prohibition in villages the prior year, in tavern-keeping. Warsaw, where Jews had "poured in from the provinces to the city, which was undoubtedly alluring from the perspective of speculation," presented the most serious problem for these officials. Warsaw's Jewish population had shot up from 28,044 in 1825 to 45,832 in 1845, an annual increase of 889 Jews per year that approached the annual increase of Christians.[66] The past year alone had seen an increase of 5,952 Jews in the capital.[67]

More elaborate justifications were offered when British Jewish philanthropist Moses Montefiore asked officials to acknowledge the impoverishing effects of Jewish quarters.[68] Several insisted that Jews had always been a foreign, itinerant, harmful people, and that their invasion of towns had deprived Christian townspeople of a means of making a living, sparked interreligious conflict, and transformed Warsaw into a veritable Jerusalem. According to their understanding of the history of residential restrictions, the Napoleonic regime had upheld residential restrictions in 1809 because it had noticed how Jews speculated and captured every trade, even the most lucrative ones, driving Christians into poverty. The regime of the Kingdom of Poland had likewise viewed Jewish residential segregation as the only solution to interethnic competition. At the same time, those Jews who desired moral reform and were able to resist the discouragement of their Jewish religious leaders and the scoffing and condemnation of their Jewish neighbors had always been able to qualify for residence on restricted streets, they pointed out without mentioning the wealth requirement.[69]

The minister state secretary of the Kingdom of Poland, in his own response to Montefiore's protest, defended Jewish quarters as a means to "prevent in this way a large accumulation of inhabitants in the cities and the resulting disease, contagion, drunkenness, and rise in the prices of vital goods, to ease surveillance of the inhabitants' morals by the Police and facilitate the beautification and cleanliness of the cities, and, finally, to limit in some measure the opportunity for the Jews to engage in all kinds of roguery and fraud at the expense of Christians."[70]

Some non-Jewish observers rejected this logic. The Jewish Committee of 1826, consisting of Poles who exhibited no great love for Jews, protested that expelling Jews from their homes and chasing them into new, separate quarters did not open up any route to their moral reform through integration with the rest of the populace.[71] In the wake of the failed 1830 uprising, the exiled Jan Czyński protested Zajączek's "arbitrary" expulsion of Jews from Królewska Street on the grounds that "many thousand Jewish families, both rich and poor, were on this account forced to remove from a spot where they found their only means of subsistence." In Czyński's opinion, "to gratify the wanton caprice of one man [Zajączek], notorious for his utter servility to the Russian government, thousands of inoffensive inhabitants were inevitably ruined, and a daring outrage committed against every shadow of justice, as well as individual liberty."[72] Another Polish exile, the aforementioned Antoni Ostrowski, protested that by being "driven from village to town, from small town to larger [town]; and in [larger] towns from one street to another," Jewish families languished in miserable living conditions and barely scraped by.[73]

In 1848, in response to Montefiore's plea, the regime did eliminate certain excluded streets in Warsaw and soften exemption qualifications.[74] But objections to the entire policy grew louder. According to the minister state secretary's extremely optimistic view, enforcing segregation was at any rate "becoming all the more difficult since, in accordance with the Government's will, [Jews] change the very clothes that distinguish them from the other inhabitants."[75] This was a reference to the "clothing decrees" (1845–1851), which in actuality contained a significant loophole: Jewish men who merely adopted the hats and longer coats of Russian merchants were permitted to keep their beards, thus continuing to distinguish themselves from their Polish neighbors.[76]

Privy Councilor Turkul' also questioned the wisdom and ethics of legal segregation.[77] The overcrowding in Jewish quarters had been exacerbated by migrations of rural Jews to cities and towns "due to the prohibition against their selling alcohol in village taverns" (in 1844). Turkul' moreover dismissed most of the original justifications of the policy:

> Frequent fires and the spread of uncleanliness in the cities could be prevented with ease through more vigilant surveillance on the part of the local Police, all the more so since the Christian homes in a city are equally prone to fires. The separation of Jews from Christians would in no way promote the decrease of contagious diseases, for this

> measure cannot counteract the frequent communication between them, and, consequently, neither can it thwart the deception and roguery that have been ingrained in the Jewish tribe since the distant past.[78]

Notwithstanding Jewish "deception and roguery," Turkul' concluded, the government should remove the cap on the number of Jewish families permitted to live on excluded streets and allow all Jews deemed deserving to move there. He also recommended allowing Jewish quarters to be established in towns possessing *de non tolerandis Judaeis* in order to reduce "the number of localities excluded from Jewish habitation, without which they will concentrate more and more in certain points, and in this way their merging with the other classes of the population will continue to become difficult."[79]

In 1858, an anonymous social commentator vividly described the effects of residential restrictions on Warsaw Jews. He promised officials that he had no great love for the Jewish poor man, who, "steeped in dark superstition, spends all his energy dreaming of zlotys and earns his living for the most part from harmful activities like smuggling." He was admittedly repelled by "the so-called Hasidic Sect, which counts the greatest number of believers among our country's Jews and appeals especially to the lowest type, and whose fanatical propaganda paralyzes every government initiative." Yet he insisted that overpopulation was a real concern to all. One only had to visit Warsaw's Jewish quarter at dusk on Sabbath eve, when religious custom demanded that every family light candles in their residences. Peering into any open cellar hatchway revealed a throng of Jews wallowing in offensive filth and unhealthy fumes. Such a state of affairs was harmful to the general population and would inevitably result in the Jews' expulsion. They should at least be allowed to build in Warsaw's Jewish quarter unrestrictedly; while Jewish quarters in provincial towns should at the very least be expanded.[80]

That same year, a new Jewish Committee concluded that the policy of exempting only wealthy Jews from Jewish quarters was morally indefensible, and recommended requiring only a gymnazium or modern Rabbinical School certificate for exemptions in all towns, save Warsaw.[81] Then the Warsaw governor himself protested Jewish quarters on the grounds that they isolated Jews and prevented their absorption into and adoption of the customs of the wider populace, which was surely not the regime's intent.[82] Fear of Jewish support of another impending Polish revolt did the rest. In 1862, the tsar's new leading representative in the kingdom, Marquis Alexander Wielopolski, proposed an end to all Jewish residential segregation as part of his pitch for a broader liberalization of Jewish legislation. His proposal became law on May 24, 1862.[83]

Conclusion: The Question of Jewish Economic Exceptionalism

To what extent did the myth of Jewish economic difference that underwrote residential restrictions correspond to reality? Given its prominence in anti-Semitic theory, discussion of Jewish economic prowess easily lends itself to a philo-Semitic reframing: economic overrepresentation becomes economic achievement, something to be admired rather than feared. Several recent scholarly treatments take this route, offering impressive snapshots of Jewish economic predominance as evidence of a unique Jewish ethos, while ignoring crucial factors like the conditions of initial Jewish settlement, Jewish legal status, kinship networks, and so on.[84] Yet the opposite tendency, the attempt to normalize Jewish history by downplaying all indications of Jewish difference in the economic realm, seems no less apologetic.[85]

Recent works on Jews in transnational trade have begun steer clear of both tendencies. Sarah Abrevaya Stein, for example, argues that "Jewishness abetted commercial alliances" in the ostrich feather trade because of "the particular skills, expertise, and contacts [Jews] possessed" as an immigrant group with experience in the textile trade.[86] Francesca Trivellato argues that state policies, both hostile and "philosemitic mercantilistic," reinforced Sephardic Jewish subgroup identities and alliances. At the same time, Trivellato appreciates the limits of this network, noting cases where Sephardic Jews forged alliances with non-Jewish "strangers" as partners and agents. The upshot is that Jewishness alone was insufficient for the formation of business alliances within Sephardic Jewish subgroups, for "cooperation among coreligionists was not based on a vague sense of belonging to the same nation but was contingent on alliances built via marriage and economic specialization."[87]

Based on the foregoing analysis, it seems possible to assert several distinctive economic advantages enjoyed by Jews during the segregation period. Those advantages were often based on mere perceptions; but those perceptions profoundly shaped realities, which, in turn, fed back into the perceptions. For example, our sources demonstrate that Polish Jewry had earned a fearsome reputation for economic competitiveness, which tended to scare off potential rivals and further enlarge their reputation. Recall, for example, G. Połbrecht's difficulty finding Christian tenants because of the presence of a Jewish-run store around the corner. When expulsions seemed to create a vacuum, they, too, indirectly enhanced the Jewish economic reputation: recall Perla Mirli Lewin's claim that prime areas in Warsaw remained desolate after they were declared off-limits to Jewish traders, or Privy Councilor Turkul's observation that it often proved impossible to find Christian buyers for Jewish homes vacated after expulsions from restricted streets. Outside observers helped perpetuate the image cycle. British travelers asserted that all retail trade in former Poland and Lithuania was carried out by Jews, "an industrious and persevering people, and of a nature that, notwithstanding the oppressive hand of government, seem everywhere to thrive."[88] In Warsaw itself, another traveler claimed, Jews managed "all the trade of the city."[89] A native Polish observer proclaimed that "no sale or purchase can transpire in Poland without Jewish participation."[90] Such perceptions could become self-fulfilling.

They seem to have derived, in part, from residential patterns: most Polish Jews—around 85 percent—resided in towns and cities for the greater part of the nineteenth century, which was almost the exact inverse of the Polish Christian demographic situation (around 15 percent).[91] On the whole, Jews formed 46.5 percent of the kingdom's urban residents by 1865 while constituting only around 10 percent of the overall population.[92] It is difficult to determine the degree to which urban migration was voluntary (that is, due to new economic opportunities) or involuntary (that is, attributable to legislative assaults on the rural Jewish liquor trade). But as agriculture was slowly displaced by industry, most Jews would certainly find themselves better positioned than most Christians. By the middle of the nineteenth century, seventeen out of Warsaw's twenty bankers and six out of Warsaw's eight department store owners were Jewish or of Jewish origin. By the beginning of the next century, at the peak of Jewish involvement in industry, 64.8 percent of Warsaw's factories were owned by Jews.[93]

Notions of Jewish economic assertiveness ("aggressiveness") were reinforced by Jewish petitioning practices. Lacking the most basic civil rights and protections, Polish Jews were of necessity proactive; and the experience of reading through government petitions, overwhelmingly authored by Jewish supplicants, cannot fail to impress the historian. Many petitions were composed by Jewish women, most of whom appeared no less skilled or experienced in business than their husbands. A Polish Jewish wife was often a junior partner in a couple's joint economic venture—in a tavern, for example, she would serve the customers, while he would deal with supplies and production.[94] In a large city like Warsaw, her lack of a beard, side-locks, and other outwardly Jewish markers that officials found so odious elevated her importance for the family venture and made it wiser for her, rather than her husband, to interact with officials and become the public face of the venture. The preponderance of Jewish working women in the kingdom's urban centers, helped by positive attitudes toward working women in traditional Jewish culture, presented Christian competitors with a double-barreled threat.

Other Jewish societal values fed the image cycle, as well. In the all-pervasive liquor trade, which I have treated in depth elsewhere, deeply rooted perceptions of Jewish sobriety conditioned Polish landowners to unanimously prefer to lease their taverns and distilleries to Jews, even after doing so became illegal. Those expectations and rewards also conditioned Jewish behavior, for example by encouraging more regulated and discrete drinking in exclusively Jewish spaces (e.g., Hasidic prayerhouses and courts). Rabbis may have felt ambivalent about Jewish tavern keeping, but many proved willing to compose legal fictions that would allow Jews to keep their taverns running on Sabbaths and festivals.[95] Overall, Jewish religious leaders seemed less ambivalent about trade and credit than their Christian counterparts. Rabbinic views were divided over the spiritual significance of wealth, but rarely condemned wealth as such.[96]

The last and perhaps most germane point about Polish Jewish economic proclivities may seem anticlimactic: Jewish residential restrictions did not seriously debilitate the Polish Jewish population. Voluntary migration into precisely those towns and cities with Jewish quarters, most notably into Warsaw, continued unabated. This does not negate the pictures of individual suffering invoked by certain outside observers. But it does mean that many Jews learned to work around residential restrictions. New forms of discrimination against a group with a long history of involvement in trade and few viable alternatives encouraged adaptation, not the desired exclusion.

Chapter 5

From Moses to Moses: Jews, Clothing, and Colonial Commerce

Adam D. Mendelsohn

Ask Londoners in 1843 to name the best-known Jew living in their city and they would likely not answer Moses Montefiore, the much-heralded savior of the Jews of Damascus, but Elias Moses, a clothier whose gas-lit emporiums, parsimonious prices, and aggressive advertising scandalized and delighted the public in equal measure. Elias's renown was not entirely of his own making. In October of that year, the London *Times* recounted the sorry case of the widow Biddell, who, desperate to feed her starving children, pawned the trousers she had agreed to sew as piecework only to be prosecuted by her employer for breach of contract. In heart-wrenching detail the *Times* lamented the misery and meager wages of needleworkers like Mrs. Biddell. Saved from debtors' prison, she and her children were nonetheless consigned to the poorhouse. In the resulting public outcry, Elias Moses was often confused with his lesser known relative Henry Moses, a leading manufacturer of ready-made garments and the man who had indirectly contracted Mrs. Biddell to sew trousers. Charles Dickens was guilty of confusing one Moses with the other. He damned Elias—a frequent advertiser in his serialized novels—as the "most impudent dog in the world."[1] The *Times* was not alone in pinning the blame for her plight on Moses and all the Children of Israel "revenging on the poor of a professedly Christian country the wrongs which their fathers sustained at the hands of ours." To save his sullied reputation, Elias Moses advertised in the *Times* (in his characteristic doggerel) that he had no commercial connections with his namesake, making no mention of the ties of marriage between the two Moses clans.[2]

While Elias sought to publicly disassociate himself from Henry Moses (in 1865 his family relinquished the blighted name of Moses for the gentrified one of Marsden), the two were bound together by much more than their public shaming and a shared surname. In different ways, Elias and Henry owed their successful careers in the clothing business to opportunities presented by the dramatic expansion of the British Empire, emigration to the settlement colonies, and colonial trade. Their twin careers offer a useful case study of the way that some Jewish ethnic niches in England were transformed by Britain's vaulting ambitions abroad. One such field, the collection and resale of secondhand clothes, had long been a staple trade of the Jewish underclass. This existing Jewish niche became increasingly elaborate and sophisticated as it adapted to new opportunities for profit at home and abroad. In the 1830s and 1840s, several Jewish used-clothing dealers hoping to profit from expanding domestic and colonial demand experimented with mass manufacturing and retailing of ready-made clothing.[3] Elias and Henry, who both began in the secondhand trade, parlayed these opportunities into great fortunes.

Even as the Jewish role in the tailoring trades—and other ethnic niches including retailing, banking, finance, and entertainment—has received recent attention from historians, their participation in international commerce in the modern era has remained relatively neglected. This lacuna is all the more surprising given the growing literature on Jewish participation in regional and long-distance commerce in the medieval and early modern periods. For much of the modern period, foreign trade involved crossing imperial boundaries or trading with colonial markets. This was true in England long before the Moses clan began to send clothing to the colonies. In the eighteenth and nineteenth centuries, Anglo-Jewish firms traded with Europe, North America, India, North Africa, the Levant, and the Caribbean. For those within the Sephardic and Ashkenazi elite who had capital and connections, international commerce provided a vehicle to make and bolster fortunes.[4]

The expansion of the British Empire provided particular opportunities for the children of this small elite. The scions of leading Sephardic and Ashkenazi families were among the early Jewish free settlers in Australia and at the Cape. Aaron, John, and Elias de Pass, for example, became pioneers of the coastal trade around Cape Town. Alongside interests in shipping, whaling, and copper mining, the brothers dominated the export of phosphorous-rich guano, harvested from the islands that dotted the western coast of South Africa, to England and the United States. The natural fertilizer was much in demand by farmers. The de Pass brothers distanced themselves from their fowl reputations by giving generously to Jewish charities in London and Cape Town.[5] John also established a beachhead in Australia, where he tried his hand as a merchant, prospector, and railway man.[6] The antipodes exerted a stronger pull than the Cape on the Anglo-Jewish elite. Unlike the majority of their penurious fellow immigrants to Australia, the sons of the Furtado, Mocatta, Montefiore, Phillips, and Samuel clans came as unfettered investors and speculators. As many as a third of early voluntary Jewish migrants to the antipodes belonged to the British communal aristocracy.[7] For footloose Joseph Barrow Montefiore, impatient at age twenty-five with his position as a broker on the London Exchange (and overshadowed by his most successful and illustrious cousin Moses), Australia was terra nova. The family was already active in the West India trade; here was the means to establish his own colonial fortune.[8] He arrived in 1829 to take possession of a vast land grant, which he supplemented with a banking and export business in partnership with his brother in London. During the boom years of the 1830s, Montefiore and his fellow pedigreed immigrants prospered, sending Australian produce to London, and trading with the United States, China, and the South Seas.[9] Montefiore's first Australian fortune collapsed in 1841, a victim of his overenthusiastic speculation and the looming economic depression in the colony. If these sons of privilege were somewhat insulated from the jolting downturns that periodically disrupted colonial growth—Montefiore returned to stake out a second fortune in South Australia in 1846—they were far from alone in profiting from empire and overseas trade. Even Jewish hawkers in London were at the bottom end of an international distribution chain that in a number of instances included Jewish intermediaries. Among the baubles sold by Jewish peddlers in the street trade were sponges from the Levant and Adriatic, ostrich feathers from North Africa, and oranges and lemons, fruits of Mediterranean commerce. Jewish secondhand clothing dealers sent cast off clothing in the opposite direction.[10]

Although English economy was particularly intertwined with colonial markets, few have examined Jewish participation in imperial trade in the second British Empire.[11] Anglo-Jewish historians are not alone in devoting little time to this subject. When historians have written about Jewish economic life in the nineteenth and twentieth centuries, they have more often focused on developments within individual imperial and national contexts than on networks that spanned borders. On the rare occasions that Jews have figured in the literature on commerce in the age of colonial expansion, historians have highlighted their role as links in an extractive commodity chain that shipped raw materials from colonial sources to metropolitan markets. Sarah Abrevaya Stein's book on the Jewish network that supplied couturiers and milliners in Paris, New York, and London with ostrich feathers is the best of this breed.[12] Even as Stein adds significantly to the existing literature on colonial commodity chains by inserting ethnicity as a unit of analysis, her choice of subject reinforces the conceptualization of imperial trade as a hub and spoke model, with agents on the periphery supplying the metropolis with colonial commodities. While Jews played a variety of roles in extractive trade, they also participated in—and arguably benefited more substantially from—the colonial commerce that sent metropolitan goods to far-off markets.

This chapter examines how the livelihoods of Jewish clothing wholesalers and garment retailers in England became inter-stitched with the fortunes of the British Empire. It takes as a case study the extended Moses family, a clan that proved particularly adroit in selling clothing to emigrants from England at several stages of the immigration process. As I will demonstrate, different branches of the family pursued contrasting strategies in response to the expansion of colonial markets. Although some members of the Moses clan became unusually successful, the transformation of the family's fortunes reflected a slow sea change within the clothing market as mass-manufactured ready-made garments gradually began to displace the secondhand trade. In England, and particularly in London where Jews were active at all levels of the exchange of castoff clothing, some were able to shift from the sale of secondhand garments to manufacture, wholesale, and mass retail. The most successful were those like the Moses family who leveraged their colonial contacts to facilitate this transition. The same was true of other Jewish clothing firms identified by observers in the early 1850s as the largest in London.[13] This chapter therefore highlights the dynamic interrelationship of Jewish economic life in the metropolis and the colony. It suggests that colonial trade had broader consequences for Jewish economic life in England than has hitherto been suggested. While the successes of the Jewish elites in London in international banking and speculation are well known, the clothing business involved a far broader swathe of Jewish society. Even as much of the Moses clan left their humble roots behind, the international scope of their businesses meant that those whom they hired as seamstresses in London—like

Mrs. Biddell—were vulnerable to changes in fickle fashions as far away as Melbourne and Montreal.

Australian Exodus

Elias Moses was born in the small market town of Bungay in Suffolk in 1783. Little is reliably known of his family and early career. As was typical of many of the Jews who became garment manufacturers in the 1830s and 1840s, Elias began by working in the secondhand clothing trade, a low status occupation with few barriers to entry. Much more is known of his career once he moved to London and entered into partnership with his eldest son, Isaac. As late as 1831, Elias and Isaac were described on insurance policies as modest slop-sellers—producing and selling rough apparel favored by sailors and workmen—and dealers in clothing, with premises in Houndsditch. Within a decade, the firm of E. Moses & Son had become one of the leading clothiers in England.[14] They did so in large part by exploiting the opportunities presented by empire. In the late 1830s, they identified an untapped and growing segment of the clothing market and introduced a combination of innovations in production and marketing to corner a substantial segment of this custom.

Paradoxically, the vast increase in the number transmigrants and emigrants leaving Britain's shores for the colonies and the United States from the 1830s onward created a new source of domestic demand. An industry developed to service the needs of these travelers, including guidebooks offering basic advice to emigrants. As early as 1823, *Godwin's Emigrants Guide to Van Diemen's Land* suggested that travelers buy slops for the voyage to the antipodes, and directed them to slop-sellers in the Minories, close to the Tower of London.[15] As the numbers of emigrants increased, they provided a boon for clothiers. These travelers typically bought what were known as "emigrant outfits" before departure, consisting of an assortment of clothing, bedding, and toiletries thought to be useful for a new emigrant on distant shores.[16] Some government-sponsored settlement schemes required emigrants to bring set quantities of clothing with them.[17] Elias and Isaac cornered a portion of this substantial market by selling several collections aimed at emigrants, ranging from a basic wardrobe of work clothes and suits for more impecunious travelers to elaborate attire intended for gentlemen who foresaw the need for clothing for shooting, foxhunting, and banqueting.[18] Their success was rooted in supplying the needs of those planning to resettle abroad; so important was this market to Elias and Isaac Moses that they claimed the emigrant outfitting department at their emporium in Aldgate was the "the root from whence sprung all those other branches [of their business] to which so many vast establishments are now devoted."[19]

This glamorous retail premises in the East End, among the first in London to use gas lighting and large plate-glass display windows, required the conversion of seven houses into a single large establishment with separate departments for different kinds of clothing. The grand interior was lined with mahogany paneling and lit by chandeliers.[20] This emporium prefigured the architecturally ornate department stores of Paris and New York and was soon followed by several others. By 1849, E. Moses & Son had eight branches in total, including stores in the industrial cities of Bradford and Sheffield. In the 1861, they had three stores in London, including one on the upmarket New Oxford Street. All closed at sunset on Jewish festivals and the Sabbath (reopening on Saturday evening until midnight).[21]

Elias and Isaac became masters of salesmanship and self-promotion. Their rhyming advertisements in the *Times* frequently improvised on current events.[22] When news reached London in 1842 that Britain had signed the Treaty of Nanking forcing China to open five of its ports to trade, they advertised in the *Illustrated London News* to solicit custom from "naval and military men, merchants, captains, and emigrants" bound for the East.[23] The firm placed its advertisements prominently within Dickens's serialized novels (supplementing the text with such poetic gems as "The Proper Field for Copperfield").[24] During the Australian gold rush, the firm advertised extensively in the shipping columns of the Liverpool press.[25] *Punch*, the satirical magazine, singled out their flagrant self-promotion for heaps of scorn.[26] Even more objective observers complained that their "Advertising now overflow [*sic*] into our omnibuses, our cabs, our railway carriages, our steamboats. . . . The emissaries of Moses shower perfect libraries through the windows of carriages which ply from the railway stations"—a comment that reveals their appreciation of advertising to a nation on the move.[27] This avid self-promotion meant that the name of Moses was well enough known for a parliamentary inquiry on Sunday trading to ask specifically about the firm.[28]

With typical immodesty, E. Moses & Son described themselves as "Monarchs of Trade" in the 1840s. Their puffery and self-aggrandizement expanded along with their empire. In 1850, they boasted of their renown "all over the world." Two years later, they were the "greatest Merchant Tailors in the Universe."[29] Although the firm trumpeted that it sent clothing "all over the world"—and by the 1870s engaged agents in Australia, New Zealand, the

Cape Colony, India, China, Japan, the West Indies, and the Americas—their success was rooted in the domestic market.[30] Without question, their enterprise left Elias and Isaac tremendously wealthy. When the Reverend John Mills published *The British Jews*, an overview of Judaism and Jewish life, in 1853, he singled out the "great clothing establishments" of E. Moses & Son as one of the most noteworthy Jewish businesses in London. Tellingly, he grouped the firm with H. E. & M. Moses of Tower Hill and Moses, Son & Davis of Aldgate, all, unbeknownst to Mills, interrelated via marriage.[31]

Go Down Moses

If Elias and Isaac Moses cornered the market in supplying outfits to emigrants departing England, Henry Moses—who ran the firm H. E. & M. Moses with his son—saw opportunity in selling clothing to consumers once they had settled in the colonies. He established a sophisticated distribution system that linked his factories in London and Colchester with retailers in Australia, New Zealand, and Canada.[32] Like Elias Moses, Henry began his career in humble circumstances. He was born in 1791 in Upper East Smithfield very close to the used-clothing market in Rosemary Lane. His father worked variously as a hardware man, dealer in sticks, sponges, and slippers, stickmaker, toy man, silversmith, and slop-seller and left less than £100—roughly £6,000 today—at his death in 1806.[33] His son followed in his footsteps, becoming a jack-of-all trades in the early part of his career—a silversmith, hardware man, used-clothing dealer, clothes salesman, and slop-seller—working in Upper East Smithfield, Houndsditch, and the Minories from at least 1813.[34] While Henry had an eye for the main chance, investing in property and speculating in sponges, his primary focus remained selling and dealing new and old clothing.

Henry's move during the 1830s to Tower Hill—two hundred yards away—reflected a fortuitous set of developments in far-off Australia.[35] An earlier misfortune, the transportation in 1827 of a ne'er-do-well nephew to New South Wales for stealing jewelry from a peddler, redounded to the benefit of his extended family. After bringing his family shame, his nephew Moses Joseph propelled it to fortune. His reports of antipodean opportunity persuaded four of his siblings and at least ten of his cousins to embark for Australia and New Zealand. The first of a stream of relatives arrived in May 1833. Within months, the general store that Joseph had opened in Sydney was advertising "trousers and other clothing" for sale, perhaps supplied by his uncle in London.[36] Henry Moses was clearly impressed by the bounding success of a nephew whose reputation had been bleached clean under the glare of the antipodean sun (and the watchful eye of the penal authorities). He also sniffed opportunity. Before their departure for the antipodes, Henry Moses provided two of his sons and several of his nephews with training and £100 of stock—a little less than three times what a general laborer could expect to make in a year—as start-up capital. This was a wise investment. The flotilla of relatives who sailed south for Australia created a beachhead for the family firm, establishing stores in Wellington, Auckland, Sydney, Adelaide, Melbourne, Hobart, and Launceston. The clothing stores they opened were supplied with lenient credit and ample stock from the family firm in London.[37]

This colonial distribution chain appears to have given the London firm a significant boost, perhaps permanently pushing Henry Moses from dealing in secondhand clothes and slops into the mass production of new clothing. Although not exclusively an exporter—he also supplied clothiers in England—the overseas market quickly became an important component of his tailoring business.[38] By the middle of the 1850s, he had at least two manufacturing warehouses in London, and another in Colchester, fifty miles away, producing clothing for wholesale on the domestic and colonial markets.[39] Like Elias and Isaac Moses, H. E. & M. Moses employed the putting-out and piecework systems, along with factory production. Like several other manufacturers, the firm contracted female inmates at the Brixton and Millbank prisons to stitch large orders of shirts and military uniforms.[40] He proved particularly adroit in profiting from the price advantage enjoyed by British clothing exporters. Higher labor costs in the United States and the colonies made British exports more competitive. By one estimate, clothing purchased in America and Australia and at the Cape was 25 percent more expensive than that in England, leaving a juicy margin for British manufacturers and exporters to exploit.[41] Labor shortages in the settlement colonies and distance from raw materials precluded cheap manufacture. The most successful merchants were those like Henry Moses, who were able to achieve vertical integration, controlling production, distribution, and retail.[42]

An immigrant preening and parading down the dusty high street of an antipodean town in a new outfit bought from a retailer in London might be aghast to discover the identical fashions on display in store windows, sometimes at cheaper prices. The Moses family stores in the colonies were supplied with lenient credit and ample stock from the warehouses in London. In turn they shipped wheat, wool, tallow, hides, old clothing, canned meat, and kauri gum back to London as return cargo to be reprocessed or sold. In 1851, H. E. & M. Moses described themselves as "agents for the sale of colonial produce."[43] This ancillary business enabled the London firm to profit twice over from its Australia connections. In colonial markets serviced by a new and still primitive banking system, and desperately short of currency and capital, such seamless arrangements between kin benefited both parties.[44] British clothiers gained access to colonial consumers (who were particularly profligate during periods of boom) through reliable agents. These additional sales supported the high-turnover and low-margin model that underpinned their manufacturing and wholesale business. These colonial branches provided Henry Moses with greater economies of scale for manufacture, access to more consumers, and the means to dispose of stock that was not selling well in England. Retailers in the colonies gained a competitive advantage over their rivals: easy credit and access to new fashions at wholesale rates and with low transaction costs. This reliance on ethnic capital to supply credit needs, bypassing credit agencies suspicious of Jewish newcomers, was also a hallmark of Jewish business networks in the United States and Canada. In Montreal, for example, Jewish businessmen turned to their coreligionists in New York, Manchester, and London to advance goods and loans.[45]

Henry Moses was far from exceptional in cultivating colonial outlets for his business. In 1845, Jews owned twenty-five of the forty-seven clothing stores in Melbourne, and a number of them acted as agents for family concerns overseas.[46] Several metropolitan Jewish clothing moguls entered the market during the gold rush, including the Moses's major Manchester competitor, Benjamin Hyam.[47] Moses Benjamin, the scion of a rival clothing family, arrived in Melbourne in 1843 with 2,000 pairs of trousers and 8,400 shirts to stock his new store.[48] Even Elias Moses established a grand edifice in Melbourne in 1852—initially an imported corrugated iron store eighty-eight by twenty-two feet in size with plate glass windows—in anticipation of "immense business." Despite replicating some of their London sales techniques—including advertising on wagons, carriages, and stagecoaches and prolifically in newspapers as far away as Hobart—Elias's Australian branch went belly-up in 1856 when the gold-rush bubble deflated.[49] Henry Moses's antipodean operation seems to have survived the crash better, suggesting that its resilient network of family-owned stores made the firm better attuned to local fashions and market conditions.

Henry Moses also cultivated a presence in the Canadian market. Two of his nephews, Edward and David Moss, moved to Montreal in 1836 and were soon joined by a third brother, Lawrence. They were likely seeded with start-up capital from Henry. Certainly they were able to open a large retail clothing store shortly after their arrival, and began to advertise ready-made apparel imported from England, probably manufactured by their enterprising uncle. Through the 1840s, they continued to rely predominantly on clothing shipped from London to stock their shelves, replicating the pattern they shared with their cousins in Australia. During this same decade, they began to break with this dependence by subcontracting locally through the piecework system. Local production was cost-effective because of the relatively high cost of clothing in Canada.[50] In the 1850s, they established their own factory alongside the Lachine Canal in Montreal. By 1856, they employed eight hundred workers in their five-story plant—by far the largest employer in the industry in the city—producing men's work apparel almost exclusively for the export market. By a contemporary estimate, over 90 percent of their annual production of £90,000 was exported, with £40,000 of clothing sent to the antipodes. The brothers cottoned on early to the spike in demand for work clothing created by the Australian gold rush, taking advantage of a tariff structure favorable to intercolonial commerce to export directly to Australia.[51] By doing so, they vastly expanded their market by selling to storekeepers in another distant colony.

There is some evidence that their antipodean customers included their siblings in Hobart and Launceston. One of these brothers, Samuel Jacob Moses, had married his first cousin (and Henry's daughter), Rosetta, and arrived in Australia in 1840 in the style that befitted the offspring of a prosperous merchant, traveling with two servants in tow. They settled in Hobart in February 1841, and Samuel entered into partnership with his brother-in-law, Louis Nathan, who had married another of Henry's daughters. Samuel and Louis were joined in Hobart for a time by Henry's son Hyam, who briefly became a partner in the firm. Nathan & Moses became one the largest importing and exporting houses in Van Diemen's Land, trading in colonial commodities—whale oil, wool, gold dust—and importing merchandise from abroad. It is very likely that clothing imported from Montreal made up a portion of their business.[52]

The Promised Land?

The clothing business brought prosperity to the Henry Moses family. His manufacturing business earned him a tremendous fortune. By 1875, the year of his death at age eighty-five, he had left his humble past in the secondhand trade far behind. He now lived adjacent to Regent's Park, the promised land for prosperous merchants, and owned scores of rental properties in the East End.[53] (The practice of investing in property in the East End was not uncommon among successful Jewish clothing manufacturers; an acute housing shortage kept rents high.)[54] His firm continued to trade extensively with the antipodes.[55] His sons changed their names to Beddington a few years before their father's death—a further step in their process of gentrification—and became communal grandees active in founding the Central Synagogue and the formation of the United Synagogue. (A cruel wit rhymed that the Moses Beddingtons "could change their names but not their noses.")[56] A granddaughter married into the Montefiore family.[57] The estate of Maurice, Henry's second son and business partner who died in 1898, was valued at over £1 million, equivalent to more than £80 million today.[58]

Ironically, the success of Henry Moses and other mass manufacturers had a more ambiguous impact on the fortunes of several of his siblings.[59] Unlike Henry, who abandoned the secondhand business in the 1830s, his brother Jacob Moses (1782–1845) appears to have remained a modest slop-seller and secondhand clothing dealer for much of his life. In 1814, he operated as a used-clothing dealer and salesman on the same street as his brother Henry, within easy reach of Rag Fair.[60] From there, their trajectories diverged dramatically. Henry's eldest brother, Moses Moses (1768–1845), appears to have been somewhat more successful than Jacob. He, too, began his career in the used-clothing trade, operating a small store attached to his home close to Rag Fair. As was common at the time, the shop stocked new and old clothing that was available for both sale and barter.[61] Moses Moses seems to have remained in the slop-clothing trade for most of his career, achieving little of the vaulting success of his brother Henry. Three of his children joined the antipodean exodus. One son remained in London and became a clothing salesman in Rosemary Lane. His son David established the London Mart in Hobart in 1836, a general store that probably sold some clothing along with fabric, hardware, and groceries. A second son, Elias Moses, was more successful, running a general store in Sydney, which expanded to Windsor and Goulburn. His business, however, seems to have been mostly local.[62] Although Henry Moses may have initially sponsored these nephews, there is little evidence that they entered into the same sort of long-range partnership that he did with his other Australian relatives. Instead, in reverse of this pattern, Moses Moses was supported with remittances from his children in Sydney,

Hobart, and Melbourne during his dotage.[63] It is quite possible that Jacob's sons, Edward, David, and Lawrence Moss, did the same for their father.

Ironically, the success of Elias and Henry Moses and other pioneering manufacturers ultimately undermined many of those who remained rooted in the used-apparel business. Competition from the new ready-made clothing emporia and declining prices of cheap garments squeezed dealers of used apparel like Jacob and Moses Moses. Although the erosion of the secondhand trade was slow—booming demand for rags used for making paper cushioned the decline of domestic sales of used garments—the domestic market gradually shifted away from old clothing. Only a tiny minority of used-clothing dealers made the transition to mass production of ready-made garments, although many more replaced dealing in old clothes with the petty retail of new attire. Emigration, which had bolstered demand for mass-manufactured cheap clothing, provided an escape for some of those whose source of livelihood had withered. Some of those on the bottom rungs of the secondhand business abandoned their limited prospects in London for a new beginning abroad.

Although both Elias and Henry Moses became leading manufacturers of clothing by introducing several innovations in production, their strategies for sales and distribution diverged substantially. If anything, Henry's reliance on an extended network of nephews acting as his agents in distant markets was reminiscent of earlier models of Jewish long-distance trade. While the scale of the trade, the manufacturing techniques, and the methods of transportation were new, Henry's kin- and trust-based business empire shared a basic template with Jewish merchant networks typical of the early modern period and before. By contrast, Elias and his son Isaac established a more modern business empire that did not rely on family members to operate branch shops. They were pioneers of mass retailing, advertising, and branding, experimenting with a variety of innovations that later became typical of department stores. For all of their innovation, however, their single foreign venture, a short-lived store in Melbourne, failed. Tellingly, those operated by Henry's Moses nephews proved more resilient.

Where Elias and Henry diverged more strikingly from earlier Jewish business networks was in the speed of their ascent. Neither was born into a wealthy family active in foreign trade or banking. Instead, both came from humble backgrounds in the used-clothing business. Paradoxically, this proved a vital springboard for their later successes. As enterprising clothing dealers, they benefited from a variety of broader changes—rising working-class incomes, the expansion of foreign markets—which were slowly transforming the garment business. These changes presented new opportunities to men willing and able to assume substantial risks. Here again, they were beneficiaries of fortuitous timing. Both were well enough established by the 1830s to devote capital to colonial ventures. Even then, good fortune arrived in a surprising guise. Henry's initial exposure with antipodean opportunity came via England's punitive legal system. Once his nephews were established in Australia, New Zealand, and Canada, Henry stumbled into the commodity trade as they shipped a variety of colonial products back to London.

Although there is no evidence that Henry and Elias ever left England, their extraordinary fortunes were the product of those who did so in large numbers. The centrality of colonial markets to their success should give us pause when considering the clothing trade, a subject that has often been examined in national and local frameworks, but rarely as a transnational enterprise.[64] This case study should also force us to scrutinize other Jewish ethnic niches that have been treated in a similar way. Likewise, this example suggests that Jews may have engaged in a variety of areas of international trade in the modern period both by creating ethnic networks and by adopting more modern business structures. No doubt, counterparts to the Moses clan operated in several other international businesses. Certainly in the clothing business, from Moses to Moses, there were none like Moses.

Chapter 6

Brokering a Rock 'n' Roll International: Jewish Record Men in America and Britain

Jonathan Karp

While rock 'n' roll, as art or business, is not mainly a Jewish story, Jews did play an outsized role in its development. The case has recently been made, for instance, for the influence of Jews on rock songwriting; studies such as Michael Billig's *Rock 'n' Roll Jews* and Ken Emerson's *Always Magic in the Air* ably recount the contributions of composers associated with the Brill Building era, including Jerry Leiber and Mike Stoller, Doc Pomus, Carole King, Barry Mann and Cynthia Weil.[1] Others have focused on the (often submerged) Jewish identities of some of rock's major performers, such as Bob Dylan, Mike Bloomfield, and Lou Reed.[2] But more profound by far is Jews' historic role as rock's brokers: agents, impresarios, promoters, publishers, small record label entrepreneurs, and big label execs. The infrastructure they provided proved critical to rock 'n' roll's emergence as a major cultural force. This brokerage role, moreover, was not limited to the United States; we find a rough parallel in the music business of the United Kingdom during the 1950s and 1960s. Indeed, precisely because Jews became significant players in both the United States and United Kingdom, they were well situated to help bridge the Atlantic divide when rock 'n' roll emerged as a global industry in the 1960s.

Rock 'n' roll, especially by that decade, had become a hybrid cultural phenomenon as well as an increasingly ramified industry. The rock music of the

1960s became both a cultural fusion of British and American musical styles and a commercial amalgamation of businesses that had hitherto largely evolved independently. The integration of these two worlds, through successive American and British musical "invasions" of each other's territories, helped make rock 'n' roll exponentially more profitable than any preceding musical form and contributed to its emergence as perhaps *the* global musical style. The role of Jews supplies one important thread in understanding this complex tapestry.

This essay has two distinct but related goals. The first is to employ a comparative analysis of Jews' activity in the music business in both postwar United States and Britain in order to compare economic behaviors and outcomes between the two Jewish populations. Jews emigrated from Eastern Europe to Britain and America at roughly the same time, although in vastly different proportions. The broad social and economic circumstances in these different locales created distinct sets of opportunities and constraints; nevertheless, what is striking is the rough similarity of the Jewish brokerage role in the music business of both countries. For this reason, the analysis here may help us draw some general conclusions about the entrepreneurial orientations of Jewish immigrants and their offspring. The second goal is to show how the parallel experiences of Jewish popular music brokers in the United States and United Kingdom eventually intersected—and indeed exerted powerful mutual influences that helped determine the evolution of the music business as a whole. In short, the first goal is to understand the economic character of Jews in the music business; the second is to gauge their historical impact on it.

The analysis opens with an overview of the development of the American popular music business scene in the post–World War II period, with a particular focus on the aspect that can be accurately characterized as a Jewish niche industry—namely, the market focusing on rhythm and blues that by the mid-1950s gave birth to early rock 'n' roll. A similar overview of the English scene follows, emphasizing the distinctive roles played by British Jews. Finally, the chapter concludes by showing how British and American pop music scenes gradually and partly merged in the decade of 1955–1965 and why contacts between American and British Jews facilitated this process.

The American Scene

Between 1940 and 1960, dozens of independent record companies owned by Jews emerged, many of which specialized in black vernacular music (until the late 1940s often labeled "race music") or black-tinged pop music. The cohort of entrepreneurs included Herb Abramson of Atlantic, Syd Nathan of King, Hy Weiss of Old Town, Florence Greenberg of Apollo, Herman Lubinsky of Savoy, Al Greene of National, Art Rupe of Specialty, and Jules Bihari of Modern—to name only some of the most prominent. It is not too much to say that the indie record labels of the rhythm and blues and early rock 'n' roll eras constituted a veritable Jewish business niche.[3] It was by no means a monopoly. There were quite a few black-owned indie labels that competed (and sometimes collaborated) with the Jewish ones throughout this period, long before Motown Records came into existence.[4] And there were important musical regions of the country where the Jewish entrepreneurial presence in popular music was smaller (although by no means absent), such as Nashville and Houston. Sun Records in Memphis, one of the most important indies, which guided the early career of Elvis Presley, was founded by Sam Phillips, of solid Methodist stock.[5] Despite such exceptions, Jewish indie record label ownership, alongside associated fields in which Jews were prevalent, such as record distribution, music publishing, booking agencies, and artist management, reflected an extensive Jewish business network in the field of popular entertainment, which operated in many parts of the United States during the middle of the twentieth century. This network exerted a marked influence on American business and cultural life for decades.[6]

The basic starting point to understanding the commercial activity of Jewish minorities in the United States and United Kingdom is the key sociological fact that unlike most other immigrant groups, European Ashkenazic Jews had never been peasants (although Jews were by no means strangers to agriculture). While most Jews in any given period or place were poor, and while many were artisans, servants, or laborers, since the Middle Ages Jews as a whole had earned their livelihoods by performing a range of commercial functions. In return, they received the tenuous protection of the state (which heavily taxed their earnings), as well as the occasional grudging appreciation of their neighbors.[7] Eastern European Jews had performed middleman commercial and managerial functions for the Polish nobility since at least the sixteenth century. Yet by the middle of the nineteenth century, the economic circumstances of this Jewry—by far the world's largest—had declined precipitously as the old feudal-commercial order crumbled. During the nineteenth century, the demographic growth of Eastern European Jews sharply outpaced that of the general non-Jewish population, while their economic opportunities stagnated. Consequently, Jews began to lose some of their former character as a middleman commercial group, with many slipping into severe poverty or approaching "proletarianization."[8] By the last two decades of the nineteenth century, the squeeze of population growth and impoverishment fueled mass emigration from eastern Europe. Amidst these complex developments, what is important to remember, however, is that, broadly speaking, Jewish emigrants to the United States, while ostensibly impoverished proletarians, carried with them the cultural and social capital that would allow them to develop business niches when confronted with propitious circumstances (after all, their economic decline had been severe but not especially protracted). Such was precisely the case for Jews who settled in New York around the turn of the twentieth century.[9]

The starting point of Jewish prominence in the music business was their role in popular music publishing, both as songwriters and owners of sheet music firms. The dense settlement of Eastern European Jews in New York City starting in the 1890s placed them in close proximity not only to the center of American garment manufacturing but also to the nucleus of music publishing, concentrated on Tin Pan Alley (initially located below Fourteenth Street, then, by 1900, on West Twenty-Eighth Street, and later on, in Midtown Manhattan).[10] Here, the timing of Jewish mass immigration proved decisive. Tin Pan Alley began to flourish during the 1890s, when changes in American copyright law made sheet music royalties potentially far more profitable than ever before and at the very moment of a technological revolution in both film and recorded sound.[11]

Initially, the New York publishing firms were dominated by printers of German and Irish descent, then slightly later by German Jews. As occurred in the garment industry, Jews of largely Central European origin whose families were already well established in the United States by the late nineteenth century facilitated the entry of newer immigrant waves of mainly East European coreligionists into the business, first as employees and eventually as competitors or successors. The names of Joseph W. Stern, Edward B. Marks, the brothers Witmark, Charles K. Harris, Leo Feist, Max Dreyfus, and Waterson, Berlin & Snyder became the early Jewish core of Tin Pan Alley.[12] Jews constituted a plurality, never a majority, let alone a monopoly, in this field. The same held true of theater ownership, management, and booking. Although Jews never wrested the vaudeville theater circuit from its architects, B. F. Keith and E. F. Albee, this shortcoming was partly redressed by the Shubert chain of legitimate theaters, by Marcus Loew's and William Fox's chains of nickelodeon movie houses, by the talent agency of William Morris, established in 1898 by the immigrant Zalman Moses, and later by the Music Corporation of America (MCA), founded in 1924 by Chicago doctor and musician Jules Stein.[13]

Jewish publishing, theater, and agency ownership facilitated wider Jewish employment in these businesses and provided models for subsequent Jewish businessmen to emulate. A kind of melding of these industry subfields took place, with individuals wending their professional way between them, moving from booking to artist management, from Broadway theater to Hollywood musical, from trade industry music journalism to publishing, and the like. More profoundly, however, an intensified integration of the different branches of the mass entertainment industries began to manifest itself in the 1920s, as movie studios increasingly swallowed up sheet music publishers with the aim of exploiting their catalogues for film music repertoires, and as broadcasting companies established recorded sound divisions and branched out into the manufacture of electronics equipment.[14]

While Jews played prominent roles in many of these areas, record companies themselves proved something of an exception, at least at first. On the whole, the Jews who helped pioneer the post–World War II record industry were not directly part of the earlier show business establishment in fields like music publishing or booking agencies. It is more accurate to say that those institutions provided an array of cognate businesses that willy-nilly served to reinforce Jews' conquest of the new record field, although at times the relationship between the establishment and the newcomers was as combative as it was complementary (as reflected, for instance, in the 1950s bitter rivalry between the Tin Pan Alley composers' performance rights society, ASCAP, and the upstart Broadcast Music, Inc. [BMI], which represented the indie record companies).[15]

While there had been a recording industry since the 1910s, in a sense the Second World War and immediate postwar period created it anew. The small independent labels of the 1920s had mostly folded by the height of the Depression, although crucially their back catalogues remained available for cannibalization by other record companies. At the same time, the major record labels—RCA-Victor, Columbia, and Decca (and slightly later, Mercury and Capitol)—adopted a highly conservative business stance in the 1940s. To some degree they were hamstrung by government-imposed restrictions on the use of recording materials considered vital to the war effort. In addition, the powerful musicians union—the American Federation of Musicians—launched a series of strikes in 1942–1943 and 1948, which restricted the recording of instrumental music. In response, the big labels increasingly confined their recording activities to established stars, especially band singers like Bing Crosby, Frank Sinatra, and Rosemary Clooney.[16]

It would be a missed opportunity for the majors, but it gave the small-time but enterprising entrepreneurs precisely the chance they needed. World War II, and later the Korean War, helped propel an upsurge in a century-long movement of rural southerners into nearby cities and more distant ones in the Northeast, Midwest, and West. Not all these migrants were destitute; on the contrary, urban factory work put spending money in pockets and fed a yearning for new forms of entertainment among both white and black populations.[17] "Hillbilly" and "race" music were, respectively, the designations that the music industry had traditionally applied to these two markets. While Jewish entrepreneurs were not absent from the hillbilly field (Syd Nathan's King Records in Cincinnati was a major purveyor of both styles, while the sheet music publisher Hill and Range, owned by Austrian Jewish émigré Jean Aberbach, became a major force in country and western song publishing), it was in the business of race music that Jews proved dominant.[18]

Why did Jews become the principal brokers of a musical form that was created by black musicians exclusively for black listeners?[19] Veteran L.A. record man Lester Sill offers a commonsensical answer:

> Look at the way big iron and steel companies threw the scraps to the Jews. . . . That's how Jews started in the scrap metal business. Same thing in music. The majors see great artists like [Blues singer] Jimmy Witherspoon as scrap. They don't want to deal with what they consider junk. Well, some of these small labels were actually junk dealers before they got into the music game. Through experience, they learned what some see as junk might actually be precious jewels.[20]

It is true, as Sill implies, that Jews have had a long history of taking advantage (or making the best) of the limited opportunities available to them. But fortuitous factors of timing and location proved crucial though uncontrollable. For instance, during the 1920s, the first generation of indie labels specializing in black music was mostly white-owned but non-Jewish companies like Okeh, Gennett, and Paramount. Many of these companies evolved out of furniture manufacturing concerns that branched out into phonograph production and subsequently the recording of race and hillbilly music.[21] It was only the circumstances of a fresh wave of black migration during World War II, the incomes generated by factory work, and the new but momentary proximity of blacks and Jews in the postwar urban landscape that triggered the Jewish indie phenomenon.

While New York, with its large Jewish population, remained a center of sheet music publishing, musical theater, and network radio, the record business would prove to be far more decentralized than most other branches of the mass entertainment industry. This was true even with regard to the major record labels. Of the big five, only RCA-Victor, Decca, and Columbia were headquartered in New York, while Mercury operated out of Chicago and Capitol out of Los Angeles. The small "race" labels established by Jews and others were even more widely dispersed: Imperial in New Orleans; Duke-Peacock in Houston; Sun in Memphis; King in Cincinnati; Vee-Jay and Chess in Chicago; Savoy in Newark, New Jersey; Aladdin, Modern, and Specialty in Los Angeles; and Atlantic, National, and Apollo in New York. These were all important destinations for the black migrant populations that tended to move roughly in a direct northward pattern from their Southern points of origin (Virginians, Carolinians, and Georgians to Washington, Baltimore, Philadelphia, and New York; Alabamans and Mississippians to Chicago, Detroit, Cincinnati, and Cleveland; Louisianans to St. Louis and Kansas City; and Texans to Los Angeles).[22] Jews had been situated in many of these Northern urban locales for decades.[23]

Jewish businessmen and women in these and other American cities had businesses in neighborhoods close to those that housed the new black populations, including liquor stores, used furniture shops, and dry good stores that also sold radios and phonographs. Postwar Los Angeles became one of the centers of race and rhythm and blues music-making. A significant black population had only recently settled there, drawn by the factory jobs fueled by the war, whereas substantial numbers of Jews had lived in Los Angeles since the 1920s. In fact, Los Angeles was something of a special case: it was a city whose postwar Jewish population more than doubled, and several of the Jewish indie label owners there were freshly minted Angelinos.[24] More typical were locales like Cleveland, Chicago, Cincinnati, and other large and medium-sized American cities outside of the Sunbelt. But although Jews in these locales were more residentially and commercially established than most blacks, they were still driven by intense economic need. By the late 1940s, many had only recently emerged from the working class or were still struggling in small businesses.[25]

Some of the characteristically "Jewish" businesses of this era formed bridgeheads into indie record label entrepreneurship—particularly scrap metal and junk dealers (Leonard Chess's father was a scrap metal dealer), used furniture (where old 78 records could sometimes be found hidden in cabinets), liquor and cigarette sales (entailing close contact with nightclubs where the latest styles of black music were performed), paint and textile manufacture (in functional proximity to record-pressing plants), and of course dry goods shops (a classic "Jewish" business in medium-sized towns across America, where both radios and records would often be sold).[26]

These and similar fields provided entry points for Jews who already possessed business and sales experience, a modest but sufficient amount of capital, and a keen sense of opportunity. Syd Nathan, the gruff founder of Cincinnati's King Records, once quipped, "All you need to get into the record business is a desk, a telephone, and an attorney."[27] Yet Nathan launched King not only with years of retail and merchandizing experience behind him, but a $25,000 loan from his relatives.[28] Brothers Leonard and Phil Chess had not only the father's scrap business to draw on, but years of experience owning liquor stores, running night clubs, and observing the tastes and spending habits of black customers.[29] The Bihari family, to cite another example, were veteran salesmen of farm machinery, who moved into coin-operated machinery, first in Oklahoma and eventually in Los Angeles, where launching Modern Records in 1945 seemed a logical extension of their pinball and jukebox business.[30]

Given that the indie entrepreneurs often moved into race music from businesses like scrap, liquor, nightclub management, and cigarette and jukebox distribution, their world exuded more than a whiff of illegality, including occasional mob associations. Fraud, bribery (in the form of payola), numbers juggling, tax evasion, and other forms of book-cooking were in fact inseparable from the business. This was clearly the case for notorious characters like National Records' founder Al Greene, a veteran of the Chicago union rackets, and Roulette Records' Morris Levy, a trusted lieutenant of New York's Genovese crime family.[31] But even on a less sensational level, illegality seems to have been pervasive and routine. Bernard Besman, the Detroit founder of Sensation Records and local distributor for the Biharis' Modern label, exaggerated only slightly when he claimed, "Everybody in the record business was crooked. Everybody. I don't care how big they are." Naturally, Besman was careful to add, "I'm not talking about me, I don't count."[32] His comment, however, reflects an unfortunate historical reality: scrupulous honesty in the indie record business would have been suicidal. In exasperated response to accusations that he had stolen musicians' royalties, black record label owner Don Robey once asked, "How can these ignorant sons of bitches think I owe them money because they hear their record on the air? Hell, I paid the deejays to play it!"[33]

For many of the indie entrepreneurs, the music made by their companies did not necessarily possess intrinsic artistic or cultural value. As Leonard Chess once put it, "If shit is gold, we'll sell shit," a statement perhaps belied by his label's track record as one of the most distinguished in the history of American music.[34] On the other hand, a segment of the Jewish race music entrepreneurs were unabashed aficionados of African American blues and jazz. As young men just after the Second World War, figures like Milt Gabler, Herb Abramson, Bob Weinstock, Manny and Seymour Solomon, Jac Holtzman, and Norman Granz devoted their free time to scouring flea markets and used furniture stores in search of nearly forgotten race records of the 1920s, particularly the New Orleans jazz and classic blues 78s that had been made by now-defunct (non-Jewish) indie record labels. These figures would become important to the development of a jazz scholarship and to the history of postwar jazz recording, which they were among the first to chronicle. A number of them started their own jazz labels.[35] But a subset of these same jazz and blues collectors branched out into recording black commercial music for profit—that is, making records for a contemporary black consumer base. The distinction is well captured by the music business journalist turned record entrepreneur Jerry Wexler in discussing his partnership with the Turkish born Ahmet Ertegun in the establishment of Atlantic Records: "[Ahmet and I] could have developed a label along the lines of Blue Note, Prestige, Vanguard or Folkways, fastidious documentarians of core American music. Bobby Weinstock, Alfred Lion, Moe Asch, Orrin Keepnews, Manny Solomon and the other keepers of the flame were doing God's work. Ahmet and I, however, didn't feature ourselves as divinely elected. We weren't looking for canonization; we lusted for hits."[36]

This rejection of musical purism could even lead to some bold experimentation. The race music niche had been built exclusively on the conservative formula of black musicians producing music for black consumers (by the late 1940s, thanks in part to Wexler, "rhythm and blues" was replacing "race" as the accepted rubric). But with the exception of Sun Records' Sam Phillips, who allegedly mused that "if I could find a white boy who could sing like a black man, I'd make a million dollars," none of these entrepreneurs evidently anticipated the crossover potential of rhythm and blues, it's possible appeal to white record buyers. This seems ironic given that Jewish and other white indie entrepreneurs earned their livings precisely by determining what product would sell to a black audience. They frequently boasted of their own "ears" for rhythm and blues hits. One is tempted to ask, if they "got it," why didn't they imagine that other whites—including white consumers—might get it too?

In fact, while Phillips was grooming Elvis in Memphis, other indie entrepreneurs were experimenting with hybrid musical forms performed by white country or hillbilly singers who sang rhythm and blues, or blues musicians who sang country songs. What drove the process was less the aesthetic attraction of creating a musical gumbo, so much as the willingness to experiment in the pursuit of profit. Sun Records had a policy of signing a wide range of white and black musical acts. The same was true of King Records in Cincinnati. As Syd Nathan's assistant at King put it, "In many ways [Nathan] was a remarkably open-minded man. He perceived this wonderful notion of American music as not being segregated into different styles, but one big cross-ethnic whole. He did that because it was a way to make money."[37] Chess Records in Chicago is famous today as the home of blues legends Muddy Waters and Howlin' Wolf. But however influential, these pioneers remained stars within the segregated world of black nightclubs and all-black radio stations. Neither exhibited crossover appeal until the folk revival of the 1960s. Instead, Chess's real innovator would be Chuck Berry, whose 1955 breakout hit "Maybelline" was based on the country song "Ida Red," a tune that label owner Leonard Chess personally picked out for Berry's debut release. Not only did it reach number 1 on the rhythm and blues charts, but it reached number 5 on the white pop charts, too.[38]

But the real breakthrough arguably took place a year earlier in New York City, in this case, too, by melding "race" and "hillbilly" styles. Milt Gabler had long been at the heart of the Jewish indie label phenomenon, though he himself was much more a broker than an owner-entrepreneur. The son of an immigrant radio and novelty shop owner, Gabler persuaded his skeptical father to open a section of the store for used blues and jazz records that had been produced in the pre-Depression golden age. Their Commodore Shop on East Forty-Second Street became a mecca for young collectors like Ertegun, Abramson, Wexler, Oren Keepnews, and Jac Holzman. Along with Eli Oberstein, Gabler pioneered the business of reissuing these rarities through mail-order purchase, eventually founding his own Dixieland jazz revival label, also called Commodore. Gabler had no big hits on that label; it was strictly for

Figure 6.1 Commodore Record Shop, New York, N.Y., c. August 1947. Left to right: Milt Gabler, Herbie Hill, Lou Blum, and Jack Crystal. Library of Congress, the William Gottlieb Collection.

aficionados. But he was no purist either. Surely, Decca Records' Jewish executive Jack Kapp must have sensed Gabler's commercial instincts when he hired him to serve as in-house producer for the label's race acts. Of all the majors, Decca was the one that jumped earliest onto the race bandwagon. Back in 1926, Kapp himself had been hired by Brunswick Records to supervise its race division, and in 1941, he acquired the Brunswick catalogue for Decca and charged Gabler with reorganizing it. Gabler became a house producer for Decca's own race recordings, subsequently creating a string of hits with the singer, saxophonist, songwriter, and rhythm and blues pioneer Louis Jordan.[39]

In 1954, Gabler applied the lessons he had learned over many years with Jordan to accent the sound of country and western singer Bill Haley, resulting in the watershed rock 'n' roll hit "Rock around the Clock." Haley was a country yodeler in the manner of Bob Wills and the Texas Playboys (prior to the Comets, his band was called Bill Haley and the Saddlemen). Around 1951, he began to experiment with performing rhythm and blues tunes in a western style, employing "slapback" bass in manner soon to be labeled "rockabilly," an obvious amalgam of black and hillbilly sounds. Gabler helped refine the style, employing the dotted eighth notes and sixteenths so characteristic of the Louis Jordan sound.[40] "Rock Around the Clock" had the advantage of playing during the opening of one the earliest of the teen-angst genre films, *Blackboard Jungle* (1955). The explosive combination transformed rock 'n' roll from a momentary fad into a veritable social movement. As we will see, it was also the opening salvo in the conquest of Britain by the new American popular music.

Yet success itself threatened to kill the goose that laid the golden egg, at least for the Jewish indie label owners. Their niche lay in exploiting what no one else had thought profitable—namely, black music. With crossover and the new hybrid form of rock 'n' roll, the stakes became obvious to all—and the other majors finally jumped in with all the resources at their disposal. Consequently, as the indies were displaced in the early 1960s, popular music appeared to revert to the kind of bland and predictable patterns that had preceded the rock 'n' roll revolution. This fit the conservative corporate strategy that increasingly held sway. It was precisely the aim of the majors, after all, to control markets through the manipulation and management of pop music fashions. Rock 'n' roll thus contained the seeds of its own infantilization. As songwriter Jerry Leiber said in a 1959 *Time* article, "At least 60 percent of our stuff is rock and roll, and we're sick of it. But consumers dictate the market: kids nine to 14 make up our market, and this is the stuff they want."[41] Make no mistake: the decline of the indies did not mark the end of a strong Jewish presence in the American popular music business. Rather, by the 1960s, a number of those Jews had become thoroughly integrated into the new corporate structure of the American music business. Mitch Miller and Goddard Lieberson at Columbia Records, Clive Davis, who rose up through the ranks of Columbia's legal department to executive status there, and Mo Ostin at Warner Brothers, who had been an economics major at UCLA, came to represent the corporate establishment. The phenomenon of Jewish indie label entrepreneurship did not die; on the contrary, we find it as late as the rap and hip-hop era of the 1980s. But by the late 1950s, Jewish indie label entrepreneurs no longer represented an insurgency of ethnic outsiders; while their function as originators of rock 'n' roll had already become a thing of the past.

The British Scene

The sequel to the story of the 1940s and 1950s Jewish indie labels is not to be found in America but in the Great Britain in the late 1950s and early 1960s.

Just as the 1955 film *Blackboard Jungle* helped launch rock 'n' roll in the United States, so too the musical play and subsequent 1959 film *Expresso Bongo* helped set the stage for the start of a new music scene in the United Kingdom. *Expresso Bongo* tells the story of a Jewish pop music agent named Johnny Jackson (played in the film by the actor Lawrence Harvey, who himself was born a Jew in Lithuania and was originally named Larushka Mischa Skikne). Jackson is a sympathetic shyster who hops on the rock 'n' roll bandwagon when he notices teenage girls going gaga over a young singing bongo player at a local nightclub by the name of Herbert Rudge (played by actual British teen heartthrob Cliff Richard). Christening the lad "Bongo" Herbert, Jackson signs him to a contract in which he as manager takes 50 percent of all earnings. In the meantime, Jackson hustles to make a deal with a record company chief, Mayer Marcus, played in the film by the Yiddish stage actor Meier Tzelniker. When Jackson inquires as to Marcus's feeling about the boy, the chief responds with a single word: "nausea." As Marcus explains to Johnny, he is "really by nature an opera man" who finds "all this kind of thing deeply sickening to [his] temperament." Nevertheless, "it so happens," Mayer continues, that "due to the irony of fate, in opera I lost my shirt." Mayer is clearly no fool. He proceeds to out-swindle Jackson and steal away Bongo, who is thereafter set on the path to rock 'n' roll immortality. But we need not feel sorry for Jackson. At the conclusion of the film, he finds his own salvation through the reappearance of an old friend to whom he had once lent a few quid, the washed-up auteur Kakky Katz. As Kakky tells Johnny in the concluding scene, "To cut off a long story short, [the Hollywood Studio] Feygele-Lox want the remake rights of my great picture *Rubaiyat*," and Kakky knows that Johnny is just the man to produce the musical numbers.[42]

The film (and the novella and stage musical that preceded it) represented a response to the inundation of Britain by American popular music and England's first fledgling attempts to combat it by creating its own indigenous rock 'n' roll.[43] By the middle of the 1950s, American recordings of Bill Haley, Elvis Presley, Gene Vincent, Sam Cooke, James Brown, and a host of lesser lights were flooding the U.K. market. This was not just the fortuitous result of infectious music reaching receptive ears; rather, it arose out of a conscious effort on the part of both American and British record company executives to exploit the untapped British market. As early as 1934, British record company executive Edward Lewis had created the American Decca Records though his partnership with a trio of American record company veterans: E. F. Stevens, and his Jewish associates Jack Kapp and Milton Rackwil

(Lewis's American lawyer, Milton Diamond, also played a major role in the company's establishment).[44] After Decca became independent, Lewis established London Records in 1947 to provide a U.S. outlet for such British acts as Vera Lynn and Montovani. But once rock 'n' roll began to dominate the U.S. charts, London's export business to U.S. markets effectively dried up, so Lewis determined to use his American company as a clearinghouse for the importation of American rock into the United Kingdom, Europe, and the British Commonwealth. His principal agent in this endeavor was a Jewish Brooklynite named Mimi Trepel, who became the key broker in securing publishing and recording copyrights from indie labels and Tin Pan Alley publishers for Lewis's company.[45] The other British majors quickly followed suit. In 1955 Britain's largest record company, EMI, purchased Capitol Records, a company that had been started in 1942 by songwriter Johnny Mercer and retail mogul Glenn Wallichs. And in 1958, Louis Benjamin, chairman of the smallest of the British companies, Pye Records, signed U.K. distribution deals with Chess and King Records and a number of other U.S. indies.[46]

The reaction to this "American invasion" was not all positive, as evidenced by the Bank of England's unsuccessful effort in 1954 to impose an outright ban on the activities in Britain of American music publishers, such as Jean and Julian Aberbach, Lou Levy, and the firms of Leo Feist and Robbins, which were said to be "draining pound sterling from the country." Similarly, the British Musicians Union made efforts to impose quotas on the number of performances permitted to American musicians.[47]

An alternative approach of appropriating American musical style so as to claim it as essentially British can be dated to the rise of "skiffle" music in the middle 1950s, defined by some of its practitioners as Britain's "indigenous" rock 'n' roll (although its key exponents, such as Lonnie Donegan, recognized its overwhelming debt to American Dixieland jazz and jug-band music). By the late 1950s, however, as the appeal of such revivalist fads as skiffle and "trad jazz" was wearing out, entrepreneurs were on the hunt for England's next musical step—precisely the moment depicted in the *Expresso Bongo* film.[48]

While *Expresso Bongo* appears as a kind of British version of *Bye Bye Birdie* (the former opened as a musical in the West End in 1958, the latter on Broadway in 1960), what is remarkable is its depiction of the English pop music business as essentially a Jewish affair. The author of the original story as well as the subsequent London stage production and film screenplay, Wolf Mankowitz, was a noted British playwright, famous for his depiction of the lives of Jewish hustlers and hucksters in the post-immigrant East End.

Mankowitz's father ran a used-book stall, which may have been the model for his short story "A Handful of Earth," about the proprietor of Moishe Music, who "had been selling second-hand records almost from the invention of the gramophone . . . on one of these short dead-end streets which lead off from Petticoat Lane like forgotten backwaters" off the Grand Canal in Venice.[49] The film itself references Jewishness from a "Jewish" insider perspective, not merely by featuring two overtly Jewish characters as its principal music business operators, but through its frequent deployment of Yiddishisms. While such allusions might have escaped most British viewers at the time, they would have been readily apparent to audience members familiar with the contemporary London popular music and theater worlds.

It would indeed be remarkable if, as in *Expresso Bongo*, the contemporary British music industry turned out to be a kind of ethnic mirror of the American, with a high degree of Jewish overrepresentation. Scholars have called attention to parallels between American and British Jews in creating entrepreneurial niches. Andrew Godley's important 2001 study of *Jewish Immigrant Entrepreneurship in New York and London, 1880–1914* shows why Jews in both countries played inordinate roles in the turn-of-the-century garment industry. Godley's study succeeds in demonstrating three things: "First, the Jewish immigrants in both host societies were upwardly mobile, considerably more so than the surrounding population. Second, they were upwardly mobile at different rates. Finally, the path of upward mobility was an entrepreneurial one."[50] But Godley's study is less about Jews than about comparisons between twentieth-century British and American entrepreneurship, for which the activities of Jews provide the control measurement. What he really seeks to prove is that while you cannot keep a good ethnic group down, the relatively slower upward mobility of London versus New York Jews can be accounted for not by the different baggage brought by these immigrant populations but rather by the comparative lack of entrepreneurial dynamism in twentieth-century British in contrast with American society. And in fact, a comparison of Jews in the pop music industries of both countries supports Godley's contention. However, such a comparison requires going well past the chronological terminus of Godley's study, which ends with the World War I. At that stage, New York Jews were already well on their way to conquering Tin Pan Alley, whereas Anglo-Jews had yet to make serious inroads into their adopted country's entertainment business.[51]

The lack of dynamism in the early twentieth-century British economy is only part of the reason for this slower rise. Equally important is the far more

Figure 6.2 Anglo-Jewish playwright Wolf Mankowitz c. 1960. Courtesy of the Wolf Mankowitz Estate.

Figure 6.3 Wolf Mankowitz in cameo role chatting with star Lawrence Harvey on the set of *Expresso Bongo*. Courtesy of the Wolf Mankowitz Estate.

rigid nature of the British class system, exemplified by the near inaccessibility of university education to the vast majority of Britons, including Jews, until well into the post–World War II era. What this meant was not that Anglo-Jews remained proletarianized. True, a substantial number were skilled manual workers in Britain well into the postwar period and significant pockets of Jewish poor (not just elderly) could be found as late as the 1960s.[52] More to the point, however, the class system ensured that Anglo-Jews remained "stuck" in the world of small business far longer than their American counterparts. Clothing continued to be a major, albeit reduced, source of livelihood for postwar Anglo-Jews, as did food services and furniture retailing. George Orwell, seeking to dispel anti-Semitic charges that Jews controlled the British economy, noted accurately in 1945 that "[Jews] remained fixed in those trades which are necessarily carried out on a small scale by old fashioned methods."[53] Given the class and economic obstacles that English Jews faced, not to mention anti-Jewish prejudice, it should not be surprising that a low overhead but accessible and highly speculative field like pop music would have attracted significant numbers of them.

If anything, the twentieth-century British economy was more protective of small business and less subject to rapid amalgamation and merger as well as to the proliferation of chain stores than was the case in the United States at the time.[54] In Britain, such tendencies proceeded less rapidly and with comparatively less dynamism than across the Atlantic (or in Germany). In theory, this should have augured well for the proliferation of indie record labels; but in fact, up through the mid-1960s, few successful British indies existed. As noted, the music industry was entirely dominated by four major labels: EMI (indeed, by 1960 the largest record company in the world), Decca (distinct from the American Decca, despite common origins), the Dutch company Phillips, and the runt of the group, Pye Records. While individual Jews were not absent from the leadership of some of these companies (for instance, Louis Benjamin was managing director and later chairman of Pye Records and partly the inspiration for Meier Tzelniker's character in *Expresso Bongo*), in no sense could these companies themselves be described as "Jewish."

Whereas the vast size of the United States ensured that its music industry would be fragmented by regionalism, with important indies launched in cities like Chicago, Detroit, Houston, Nashville, and Los Angeles, in Britain, all roads led to London. No other British city could compete with or remain free of its domination. To be sure, local and regional music scenes existed throughout Britain, in clubs and dance and concert halls, but even regional sounds, including the Merseyside beat that would bring the Beatles and other Liverpudlian bands to the world, were all mediated through the offices of London record companies, recording studios, music publishers, and advertising agencies. Compounding this situation was the centralization of British radio. In postwar America, in part because of the advent of television, local radio stations flourished. Attuned to nearby musical talent, tied in with surrounding businesses, such as record stores, these stations were integral to the rise and success of indie labels.[55] Britain, in contrast, had what was effectively a radio monopoly, at least through much of the 1950s. The BBC had been established in 1927 by royal charter as a "public corporation," neither privately nor state-owned, and its mission of serving the public's interests was construed to mean the precluding of crass commercial ones. In the postwar years through the early-1960s the monopoly held virtually airtight. This changed only slightly, starting in 1962 with the appearance of "pirate" stations that operated by ship from international waters—before these, too, were shut down by the Royal Navy in 1967. Throughout the postwar decades, only Radio Luxembourg remained a defiant exception, but its reception could be spotty and its authorized playlist was limited to releases by major labels.[56]

For these reasons, Anglo-Jewish pop music entrepreneurship could not express itself through the creation of little labels, as in the United States. Rather, there were two principal avenues of Jewish involvement in the business side of British music. First, we find a parallel to American Jews' historic involvement in sheet music publishing, with London's Denmark Street serving as the counterpart to New York's Tin Pan Alley. But as Irving Berlin discovered, while Denmark Street had had Jewish sheet music publishers as early as the turn of the century (for example, his British publisher, B. Feldman, Elkin & Co., as well as Sidney Bron), its sales and promotional techniques were primitive compared to the heady New York scene.[57] As a generalization, it is fair to say that the sleepy and passive character noted by Berlin remained typical of Britain's music business up through the era of rock 'n' roll. Indeed, the infusion of Jews into the business during the late 1950s, and growing coordination with their American coreligionists slightly later, helped bring about a fundamental change in this regard. The increased role of Jewish music publishers would be part of this development, as we will see.

The second important place of Jews in the business, as *Expresso Bongo* suggests, was that carved out by pop music agents and managers. No one expressed the stereotype more than Larry Parnes, loosely the model for *Ex-*

presso Bongo's Johnny Jackson. Born in Willesden (Northwest London) in 1930, Parnes came from a family of clothing shop owners who subsidized his own start in the same business. It was not the first time (or the last) that clothes retailing pointed the way to show business for enterprising Jews. A number of the Hollywood moguls and sheet music publishers had started as salesmen in New York's *shmata* business, the obvious link being merchandizing and fashion.

Coffee bars were then the rage in Soho (hence the title of *Expresso Bongo*), and Parnes frequented them in search of a raw talent to recast and refine into gold. The 2i's was the most important of these espresso bars; its interior design was created by Jewish songwriter and playwright Lionel Bart (born Lionel Begleiter), a key figure in the early British rock 'n' roll scene and later the composer of the hit musical *Oliver!*.[58] Just as *Expresso Bongo*'s Johnny discovered young Rudge in a Soho coffee bar, so, too, in 1955 Parnes found singer Tommy Hicks in the 2i's and swiftly proceeded to rechristen him Tommy Steele, Britain's first home-grown rock 'n' roll star. Such rebranding would become a standard feature of the Parnes method: espresso bar discovery Reg Smith became Marty Wilde; Roy Taylor became Vince Eager; Roy Wicherley was remade as Billy Fury; Richard Kneller emerged as Dickie Pride; Clive Powell as Georgie Fame; and so on. The Parnes formula was so successful that the British press dubbed him, "Parnes, Shillings and Pence."[59]

But Parnes' real importance was to create the original model of the pop Svengali, the impresario as creative artist whose imagination and gift for presentation constitutes the truly artistic component in the otherwise ephemeral and disposable genre of pop music fashion. In this regard the fact that Parnes was Jewish and homosexual was in no way an obstacle to his success. Despite a still robust anti-Semitism in England and the persistence of anti-sodomy laws there until 1967, these transgressive identities lent an exotic mystique to an otherwise rather mercenary business. Moreover, the combination of Jewishness and homosexuality appears to have offered a double measure of access to commercial networks in the entertainment industry. As Paul McCartney put it with regard to the Beatles' own manager, Brian Epstein, "I think in many ways [Epstein's homosexuality] was a plus because there's a gay network in show business. There are a lot of people who are gay so that a lot of the TV producers we would find ourselves working with we'd later find out were gay. So now I can see that Brian was networking. I think it was only ever a plus. It was never negative."[60]

Parnes fashioned the image of the manager as a cross between *Pygmalian*'s Professor Henry Higgins and a Cub Scout den mother. As Parnes indicated in an interview from the 1980s, the manager's role was to transform the crude, raw human material into a refined "artiste":

> They go through a very extensive grooming. It is sometimes five months before they appear on stage or three months before I let them do any recording. To start with, they have physical grooming. I have their hair cut—that is very important. Sometimes, they may have bad skin which has to be attended to. Then I get them suitable clothes and provide them with comfort. I like them to have a touch of comfort from the start so that if they make the big time they don't lose their heads. I like them to live in a good home, get three good meals a day, get to bed early and have plenty of fresh air.[61]

Curiously enough, it was not only the actual Parnes who solidified this image, but the faux Parnes depicted by the handsome Lawrence Harvey, himself both Jewish and homosexual, who inspired emulation. A number of the major rock managers of the 1960s and 1970s—including those of Jewish background, such as Brian Epstein of the Beatles, Andrew Loog Oldham of the Rolling Stones, and Malcolm McLaren of the Sex Pistols—self-consciously modeled themselves to one or another degree on Parnes and Harvey.[62] All of these individuals exhibited a sense of style and cultivated a personal mystique that at times threatened to outshine the acts they managed.

We will return to look more closely at the prevalence of this Jewish and homosexual mystique among a segment of aspiring British music managers. But first we must consider a very different—if at times also overtly Jewish—model of musical middleman. If Larry Parnes provides the rough Anglo-Jewish parallel to intellectual Jewish record men like Gabler and Wexler in America, then Don Arden is surely the equivalent of such American Jewish street toughs as Al Greene and Morris Levy. Arden's story touches on several core stages in the development of a British rock 'n' roll industry and bears close examination.

Born Harry Levy in one of the roughest areas of Manchester to immigrant parents from Riga, Arden began as a professional entertainer himself, an impressionist and singer, who claimed to have honed his performance skills in the male choir of his Manchester synagogue. As he explains in his autobiography, *Mr. Big: My Life as the Godfather of Rock*, "singing in the synagogue gave me some invaluable early experience of what it was like to stand before a crowd of very critical people and sing for them convincingly. It gave me a taste of what that might be like in an actual stage show, and I began to dream of bigger and better things."[63] In fact, after he had been blackballed from regular stage work for striking a theater manager who had called him a "fucking Jew boy," Arden labored for two years singing Hebrew and Yiddish songs in British synagogues and community centers.

As Arden approached his thirtieth birthday, an event occurred that would change both his life and the British music scene permanently. In December 1955, Milt Gabler's production of Bill Haley and the Comets's "Rock Around the Clock" smashed through the British music charts, becoming the first single in U.K. chart history to sell more than a million copies. The cultural impact of the song cannot be separated from two movies that featured it: the 1955 *Blackboard Jungle*, directed by Richard Brooks (a.k.a. the Jewish born Ruben Fox), and the 1956 Sam Katzman film *Rock Around the Clock*, featuring both Haley and rock 'n' roll disk jockey Alan Freed. Along with Marlon Brando's *The Wild One* (1953), these films created a new iconography of teen alienation and rock 'n' roll salvation. This was particularly true in 1950s Britain, where American imported rock inspired not merely rebellious poses but several actual teen riots.[64]

For a thirty-year-old schooled in the antiquated singing style of Frankie Lane, rock's advent meant the time was right for Arden to retire from performance and enter the field of promotion. Arden was well prepared for the change. He had spent part of his military service during World War II booking acts to entertain troops training in England (he spent the rest of the time in a British hospital feigning illness). He now drew upon this experience by booking musical acts for troops stationed in Germany. "Until then," recounts Arden, "army officials had relied on local German agents to provide the talent. But the war was still fresh in everybody's mind and, because all the big American stars were handled by Jews, these German agents had no chance. The old American Jews who ran the business—all of whom came from families that had been persecuted somewhere down the line by Jew-hating fascists all over Europe—wouldn't even take their calls. The U.S. soldiers would ask for Elvis and end up with Fritz the local yodeler and his dancing bear." As Arden reasoned, "all the Americans needed, it seemed to me, was someone they could deal with who didn't have a German accent! Someone, in fact, just like them: a show-business Jew. Then everyone would be a winner: I, the Germans, the Americans, the artists and most of all the soldiers stuck out there on those dreary bases."[65]

As this anecdote suggests, by Arden's day, the parallel and even interconnected networks of American and Anglo-Jews in the entertainment business were already in place. We have previously noted that New York's Tin Pan Alley had its counterpart in London's Denmark Street. But it was only by the 1950s that Anglo-Jews began to approach the status in British pop music publishing achieved by American Jews decades before, culminating in the career of English-born Dick James (born Isaac Vapnik), whose Northern Songs became the publisher of Lennon and McCartney.[66] Here, the specific causal relationships are especially important. Modern popular music publishing was by its nature an international affair. The job of music publishers is to promote songs and to ensure for its copyright holders the collection of royalties of different kinds, including those that accrue from overseas performances. For this reason, it was commonplace for successful music publishers to establish branches in major foreign cities. The domination of New York's Tin Pan Alley by ethnic Jews in the 1910s and 1920s seems to have contributed to the growing involvement of European Jews serving as overseas representatives New York firms and eventually starting their own. One of the major British music publishing firms, Bertram Feldman, started this way. But there were also important examples of French, German, and Austrian Jews getting their starts as agents of American firms, including the brothers Jean and Julian Aberbach, who would eventually establish a major publishing company, Hill and Range.[67] With the rise of fascism, some of these European publishing agents used their American business connections to shift operations to New York. Others became part of a larger wave of Central European Jews who entered Britain in the 1930s or who came after the war as survivors.

Although Aberbach and his partner-brother, Julian, fled to the United States prior to World War II, a number of European Jews active in prewar publishing wound up in London. David Platz was a German-Jewish refugee who became the London agent of another large American Jewish music publisher, Howard Richmond (who early in his own career had worked for both the Feist and Robbins publishing firms on Tin Pan Alley and who was the nephew of another significant Jewish music publisher, Abe Olman).[68] Freddie Bienstock played a similar role for the Aberbachs' firm Hill and Range. Bienstock was a Swiss-born Jew and the Aberbach brothers' cousin; he served for many years as the Aberbachs' principal publishing liaison to Elvis Presley, later running the London branch of their firm, Belinda Music, before acquiring it in his own right in 1966.[69] Bienstock's wife, Miriam, had been a pioneer of the American indie record phenomenon; along with her first husband, Herb Abramson, she was a cofounder of Atlantic Records with Ahmet Ertegun. Finally, Eddie Kasner was, like the Aberbachs, an Austrian Jew who was already employed in music publishing prior to fleeing Europe for London. There, he formed a partnership with an older London Jewish publisher, Sidney Bron, before striking out on his own in 1952.[70] His great coup came in 1955, when he managed to acquire the world publishing rights to "Rock Around the Clock." As Kassner proudly informed Ray Davies, lead singer and songwriter of the 1960s band The Kinks, "It was then that the Kassner Empire was formed."[71]

Don Arden's account itself focuses not on publishing but on booking and management. Here, too, Jews were both prevalent and prominent, and they included Hyman Zahl, Danny Betesh, Howard Lisberg, Sid Sax, Charlie Katz, and Joe Collins (the father of writer Jackie Collins and actress Joan Collins). While Anglo-Jews independently created their own niche of booking agents and musical contractors (known as "fixers" in the London business), by the late 1950s, this homegrown Anglo-Jewish phenomenon was beginning to converge with its American Jewish counterpart. Thus, to secure American acts, Arden reconnected with *his* old agent, Hymie Zahl, who had an exclusive agreement with the most important American talent agency, William Morris. The latter agency, it must be noted, founded by a German Jew in 1898, had remained overwhelmingly (indeed, almost exclusively) Jewish through the 1960s. At any rate, Arden persuaded the aging Zahl to arrange a meeting for him with representatives of William Morris in New York. When Arden returned to London, it was in possession of a contract naming him sole U.K. and European representative of the agency. Importing acts like Gene Vincent (whose personal manager Arden became), Eddie Cochran, Fats Domino, Chuck Berry, Bill Haley, and Sam Cooke, Arden now claimed the title of "Britain's Mr. Rock 'n' Roll."[72]

While Arden went on to later fame—or infamy—as the thuggish manager of late 1960s British groups, such as The Small Faces, The Move, Electric Light Orchestra, and especially Black Sabbath (Arden's daughter, the future Sharon Osborn, eventually wrested management of that band from her father and married its drummer, Ozzie Osborn), he was in no way the pioneer of a distinctly British sound. Nor, for that matter, was Larry Parnes. From the standpoint of pop music history, Parnes's significance was to recognize that despite the British public's admiration for pioneering American performers like Bill Haley, Gene Vincent, and Eddie Cochran, at heart they yearned for rock 'n' rollers of their own. Parnes himself insisted that his first great discovery, Tommy Steele, was the true savior of British rock 'n' roll as well as an artist of superior quality compared to Elvis Presley.[73] The problem with these claims to parity with American rock was that musicians like Steele demonstrated no appeal whatsoever outside of Britain. The same could be said of other contemporary British pop idols, such as Marty Wilde or even Cliff Richard. Britain's attempt to cast off American tutelage was bound to fail so long as its own popular music scene remained provincial.

This was the real importance of Brian Epstein, the Liverpudlian scion of a family of well-off and religiously observant Jewish furniture retailers. Epstein, who entertained youthful aspirations to a career in the fine arts, wound up taking over the retail record department in his father's business. Not only did his vantage point as a record department manager alert him to his young customers' fanatical enthusiasm for a new local band, but having persuaded the Beatles to let him act as manager, Epstein exploited his position as an important record salesman for the north of England to win them a recording contract.[74] From the start, his goal was to conquer not just the U.K. market but that of the United States as well, something most of Epstein's contemporaries considered to be an audacious if not quixotic goal.[75] The Parnes model had focused on grooming, but remained idiomatically English, owing as much to the music hall as to the nightclub. In contrast, Epstein's method was to let the Beatles develop themselves as well-defined individual personalities, who meshed so perfectly that they could finish each other's jokes and harmonize seamlessly. The bridging of contrasting moods and styles, scruffy but clean, amusing but earnest, self-deprecating but serious, hinted at a new sensibility emergent in Britain, one that sought to break down age-old class rigidities unencumbered by any heavy-handed left-wing ideological message. However Britons may have understood the band, for Americans they were truly a breath of fresh air. For once, the winds of fun and freedom seemed to be moving from East to West, rather than the other way around.[76]

Andrew Loog Oldham, the manager of the Rolling Stones, further refined Epstein's method. He was raised by his Jewish mother and a Jewish stepfather who, like Epstein's, owned a furniture business. According to the London songwriter Jeremy Paul Solomons, who knew Oldham just prior to his involvement with the Stones, "He was very proud of his Jewish ancestry . . . ;

in the 1950s there was a lot of talk about money and Jewish businessmen doing very well. He wanted to be a part of that."[77] Once again, we see that the atmosphere of post-austerity Britain seemed to offer at least a momentary lifting of traditional prejudices and hierarchies, at least at the level of music and fashion, the two fields where Oldham hoped to make his fortune. Young Oldham worshipped not only Laurence Harvey, especially in his Johnny Jackson incarnation, but also Tony Curtis (another Jewish actor with a gentile stage name) in the role of Sidney Falco, the seedy press agent from the 1957 film *Sweet Smell of Success*. The American music producer Phil Spector was yet another model for Oldham. Harvey, Curtis, and Spector were Jews who had overtly disguised their identities while covertly exposing them in the pursuit of fortune and fame. At least, that is how Oldham saw it.[78] Like Parnes, Spector, and Epstein, Oldham also viewed the "artiste" as product of his own—that is to say, the manager's—creative brilliance.[79] The brash and handsome go-getter, who had done a stint working for designer Mary Quant, sought to present himself as a fashion symbol like the members of his band, who, after all, were only slightly younger than he. Finally, like Epstein, Oldham was keenly aware of the vast American market as the ultimate target. While the Stones no less than the Beatles were satisfied to simulate the sounds of the black rhythm and blues musicians of the Chess era whom they worshipped, such as Muddy Waters, Howlin' Wolf, and Chuck Berry, their manager spurred them on to write their own material in a manner that evoked but did not emulate their idols. He moved them beyond homage to originality. This proved to be the essential precondition for the British Invasion of American pop music markets.

Conclusion

The tandem forces of differentiation and convergence describe the manner in which the (largely) Jewish record men brokered a rock 'n' roll international. Differentiation occurred through the cultivation of a distinctive British sound, rooted in American rock 'n' roll but marked by original songwriting and the creation of bands with recognizable identities: the Beatles as witty, charming, and unthreatening tunesmiths; the Rolling Stones as dangerous bad boys drenched in white rhythm and blues; the Who as purveyors of working-class youth angst. This seems to indicate another parallel with the activity of Jews in the American side of the music business. Whereas for a time American Jews served as the preeminent mediators of black music to commercial markets and eventually to the cultural mainstream, in Britain Anglo-Jews tended to broker not the music of blacks (whose numbers there were small in the 1950s and early 1960s) but instead members of the white working class (who themselves were emulating American blacks!). Given the rigidity of Britain's class system, the analogy appears sound. American blacks enjoyed limited access to markets due to racial exclusion; English working-class whites suffered from a less severe but not dissimilar class confinement. Jews could succeed by helping both to bridge the gap.

At the same time, the British Invasion (encompassing in its first wave not only the aforementioned groups, but also The Animals, Gerry and the Pacemakers, The Dave Clark Five, The Tremeloes, Freddie and the Dreamers, and The Kinks) both reflected and intensified a process of convergence between the British and American sides of the music business—this, too, a development in large part mediated by Jews. First, the invasion further weakened the position of indie labels in the United States, since they lacked the distribution networks to act as effective nationwide agents of British acts, while at the same time their own bread and butter, the black and black-influenced musical talent in their own backyards, was now being displaced by imports from across the pond.[80] Second, while corporate centralization along the lines of the British music industry proceeded apace in 1960s America, the style of management pioneered by Parnes, Epstein, and Oldham now found its most forceful exponent in a Jewish American manager, Albert Grossman, whom historians generally regard as the most important and creative rock manager of the 1960s.[81] Focusing initially on Bob Dylan, Grossman did not just cultivate a special identity for his musical acts à la Parnes; he elevated them to the status of creative artists of the first magnitude, entitled to complete freedom of expression and creative control from the record companies. While most musicians could not hope to receive such pampering, Grossman's approach vis-à-vis Dylan and others established a new paradigm. It marked the full transition from 1950s-era rock 'n' roll to the counterculture rock music of the 1960s, in which the 45 hit record was displaced by the 33 and 1/3 LP.

A parallel development occurred in music publishing. Here Grossman must share credit with an unlikely music business pioneer, the independent accountant Allan Klein. Described by music writer Peter Guralnik as "a kind of Robin Hood with a slide rule," Klein had been raised in Newark's Hebrew Orphanage and Sheltering Home and, due to his own troubled childhood, professed a deep personal sympathy with victimized African Americans and exploited musicians. Klein decided to apply his accounting expertise to the field of pop music management through the influence of his fellow Upsala College graduate, music publisher Don Kirshner, who would become the central figure in creating the "Brill Building" stable of youthful New York Jewish songwriters in a veritable reconstitution of Tin Pan Alley for the early 1960s. Starting with Kirshner's client, singer Bobby Darin, Klein managed to carve out a remarkable business for himself by offering to examine the books of record companies and publishers on behalf of clients, uncovering abuses, winning restitution, and frequently renegotiating far more favorable contracts.[82] Whereas Grossman had set Dylan up with his own publishing company (Dwarf Music), cutting out the traditional publishing firm as the middleman (while taking a substantial cut of Dylan's royalties for himself), Klein subjected both record companies and publishers to unprecedented levels of financial scrutiny (while lining his pockets with gargantuan fees).

The net effect of these changes proved in no way punitive to the record business. On the contrary, while 1950s rock 'n' roll was a windfall to a struggling industry, the creative explosion of the 1960s struck a proverbial goldmine. Whereas record sales increased yearly by an average of 25 percent from 1955 (the year "Rock Around the Clock" was released) to 1960, in the subsequent decade, annual sales rose from $6 million to $1.2 billion.[83] They would continue to increase exponentially until the middle of the 1980s. While the exploitation of artists and other abuses continued apace, the elevation of rock into an art form and pop cultural mainstay transformed it into a billion-dollar industry of truly global proportions. Yet the successful convergence of the British and American music business wings also had its peculiar ironies. If by the late 1960s, Allan Klein had pushed aside Andrew Loog Oldham as manager of the Stones and succeeded Brian Epstein as manager of at least three of the four Beatles (excluding McCartney),[84] by the late 1970s, the major American record companies had all been subsumed by British and European ones (and eventually Japanese ones, as well).

The foreign conquest of the U.S. record labels would seem to have provided the ultimate revenge for America's postwar economic and cultural domination so powerfully exemplified by its exportation of rock 'n' roll. But throughout the remarkable changes that occurred in the global popular music business of the 1950s, '60s, and '70s, one thing long remained the same. Jews, especially in America but in Britain, too, continued to function as music business leaders in numbers far beyond their percentages of the general population.

Historians who assume the incompatibility of modern corporate capitalism and ethnic commercial networks have not properly considered cases like the music and entertainment businesses, where Jews continue to be overrepresented across generations. The centuries-long history of Jewish middleman activity in the West just may have found its surprising climax in brokering the rock 'n' roll international.

PART II

Philanthropy, Money, and the Deployment of Power in Jewish Economic History

Chapter 7

The "West" and the Rest: Jewish Philanthropy and Globalization to c. 1880

Abigail Green

Looking back on the middle years of the nineteenth century, Ludwig Philippson—Reform-minded rabbi and editor of the *Allgemeine Zeitung des Judentums*—was struck by the rebalancing of philanthropic activity between the global and the local in the Jewish world.[1] "In recent times a feeling of solidarity has developed among the Jews," he wrote in 1872.

> Without directly reducing interest in the local community, for which the Jew makes great sacrifices and whose welfare institutions have been quite unusually enhanced, public spiritedness towards all, even the most distant branches of the Jewish religious community has increasingly developed and grown. We do not need to recall the bloody events of Damascus in the early 1840s . . . , but need only point to recent times, when from the West Coast of America throughout the rest of the world attempts were made to intervene . . . in Romania. . . . When famine raged in Western Russia . . . , then money flowed in from all over the world, as we debated how best to put an end to the distress of the poor Jewish population, transporting a significant number of orphaned children to Germany and France, in order to raise

> them as practical people. When war broke out in Alsace and Lorraine and hit the Jews hard in many places, their German coreligionists readily made sacrifices to come to their aid. Just now came an appeal from Persia on behalf of the starving Jews there, and at once committees formed in our cities to make collections, and the Jewish press fostered this charitable instinct.

This rebalancing between local and global Jewish philanthropy is the central focus of this chapter, and Philippson's 1872 article highlights several issues I wish to examine.

First, it invites us to consider the degree of continuity between nineteenth-century expressions of global Jewish solidarity, and the transnational networks of the early modern era. For Philippson saw this globally oriented, public-spirited activity as "a beautiful development of the modern era." Now that historians are inclined to question the "modernist fallacy" and stress at least the eighteenth-century origins of nineteenth-century developments, we should ask if he was right.

Second, it reflects the gray areas between charity, philanthropy, and mobilization—listing the Damascus agitation, the Romanian campaign, the famine relief efforts in Lithuania and Persia, and support for Jews impacted by the Franco-Prussian War as varying expressions of the same phenomenon.

Finally, Philippson's article suggests a genuinely global phenomenon: he talks not just of Damascus and America, but of Romania, western Russia, Alsace-Lorraine, Germany, and Persia. But were such different Jewish communities all equal players in the new game of transnational Jewish philanthropy? Almost all these examples suggest a one-sided effort of political and financial mobilization by the "modernizing" Jews of the West on behalf of their brethren in the "traditionalist" heartlands of eastern Europe and the Muslim world. Such a pattern is unsurprising in the light of the rebalancing of economic and political power between the West and the rest during this period. Studies of bodies like the Alliance Israélite Universelle are at pains to stress the relationship between international Jewish organizations and Western imperialism.[2] Yet the new imperial history lays great emphasis on indigenous agency. Should we rethink the role played by "donor" and "recipient" communities in the Jewish world?

In addressing these issues, I wish to elaborate an argument I have made elsewhere: namely, that the decades between 1840 and 1880 saw the rise of what I call the "Jewish International," a quasi-global Jewish lobby, rooted in civil society but dependent on European economic and political expansion, the communications revolution, new patterns of migration, and the development of a global public sphere.[3] In the 1840s and 1850s, this was still an intermittent reality, requiring leaders like Sir Moses Montefiore, Adolphe Crémieux, and Philippson himself to spur it into action.[4] With time, more permanent clusters of philanthropic, political, and journalistic activity arose in London, Paris, Berlin, Vienna, Philadelphia, New York, Budapest, St. Petersburg, Odessa, Warsaw, and Constantinople. As the Jewish press spread from the acculturated communities of the West to the orthodox heartlands of eastern Europe and the Ottoman Empire, so the connections forged between these clusters in times of crisis became more tightly linked and found institutional expression in the Alliance Israélite.[5] By the late 1860s, the activities of established Jewish leaders were merely one facet of the increasingly confident, diverse, and autonomous body that was world Jewry. Thus, the global forces of civil society empowered obscure individuals to follow in the footsteps of Montefiore, Crémieux, and Philippson. In 1868 Isaac Rülf, a provincial rabbi from East Prussia, raised 630,000 marks for the starving Jews of Lithuania. Three years later, a Jewish journalist from Cleveland could muster enough money and political connections to defend the cause of Jews in Romania as United States consul in Bucharest.[6] In the years between 1868 and 1872 (the date of Philippson's article), what I call the "Jewish International" assumed critical mass.

This new configuration drew upon traditional communal institutions and practices, while remaining distinct from them. It was, essentially, a cluster of voluntary transnational organizations and representations crystalizing around international issues, in which both "ordinary" Jews and religious specialists could serve as protagonists. Indeed, the Jewish experience was only one aspect of a much broader outward projection of religious energies into modern society and the global arena. This entailed the re-forging of religious identities in transatlantic or imperial encounters and the emergence of new forms of sectarian politics, philanthropy, and the press. For Christians and Muslims, as well as Jews, the interaction of traditional religious structures and identities with wider processes of political, social, cultural, technological, and economic change promoted the transformation of communities of believers into communities of opinion.

How far did these developments draw on early modern Jewish networks, practices of Jewish solidarity, and patterns of transnational activity? Less, perhaps, than one might think.

Of course, neither international Jewish solidarity nor transnational mobilization around Jewish issues was a nineteenth-century novelty.[7] Rather, the politicization and diversification of these practices was very much a product of the early modern era. For, as Jonathan Israel has argued, the expulsions and forced migrations of the fifteenth and sixteenth centuries created an unprecedented degree of cohesion in the Jewish world.[8] In an atmosphere of intermittent crisis, these more intense intercommunal contacts promoted the institutionalization of trans-Judaic solidarity and the creation of support networks designed to (1) send alms (known as *halukah*) to relieve Jews living in Eretz Israel; (2) ransom Jewish captives being sold in Ottoman and North African slave markets; (3) relieve Jews left starving or homeless by war and natural disasters; and (4) intercede with secular authorities.

As ongoing commitments rooted in religious obligation, the first and second endeavors generated the most formally articulated networks of solidarity. Egyptian Jews began organizing financial support for Palestine in the early sixteenth century, and 1532 saw the first *halukah* committee established in Venice.[9] There were others in Istanbul, Rome, and Poland by 1600, with special treasurers for Eretz Israel appointed in every Moroccan congregation soon after. The money could be transferred via smaller Jewish communities to larger ones, through private individuals, and through officially certified Palestinian emissaries (*shlichim*). The latter were ubiquitous, reaching Cochin in India in 1740, and New York for the first time in 1759.[10] From 1729, the Istanbul officials acted as a clearing house for *halukah* and assumed ultimate responsibility for all the communities in Palestine. By 1800, equivalent committees had been established in cities like Amsterdam, Vilna, and Brody. Interestingly, many *halukah* committees were also responsible for ransoming captives. Here, too, a formal structure had evolved by 1640, when the communities of Livorno, Venice, and Istanbul assumed overall responsibility for western, central, and eastern Mediterranean zones. Geopolitical upheavals inevitably threw this system into turmoil. The Chmielnicki massacres of 1648 in the Ukraine sent a flood of Ashkenazi captives onto the slave markets of Istanbul, overwhelming the local community's resources and diverting scarce funds from redemption efforts farther west and from the competing needs of Palestine.[11]

Such crises called for a different kind of management. In the late fifteenth century, Rabbi Joseph Colon declared aid for another community an obligation under Jewish law when it might reasonably be supposed that the danger facing that community was likely to strike others, too. This attacked the principle of absolute communal autonomy by highlighting the common vulnerabilities underpinning trans-Judaic solidarity during an age of persecution and insecurity.[12] The mid-sixteenth-century international banker Doña Gracia Nasi established an escape network that saved thousands of her fellow crypto-Jews from the Inquisition, spearheading a Jewish commercial boycott of Ancona after a wave of persecution.[13] More generally, communities appealed for aid on an ad-hoc basis: first through emissaries, later by letter. The Chmielnicki refugee crisis, the epidemic of 1680 that killed three thousand Jews in the Prague Judenstadt, and the Austrian sack of Budapest and Belgrade in 1686 and 1688 all elicited concerted (if occasionally reluctant) collaboration among far-flung communities across the Sephardi-Ashkenazi divide.[14]

Arguably the collapse of Dutch Brazil, the Ottoman-Venetian War, and the Spanish financial crash of 1647 prompted a similar relief effort in the mid-seventeenth century.[15] These events unleashed large-scale migration, placing Sephardi communities in northwest Europe and Livorno under severe pressure and prompting key figures in Amsterdam to seek alternative outlets. Fusing disaster relief with mercantile ambition and a messianic desire to complete the geographical process of Jewish dispersion, João de Yllão, Abraham Drago, and David Nassy negotiated Jewish settlement in Curaçao, Cayenne, and West Guyana. They publicized their activities through Livorno, and Jews in Italy formed the bulk of the colonists. De Yllão even petitioned Charles II for a safe conduct to ship fifty Jewish families to Palestine since "God in his mercy has begun to gather in his scattered people."[16] Curiously, Doña Gracia had also petitioned the sultan to found a textile-working colony for refugees near Tiberias.[17]

Such high profile individuals are best understood as *shtadlanim* (intercessors).[18] Though most *shtadlanim* operated more locally, these examples suggest that even in the sixteenth and seventeenth centuries, some forms of intercession transcended political boundaries. This was certainly the case by 1744–1745, when the threatened expulsion of Jews from Prague and Bohemia prompted simultaneous attempts to obtain diplomatic intervention in six different communities, after an initial appeal from Prague was disseminated through Germany, Italy, Britain, Denmark, and Holland.[19]

How regularly structures of solidarity crossed the Sephardi-Ashkenazi divide is another story. Dowry societies established in Venice (1613) and Amsterdam (1615) adopted Sephardi lineage as a criterion for eligibility.[20] Conversely, the eighteenth-century Sephardi *shaliach* emissary Rabbi Haim

Joseph David Azulai discovered belatedly that German Ashkenazim claimed the right to give exclusively to Ashkenazim in Jerusalem. His contemporary Moses Hagiz regretted that targeting *halukah* to members of a particular subethnic group was now common practice.[21] Paradoxically, however, the life stories of both Azulai and Hagiz confirm the extent to which practices like *halukah* drew on genuinely intercultural Jewish networks—not just the commercial and family ties that underpinned the Atlantic and Levantine diasporas of Doña Gracia's world, but the individual, dynastic and intercommunal connections created by itinerant rabbis, scholars, and religious ministrants, which characterized (and to some extent bridged) both Ashkenazi and Sephardi spheres.

Of course, these connections remained important. Yet it is worth pointing out the fundamental discontinuities between the geopolitical structures and networks that underpinned early modern forms of Jewish internationality and the Jewish International as it emerged in the mid-nineteenth century. Here, I wish to make two key points.

First, this was an age of empire, but despite the participation of the United States in a broader Anglo sphere, there was surprisingly little continuity between the imperial configurations of Western Europe in the eighteenth and nineteenth centuries. Jews had played a key role in the Atlantic during the first British Empire and the great Hispanic Empires, but the mid-eighteenth century saw the decisive retreat of the Western Sephardi diaspora, while the Atlantic of the nineteenth century was no longer such a contested imperial zone. Yet the growth of informal (and increasingly formal) British and French Empires in the Middle East between 1830 and 1882 created new synergies between Jews and empire.[22] Changes in the Ashkenazi world were similarly far reaching. The partitions of Poland divided the east European heartlands in new ways, while the rise of emancipated and self-consciously patriotic "national" Jewries within the emerging European framework of nation-states created the potential for genuinely international forms of Jewish activity. Meanwhile, the mass migration of Ashkenazi Jews to the New World formed the basis for an entirely new set of global connections.

Second, the birth of the Jewish press created a new—and self-consciously global—arena that enabled Jews in very different parts of the world to (re) connect with each other. This again, was different from what came before. For, as we shall see, the emergence of a Jewish public sphere around 1840 provided a coherence and focus that premodern expressions of transnational Jewish activism lacked.

The speed of this development is particularly striking. In 1838 Philippson's *Allgemeine Zeitung des Judentums* was the only Jewish newspaper; by 1880 there were over a hundred.[23] As Jonathan Frankel has noted, such newspapers usually sold in the hundreds rather than the thousands: the *Allgemeine Zeitung* boasted 400 subscribers in 1841, the Philadelphia-based *Occident and American Jewish Advocate* 500 in 1845, *Der Orient* 550 in 1850, the London-based *Jewish Chronicle* 1,000 in 1855, the Russian *Raszvet* 640 in 1860–1861. In practice, the impact of these newspapers was far greater: copies passed eagerly from hand to hand, and the news and views they disseminated spread rapidly by word of mouth.

At first, the Jewish press appeared to be divided on national lines. Newspapers and periodicals like the *Allgemeine Zeitung des Judentums*, the *Archives Israélites*, the *Univers Israélite*, the *Jewish Chronicle*, and the *Occident* were written in the vernacular, primarily served the Jewish readership of a particular country, and necessarily paid disproportionate attention to domestic Jewish politics. Yet this national bias did not prevent the internationalization of the Jewish public. For one thing, these newspapers effectively addressed linguistic communities—above all, the emerging world of modern Hebrew letters, the German speaking communities of Ashkenaz and, as Adam Mendelsohn has demonstrated so convincingly, the emerging Anglo sphere.[24] Moreover, for those actually producing early Jewish newspapers, active participation in a global Jewish endeavor was a central aspect of the enterprise. In 1842, the London-based *Voice of Jacob* informed its readership that a Ladino newspaper was to be launched in the Jewish community of Smryna in Turkey. It welcomed the projected *Buena Speranza* as "an additional and important link to the great chain of communication which we hope to see established between Jews all over the world."[25]

This incident points to the dual role of the Jewish press as a forum not just for news and debate but for mobilization, an issue highlighted by Jonathan Frankel's seminal study of the Damascus Affair. Indeed, mobilizing Western public opinion became a key function of this new Jewish press—directed against Russia in the 1840s, against the Papal States during the Mortara Affair, and against Morocco and Romania during the 1860s and 1870s. But the ability of Jews to shape policy in authoritarian regimes remained limited, particularly outside zones of informal empire: Western opinion was influential only where Western governments were able to intervene. These mobilizations served to internationalize the so-called Jewish Question, but they also had a transformative impact *within* the Jewish world.

Here, some reflections are in order on the changing relationship among charity, philanthropy, and advocacy. If charity is usually taken to describe individual giving within the traditional framework of *tzedakah*, philanthropy describes more modern forms of Jewish giving, shaped by practices current in Western capitalist society and often institutonalized on a larger scale.[26] Advocacy, meanwhile, suggests the informal influence exercised by Jewish plutocrats, who leveraged their financial clout to shape government policies. But what might these distinctions mean in practice? Transnational charity is easily linked to the traditional *halukah* donations sent from the diaspora to support prayer and learning in Eretz Israel. Philanthropy captures the different quality of attempts to productivize the Old Yishuv through agriculture and modern education—and entirely new arenas of transnational Jewish activity, most famously the educational networks founded by the Alliance Israélite Universelle. Advocacy describes the informal activities of men like Bleichröder and the Rothschilds during moments of crisis—and the more public activity of formally constituted bodies like the Board of Deputies, both as continuations and reinventions of *shtadlanut*.

Yet none of these categories seem to capture the marriage between the Jewish press and mass-subscription fundraising that was, for me, the lifeblood of the Jewish International. Here we see a real break with past practice in the mobilization of *collective* Jewish wealth across political and geographical borders: subscription fundraising facilitated giving by the poorer many, not just the wealthy few. Including this fourth category widens the scope of our inquiry. For the Jewish International sometimes mobilized around issues that were not explicitly philanthropic—or even explicitly Jewish.

In 1860, Crémieux launched a major international appeal in response to the widely publicized massacres of Syrian Christians. His staggering success in raising money from exclusively Jewish sources for a group that had instigated the Damascus blood libel twenty years earlier highlights the difficulties attached to the concept of "Jewish" philanthropy. Little of this generosity was disinterested. Donations came from as far afield as St. Petersburg, Zhitomir, Corfu, Gibraltar, and Livorno, ostentatiously underlining the Jewish commitment to universal humanitarian values. In Florence and Paris, the politics of the Jewish gesture was an act of gratitude for emancipation; in Russia and Rome, it was a challenge to the status quo. Some thought the campaign a travesty of Jewish philanthropy. Philippson noted bitterly, "an appeal from Jews to Jews for a purely non-Jewish goal is a new form of exclusion, which merely serves to keep the old forms that much more fresh in our memory!"[27]

At issue here is the distinction between philanthropy and advocacy, or philanthropy and politics—and occasionally the role of philanthropy *as* politics. In 1840, it was still hard to differentiate between these strands of activity. The campaign to finance the Jewish mission to the East during the Damascus Affair was perhaps the first example of international Jewish subscription fundraising, raising nearly £7,000.[28] *Pikuach nefesh* is a sacred obligation, and the Damascus mission falls within the traditional category of activities for the redemption of Jewish captives. Yet contemporaries never qualified it as "charitable" or "philanthropic": this was a humanitarian mission, clearly motivated by the political concerns of Western European Jewry. The pogroms of 1881–1882 called forth a similar combination of philanthropy, self-interested politics, and large-scale mobilization. With the birth of the pre–state Zionist movement, the distinction between politics and philanthropy became much less elusive—but the focus on mass-subscription fundraising allows us to trace continuities. Locally, the Hovevei Zion drew on patterns of association and party formation in their immediate contexts; globally, they plugged into the networks and practices of the Jewish International. The decision to raise money through selling pictures of Montefiore exemplifies this connection.

The emergence of philanthropy *as* politics was not the only paradigm shift. In retrospect, the Damascus crisis heralded a dramatic renewal of the structures of Jewish solidarity: Jewish newspapers chipped away at the fundraising monopoly exercised by the Amsterdam committee over diaspora charity in Palestine, while the birth of modern subscription fundraising on an international scale, through initiatives to support beleaguered communities like those of Smyrna and Mogador, enabled the recipients of this charity to make direct contact with a much broader sector of the Jewish world. Crucially, as we shall see, subscription fundraising served as a catalyst for the engagement of traditional Jewries with their Western counterparts through active involvement in the Jewish International. Money mattered. Both the fundraising potential of the new Jewish public and the philanthropic interventions of Western Jewries forced Jews in eastern Europe and Muslim lands to find new ways of doing business with their brethren in wealthier parts of the world.

Here, the experience of Palestine was paradigmatic. Debates over the relative merits of *halukah* and productivization acted as a kind of barometer for public willingness to reject Jewish religious tradition and embrace Western norms. Faced with a barrage of criticism from their enlightened brethren in Britain, France, Germany, and North America, the devout communities living in Palestine adopted and adapted the strategies of their opponents in a bid to defend their income and way of life. Their willingness to innovate on their own terms undermines the ideological dichotomy between "traditional" and "modernist" camps.

These complexities first became apparent during the 1830s and 1840s, with the arrival of an economically dynamic wave of east European immigrants to Palestine.[29] They brought fresh ways of doing things, retained close ties with their communities of origin, and imported the traditionalists' fear of the Haskalah. Such men also mediated among Western Jewish philanthropists, the local community, and the wider public sphere. One of these was Israel Bak, a Hasid from Berdichev, who, with Montefiore's help, established the first Hebrew press in Palestine and worked to strengthen Montefiore's links with the Rabbi Israel of Sadgora. Another was J. A. Rosenthal, a Prussian in Jerusalem, whose articles in the press stressed the need for economic self-sufficiency and who was later dispatched by Montefiore to England to learn weaving techniques. The Sephardim, too, learned to do business with the Fourth Estate. Born into an Ottoman rabbinical family, Moshe Hazan travelled through Europe to raise money for a hospital in Jerusalem as a traditional *shaliach* (or emissary). On his return in 1846, he began corresponding directly with the *Voice of Jacob.* The presence of a similar *shaliach* in North America underlines the extent to which concurrent processes of globalization transformed the networks of the Jewish world.

At a very early stage, then, the leadership of the Old Yishuv recognized that the new Jewish public was a force to be reckoned with. They grasped its potential, but also the risks it posed to their values and lifestyle. When Philippson launched a dramatic appeal in 1842 to found a Jewish hospital in Jerusalem, the French Rothschilds promised 100,000 francs if the foundation was combined with an industrial school. Indeed, Philippson's initiative can be seen as marking the dawn of a new age of more interventionist Western Jewish philanthropy in Palestine. Possibly as a result, it proved unacceptable to local Jewish leaders. Where the Perushim simply expanded their existing Bikur Holim, Israel Bak initiated a joint Hasidic-Sephardic venture—explicitly rejecting Philippson's initiative because "an establishment conducted upon principles such as advanced by the author of the German article [in the *Allgemeine Zeitung des Judentums*], would be misleading them in the performance of religious duties."[30] When the Hasidic-Sephardic hospital opened a few months later, its founders sent Montefiore and his wife a copy of the regulations, alongside a document signed by Israel Bak and Moshe Hazan appointing them as "patrons."[31]

Such interactions gathered pace during the 1850s and expanded dramatically during the Crimean War.[32] These years saw a procession of Western Jews descend on Jerusalem to implement modern philanthropic projects, including men like the Paris-based orientalist Albert Cohn, the Anglo-Jewish Montefiore (who raised £20,000 through international subscriptions), the North American Gershon Kursheedt, and the Austrian, Ludwig August Frankl. Their initiatives marked a break with established philanthropic practices, while the physical presence of so many Western Jewish leaders in Jerusalem was itself an inversion of the traditional relationship between Palestine and the diaspora.

The launch of the weekly *Hamagid* added a further dimension to this phenomenon. For *Hamagid* gave voice to less acculturated Jewish circles, enabling them to adapt Western strategies while remaining ambivalent toward—or even hostile to—Western values. Few things testify more effectively to this process than the extensive space *Hamagid* devoted to the mission of Rabbi Azriel Selig Hausdorf to raise money to build new houses for Jerusalem's Jewish poor. The whole structure of the Hausdorf campaign betrayed the hallmarks of Montefiore's modern approach to fundraising: committees established in major European cities like Berlin, Paris, Brussels, and Amsterdam; subscription lists reproduced faithfully in *Hamagid*; and endorsements from relatively acculturated Jewish leaders. Like Montefiore, Hausdorf also looked beyond the continent of Europe, setting sail for North America in June 1859. But Hausdorf's mission sprang from the heart of Jewish Jerusalem. And with other Ashkenazi immigrants like Moshe Sachs and Zvi Haim Sneersohn embarking on similar missions, it was far more than a one-man show.[33]

In other ways, too, the ongoing debate about diaspora funding for Jews in Eretz Israel proved critical to the broadening and deepening of the Jewish International. In 1863, the launch of *Ha-Levanon* testified to the emergence of a more radical and self-consciously Orthodox Jewish public that was similarly global in orientation. Debates about *halukah* were in many ways its raison d'être. Founded by *mitnagdim* in Palestine, but later published in Paris, Mainz, and London, *Ha-Levanon* engaged in vigorous debate with secular figures like Charles Netter, and promoted the right of Jews in Palestine to devote themselves to prayer and Torah study. In Jerusalem, moreover, it stimulated the publication of *Havazelet*, a rival Hasidic organ that conducted a vigorous campaign against the system of *halukah*. Thus, the need to redirect Jewish patterns of giving and/or preserve access to diaspora moneys repeatedly acted as a catalyst for the attempts of "traditionalists" to appropriate the new Jewish voluntarism and shape global Jewish opinion. Nor was this pattern restricted to the Jews of Palestine.

In Tangier, for instance, the ability of Western Jews to raise vast sums of money on behalf of their Moroccan coreligionists demonstrated to members of the communal elite the desirability of establishing their legitimacy in Western eyes. In a letter to the Board of Deputies written a year after the Moroccan Jewish Relief campaign of 1859, the newly created Governing Committee of the Jewish Congregation of Tangier (Junta) undertook "to conduct all affairs upon a system similar to that observed in Europe," recognizing that as the objects of widespread public solicitude, it was incumbent upon them to "govern our communal affairs in a way best calculated to elicit from our Brethren in Europe their approbation."[34] The origins of the junta were more complex than this implied, but the willingness of its leaders to present themselves in this way reflected their ability to engage with the new structures of world Jewry in appropriate ways.[35] On one level, their initiative can be read as the response of a subaltern group to a political environment colored above all by informal Western imperialism; on another level, it can be seen as an attempt to seize the initiative—both vis-à-vis Western Jews and vis-à-vis their Moroccan rulers.

Conversely, when the Alliance Israélite launched its first campaign in 1860 on behalf of the Christian victims of large-scale ethnic violence in Syria, the appeal resonated most powerfully among those communities that had themselves appeared in the news. Contemporaries would have had no difficulty relating the Corfu contribution to the ongoing controversy over the status of Jews in the Ionian Islands or the participation of Jews in the Gibraltar Syrian Relief Committee to the welcome accorded Moroccan Jewish refugees there six months earlier.[36] The famine of 1868 would unleash a similar process among the Jews of Lithuania, whose plight galvanized an unprecedented level of institutional coordination among French and German Jews and a worldwide fundraising campaign. When Montefiore appealed for funds on behalf of the starving Jews of Persia four years later, the subscription lists that began to appear in *Hamagid* included the names of some forty thousand Jews living in the Pale of Settlement.[37] The high concentration of donors in places that had benefited from Rabbi Yithak Rühl's international fundraising campaign highlights the interlocking nature of these initiatives as international Jewish activism came of age.

Throughout eastern Europe and the Muslim world, then, transnational Jewish philanthropy of various kinds acted as a trigger for the engagement of traditional Jewries with their Western counterparts via the Jewish International—and here I use the term "philanthropy" as a catchall phrase. This engagement certainly built on preexisting commercial, scholarly, familial, and publishing networks, as well as on the broader religious and historical traditions that united the Jewish world. But we should not forget the intense localism and cultural fragmentation of an early modern Jewish world that was divided into a patchwork of ethno-religious communities—a conglomeration of "diasporas within the diaspora," to use Jonathan Israel's phrase. To give just one example: Jews in Russia, Morocco, and Britain lived in different worlds until international coverage of Montefiore's mission to Marrakesh in the early 1860s allowed the readers of eastern (and western) European Jewish newspapers to reconfigure the relationship between these worlds in their collective imagination. Thus, the birth of global civil society and a set of interlocking global publics provided a space in which Jews of the East and West could connect in new and fundamentally transformative ways.

* * *

What does the mobilization of Jewish financial and political resources on a global scale tell us about the reality and perceptions of Jewish power in the age of emancipation? Here, I would highlight three important issues: a shift from covert to overt attempts to exert Jewish influence; the role of subscription fundraising in subverting the power exercised by communal elites; and responses to these developments in the non-Jewish world.

The emergence of the Jewish International reflected a fundamental shift in the nature of Jewish politics—away from the politics of *shtadlanut*, dependent on the personal connections of wealthy individuals, and towards the politics of the public sphere.[38] The democratization of Jewish politics was an inevitable byproduct of this transition. Of course, wealthy Jews retained disproportionate influence, both within their own community and outside it; but financiers like Montefiore, Baron James de Rothschild, and Sir Francis

Goldsmid now worked in tandem with organizations like the Board of Deputies, the Consistoire Central, and the Alliance Israélite. As public opinion grew in importance, the ability of Jews to plead the cause of Jewish relief no longer depended exclusively on money and personal connections. The relationship between Bismarck and his Jewish banker, Gerson von Bleichröder, may have harkened back to an earlier era, but success in obtaining diplomatic support for Romanian Jewry at the Congress of Berlin owed as much to the rise of international Jewish activism since 1840 as it did to Bismarck's willingness to lend Bleichröder an ear.[39] Not money alone, but decades of campaigning on behalf of oppressed Jewry had helped to render the treatment of religious and ethnic minorities a precondition for acceptance into an international state system that was increasingly governed by Western norms.[40]

In a sense, of course, the Jewish International remained an elite phenomenon. There is no denying the central role played by Jewish religious, intellectual, and financial elites during the initial period of takeoff—a role that is entirely consistent with the broad contours of non-Jewish politics and the "bourgeois" nature of the public sphere in mid-nineteenth century Europe. Even in countries like France and Germany, which operated under systems of universal suffrage, it was not until the 1890s that the masses really began to make their presence felt in the world of mainstream politics. If anything, this was even more true of the Jewish world. In Britain, a small and wealthy "cousinhood" of elite, interrelated families proved well able to defend its oligarchic position even after the onset of mass migration from eastern Europe in the 1880s and 1890s.[41] In Russia, the decline of communal self-government undermined the alliance of communal magnates and rabbinical authorities, but the opportunities now available to Jews created a different kind of partnership between a new class of more acculturated Jewish plutocrats, like the Gintsburgs, and the *maskilim*.[42] This was in some ways merely a reconfiguration of the alliance between brains and money that had long characterized the Jewish communal elite. Certainly, the collaboration among Jewish financiers, secularizing intellectuals, and the bureaucrats employed by national and international Jewish organizations was to prove critical in the decades to come.[43]

Yet mass-subscription fundraising channeled through the Jewish press had an inherently subversive potential. It enabled journalists and rabbis like Philippson and Rülf to take the lead in the cause of Jewish relief alongside communal oligarchs like the Rothschilds and Montefiore. It enabled whole swathes of the Lithuanian Jewish public to demonstrate their sense of solidarity with Jews in countries as culturally and geographically remote from their own experience as Persia. And it enabled recipient communities in places like Palestine to bypass the traditional channels of *halukah* through innovative fundraising appeals like the Hausdorf house-building campaign. This was a process entirely analogous to developments within the non-Jewish world, where association formation enabled the middle classes to punch collectively above their weight in fields as varied as social welfare, cultural patronage, and politics.

Not all contemporaries viewed these developments with the enthusiasm of Ludwig Philippson, however. From the Damascus Affair onward, the emergence of the Jewish International was viewed with fear and loathing by those who were, in any case, instinctively unsympathetic to the Jewish cause. In particular, Judaeo-phobes highlighted the role of Jewish money in buying influence in the non-Jewish press. As early as 1840, the ultramontane *Univers* saw the success of the Jewish intervention in the Damascus Affair as proof of the disturbing reach of Jewish "money and intrigues."[44] The Mortara Affair of 1859 called forth a similar Catholic polemic. Writing in the *Univers*, Louis Veuillot blamed public outcry over the fate of Edgardo Mortara on the agents of Mazzini, financed by the Jews. "Everywhere that eastern race rules supreme. They have purchased the copyright of all the important newspapers in Europe: the *Times*, *Constitutionnel*, *Débats*, etc."[45] Ten years later, the father of Prince Carol of Romania warned his son at the height of the furor over Romanian Jewry that the Jewish question was "a Noli me tangere, because the Jews have money and [own] the entire press."[46] A month later, he elaborated: "This reality is a symptom of Europe's disease, but it must be accepted as a reality; there is nothing to be done about it, because the whole European press is dominated by Jewish financial power. In a word, Jewish finance [*das Geldjudentum*] is a Great Power, whose . . . displeasure is dangerous!"[47] Unsurprisingly, when the first International Anti-Jewish Congress at Dresden turned its attention to Montefiore, delegates indicted him above all for his ability to shape public opinion, attributing Jewish control of the Continental press to his malign influence.[48]

Perceptions of Jewish press control reinforced concerns about other kinds of international Jewish activism as the appeal of Iakov Brafman's *Book of the Kahal* in Russia demonstrated. Writing in the late 1860s, Brafman claimed that Jews maintained their separatism through a secret internal organization known as the *Kahal*. This unsavory organization had long oppressed the Jewish masses through its abuse of Talmudic authority, but in recent years it had acquired national and international significance through the creation of five international brotherhoods. Superficially committed to enlightenment, modernization, and integration, the real aim of societies like the Society for the Promotion of Enlightenment Among the Jews of Russia (OPE) and the Alliance Israélite was to prepare Jews for citizenship of a future Jewish kingdom.[49] Thus did Brafman build on the realities of globalization, Jewish associational life, and the longstanding tradition of Jewish self-government to present a definitively hostile interpretation of international Jewish activism. It is surely no coincidence that he was writing just as the Jewish International assumed critical mass.

And here, it may be appropriate to return once again to the thoughts of Ludwig Philippson. Responding to news of the establishment of the Alliance Israélite in 1860, the editor of the *Allgemeine Zeitung des Judentums* was torn between enthusiastic support for this new sign of Jewish vitality and alarm at the hostile response he anticipated from the non-Jewish public. For, as Philippson noted, the fear of a secret Jewish understanding directed against non-Jews was one of the most deep-rooted forms of anti-Jewish prejudice: "and this is the greatest cause for concern aroused by the foundation of an 'Alliance Israélite Universelle.' . . . Just the name strikes fear into the hearts of thousands of Christians. . . . Hundreds of real episodes when Jews helped unlucky, persecuted Jews, when a Montefiore traveled to Damascus, a Crémieux to Alexandria, a[n Albert] Cohn to Morocco, have no [negative] consequences because they seem entirely natural and transparent—but the name 'general Israelite association,' [and] the existence of a permanent organizational tie will call forth the most diverse speculations, a thousand suspicions."[50] In assuming that the activities of men like Montefiore invariably met with a benign reception, Philippson proved misguided. In anticipating the hostility new, more public forms of Jewish power and associational activity would arouse, his anxieties were by no means misplaced.

Chapter 8

Rebels Without a Patron State: How Israel Financed the 1948 War

Derek Penslar

> To wage war, three things are necessary: money, money, and yet more money.
>
> —Gian-Jacopo Trivuzio (1499)

> A state exists chiefly in the hearts and minds of its people; if they do not believe it is there, no logical exercise will bring it to life.
>
> —Joseph Strayer (1970)

No state ever won a war without money or arms. The challenge of acquiring sufficient resources to fight is especially acute for rebels, revolutionaries, and Guerrillas who enter armed struggle at a vast disadvantage compared to the states or colonial regimes that they strive to overthrow. (For convenience's sake, I will use the term "anti-regime actors" to describe any group that seeks to overthrow an existing state power structure, be it the central government or a colonial offshoot.) In order to acquire weaponry and supplies anti-regime actors have a limited number of options. They can steal from the police or military of the sovereign, appeal for aid from sympathetic states or their ethnic kinsfolk in other lands, extract revenue and resources from the local population, or develop homegrown arms production.

Scholars of Israel during the 1948 war compare it mainly to its Arab foes, thereby presenting the war as a struggle between a state in the making and an array of sovereign states. They have not engaged in global or diachronic comparisons, nor have they seriously considered Israel as an element in the matrix of anticolonial and revolutionary movements of the interwar and postwar periods. One could of course argue that Israel's struggle for statehood does not fit into a comparison with anticolonial movements. The colonial power, Britain, had in 1917 officially pledged to promote the Zionist cause and did so with only occasional lapses until 1939. What is more, while the pre-state Jewish community in Palestine, the Yishuv, waged a guerrilla campaign against the British after World War II, the principle target of fighting in 1948 was Palestine's native Arab majority and the Arab states that claimed to be protecting it.

Israel's situation was in some ways akin to that of the nineteenth-century Afrikaner republics that simultaneously resisted British colonial expansion while fighting colonial wars against black natives. In South Africa, however, the two sets of conflict occurred simultaneously, while in Palestine, they came in succession, with the British largely out of the picture by the time the Palestine war began towards the end of 1947. What Israel calls its "War of Independence" was an effort to seek independence not from the British, nor from the Arabs, but from a far more amorphous and venerable antagonist, diasporic existence itself.

Culturally, the Yishuv of early 1948 was a community of immigrants who had developed a fiercely powerful sense of rootedness in the land. The Zionist project was attached to both its European heritage and the Middle Eastern environment. *Situationally*, however, the Zionist struggle for statehood was part of the era of postwar decolonization and was successful due to the rapid development of autonomous political and military institutions. In all cases of struggle against colonial domination, success or failure depended on the ability to marshal funds and acquire weaponry. In some ways, Israel was more poorly positioned to gain international financial support than other anti-regime actors of the time. In other ways, its position was vastly superior. In 1948, Israel did not receive direct aid from foreign states, but it had well-developed mechanisms of taxation and marketing public debt. No less important, Jews in the diaspora purchased weaponry, provisioned the armed forces and augmented them with experienced and technically expert personnel, and sustained the civilian economy of the fledgling state of Israel. Money and men, financial and human capital, were inseparable components of the diaspora's contributions to Israel in 1948.

* * *

I begin by constructing a typology of funding and arms-acquisitions schemes by anti-regime actors in the early to mid-twentieth century. My main comparison situations are: Ireland during the Anglo-Irish and Irish Civil Wars (1919–1923); Algeria during its guerrilla war against France (1954–1962); Vietnam during the First Indochina War (1946–1954); and Kenya during the Mau-Mau rebellion of 1952–1956. These cases come from four distinct regions of the globe—northern Europe, northern Africa, east Asia, and sub-Saharan Africa—yet share common traits as sites of anticolonial struggles in which the colonized suffered from a severe material disadvantage at the outset of hostilities.

The guerrillas' first tactic was to scrounge for weapons within their communities and to steal them from the police or military of the colonizing power. In the early days of the Algerian war, the Armée de Libération Nationale (ALN) was so short of weaponry that at times it had to make do with hunting rifles and knives.[1] In Kenya, urban Kikuyu civilians employed by the government at police stations, prisons, and railway yards had abundant opportunities to pilfer weapons and supplies, which they then passed on to the guerrillas. In Nairobi, prostitutes sympathetic with the rebel cause demanded bullets in payment for their services.[2]

Such heroic gestures could not generate the kind of resources required to overthrow a deeply rooted colonial regime. In 1946, Thai arms merchants offered the fledgling Democratic Republic of Vietnam (DRV) thirty thousand war-surplus Japanese rifles, but the cash-strapped DRV could afford only a third of that number.[3] In Kenya, the Mau Mau's small arms were no match for the British military, which crushed the rebels with armor and air power. The eventual British withdrawal from Kenya was less a direct response to the Mau-Mau rebellion than an acknowledgment of the unsustainability of a colonial presence in Kenya or pretty much anywhere else in the world. The French authorities and European settlers in Algeria, however, were less willing to sacrifice a territory that, since 1848, had been considered an integral part of France rather than a colony. In order to drive the French out, the Algerian nationalists depended on foreign aid, our second source of material support for anti-regime actors.

In 1958 the Arab League pledged $34 million to the Algerian resistance movement's political arm, the Front de Libération Nationale (FLN). It is not clear how much of that money actually materialized, but toward the end of the war, China contributed substantial sums.[4] (China's Communists themselves had, during their years of struggle against Chiang Kai-shek's Nationalists, benefited from Soviet financial assitance and weapons that the Soviet Union had taken after World War II from the Japanese.)[5] During the 1950s, Czechoslovakia was a conduit for small arms for the ALN just as it had provided heavy weaponry to Israel in 1948. In both cases it acted with the Soviet Union's express approval. Foreign aid to the Algerian rebels could also take the form of logistical support. During its first years, the ALN needed Egyptian help in running the camel caravans that transported arms across the Sahara and engaged in a constant cat-and-mouse game with French forces in Algeria and Tunisia.[6]

Vietnam provides a particularly useful example of the many different forms that foreign assistance could take. From its postwar beginnings, the Democratic Republic of Vietnam (DRV) received miltary stock from the Soviet Union and, to a far greater extent, China. Between April and September of 1950, China supplied the Viet Minh with 14,000 hand guns, 17,000 machine guns, 150 cannons, and 2,800 tons of grain, plus ammunition, arms-manufacturing machinery, medicine, and medical equipment. Aid levels grew even further after the end of Korean War in 1953. In addition to providing military and civilian aid as an outright grant, China was also Vietnam's most important trading partner, with commerce handled via the DRV's Bureau of Foreign Commerce. In May of 1947 alone, the bureau purchased over twenty-five-million yuan worth of supplies, ranging from uniforms, petrol, radio equipment, and medicine to small arms and explosives. This trade took place in a gray zone between the black and free markets; some of it was contraband, and the transactions had a strong governmental imprimatur.[7]

Last and not least, China enhanced the Viet Minh's human capital. China's celebrated Huangpu military academy, which had been built in the 1920s with Soviet assistance, authorized Ho Chi Minh to send dozens of Viet Minh cadres to China for training in Soviet military science. In April of 1950, the DRV's defense ministry transferred its own Tran Quoc Tuan military academy to southern China, where thirty thousand Viet Minh were transformed from undisciplined guerrillas into soldiers and officers familiar with command structure, large-scale operations, and strategic planning.[8] This direct intervention by a powerful state into the operations of a guerrilla force differed in intent, but not in ultimate benefit, from the case of ALN leaders who had fought for France or the thirty thousand Jewish residents of Palestine who had served in the British forces during World War II. The more thoroughly anti-regime actors have been trained in military operations, the more likely their movements are to succeed, even if it means overthrowing those who trained them.

In most cases, state aid has overpowered the third type of assistance I wish to analyze: contributions from diaspora communities sympathetic with the anti-regime actor's cause. During the 1950s, the eastern Thai provinces were home to some fifty thousand ethnic Vietnamese who rarely donated money but did facilitate trade with the DRV and arranged for the transportation of purchased items. This was a profitable business for the ethnic Vietnamese and so cannot be considered a form of ethnic or nationalist philanthropy, although some diaspora Vietnamese volunteered their time for translation and administrative services on behalf of the Viet Minh.[9] Given the extent of Russian and Chinese aid to the Viet Minh, the role of diaspora aid was modest and of little consequence. The situation was different for the rebels in Algeria, where in addition to support from China, Czechoslovakia, and the Arab states, a significant smuggling network operated out of France. Between 1957 and 1960, the network led by the journalist Francis Jeanson smuggled money, forged identification documents, and small arms into Algeria. Donations of money and services came primarily not from an Algerian diaspora but from a wide spectrum of French sympathizers of the FLN. Jeanson claimed that in 1958 the network smuggled about five billion old francs ($10 million) into Algeria but dismissed that sum as negligible in the face of the costs of a long-term war and the establishment of the Algerian provisional government.[10]

Our own era is filled with ethnic diasporas funneling money to separatist and liberation movements in the homeland. (To provide but one example, Tamil Canadians had a long and chequered history of financial support for the Tamil Tigers prior to their decisive defeat by the Sri Lankan government in 2009.) The significance of diaspora aid is, however, often questionable. During the 1970s and 1980s, Irish Americans vigorously solicited funds for an organization known as Northern Aid (NORAID), allegedly for families of incarcerated or killed Irish Republican Army (IRA) fighters, although the money was in fact used for the purchase of arms and explosives. The total amount raised over this period was about $3.6 million, a minuscule sum when compared with the IRA's *annual* income of some $10 million, most of which came from criminal activity such as bank robberies, extortion, and kidnapping for ransom, as well as a network of legitimate small businesses.[11]

During Ireland's struggle for independence earlier in the century, the Irish diaspora in North America was a significant source of philanthropic aid. The American Committee for Relief in Ireland raised over $5 million to feed, clothe, and house Irish civilians between the committee's establishment in December 1920 and the summer of 1922.[12] It is far less clear, however, how much Irish Americans donated to arms-smuggling operations in the United States, or how important the smuggled weapons really were in Ireland's struggle for independence. The American-made Thompson submachine gun that went on the market in 1921 has acquired a legendary status in Irish collective memory, but in fact very few of the guns were sent to Ireland during the time of the Ango-Irish War. The Irish White Cross chartered a ship to carry a load of five hundred Thompsons disguised in sacks labeled "leg of lamb," but the contrabad was found before departure from New York. Joseph McGarrity, a major fundraiser for the IRA in New York, managed to send a few score of Thompsons to Ireland during the 1930s, long after the country had achieved independence. In addition to being thin on the ground, the guns were inaccurate, unusable beyond a range of a few hundred yards, and often unreliable.[13]

As Peter Hart has argued, the Irish Republicans fought the English with assassinations, not firefights, and in their attacks on British targets, they relied primarily on pistols, shotguns, and explosives rather than on automatic rifles. After mid-1921, the Republicans stopped trying to manufacture even these relatively simple weapons themselves, and they were in fact very much dependent upon arms and munitions smugglers, but their saviors were across the Irish Sea, not the Atlantic. Small, informally yet tightly bound groups of Irishmen in England acquired and crated hundreds of pistols and sticks of gelignite, while Irish stevedores in Liverpool turned a blind eye to the contraband bound for Dublin. It is difficult to describe these actors as part of a diaspora, given Ireland's proximity and, even more important, its political attachment to Britain. This was an unusual case of what Hart calls "a guerrilla movement arising from an immigrant population as part of a struggle against the host country's rule of their 'native' land."[14] The Irish war of independence was therefore much more of a geographically delimited guerrilla war than a global battle drawing on the resources of a distant diaspora.

As the Provisional IRA of the 1970s shows, crime can pay well—so well that the PIRA was able to purchase vast quantites of arms, first on the private market in the United States and then from the Libyan government.[15] In most cases, however, successful anti-state actors have invested less effort in crime than in developing predictable, routinized flows of income and materiel from their own populace. Access to taxation revenue, credit, raw materials, and manufactured goods from within the homeland constitutes a fourth and final means by which anti-regime actors sustain their armed struggle.

Resource extraction can in and of itself be seen as a form of "organized crime," as Charles Tilly observed in a classic article from 1985.[16] "Banditry, piracy, gangland rivalry, policing, and war making all belong on the same continuum," Tilly claimed, referring to immature states' tolerance of multiple agents of violence (such as privateers and bandits in early modern Europe) in struggles with their external enemies and the encouragement of soldiers to plunder the foe's civilian population. Within a polity, states, like criminal gangs, offer protection to their populace and extract a price in return. Extraction enables war-making, which, even when unsuccessful, strengthens the development of governmental institutions. Stronger states augment the technology of extraction, thus improving their abilities to make war and enhancing the power of the state even further. In our day, the ongoing brutality of the extraction process is apparent in authoritarian states in the developing world and in the armed militias that spring up to oppose them. In such cases, both states and anti-state actors can have access to highly valuable natural resources (such as diamonds, coltan, coca, opium). In the cases from the mid-twentieth century under review here, however, usable raw materials were usually limited to those obtained from agriculture or forestry.

The process by which these products were collected could at times be coercive and extortionate, as in the Soviet Union under War Communism, the brutal economic regime of enforced food requisitioning during the civil wars of 1918–1922.[17] A quarter-century later, Maoist rebels in China combined the carrot with the stick, destroying the old rural elite and winning the support of the peasantry through land reform. A newly empowered peasantry took on the tasks of tax collection and organizing the flow of money, food, and supplies to the People's Liberation Army.[18] For the FLN in Algeria, during the tough years before foreign aid started to arrive in 1958, the key to survival lay in developing regional authorities with powers of taxation. The

FLN was an elite revolutionary movement, to which most of Algeria's Muslims did not belong, but they supported it as the most effective and likely means to shake off French rule and domination by the European settlers, the *pieds noirs*. There was no separation between government and party, so dues-paying members of the FLN provided a secondary stream of revenue for guerrilla activity. Collected funds were deposited in local banks and then transferred to the banks' branches abroad, where they were used to purchase weapons and supplies.[19] Ironically, the Algerian revolutionaries benefitted from Algeria's political status as an integral part of France in that Algeria used the French franc, a major, widely accepted world currency. Arms merchants in any country would be happy to take francs, although the cost of weapons rose consistently due to the inflation that throughout the 1950s steadily eroded the franc's purchasing power, so much so that in the currency reform of 1960 the new franc replaced the old at a value of one hundred to one.

A corollary to independent taxation authority is the ability to manufacture one's own weapons. Large-scale arms production, however, has not been common amongst anti-regime actors in the twentieth century. As we have already seen, the IRA ceased munitions manufacture in mid-1921. Mau-Mau blacksmiths manufactured pistols and rifles, but they were notoriously unreliable. The Viet Minh were exceptional in the quantity and quality of their artisanally produced weapons, which amounted to some seven thousand tons of grenades, bazookas, bombs, and other small arms over the period of the First Indochinese War.[20]

How does the Zionist project fit into our *tour d'horizon* of anti-regime actors? We have seen that no one type or combination of funding and acquisitions mechanisms assured success for an anti-regime actor. The most important variable—the military capacity, determination, and ruthlessness of those they were fighting against—was out of the rebels' hands. But historically, the most significant source of money and munitions was aid from patron states, and in 1948, the Zionists had no patron. Czech arms sales to Israel in 1948 could not have taken place without Soviet authorization, but these were cash transactions, not gifts. The Zionists had to either buy weapons or make their own. Nor could the Zionists hope to get very far with small arms alone, whether acquired by theft, gift, or purchase. Guerrilla warfare waged with handguns and explosives had sufficed to drive the British out of Palestine, just as similar tactics had worked for the Irish Republicans during the Anglo-Irish War. Both the Irish and Israeli wars of independence followed shortly upon world wars that exhausted and financially strained the British government. Both wars were the final chapters of independence movements in which Britain had been enmeshed for decades (Home Rule to the 1870s, Zionism to 1917) and which had attracted worldwide public attention. Finally, the British were not willing to apply the level of force to the Irish and the Jews that they had unleashed upon the Mau Mau in the mid-1950s. The Black and Tans and the Auxiliary Division of the Royal Irish Constabulary terrorized the Irish population, but their crimes were dwarfed by British actions in Kenya: the use of bomber aircraft, massacres or executions of thousands, construction of labor camps for political prisoners, and forced resettlement of a million Kikuyu in villages surrounded by barbed wire and deep trenches—in effect, open-air prisons.[21] The British supression of the 1936–1939 Palestinian revolt had many of these features. In contrast, British actions against the Zionist militias appears quite tame, even when taking into account the twelve Irgun and Lehi guerrillas who were executed by the British or who committed suicide in prison in order to cheat the hangman.

Compared with the successful guerrilla movements we have been looking at, the Palestinian militias that fought against the Zionists in 1947 and 1948 were not a formidable foe. Over the course of the Mandate period, the Palestinians were riven by factional and ideological rivalries and failed to develop a hegemonic revolutionary organization that could assume protogovernmental functions. During the Palestinian Arab revolt of 1936–1939, the British killed or deported many of the rebellion's leaders and captured much of their weaponry. Internecine warfare amongst Palestinian factions reduced the leadership even further. In 1947–1948, the Palestinian armed resistance was divided into numerous bands and militias, most of whose members were untrained, inexperienced, and poorly equipped. The Arab Liberation Army, a volunteer force assembled under the authority of the Arab League, had able leaders but was a small force (at most five-thousand strong) whose main function was to thwart the expansionist ambitions of King Abdullah of Jordan. The Arab states strove to throttle, not nurture, autonomous Palestinian military power.[22]

Despite their small numbers and limited firepower, the Palestinians enjoyed important tactical advantages over the Jews in the late fall of 1948 and winter of 1949. Jews controlled less than 10 percent of Palestine's territory and were outnumbered two to one. Palestinian fighters could travel with ease throughout the countryside, taking shelter in hundreds of Arab villages (whether the village folk wanted them there or not). Jewish agricultural settlements were highly vulnerable to attack, as was the road to west Jerusalem, which was virtually impassable due to Palestinian sniper fire. In order to break the siege of Jerusalem and defend the Jewish rural settlements, and even more so in order to push back the Arab states that attacked in May of 1948, the Zionists required transport vehicles, artillery, armor, and aircraft in addition to massive quantities of small arms. The Yishuv successfully marshaled the necessary resources to provision its troops and maintain the civilian economy via the public institutions it had developed throughout the period of the British Mandate. As soon as it was born, Israel assumed the responsibilities of a full-grown state, but it would have died in the cradle without a foreign patron. As no state came forward, the diaspora took its place, and to an extent unrivaled in the history of the twentieth century.

* * *

Fighting the 1948 war was a far more expensive affair for Israel than for the Arab states that attacked it. The Arab states deployed only portions of their armies, and with the exception of brief fighting in the Sinai, the war was carried out entirely on the soil of the lands designated for the Jewish and Palestinian states. Nonetheless, Jordan and Iraq were plummeted into financial crisis by the war—a crisis Israel avoided by mobilizing its entire population and economy in what Moshe Naor has described as a situation of total war.[23] Israel extracted almost three-fourths of the $300 million direct costs of the war from its own citizens—through loans (subscribed by patriotic individuals, especially the Yishuv's small entrepreneurial class of bankers and manufacturers), taxes, and bonds (bought by patriotic and desperate banks).[24] Since Israel's very survival was far from certain, the purchase of government debt was an expression of fervent patriotism, collective solidarity, and desperate hope. Even the robust civic spirit of the Israeli population, however, could not compensate for the exclusion of the Palestine pound from the Sterling bloc in February 1948, which rendered the Israeli currency nonconvertible on the international market and severely limited the country's foreign trade.[25] Israel was thus more poorly positioned to purchase arms than guerrilla movements operating within the penumbra of the colonizing power's currency (for Algeria, the French franc; for Ireland, the British pound).

The final and crucial quarter of the costs of Israel's War of Independence had to come in the form of hard currency, which was supplied by diaspora

Jewry. In addition to raising funds, diaspora Jews worked closely with Zionist emissaries, mainly from the Haganah, in the acquisition of arms both before and during the war. Despite the many challenges facing Israel in 1948, with respect to arms purchase its situation was superior to that of the Arab states, which did not have arms-acquisition networks abroad. Before the war, Arab states had been able to buy high-quality heavy weaponry from the United Kingdom and other countries, but they were denied access to weapons after the imposition of embargoes on arms sales, first by the United States (declared on December 14, 1947, and strengthened by Executive Order, effective April 15) and then by the United Nations (May 29).

The story of diaspora Jewry's military assistance to Israel predates the state's creation by three years. On July 1, 1945, United Jewish Appeal director Henry Montor convened a meeting at the New York home of industrialist Rudolf Sonneborn. The meeting was attended by seventeen prominent Jewish businessmen and Zionist activists. The guest speaker at the meeting was David Ben Gurion, who told the gathered guests that Great Britain would leave Palestine within three years and that an Arab invasion was sure to follow. He called upon the assembled to raise money for arms purchase. All present at the meeting agreed to take part in this largely illegal activity. The meeting resulted in the creation of a steering committee that established what became known as the "Sonneborn Institute."

The July 1, 1945 meeting has become the stuff of legend. Memoir accounts differ widely as to the composition of the meeting as well as its participants' later activities. Late arrivals to the Sonneborn Institute depict themselves as present from its creation, and peripheral characters claim to have played central roles. There is also a confusion of the institute's illegal activities, such as raising funds to acquire arms-production machinery and smuggle it out of the country, and the legal collection of tents, clothing, and other nonmilitary materials. Fortunately, despite the secrecy attached to the meeting and its outcome, an archival document with the guest list has survived.[26] This list can serve as a point of departure for exploring what kind of prominent American Jew would commit himself to breaking the law to assist in the founding of a Jewish state.[27]

Most of those present were already deeply involved in Zionist affairs. Some were modestly successful attorneys or businessmen, like Atlanta's Howard Travis, president of the Zionist Organization of America's southeastern region and a founder of Camp Judaea in North Carolina, or Cleveland's Ezra Shapiro, who was to become world chairman of Keren Hayesod–United Israel

Appeal.[28] Eleven of the seventeen, however, were highly affluent, and several had penetrated American elite society. Sonneborn himself was "old money," being the grandson of an immigrant who became a prosperous textile manufacturer. Like his father, Rudolf Sonneborn attended the elite Johns Hopkins University, and once in business, he turned the family concern successfully from textiles towards petrochemicals. He also married into the German Jewish aristocracy, becoming the fourth husband of Dorothy Schiff, the granddaughter of financier Jacob Schiff. Charles Rosenbloom, son of an immigrant Jew from Lithuania who became a liquor distributor in Pittsburgh, attended Yale, became an attorney, and then went into business with his college friend Alex Lowenthal, who also was present at the July 1, 1945 meeting. Lowenthal was a developer and pillar of Pittsburgh civic affairs; he amassed sufficient wealth to retire at the age of fifty. Rosenbloom was at least as successful as a financier and developer and became a trustee of Carnegie Mellon University. He donated masterpieces of European art from his private collection to both Carnegie Mellon and Yale. Shoe magnate Philip Lown, perhaps best known today for his endowments to Brandeis University, was an immigrant from Lithuania but a graduate of the University of Maine who had worked in the army's chemical warfare service during World War I. William Sylk owned a chain of drug stores in Philadelphia, and Julius Fligelman was a wealthy furniture manufacturer from Los Angeles.[29]

These men were, as a whole, not only well to do but, by the standards of a mid-twentieth-century American immigrant community, reasonably genteel. True, one of the most active leaders of the group, Shepard Broad, had been born into poverty in Pinsk and clambered his way to great success as a banker, lawyer, and real estate developer in Miami. Broad had a reputation as a tough, savvy businessman who was not unaccustomed to skirting the edge of the law, but he was also a pillar of the Miami business and philanthropic community. Although the men of the Sonneborn group were mostly of eastern European origin, and several were first-generation immigrants, they were all respected figures within a variety of communities outside the Jewish realm and were unlikely to have flouted the law in any serious way.

The Sonneborn group created a bourgeois underground, replete with decentralized cells, safe houses, and *noms de guerre*. Some of the group's leaders had been involved in weapons production and supply during the Second World War, and they hired a staff of technical experts to locate surplus army machinery for manufacturing guns and bullets. Zionist youth volunteered to package munitions in deceptively marked crates; respected lawyers rented warehouse space for the production of weapons and stored vast amounts of cash in their office safes. With over three-fourths of the American trucking industry in Jewish hands, and many of the truck-line owners supportive of the Sonneborn project, licit goods like tents and foodstuffs were easily transported to New York and thence to Palestine.[30]

In its organizational sophistication, the Sonneborn Institute resembled the Jeanson Network, but it mobilized a larger network of operatives. The Jeanson Network had some forty full-time mules and a support network of hundreds, but through word of mouth, the Sonneborn Institute's grew to several thousand, with professional connections to key industries like textiles, naval surplus, and telecommunications (for radio transmitters and walkie-talkies; ten thousand of the latter were smuggled to Palestine). Sonneborn created a permanent administrative structure, with a finance department headed by stockbroker Louis Rocker. Within the first four months of 1947, the group had raised half a million dollars and had purchased, among other things, two Canadian corvettes and a freighter, the *President Warfield*, later to be rechristened *Exodus 1947*. By the end of 1947, $2 million had come in, and total fundraising by 1948 was $6 to $7 million. The money went to the acquisitions of ships for illegal immigration, airplanes, especially transport craft, and, most important, equipment for arms manufacture. Seventy percent of Israel's machinery for the production of small arms and munitions was bought in the United States through these mechanisms.[31]

The Sonneborn project was tightly linked with Haganah efforts to raise funds and acquire arms and arms-manufacturing equipment in the United States. Between 1946 and 1949, three Haganah bureau chiefs—Yaakov Dori, Shlomo Shamir, and Teddy Kollek—and a staff of experts headed by Yehuda Arazi nominally supervised the operation, but in fact they and the Americans operated as equal partners. The Haganah engaged in fundraising on its own, pulling in some $3 million between 1945 and 1948.[32] But its acquisition operations were not only dependent upon, but also symbiotically linked with, American Jewish activists. Haim Slavin, who headed up arms machinery purchases until the end of 1946, knew a lot about engineering from his work for the Palestine Electric Company, but he knew nothing about North America, let alone its arms industries, and could not speak English. (He taught himself by reading Sherlock Holmes stories.) Hence Slavin's need for Harry Levine, a millionaire plastics manufacturer from Massachusetts with extensive wartime experience in arms manufacture. Levine made connections with arms merchants throughout the United States and rented a warehouse in the

Bronx to house contraband. He also rented factory space in downtown Toronto, where Slavin and Karl Ekdel, a Swedish arms expert, crafted a prototype machine gun. Slavin's aide, a mechanical engineer named Phil Alper, was able, as an American citizen, to purchase military surplus equipment, including machinery for the production of arms and munitions.[33]

At times, it was simply impossible to determine if an initiative originated from a "Palestinian" or an American Jew or as a result of interaction between them. This is particularly true if we look beyond the philanthropic elite within the Sonneborn group to the scores of American experts who assisted the Haganah's acquisitions operations. For example, although Haganah commanders in Palestine were from the start enthusiastic about the import of machinery for manufacturing light arms, until late 1947, they were reluctant to think in terms of a multistate Arab invasion and the need for air power for ground troop support or transport. The idea of buying airplanes came from the United States, most likely from Al Schwimmer, a former TWA navigator who founded Service Airlines, a front corporation that purchased aircraft and then flew them to Palestine. Schwimmer also directed the recruiting of American airmen, rendering his contribution to the war all the more essential.[34]

With the American arms embargo in place and firm restrictions on foreign involvement in arms purchase and transfer established, American Jews assumed most of the legal responsibility for the acquisition project, reasoning that if they were caught, the consequences would be far less grave than for the Palestinian Jews. In fact, on several occasions, the Americans, like the Irish Republicans in the early 1920s, were caught red-handed. Crates filled with dynamite spilled open on a New York dock; Royal Canadian Mounted Police at Niagara Falls apprehended the prototype submachine gun being smuggled from Toronto; volunteer pilots were apprehended while trying to fly planes from the United States to Europe and thence to Israel. Yet out of all these incidents, only one participant in this vast enterprise went to jail. Schwimmer was convicted of conspiracy, fined heavily, and stripped of his civil rights, but was not imprisoned. (He was pardoned by President Clinton in 2001.) Many others received suspended sentences or fines, at times nominal.

In the United States, the courts were sympathetic to the Zionist cause, the defendants had astute legal representation, and the FBI was never able to pierce beyond one local cell and expose the national operation in its entirety. Apparently, it did not try very hard once FBI director J. Edgar Hoover had ascertained that the weapons would not be used within the United States.[35] In contrast, in France in 1960, an enraged and fearful government bogged down in the Algerian war put twenty-five activists in the Jeanson Network on trial. Sixteen received stiff jail sentences.

The American Jews involved in the Sonneborn project did not know in advance whether or not they would be prosecuted. They were aware of possible repercussions but felt morally compelled to act as they did. They saw themselves as leaders of an American Jewish home front, an extension of the massive home-front campaigns of the recently ended world war. There is also an obvious parallel to the Irish Americans who funneled money and arms to the Irish Republican Army during the Anglo-Irish and Irish Civil Wars. Irish and Jewish Americans also shared a self-perception as historic victims and a view of the national struggle as a righting of ancent wrongs. Al Robison, a textile merchant from New Jersey and one of the major figures behind the Sonneborn project, described it thus: "Here was an opportunity that happened maybe once in a lifetime, maybe not even once in a lifetime. That we could be cloak-and-dagger people, that we could live dangerously and feel highly virtuous about it, that we could actually make history."[36] Another member of the group expressed his feelings even more viscerally: "Haganah is the biggest romance; it is the greatest thing certain Jews had had happen to them in this country. I have known Jews all my life who were waiting for the day that they could point to another Jew that carried a gun and say, 'he represents me.' Meaning not to a gangster but a hero, and in the last few weeks the papers have come forth and they mention Haganah with respect."[37]

The Sonneborn group's activities were curtailed by secrecy, competition with public Zionist fundraising, and a lack of tax-deductible status for donations. Moreover, much of the arms and equipment purchased in the United States was confiscated by federal authorities, was lost or pilfered en route, or arrived too late to be of use (fighter airplanes, for example, as opposed to transport planes, which did make it and played a major role). Yet this network of Jewish businessmen and Haganah agents certainly accomplished more than its counterparts in the Revisionist militia, Etzel, who managed to raise only several hundred thousand dollars.[38]

The businessmen were also more generous and effective than the Jewish gangsters whose donations, both in cash and in kind (namely, guns) are the subject of many tales of dubious accuracy. Yehuda Arazi, head of the Haganah's arms-acquisition operation, claims that Meyer Lansky and an Italian named Anastasia with influence on the New York docks ensured that weapons headed to Arab lands would not get shipped or would meet with accidents. It is not possible to verify this assertion. More likely is the connection between the Miami-based gangster Sam Kay and the president of Panama, Enrique Adolfo Jiménez, who agreed to let the Israeli arms ships fly under the Panamanian flag. As to fundraising, Reuven Dafni of the Haganah claims to have met Bugsy Siegel, who arranged to go weekly to a restaurant on La Cienega Boulevard in Los Angeles and pick up suitcases stuffed with cash. Dafni claims the total amount raised was $50,000. Murray Greenfield of the Haganah's agency for illegal immigration, Ha-Mosad le-Aliyah Bet, claimed to have received $90,000 in an evening from a group of Jewish gangsters in Baltimore. Irgun activist Yitzhak Ben-Ami, who visited the United States under the aegis of the American League for a Free Palestine, claims that he received some $120,000 from gangster Mickey Cohen and other hoodlums, who extorted businessmen, gentile and Jewish, to come up with the cash. Even if these stories are true, the totals are paltry in comparison with the funds raised by the Sonneborn group. What's more, Jewish gangsters did not always display a sentimental attachment to Israel; in 1951 two Detroit Jews, Arthur Leebove and Sam Stein, were convicted of trying to smuggle twenty-one U.S. warplanes from Newark to Egypt during the 1948 war.[39]

The contributions of not only Jewish gangsters, but even the more civilized members of the Sonneborn group, paled in comparison with the massive United Jewish Appeal fundraising drive of 1948. It was here that the Jewish diaspora's financial contribution to Israel in 1948 diverged most drastically from other cases of diaspora assistance to the homeland's battles.

From the start, relations between the Haganah arms-acquisition operation and the Sonneborn group, on the one hand, and official (and legal) American Zionist organizations, on the other, were complicated. Several professional Zionist functionaries attended the July 1, 1945, meeting, which was facilitated by the UJA director, Henry Montor. Yet the meeting was kept secret from the American Zionist Emergency Council and the American Jewish Agency Executive.[40] Nonetheless, in 1946 the Haganah's arms-acquisitions initiative received a $400,000 loan from the UJA, with subsequent separate loans of $1 million and $2 million.[41] Over time, Abba Hillel Silver, president of the Zionist Organization of America, and other mainstream American Zionist officials grew worried about the exposure of illegal activity (like dynamite spilling onto the New York docks) and the negative consequences it could have on Zionist activity as a whole within the United States. Silver's Revisionist Zionist sympathies may have also turned him against blanket

American Zionist support for an operation run by and for the Haganah. In early 1948, the Jewish Agency declared its desire to take public responsibility for the arms-acquisition project by focusing on the entirely legal goal of raising money to be sent to Israel, with the understanding that much of it would go to buying arms abroad.

In 1948, the United Jewish Appeal set itself the astronomical figure of $250 million as its annual campaign goal. The campaign did reach $150 million, which exceeded previous years' tallies five- or even tenfold. Whereas in previous years, only some 20 to 35 percent of the total campaign receipts were allocated to the United Palestine Appeal, in 1948, the UPA received 45.5 percent, or almost $70 million, of which $41 million were dedicated specifically to arms purchases for Israel. In addition, $15 million from the American Jewish Joint Distribution Committee's UJA allocation that year went to civilian needs in Israel, and millions more came in to Israel from more than one hundred different American Jewish organizations.[42] The UJA's stunning tally was four times greater than the American Red Cross's entire annual campaign, and twelve times greater than that of the American Cancer Society.[43] The campaign's success was at least in part the product of Golda Meir's charismatic speechmaking and negotiations with the UJA over the percentages of receipts to be allocated to the Jewish Agency in general and arms purchase in particular.[44] Meir helped whip up a veritable frenzy of Jewish giving to Zionist causes, which historian Haim Barkai has estimated, amounted to approximately 2.5 percent of American Jewry's aggregate net disposable income.[45]

Barkai came up with this sum by calculating the net disposable income of the United States' entire population, assuming 4 percent of that sum represented American Jewry, and then dividing the Jews' alleged collective income by the total amount of money contributed to Palestine/Israel in 1948. This is admittedly a highly imperfect calculation, as aggregate Jewish income may have been greater or less than the mean, giving patterns among Jews varied greatly, and not all funds for Palestine in 1948 necessarily came from Jews. For example, in 1946, John D. Rockefeller gave $100,000 to the UJA, and similar large gifts may well have come from non-Jews in 1948.[46] However, since American Jews in the late 1940s were not a particularly affluent community, it may well be that the total percentage of Jews' disposable income that went to Palestine was greater than 2.5 percent. In past campaigns, a small percentage of Jews had contributed the bulk of annual campaigns; for example, in the New York City Federation Drive of 1940, nine hundred individuals, less than 2 percent of all donors, provided 51.5 percent of the total receipts.[47]

But it is difficult to imagine 2 percent of American Jewry providing half—that is, $75 million—of the funds raised by the UJA in 1948. The giving must have been more widely distributed.

Total arms costs for Israel in 1948 were $78 million. Between the funds raised in the United States and another $15 million that was raised in Europe, 86 percent of the cost of Israel's arms purchased abroad in 1948 was born by foreign sources. These funds paid for heavy arms and equipment purchased in France, Italy, and eventually Czechoslovakia. (The last of these receives the most historical attention, but it was the purchase in the spring of 1948 of west European armor that allowed Israel to withstand, although just barely, the first Arab assault of May and June.)[48] The funds also paid for more modest purchases such as machinery for the manufacture of small arms and munitions, which proved to be of immense benefit to Israel since the Arab states began the war with superior weaponry but soon ran out of spare parts and ammunition.

While Jewish businessmen were doing their utmost to smuggle materiel into Palestine, some 3,500 volunteer fighters (Machal) went to Palestine, then Israel, to take part in the war. National liberation struggles frequently attract sympathetic volunteers as well as mercenaries and serial soldiers, men who go from conflict to conflict in order to continuously experience the thrill of battle. There were some mercenaries among the Machal, particularly gentile pilots who were paid as much as $550 per month.[49] But the vast majority of the Machal were truly volunteers who received only a token wage. They hailed mainly from the United States, Canada, and South Africa, but volunteers came as well from North Africa.[50] The South African and North American men of the Machal forces supplied the bulk of the pilots and crew for Israel's embryonic airforce, which played an indispensable role in transporting supplies to besieged Israeli communities in the Negev and transporting arms purchased abroad to Israel (as in the case of operation Balak, which brought Czech arms to Israel).[51] Machal airforces did not, however, provide a significant level of tactical support for ground troops, nor did they engage in decisive aerial raids, as the Arab states' planes were quickly grounded due to a lack of spare parts.

Machal forces were highly overrepresented in Israel's embryonic navy. Paul Shulman, first commander of the Israeli Navy, was an Annapolis graduate who received his appointment at the age of twenty-six after going to Palestine to work in illegal immigration activity. Machal commanders served in ground units as well, as in the Eighth Armored Brigade, which had an English-speaking heavy-tank company and a light-tank company comprised of Russian speakers. (The brigade commander, Yitzhak Sadeh, communicated with this company's commander in Russian.) Benjamin Dunkelman, a major in the Canadian forces in World War II, commanded the Seventh Brigade in the Lower Galilee, and two of his battalion commanders, Joe Weiner and Baruch Friedman-Erez, were also volunteers.[52] The most celebrated Machal ground commander was David (Mickey) Marcus, a West Point graduate who had served with distinction in both the Pacific and Atlantic theaters during World War II. As a volunteer in the newly formed Israel Defense Force, Marcus commanded the Jerusalem front with the rank of Major General before he was mistakenly killed by a Palmach sentry at Abu Ghosh on June 10, 1948, on the eve of the United Nations truce.

Despite the highly sympathetic stance towards the Zionist project taken by all major Jewish organizations in the wake of the war, American Jewish volunteer rates for the Machal were only a fraction of those from other countries. Whereas one in five thousand American Jews volunteered, the ratios were one in a thousand for Canada, about one in five hundred for Britain and France, and a stunning 1 percent for South African's Jewish community, which was even higher if one takes into account the streams of South African Jewish youth who volunteered but were not mobilized.[53] The United States sent slightly more American Jews to the International Brigades during the Spanish Civil War (1,250) than to Palestine in 1948 (1,100). Why was this the case? One could argue that America's Jewish veterans were weary after their service in World War II, concerned about the possible illegality of fighting for a foreign power, and cosseted by protective Jewish parents. But the same was true for Jews elsewhere in the world. Canadian and South African Jews were far more likely to have been involved in pioneering youth movements and to have a familial connection with, or previous life experience in, the Yishuv. (Some 15 percent of the Machal, many of them South African, stayed in the country after the end of the war.)[54] American Jewry was thus less connected with Palestine than was its diaspora counterparts, and its Zionism was far more likely to be philanthropic, manifested through donations of money, not bodies. It was precisely these donations, however, that made possible Israel's victory in 1948.

* * *

The Zionist project aspired to negate the diaspora by establishing a sovereign state in the ancient Jewish homeland. According to classic Zionist ideology, a people that had survived across the ages thanks to its utility as merchants and financiers would now wrest its livelihood from agriculture and industry. Jews would no longer live at the whim of their host societies, enduring constant prejudice and frequent persecution. They would determine their own fate and develop the military means to do so. Yet the state of Israel did not give birth to itself. It was as much a continuation as it was the antithesis of the diaspora. The institutional structures in the diaspora that generated the money that sustained Israel in 1948 were not new. They were the same informal business and social networks that throughout modern history had brought Jewish activists together to engage in welfare activity on the local, national, and international level. The United Jewish Appeal grew directly out of the tradition of bureaucratized, professionalized philanthropies that Jews in Europe and North America had been developing since the 1880s. At the fin de siècle, the dense network of Jewish philanthropies in the western world's major cities consistently provided higher levels of aid than those provided by municipal charities.[55] Between 1914 and 1939, the American Jewish Joint Distribution Committee disbursed over $100 million for relief, reconstruction, and aid to refugees in Europe and Palestine. During the Second World War, the committee raised an additional $70 million.[56] It is no surprise that in the wake of the Holocaust, American Jews reached more deeply into their pockets than ever before and surpassed their already remarkable levels of charitable giving.

Placing this story in the framework of twentieth-century struggles for national liberation highlights certain unique aspects of Israel's creation. As much as colonized peoples suffered under the yoke of their colonial masters, the genocide of two-thirds of European Jewry infused into the Yishuv an overwhelming yearning for collective sovereignty and compelled diaspora Jewry to give the utmost of their material resources to enable Israel's creation and survival. The Zionist project also differed from anticolonial movements in that it aspired to liberate the Jews not by overthrowing their oppressors in their lands of residence but by engineering a mass immigration of Jews to a distant land—a land ruled by a foreign imperial authority and inhabited by an indigenous people with a growing national consciousness of its own. For the Zionists, liberation came at the expense of not only the Ottoman and British Mandatory regimes but also the Palestinian Arabs. In order to achieve collective liberation, the Zionists engaged in decades of nation-building, constructing political and economic institutions of sufficient strength and flexibility to be able to withstand the punishing assaults of 1948. Relying on their own resources and those of diaspora Jews, the Zionist leadership successfully created the preconditions for the state of Israel's existence.

Our comparative approach highlights similarity as well as difference. The Zionist project was as much a product of the era of post-1945 decolonization as it was of colonialism's zenith in the early twentieth century. The British Empire nurtured the Jewish National Home, yet it was empire's collapse that made possible the state of Israel's birth. The nascent state of Israel generated a revolutionary torque akin to that which caused the overthrow of tyrannical regimes and expulsion of colonial masters throughout the world. Like other revolutionary projects of the last century, Zionism displayed hubris and cruelty, but also an unshakable faith in humanity's capacity to re-engineer itself. Some historians of the 1948 war have described the Yishuv as a well-oiled machine that aligned its entire population into a dedicated fighting force. Not only are such explanations exaggerated, they also overlook the fact that other national liberation organizations such as the FLN or Viet Minh were highly successful at organizing the extraction of revenue and resources from the population and developing an effective fighting force. Compared with the Arab world, Israel in 1948 was indeed exceptional, and the war that secured sovereignty for Israel also brought catastrophe upon the Palestinians. When observed on a global level, however, Zionism's resemblance to anticolonial and national liberation movements becomes apparent, not only in self-conception but also in method.

Chapter 9

Orthodoxy Through Diamonds: Jewish Life in Antwerp after World War II

Veerle Vanden Daelen

Since the mid-twentieth century, Antwerp's Jewish life has been characterized by a highly visible Orthodox presence, geographically situated in and around the city's diamond district and its immediate surroundings. I argue that the intertwining of religious practice and economic practices in postwar Jewish Antwerp ensured communal cohesion and facilitated an unusual development of Orthodoxy in western Europe.[1] Economic factors, specifically those pertaining to the diamond sector, afforded Antwerp's Orthodoxy the means and capabilities to revive in the immediate aftermath of World War II. This contribution analyzes how this specific development occurred and traces how a community's economic foundation within a major industrial sector influenced Antwerp's Jewish life. What can the diamond sector tell us about Jews' understandings of their economic and political power in Europe from the interwar until the postwar period? How did economic networks operate in the twentieth-century Western world, even during wartime? The foundation and development of Orthodox Jewish life is another part of this story. I examine the development of Orthodoxy in Antwerp before World War II and its quick reconstruction and financing in the immediate postwar period, a time of widespread crisis and emergency throughout the Jewish world. Here, the central focus is religious practice and financing in postwar Antwerp in relation to economic practices and networks.

This chapter, rather than entering discussions concerning economic niche theory or theories about middlemen minorities, focuses on how economic networks function, especially in diasporic settings. It extends beyond an economic analysis of the diamond business so as to include social, religious, political, and familial networks and membership in organizations that connect people in relationships of trust (or not). Such networks influence the outcomes of economic processes, though these influences are sometimes difficult to discern, not least because of the private nature of what are often nonofficial connections. The inherent slipperiness of concepts such as "reputation" compounds the difficulty.[2] In focusing on local and international networking, this study proceeds along theoretical lines developed magnificently in two seminal studies, namely Sarah Stein's *Plumes* and Francesca Trivellato's *The Familiarity of Strangers*.[3] Like Stein's and Trivellato's analyses, this study examines economic successes and setbacks. Looking at how business and religious praxis reinforced each other in the twentieth century, it assesses the role that networks played therein.

In what follows, we will first see that the demographic development of Antwerp's Jewish population paralleled the diamond sector's rising position in the city, particularly in the prewar period. The specific work environment of the diamond sector and the local availability of basic accommodations necessary for Orthodox lifestyles helped to establish Antwerp as an attractive destination city for Orthodox immigrants. However, until the eve of World War II, Orthodoxy did not form the singular dominant characteristic of Jewish life. This development emerged in the years after the liberation. As I will show, apart from a certain serendipity, it had much to do with networks and personal contacts. A related factor is that once a sizable number of (ultra-) Orthodox Jews had settled within Antwerp's diamond milieu, the city became increasingly attractive to Orthodox Jews as its appeal to non-Orthodox Jews diminished. This contribution focuses on the interaction between an economic base and characteristics of Jewish community life and thereby sheds new light on key economic dimensions of the Jewish past, including communal economic agency.

Diamonds: The Foundation of Antwerp's Jewish Life

Jews in Antwerp have been significantly involved in the city's diamond sector throughout the modern period. In the nineteenth century, many Dutch Jews in Amsterdam who were active in diamonds relocated to Antwerp, where the sector was beginning to develop. By century's end, this group in Antwerp had been joined by Jewish immigrants, most of whom were from Russia, Austria-Hungary, or Germany. These immigrants included wealthy, established diamond traders, as well as people unaffiliated with the industry who were now entering the sector's workforce. Waves of Jewish immigration continued in the following years, a development that went hand in hand with Antwerp's emergence as a center of the international diamond trade. Parallel with the first migration waves, between 1898 and 1929, five diamond exchanges were founded, with Jews holding major positions in the four largest and most important ones.[4] In 1880 there had been about 1,200 Jews in Antwerp. Shortly after the turn of the century, this number had increased to around 8,000 persons, and by the outbreak of World War I, the figure was approximately 20,000.[5] Jewish immigration to Antwerp continued during the interwar years, initially mostly from Poland and later supplemented by refugees from the Third Reich. By the eve of World War II, the total number of Jewish inhabitants in Antwerp was estimated at 35,500.[6] In the postwar decades, the number of Jews in the city fluctuated around 10,000. In 2001, Antwerp was home to an estimated 15,000 to 20,000 Jewish inhabitants.[7]

Besides entering numerous other professions (including those that were considered typically Jewish, such as the textile and leather industries), rising numbers of Antwerp's Jewish population became active in diamonds.[8] The highest percentages of Jewish involvement in this sector were noted in the 1950s and 1960s, when, according to some estimates, 75 percent to 80 percent of Antwerp's Jews earned income directly or indirectly from diamonds.[9] Of course, this does not mean that Antwerp's diamond sector was uniformly or even predominantly Jewish. For example, although the majority (80 percent to 90 percent) of the diamond management was Jewish before World War II, most (approximately 75 percent) of the sector's workforce were non-Jews.[10] By the end of the 1920s, approximately 25,000 people worked in diamonds; about 100,000 people earned their living directly or indirectly from the industry. Indeed, at that time, the diamond sector provided more jobs than the city's international port, itself one of the largest in the world. Although the sector's workforce diminished dramatically in the postwar period and then again especially in recent decades, as the industry came to be relocated in India and elsewhere, the sector nonetheless constituted 5 percent to 8 percent of Belgium's exports throughout the twentieth century, and it continues to play a key role in the national economy.[11]

The economic importance of the diamond sector ensured those involved in it (Jews and non-Jews alike) enjoyed a favorable position vis-à-vis the local and national governments.[12] For newcomers, in particular, this was an invaluable advantage. Immigrants who had previously been active in diamonds usually encountered significantly fewer problems in obtaining residence and working permits. In order not to hinder the unique workings of this sector—where, for example, deals are typically sealed by a handshake and a spoken word (*mazal*, or *mazal un brokhe*)—the government tempered its control and oversight of the sector's bookkeeping, adherence to work laws, and so on. The importance of the sector became especially clear during World War I, when, due to the lack of rough supply and because many Jews in the local industry were of Russian nationality, the Antwerp diamond industry left the country and resettled elsewhere, primarily in the unoccupied Netherlands and in London. After the war, Antwerp struggled to regain its leading position. Governmental officials and those who remained in the sector worked together to convince the diamond diaspora to return to the city. Pull factors, from a combination of private and official governmental initiatives, included a wage increase of 33 percent; the guarantee of Belgian citizenship to non-Belgian diamond dealers; and, for those who lacked start-up capital, a return bonus and rough supply at competitive prices.[13] As will be discussed later in this chapter, these circumstances and measures were not forgotten at the time of World War II.

Factors that attracted Jews from various backgrounds to the diamond business in Antwerp included the government's flexible attitude towards the sector, the fact that the diamond sector did not present language problems, and the assurance that jobs in the sector not only could be learned quickly, without necessity of any special higher diploma, but would provide stable income within a short time. That the newcomers offered a source of inexpensive, nonunionized labor and often worked unofficially likely played a role as well. Moreover, the business was a "closed" one in the sense that a solidly credible introduction by family and/or friends or a recommendation (especially a written one) played a critical role. Thus, ethnic solidarity has always contributed significantly to helping Jews enter the sector in Antwerp. Of course, such networks did not guarantee an immigrant's success. As Esther Kreitman describes in her novel *Brilyantn*, "The errand boys with long beards had to deliver the goods, while nostalgically remembering the time when they had arrived in Antwerp with their dowry in their pockets, full of hopes of becoming rich. But, having no talent, they were soon fleeced in the Bourse or at the Club. And now this is how they made their livelihood. . . . They called out their miserable wares as if they were chanting from the *Gemara*."[14] The overall story, however, was one of success and upward economic mobility. For Orthodox immigrants and their descendants the sector was appealing for yet another reason: working hours and workplaces were adaptable and thus adjustable to the requirements of observant Orthodox Jewish life. The regular working week in Belgium at this time was from Monday through Saturday, but the diamond sector was flexible in its adherence to any sort of state-mandated scheduling: diamond cleavers, for example, could work anytime and anywhere.[15] Likewise, the economic possibilities facilitating an Orthodox lifestyle—along with the already established Orthodox facilities in the city—attracted Orthodox Jews to the Belgian port town, and a sizable, well-developed Orthodox religious life developed there. Indeed, throughout the modern period, all state-recognized and subsidized Jewish religious life in Antwerp has (officially) fallen under the denomination "Orthodox" (unlike in Brussels, for example, where a liberal community has been state-recognized and subsidized since the 1990s). The oldest community was officially recognized in 1816, when the city was under Dutch rule (1815–1830). Two other communities were officially recognized in 1910. Along with official religious communities, private prayer houses and study facilities appeared and flourished from the last quarter of the nineteenth century onwards. By the eve of World War II at least eight Hassidic groups had settled in the city. This was quite remarkable, especially for a western European city whose Jewish community, although itself one of the largest in western Europe, constituted only a small (and minority) portion of the local population.[16] However, these developments should not lead one to believe that every Jew in Antwerp adhered to observant Orthodoxy. Indeed, the city was also home to a vibrant leftist (Zionist and Communist) nonreligious Jewish life, as well as to Jewish workers' unions, sports clubs, cultural organizations, and other such groups. This variety in Jewish life gave rise to a multilingual, varied Jewish press.[17] Official communal Jewish religious life, however, adhered to Orthodox standards.

The Return of the Diamond Sector After World War II: Its Socioeconomic Evolution and Consequences

The Second Antwerp Diamond Diaspora

In early 1940, leading figures in the Antwerp diamond industry, along with Antwerp and Belgian governmental bodies began preparing for the evacuation of the sector in case of a new conflict. Two evacuation plans soon lay on the table: one direction was London, the other, France. The first was preferred by Antwerp's mayor, the Socialist Camille Huysmans, and by the Antwerp diamond organizations with predominantly Jewish membership, especially because Ernest Oppenheimer, of the Diamond Trading Company (DTC), had guaranteed adequate supply of rough diamonds and offered assistance for refugee aid efforts (especially housing). (The DTC coordinated sales and distribution of rough diamonds for De Beers, and thus was a key rough supplier in the international diamond sector.) Nonetheless, the other scenario, which was supported by, among others, the Ministry of Economic Affairs in Brussels and the main extraction company of the time, the Société Générale de Belgique, Forminière, prevailed. The exact reasons for the choice of Cognac, France, for the destination for the sector's relocation remain unclear. The actual evacuation, however, soon became a disaster, and the Antwerp diamond diaspora spread in multiple directions, including to Brazil, Cuba, the United States, the United Kingdom, Palestine, and, for some, back to Antwerp. This dispersal of the city's diamond industry affected power balances in the wider Jewish world and in the international diamond industry.[18]

Among those in management positions in the diamond sector, two figures in particular came into prominence during the German occupation, namely Romi Goldmuntz and Herman (Gedalia) Schamisso. They were close friends with Mayor Huysmans, and the three worked together to relocate as many Antwerp diamond people, from management and the workforce, as possible to London, in the hopes of keeping Antwerp's diamond sector alive. Who were these three men? Camille Huysmans (1871–1968) was a Socialist politician and freemason; he started his political career as a Brussels city councillor (1908–1921) and was mayor of Antwerp from 1933 until 1940, and again from 1944 until 1946. Both before and after the war, he served as president of the Belgian Parliament, of which he was a member from 1910 until 1965 (an exceptionally long time for Belgian politics). Huysmans was prime minister from 1946 to 1947 and minister of education from 1947 to 1949. During World War II, he was the president of the Office Parlementaire Belge, a nonofficial organization that united members of the country's Parliament-in-exile in London. Despite his advanced age, Huysmans remained active in politics until well after World War II.

Benjamin Remi (Romi) Goldmuntz (1882–1960) moved as a young child from Krakau, his birthplace, to Antwerp in 1888. He began cutting diamonds at age fifteen and worked his way up in the sector. He spent World War I in

London and the Netherlands. During the interwar period, he and his brother Léopold ran a firm, which thrived, and the Goldmuntz brothers became two of Antwerp's most important—if not the most important—diamond dealers and managers. Their firm also operated offices in Shanghai and Tianjin (Tien-Tsin), New York, Amsterdam, and London. They were important networkers, working with both Jews and non-Jews (the managers in China were non-Jewish Belgians, for example). The experiences of the Goldmuntz brothers and similar figures in the Antwerp diamond industry underscore Trivellato's premise concerning the "familiarity of strangers" and the ways that Jews have built their trading networks according to the needs of specific situations.[19] Romi Goldmuntz received Belgian nationality in 1926, four years after submitting his request.[20] Léopold Goldmuntz moved to New York the same year, where he became Huysmans's main councillor for diamond-related affairs. Romi, who continued the business on his own in Antwerp, was among the most important DTC *sightholders* (a company on the DTC's list of authorized bulk purchasers of rough diamonds). During World War II, with Romi in London and Léopold in New York, the Goldmuntz brothers had unrivaled connections in each city and elsewhere. Among the most important for the revival of Antwerp's diamond sector proved to be their friendship and contacts with Ernest Oppenheimer of the DTC.[21]

The third figure in this story was Herman (Gedalia) Schamisso (1889–1957), a respected diamond dealer of Russian origin who moved to Belgium in 1909. Like Romi Goldmuntz, he had spent World War I in the Netherlands and received Belgian nationality in the interwar period, in 1930. Schamisso, a practicing Orthodox Jew, was actively engaged in myriad aspects of Jewish communal life (Jewish social welfare, the religious community, and so on), and through his charisma, he was able to help bring about greater unity in Antwerp's Jewish life and its wartime diaspora.[22] In their individual and combined efforts to protect and preserve the city's diamond sector, these three figures successfully merged political, economic and religious contacts and networks.

At the initiative of Huysmans, the three men formed the Correspondence Office for Diamond Industry (COFDI) in late October 1940. COFDI's main goal was to maintain the status quo—that is, to make arrangements such that after the war, Antwerp would regain its leading position in the international diamond industry. In practice, they worked on keeping the diamond diaspora together—or at least keeping its members in touch with each other—during the war. They also worked to prepare for the diamond diaspora's return to Antwerp, as soon as conditions allowed, by securing Antwerp's rough supply, infrastructure, and the return of the diamond sector's management and workforce.[23] As a politician, Huysmans had clear reasons for being involved in this endeavor, not least of which was the economic importance of the sector for his city and country, as well as the significant number of jobs it created directly and indirectly for the local population of Antwerp and its surroundings. The Antwerp Socialist Party could not afford to lose this vital employment base. For Goldmuntz and Schamisso the motivation for establishing COFDI was somewhat different. They feared competition from other diamond centers that were rapidly developing during the war years, especially in New York, Palestine, Brazil, and Cuba. The vacuum that Antwerp's absence caused in the overall, international sector was quickly filled by other diamond centers, and this led to worries among those who wished for the postwar revival of Antwerp. The most effective means to guarantee their city's postwar position in the diamond world was to control the rough supply. Goldmuntz in particular was in a strong position to do so, given his friendship with Oppenheimer. At the same time, the British were also concerned about losing their control over rough supply[24] and were thus eager to talk to COFDI, which connected Belgian officials and people within the diamond diaspora who were interested in maintaining the industry's prewar balances of power.

COFDI united three individuals of great vision, networks, and power; together they made preparations and decisions at a time when nobody could have foreseen the developments and outcomes of the war. While Huysmans was a well-connected important politician, neither Goldmuntz nor Schamisso was a politician. Goldmuntz was, however, extremely adept at establishing business contacts and negotiating agreements—although unfortunately for historians, his way of doing business was almost entirely through oral contact. Consequently, we have no written documentation of his efforts, only information from interviews (gathered years after the fact) and the outcomes of negotiations. Residing at the Mayfair Hotel in London, Goldmuntz led the life of a bon vivant and frequently organized and attended social receptions, festivities, and other such get-togethers. Goldmuntz's tactics of informal social networking and negotiations were highly successful.[25] As he explained to Schamisso, (as quoted by Schamisso's son, Maurice, who related the exchange to me): "Look, negotiations and conversations with officials are best conducted over a good meal. Come along with me, and we will be able to stretch our point."[26] Maurice Schamisso further explained: "Romi

Goldmuntz and his wife had no children, they were very wealthy, he knew all the places and he spent the money. . . . My mother [an Orthodox woman] was desperately scared of my late father attending all these dinners, having fun after dinners, going to nightclubs, and she was trying to talk him out of going. So, he only went once in a while. Because of that, my late father was very much less—I would put it—in the thick of things, so some parts which he was missing, he only heard secondhand from Romi."[27] Another useful source of information for Schamisso was his youngest daughter, who worked as a secretary in the Office Parlementaire Belge in London.[28] Schamisso thereby profited from two valuable sources of secondhand information. Connections with Antwerp's Jewish diaspora, which included many people from the diamond industry, were ensured from the end of 1943, with the founding of the Belgian Jewish Committee (BJC) in London. Schamisso and Goldmuntz were, respectively, the president and the treasurer of the committee.[29] Of the three central persons in the COFDI, it was Schamisso who formed a direct link between diamonds and Orthodoxy. Together, Huysmans, Goldmuntz, and Schamisso formed a masterful network, with negotiations centered on the three of them.They knew and trusted each other, and each facilitated a separate but essential component of the mission to preserve relationships in the diamond diaspora and thus to safeguard the pre-war position of Antwerp as a diamond center after the war, even, as will be seen, when negotiations were hardly easy or straightforward.

Negotiations to Maintain the Status Quo

Indeed, the COFDI's negotiations to prepare for the return of the diamond sector to Antwerp after World War II with the Belgian government-in-exile in London were initially not especially successful. There was a great deal of reticence on the part of the Belgian ministers in London, in part owing to their tense relationship with Huysmans, who had established the Office Parlementaire Belge in London before the government members had arrived. Although this parliamentary office never gained official status, it did remain active for the duration of the war. It was not until July 1942 that the Belgian government-in-exile followed the COFDI's recommendations to ensure rough supply to Antwerp after the war and to stay in touch with the diamond diaspora in preparation for repatriation to Belgium. The organization received an official mandate from the Belgian government, the British Ministry of Supply, and the Diamond Trading Company to prepare for the renewal of the postwar diamond industry in Antwerp. Negotiations were conducted with Forminière, Dicorp (Diamond Corporation Ltd., a subsidiary of De Beers), and the British authorities, among others, to maintain the contracts for rough supply that had been in place before the war. The COFDI also managed to have diamond people (regardless of nationality) recognized as a special category for immediate repatriation. Indeed, the postwar rehabilitation of the diamond industry in the former German-occupied territories became a "declared war aim of the United Nations." Governmental officials (ambassadors, ministers, and so on) began communicating about these intentions with the Antwerp diamond diaspora, primarily in London and New York, in hopes that the sector's management—many of whom were now thriving outside of Antwerp—would be willing to return to Antwerp after its liberation.[30]

For much of the Antwerp diamond diaspora in America, especially for the segments in New York, returning to Antwerp had largely ceased to be part of their personal or professional plans. The Antwerp diaspora in New York, being at such great distance from their former "home," had quickly developed its own communal and organizational life. In 1942, they founded a Belgian Jewish Representative Committee (BJRC, discussed below) in 1942, and unlike the Antwerp diaspora in London, Jewish diamond immigrants in New York established their own congregation and burial society (the Orthodox Kehillath Morya) and their own diamond exchange, the Diamond Center. The Antwerp diamond business-in-exile and Jewish Orthodoxy were strongly intertwined. As Ethel Blitz, a member of the Kehillath Morya and of the Diamond Dealers' Club of New York, remarked: "You know, the history of [Kehillath] Morya is really the history of the Antwerp diamond community of New York."[31] Kehillath Morya was initially led by Rabbi Brodt, who had been the rabbi of the Shomre Hadas community in Antwerp until he fled Belgium. Brodt was Mizrachi, albeit of Hassidic background, and in this sense embodied major characteristics of the Antwerp Jewish refugees. This expatriate community, which counted among its members some of the more affluent diamond merchants of New York,[32] was nonetheless a group of immigrants from the same origin, like the typical *landsmanshaftn* (associations of Jewish immigrants from the same city, region, or country). Two members of the Kehilla, who had left Antwerp for New York, told me: "*Old Antwerp was here.*"[33] Already in November 1943, the *New York World-Telegram* had declared "They're Here to Stay" in the headline of an article about the Antwerp diamond merchants then operating in the city.[34]

In 1945, the diamond business in New York was flourishing, providing at least 6,000 people with jobs, as compared to about 300 in the prewar period; likewise, the United States now held 70 to 80 percent of the world's diamond production.[35] By the end of May 1945, 70 percent of the members of the New York Diamond Center were from Antwerp. A significant proportion of this immigrant group either did not return to Antwerp after the war or partially retained their businesses in New York. Indeed, for many diamond companies, which were often family businesses, the period after World War II was when they began operating branches in both New York and Antwerp, a strategy that created stable trading networks.

Antwerpians in New York were not the only ones unsure and unconvinced about a possible return to Antwerp. Even after Antwerp's liberation on September 4, 1944, the city remained under V-bomb attacks from October 25, 1944, until May 1945, which made immediate return of the diamond diaspora impossible. When relocation to Antwerp finally became a feasible option, stories of wartime discrimination, spoliation, persecution, and annihilation of Jews in Belgium and elsewhere had begun reaching the outside world. Such information led even the London Jewish diamond diaspora to question whether returning to Antwerp was advisable. Moreover, the Belgian government was not especially helpful in facilitating repatriation of Jews who were not active in diamonds.[36] The BJC's aim had always been to help all Jews who had legally resided in Belgium before the war. Clearly, however, the government's intentions were—as Trivellato also states in regards to crosscultural trade in the early modern period—purely economic. Among the general public, there was little sympathy for the persecuted Jewish victims; for the government, the main goal was to bring back the diamond business (and therefore its "diamond Jews"), not Belgian's prewar Jewish population. To this end, the government adopted measures intended to encourage the diamond diaspora to return, including tax exemptions and return visas, as well as assurances of a minimum of state control, full permission for importing and exporting, and various other exceptions and accommodations concerning financial arrangements.[37] Moreover, Belgian officials paid visits to the Belgian Jewish organizations in London and New York to convince them of the goodwill of the Belgian authorities and local population. These officials sought to reassure the diamond management about issues concerning repatriation and working conditions, as well as the stance of governmental bodies towards war crimes against Jews and their attitude concerning anti-Semitism and restitution and compensation policies of goods spoliated during the war. Negative rumors concerning Antwerp's safety and suitability for returning Jews were addressed.[38] As one representative stated, albeit with a considerable degree of exaggeration, "The population as a whole is eagerly waiting to welcome back their Jewish friends."[39] It is telling, however, that only in the diamond sector did compensation and restitution cover most of the wartime losses.[40] Most other Jewish businesses, including Hirsch & Cie., a huge department store in Brussels, would struggle for decades before receiving minimal compensation.[41]

Probably the most decisive factor in the revival of Antwerp's diamond sector was Goldmuntz's effectiveness in arranging Antwerp's rough supply, which allowed for the restoration of the market after the war. Practically the entire London diamond diaspora returned to Antwerp, as well as diamond merchants who had gone elsewhere, such as Cuba. The return from New York was only limited; however, those who remained there, along with those whose return from other places was delayed, provided the Antwerp Orthodox community an asset beyond value: financial backers and support from abroad for the reconstruction of religious facilities and support for Orthodox needs, at a time when international Jewish organizations could generally offer only emergency aid.

The Reconstruction and Rise of Orthodoxy in the Immediate Postwar Period: Diamonds, Networks, and Politics

By the end of the occupation, only a small number of Jews remained in Antwerp, mostly in hiding; officially, the city was *judenrein*. The Jewish resistance was a diverse group of mostly (but not exclusively) leftists; at least one Orthodox Zionist (Mizrachi), Josef Sterngold, was also involved.[42] They were the first to restart official Jewish life in the city by establishing a central office for information and registration. They also installed a kitchen, dormitories, a clothing supply service, and other services in the buildings of the Tachkemoni School (which had been preserved during the war, having been used as a school by a Flemish collaboration movement). Romi Goldmuntz and other Jews who had survived the war in London managed to visit Antwerp in late 1944. Their reports on the local situation informed not only the BJC in London but also the BJRC in New York and the Antwerp diaspora elsewhere. These updates caused shockwaves throughout the diaspora as the consequences of the German occupation and anti-Jewish policies became painfully clear. The diminishing uncertainty about the fates of so many fellow Jews from Antwerp, combined with information from the Allied forces, gradually enabled fuller understanding of the war's impact on Antwerp's Jewish population. Such realizations led not only to emergency help to the survivors: Among the first actions undertaken by the BJC in London was to donate money for the ritual burial of Antwerp Jews who had been interred during the war in places like gardens or in non-Jewish cemeteries and without Jewish religious rites. Schamisso urged for the rebuilding of Orthodox institutions and reinstallation of Orthodox rituals. The BJC committee, comprised mostly of Antwerp Jewish diamond merchants in exile, donated substantially and generously to these ends.[43] The BJRC in New York—the other major group of Antwerp Jewish diamond merchant exiles—sponsored the establishment of an Orthodox Jewish orphanage in Antwerp, which the Belgian Jewish aid agency in Brussels had not wished to fund. On October 5, 1944, just a month after the liberation of the city, Antwerp Jews opened a Jewish day school. However, like all other Antwerp schools, it was obliged to close from October 25, 1944, until May 1945, due to the German bombardments on the city. When schools in Antwerp were allowed to reopen, the two prewar Orthodox Jewish day schools restarted their activities and were sponsored by, among other means, money collections from the Antwerp diamond milieu in New York.[44]

The fact that these diamond diaspora milieus not only had remained active but had been doing good business during the war afforded postwar Antwerp with the sort of support and benefactors that few other decimated and devastated communities in Europe could rely on. The expatriate diamond milieus from Antwerp supported their former city through their respective Jewish committees, namely the BJC and BJRC (rather than through the diamond exchanges), through funds collected by eminent people from the expatriate community (such as rabbis who lived in exile), and through individual initiatives and donations.[45] These sources of support also suggest why not all forms of Antwerp's diverse and colorful prewar Jewish life were able to reestablish themselves after the war. Nearly everyone among the London and New York committees—who could be labeled the "elite" of the Antwerp diaspora—had held leading positions in either Antwerp's prewar Jewish social welfare or its Orthodox religious life and thus had a significant head start in reconstructing and reviving their activities in Antwerp. Other groups, such as the Communists and Socialists, had far fewer, if any, resources with which to restart, and generally did not survive through the postwar period.

Moreover, via these networks the Antwerp Jewish elite enjoyed beneficial connections to international Jewish aid organizations after the war. The most important of these was the American Jewish Joint Distribution Committee (JDC). Through its (Orthodox) diaspora, Antwerp managed to reorient the JDC's initial plans for relief and aid in Belgium so as to receive far more financial support than initially foreseen.[46] Similarly, through its connections in New York, Antwerp was engaged by other international Jewish organizations to help challenge JDC's monopoly on overseas welfare. As the JDC aimed to be the central Jewish overseas aid organization, it sometimes acquiesced against its own principles to Antwerp's requests. I illustrate these negotiations via three examples: the Belgian Jewish Representative Committee (BJRC) and its associations with the World Jewish Congress (WJC); the Comité Centrale Israélite pour la Réorganisation de la Vie Religieuse en Belgique (CCI) and its connections to the Union of Orthodox Rabbis; and the Save-a-Child Foundation/Children's Salvation. Each organization dealt with the education of Jewish children (for example, through orphanages and schools). Such educational endeavours constituted a highly sensitive point, as this new generation would determine the outlook and future of the Jewish world. The first two evidence Antwerp's success in negotiations; the third offers a counterexample.[47]

The JDC aimed to have one centralized organization in each of its countries of operation; this organization would coordinate the JDC's aid to that country. For Belgium, the JDC had opted to have its base in Brussels, since, at the moment of the liberation and even until today, this was, and is, the city with the highest number of Jewish inhabitants in Belgium. Antwerp became a JDC subdivision, dependent on the main Brussels office.[48] This was very much to the disliking of Antwerp, not least because until World War II, it had the country's largest Jewish population and because during the interwar period, the Antwerp Jewish community had established a tradition of centralized welfare unique for western Europe at the time (neither Brussels nor Amsterdam nor Paris had succeeded in such efforts). Moreover, Antwerp's centralized social welfare tradition respected Orthodox principles, which was in stark contrast to the pragmatic attitudes and the mostly nonreligious tendencies (or at least non-Orthodox tendencies) of the Brussels office and of the majority of the JDC. Difficulties quickly arose. For example, in the view of many in the Antwerp community, it was problematic that *frum* Orthodox men from Antwerp were now supposed to discuss the needs for Orthodox facilities with young, often unmarried, nonreligious Jewish female JDC representatives, who usually held professionally pragmatic attitudes towards such ventures.[49] Part of the solution to achieve its goals lay in appealing to the Antwerp diamond diaspora contacts and Orthodox networks in the United States for their support and cooperation.

When Antwerp sought to open a Zionist-Orthodox orphanage and to have the orphanage's children attend the (Mizrachi) Tachkemoni school, the Brussels office, especially wary of the children being sent to a Jewish day school, declined to offer financial support.[50] The Antwerp committee complained about this and appealed for help from the Belgian Jewish Representative Committee (BJRC). This committee, which after the war also operated under the name "Relief for Belgian Jews," was based in New York, and most of its members were from Antwerp. Whereas in 1942, seventeen of the twenty-six members were from Antwerp, by 1946, more Antwerpians had joined, including Léopold Goldmuntz (Romi Goldmuntz's brother) and other well-known individuals from Antwerp's Orthodox circles, such as Chaim Finkelstein and M. Ratzersdorfer. These three figures had been eminent leaders in the prewar community (Zionist and Orthodox) and were involved in the diamond business.[51] Finkelstein was "a wealthy and extremely Orthodox activist" and an active member of Kehillath Morya (discussed earlier), as was Ratzersdorfer.[52] After the liberation in Antwerp, this New York–based organization sought to help cover the religious communities' deficit and to aid in the reparations of its buildings.[53] The BJRC was affiliated with the World Jewish Congress (WJC) and contacted it (as did other Antwerpians, on a personal basis) with requests. The BJRC wired money via WJC to Antwerp in order to open the previously mentioned Zionist-Orthodox orphanage.[54] The JDC (which had refused to fund the orphanage) described the BJRC as "a *landsmanshaft* type of organization primarily interested in the Antwerp Jewish Community. They have sent supplies through the American Relief for Belgium and have also sent funds to the Antwerp Committee. The group, although affiliated with the World Jewish Congress, claims it is non-political in its activities. They complain that the Antwerp community is receiving a very minor part of the relief which is being sent into Belgium by the JDC."[55]

The WJC's secretary and the head of the BJRC was Léon Kubowitzki (Aryeh Kubovy), a Zionist, Socialist, and personal friend of Mayor Huysmans. During the interwar period, Kubowitzki had established himself in Antwerp as a lawyer and become a Socialist councillor (thereby facilitating his contacts with Huysmans).[56] The Orthodox elements in Antwerp did not play a key role in Kubowitzki's efforts and negotiations; however, Antwerp's Jewish and Socialist networks, combined with WJC politics, certainly did. The request from Antwerp to support the orphanage played into the hands of the WJC, as it was seeking to challenge the JDC's monopoly of overseas Jewish welfare. For example, the WJC had earlier tried to establish its Child Care Committee as the central organizing body for all such groups in Europe (by, among other measures, establishing a Jewish Foster Parents Plan for Europe).[57] For an organization to become a key player in overseas welfare, it needed recognition and financial support from within the United States. Therefore, making a favorable impression on the diamond milieu in New York, which included many people from Antwerp, was crucial for the WJC. As Kubowitzki wrote to his brother Isaac, in Brussels: "Has it not been possible yet to establish an Antwerp committee that is sufficiently representative to impress the Antwerpians here [in New York]?"[58]

However, realizing that the JDC was willing to grant Antwerp both financial self-determination (that is, by rendering Antwerp accounts directly to the JDC rather than via its Brussels office) and the freedom to organize the orphanage according to their own (Orthodox) standards, Antwerp agreed to work with the JDC. The Antwerpians in New York as well as those in Antwerp soon had the orphanage they had sought, regardless of the WJC's financial support. Indeed, the orphanage's letterhead would read: "Home for Jewish Children, Maurice Finkelstein Foundation, rebuilt by: Belgian Jewish Committee, NY, assisted by: American Joint Distribution Committee." The WJC, through which the BJRC had wired its financial support, was not mentioned, and disappeared from the situation, despite trying to stay involved in the case.[59] Kubowitzki and the WJC would never succeed in becoming a major player in overseas welfare, and its Foster Parents Plan was subsumed into the JDC in April 1947.[60] For an organization or individual to become a major player in such matters, political and Jewish connections alone were insufficient, unless they included abundant Orthodox (or at least Orthodox-respecting) connections.

Another organization, the Comité Centrale Israélite pour la Réorganisation de la Vie Religieuse en Belgique (CCI), similarly disagreed with the JDC's policies and practices. The CCI founded two Orthodox children's homes in Antwerp and one in Brussels; it was financed by Vaad Hahatzala/Rescue Children,[61] an organization founded by the Union of Orthodox Rabbis in the United States. The JDC, as part of its efforts to further unify overseas Jewish welfare under its lead and management, sought to incorporate these homes. This was achieved after negotiations with the Orthodox leadership in the

United States during the course of 1947–1948. However, after strong protests, those in charge of the CCI homes managed to remain independent from the JDC's Brussels office. They instead received money directly from the JDC's Paris office, which exerted little control over the orphanage. The CCI remained in charge of the orphanage, thereby preserving its Orthodox character. This was a fairly exceptional arrangement, and may have been connected to the fact that the Antwerp CCI leader, Jozef Rottenberg, was a representative for the Union of Orthodox Rabbis.[62] The history of the JDC's takeover of Orthodox homes in France evidences the extent to which the CCI's ability to retain control of its Antwerp orphanage was exceptional. As Maud Mandel details,

> Representatives of the Agudath Israel . . . complained that the Joint [JDC] had chosen to "liquidate" their *maisons d'enfants* [children's homes] and to distribute the resident children into nonreligious or even non-Jewish homes. While not necessarily hostile to Orthodox groups, Joint officials sought to ensure the greatest efficiency in their operations. By supporting the agencies that they dubbed most successful—in this case nonreligious homes—the Joint proved uninterested in the sectarian divisions that characterized Jewish life in France. Those agencies unwilling to accept Joint guidelines or that proved less capable of meeting its standards of operations ultimately lost financial support."[63]

Yet not every Orthodox initiative could count on general support in Antwerp. For example, the Save-a-Child Foundation, an organization affiliated with Agudath Israel in New York, was founded shortly after the war to trace Jewish children who were still living in the non-Jewish environments in which they had survived the war. Its main overseas office was in Brussels, but it had an especially active Antwerp department. When the organization's funding ran out in the early 1950s, it was two Orthodox diamond-trading families (Finkelstein and Bande), both of whom had connections in Antwerp and New York, who took over the organization and renamed it Children's Salvation. Their requests for support from the JDC never garnered anything more than what they called "hush money"—that is, small sums that did not help their work significantly but that nonetheless precluded them from telling the outside world that they had not received support from the JDC. The JDC's financial assistance was provided via the Antwerp Jewish social welfare agency, which itself did not desire any official connection to the Children's Salvation's actions. (The reason for this distancing was that, by the time Children's Salvation had initiated its project in the 1950s, the children in question were already teenagers or older and had lived most of their lives, or at least ten years, in non-Jewish environments.) The officially organized Jewish life in Antwerp was following Orthodox standards, yet this ultra-Orthodox initiative could find only small-scale support. This is also the likeliest reason why the organization received only so-called "hush money" instead of an actual working budget.[64]

Nevertheless, the Orthodox mainstream, financed by Orthodox or Orthodoxy-respecting people such as Schamisso and Goldmuntz, caused an avalanche effect with regard to other, more strictly Orthodox initiatives. Such initiatives, despite not always being to the liking of this mainstream, usually did eventually receive financial support. The successful efforts of the Orthodox mainstream to convince the JDC to financially support Antwerp's Orthodox Jewish day schools—after years of refusal from the JDC, on grounds that Jewish children could attend the city's public schools for free—resulted, by the end of the 1950s, in the JDC (together with the Claims Conference) extending such support even to Hassidic schools.[65] This is further evidence of how Antwerp's Jewish life after World War II increasingly came to center around Orthodoxy.

"Jerusalem of the North"

After World War II, the three prewar (officially Orthodox) religious communities in Antwerp revived. Thanks in large part to the existence of a wide range of Orthodox facilities in the city—including kosher shops, Jewish day schools, yeshivas, and an eruv—and to the better chances of finding work (especially in the diamond sector) compatible with an Orthodox lifestyle, Antwerp once again attracted Orthodox Jews, among whom were numerous Hassidic groups (mostly of Polish or Hungarian origin). Jacques Gutwirth notes that what had been a small number of Hassidim from various groups in Antwerp in the immediate postwar period soon expanded dramatically.[66] By 1955, there existed at least nine private prayer houses in the city, five of which were maintained by Hassidic groups (Belz, Ger, Satmar, Tschotkow, and Wischnitz, respectively). In 1990, more than one third of all Hassidic groups worldwide were represented in Antwerp. No other western European city in the postwar period has been home to as many Hassidic groups or counted as high a percentage of Hassidic Jews among its total Jewish population.[67] This vibrant Hassidic life, as Gutwirth explains, was significantly enabled by the presence in Antwerp of the non-Hassidic majority: for example, most Hassidic children attended the Orthodox day schools; there was a well-developed Jewish social aid system, as well as burial societies and other such institutions; and the Jewish presence in the diamond sector allowed for easier introduction into its businesses. This economic factor was of key importance, especially for Hassidic groups, as their religious practices and observances considerably restricted their choice of professions. Moreover, the liberal atmosphere and religious freedom of the Belgian state afforded a welcoming climate for the creation and management of Hassidic institutions. Likewise, the Belgian social and legal system, in determining financial support and tax deductions per the number of children in a household, was a source of considerable support for traditionally large Hassidic families.[68] At the same time, this growing Hassidic presence strengthened and expanded the Orthodox infrastructure and tincture of Antwerp's Jewish life.[69]

Parallel to the evolution through the twentieth century of the growing importance of Orthodoxy in Jewish Antwerp was the emergence of Jewish day schools. These schools, which even before the war had constituted an important indication of the character of Jewish life in the city, flourished again after World War II. In 1941, before Jewish students were banned from non-Jewish schools, two Orthodox day schools (one Mizrachi, one non-Zionist Orthodox) had included about 30 percent of the Jewish children present in the city.[70] The schools closed during the war, but reopened shortly after the liberation of the city; other Orthodox, mainly Hassidic, initiatives also commenced and developed successfully. By the end of the 1950s, enrollment in Jewish day schools was estimated to include 80 percent to 90 percent of the city's Jewish children.[71] In comparison, not even 20 percent of Jewish children in France attended Jewish day schools during the same period. In the 1960s, the JDC estimated that 40 percent of Jewish children in Europe received Jewish education.[72] Today, Antwerp counts, besides the various facilities of the three state-recognized religious communities, about thirty prayer houses, of which about twenty belong to Hassidic groups. There are eleven Jewish day schools, and all facilities necessary for leading an observant Orthodox Jewish life are available.[73] Such an Orthodox revival is not necessarily exceptional in western Europe, where other Orthodox communities exist there. But the extent to which Orthodoxy has come to characterize Antwerp's Jewish life and the timing of the establishment of these Orthodox facilities in the immediate postwar period are remarkable and unique. I argue that the reconstruction of Orthodoxy and its postwar development are a consequence of the Antwerp diamond diaspora's negotiations, networks, and contacts during and immediately after World War II.

The leftist elements, which had been important during the war and immediately after the liberation, were soon removed from leading positions in Antwerp's Jewish community life. Similar diminishments occurred in other Jewish communities, for example, in the Netherlands and in Vienna.[74] Even when these leftist Jewish elements sought to reestablish themselves in Antwerp, they generally remained frustrated in their efforts. This was partly because of the decimation of Antwerp's prewar Jewish population and changes in socioeconomic circumstances. I would argue that it was largely due to developments in religious and business practices in the diamond business and to their interconnectedness. Judith Tydor Baumel's observations about New York—including the informal connection there between the religious community's solvency and the fluctuations of the diamond business, the fact that all issues in the Kehillath Morya were resolved in a manner typical of the diamond community, and that various members (and board members) of the Kehillath Morya held leading (and quite wealthy) positions in the diamond business—also apply to Antwerp.[75] The non-Orthodox tendencies in Antwerp, in contrast, did not have effective access to such financing or adequate connections to such resources.

During the postwar years, non-Orthodox Jews in Antwerp either became official members of the city's Orthodox communities and began sending their children to Jewish day schools (though they did not necessarily adjust much in their private daily lifestyles), or they disappeared into general society, thereby becoming untraceable for researchers. Some moved out of Antwerp, very often to Brussels, where a nonreligious and leftist Jewish life existed alongside more religious tendencies. The secular Centre Communautaire Laïc Juif (Jewish Community Center, or CCLJ) was founded there in 1959, by one such migrant from Antwerp, the diamond dealer David Susskind, who had been born (in 1925) into an Antwerp Orthodox family.[76] In contrast, non-Orthodox newcomers to Antwerp were now soon immersed in Orthodox life. Newly arrived Jewish children were sent to Jewish day schools, with special teachers assigned to help them catch up in their Jewish education so as to be at the level of their peers. In 1959, the two largest Jewish day schools in Antwerp asked the Claims Conference for financial aid to pay for these extra teachers.[77] For the adults in the community, where such a high concentration of them were active in diamonds, Orthodoxy was similarly encompassing. In the postwar years, the diamond sector began to display respect for the Orthodox calendar, for example, by closing on Friday afternoons and on Saturdays. Jewish communal and business life became almost completely intertwined.[78] However, this did not preclude business deals between Orthodox Jews and non-Jews, or, as it was explained to me: *mekhutn is mekhutn, gesheft is gesheft* (family is family, business is business).[79] The industry's first and foremost goal is to generate economic profits, and so it moves to where cheap labor and favorable governmental attitudes towards the business (that is, little control) are available. This explains the industry's turn in recent years towards Mumbay (for trade) and Surat (for industry).[80] As Trivellato's research concerning the early modern Period has demonstrated, Jews have time and again entered crosscultural trades, especially in places where few if any Jews resided.[81] Indeed, this is key to understanding how Indian diamond merchants have been able to break into the "Jewish monopoly" in Antwerp's diamond trade. Sarah Stein's observation—that Jews were hugely overrepresented in the global exchange of luxury goods because they were members of diasporas, with contacts spanning oceanic, cultural, and political divides and holding marketable and portable skills through which they could fill mercantile and industrial niches—is similarly valid for Antwerp throughout the twentieth century.[82] The case of the Antwerp diamond industry offers a sector that, rather than disappearing (as did the ostrich feather trade, in which Jewish merchants had been similarly prominent), saw other cities and other minorities become increasingly successful in the industry and begin to take over leading positions.

One fact, however, is central to understanding the specific Antwerp Jewish setting, and it adds extra perspective and new insight about Jews as global and intercultural traders. This concerns the consequences of a trading network in which Orthodox and Orthodoxy-respecting Jews hold key positions. In the Antwerp diamond sector, Orthodox Jews distinguish between Jewish and non-Jewish work relations. Consequently, anyone who seeks to engage in a business partnership with an observant Jew in Antwerp must understand that Orthodox rules will need to be observed to a certain extent. However, such rules apply differently to non-Jews than to non-observant or less-observant Jews. For example, a non-Jewish partner can work on Shabbat, provided that the day's profits go only to him and not to an observant Jewish partner. However, a Jewish business partner, even if entirely non-observant, is not be permitted to engage in company business at any point during Shabbat. He is free to do other things—play golf, for example, as such activities are his own business and are unrelated to the partnership—but having an Orthodox partner would preclude any related business deals or transactions being pursued or sealed on the Sabbath or during other similar times of prohibition. Such restrictions are a direct consequence of observant Orthodox Jews' religious practices, which prohibit them from encouraging or aiding other Jews to violate Jewish law (such violations include working or handling money on the Sabbath). Conversely, when an observant Jew works for (as opposed to partnering with) a non-observant or non-Jewish person, he must make his own arrangements by which to adhere to religious law. However, the considerable presence of Orthodox Jews in Antwerp's diamond industry has resulted in much of the sector following certain elements of strict Jewish religious life, though not necessarily out of any religious inclination. This includes the moral duty of *tsedaka*—the responsibility to donate to welfare organizations, schools, and other community needs, which has become a common practice among in the Antwerp diamond sector. Interestingly, the fact that observant Jews differentiate between Jews (observant or not) and non-Jews in their business relationships makes for a "Jewish-Jewish subgroup" within the already general "Jewishness-respecting diamond sector."[83] The consequences of this are an important additional element in our understanding of Jewish and non-Jewish economic networks and relationships.

Conclusions

Diaspora and its networks can strengthen a group's position considerably.[84] This study has sought to demonstrate how Orthodoxy in Antwerp—despite the community's devastating losses in the Holocaust—was able to reconstruct and develop itself further after World War II through its numerous contacts and business relations in the diamond sector in London, New York, and elsewhere. The community's diaspora in London prepared and ensured Antwerp's status quo as a diamond center after the war; the diaspora in New York provided Antwerp diamond dealers with important business connections and partnerships, often within family firms. This study thus confirms Sarah Stein's position that thinking about global commerce can help us better appreciate the material ties that have bonded many modern Jews to one another.[85] It also extends Stein's analysis so as to include consequences of Orthodox dominance in key positions of (a particular international segment of) this global commerce. As the main players in this story were either Orthodox or

Orthodoxy-respecting Jews, the combination of their respective economic positions and ways of being Jewish helps explain how Antwerp's Jewish life developed during the postwar period. Indeed, their success and connections during and immediately after the war made for a strong foundation on which to rebuild Orthodox Jewish institutions, at a time when much of the Jewish world had negligible means, financial and otherwise, for such endeavors. International Jewish organizations focused, understandably, on immediate emergency aid to survivors in displaced persons camps and scattered throughout Europe. Very soon, the organizations' attention and distribution of financial resources and staff were divided between the ruins of the Jewish world in Europe and the political developments in the Middle East stemming from the efforts towards establishment of a Jewish state in Palestine. Nevertheless, the Antwerp diamond milieu and its contacts in New York, as well as the politics and rivalries of international Jewish aid organizations, made it possible for Antwerp's Orthodox community to receive support for particular projects, such as Orthodox orphanages and day schools, which would likely not have been considered otherwise. Orthodox Antwerp navigated smoothly and effectively between these myriad sensibilities, interests and policy issues so as to receive what it needed and wanted.

The city's reviving diamond sector, combined with the various available and operative Orthodox facilities, became a major pull factor for other Orthodox Jews to settle in Antwerp. Indeed, by the early 1960s, Hassidic Jews constituted about 12 percent of Antwerp's total Jewish population, an especially high figure for western Europe at the time; by 2004, the figure had risen to 25 percent.[86] For observant Jews, Antwerp, with its array of Orthodox facilities and renowned diamond sector, "was like heaven."[87] Especially critical in this respect was that one could take a job in a predominantly Jewish milieu that promised a stable and sufficient income, did not require a fixed working schedule, and allowed ample time for study and prayer. The diamond industry's ups and downs, with diamond dealers finding success in business at some moments, but failure at others, was the major factor determining Jewish socioeconomic life in Antwerp from after World War II until the 1980s, when it became clear that the industry was rapidly relocating to India and elsewhere. In recent years, the sector's management has seen growing numbers of non-Jews rising through the highest positions. The effects of the diminishing impact of Jews on the business, and the severe reduction in the processing aspects of the sector (such as cutting and polishing) in Antwerp have tremendously affected Jewish life in the city. Given the high percentage of practicing Orthodox Jews, reorienting the community, in terms of its traditional jobs and employment prospects, is not an easy or simple matter. Poverty in Antwerp's Jewish community has increased markedly in recent years, and it has become unclear whether this island of Orthodoxy in western Europe will be able to survive absent its earlier established economic position in diamonds.[88]

This contribution, in endeavoring to shed light on the development of Antwerp as a major center for the international diamond sector, has discussed the importance of economic considerations in political matters, especially as related to the diamond sector's maintenance and reestablishment during and immediately after World War II. Indeed, economic considerations had high priority in the attitudes of the local Antwerp and national Belgian governments. Moreover, the economic position of the minority group examined here facilitated a favorable negotiating position, not only in a political context (interactions with political actors and organizations), but also in a Jewish context. Thus, this local study foregrounds the reality that a successful economic position does not necessarily lead to assimilation into general society. In fact, it can have the opposite effect, as seen in Antwerp, where Jewish individuals in the diamond sector, religious and nonreligious alike, as well as their non-Jewish colleagues, accommodate elements of Orthodoxy. The economic niche in the local diamond industry allows for maintenance and conservation of cultural and religious traditions. The story of Jews and economic networks is certainly not a straightforward narrative, not least because it is a global history with myriad storylines. This contribution focuses on one of these international storylines, that of a specific Orthodox diamond diaspora that succeeded, via its religious, political, and economic networks and connections, in shaping both the specifically Jewish history and the more general history of a major Western European city, throughout the twentieth century.

Chapter 10

Faith Meets Politics and Resources: Reassessing Modern Transnational Jewish Activism

Jonathan Dekel-Chen

Jews in the West have for generations mobilized transnational philanthropic efforts and political advocacy campaigns on behalf of target communities of embattled coreligionists abroad. These mobilizations for distant brethren have intersected with the ebb and flow of Jewish economic life and communal politics. Such campaigns may not have changed the course of history. In fact, many of them did not achieve their declared goals. Nevertheless, these transnational efforts have deeply impacted the communities that launched them and have altered trajectories of Jewish politics.

Scholarly discussions of these issues in relation to modern economic life tend to focus on two distant poles. At one end, some study the "heights" of philanthropy and advocacy through the biographies of prominent individuals or groups. At the other pole, there is a focus on the support networks forged by Jewish working classes and their road to political radicalization. In this way, the foci of Jewish economic history have oscillated periodically between "haves" *or* "have-nots." Using a wider-angle lens, however, one can see that philanthropy is a rare thread that connects these two socioeconomic poles.

Transnational philanthropists in the West were best characterized in the premodern era as male intercessors (*shtadlanim*, in Hebrew), usually possessed of significant wealth and political cachet in their home societies; they engaged in this activity for multiple reasons, among them to perpetuate class and ethnic divisions.[1] But starting in the mid-nineteenth century, transnational philanthropy and advocacy in the West democratized. By the mid-twentieth century the democratizing process had brought these organizations to reflect the complex social realities in their home communities, wherein the leverage that could be deployed through finance gradually gave way to the weight of public opinion. Hence, from the late 1800s the modest *pushke* at home and synagogue began to constitute a parallel, if not equal, fundraising tool in modern Jewry compared to that of the salons and social circles of Jewish elites. Focusing on the later, more contemporary end of this progression in transnational advocacy, we will examine in some depth the Soviet Jewry movement of the 1960s–1980s, a case in which the personal wealth of the activists played a much smaller role in the campaign.

Within the realm of democratized activism, it is important to note the distinction between political advocacy and lobbyism: while both require engagement with political regimes, the former is fundamentally altruistic whereas the latter is pursued for one's own benefit. Moreover, advocacy is almost always a sustained effort, not a reflexive response to sudden crises. Advocates usually attempt to influence governments, but are not directly engaged in governance.[2] Furthermore, unlike conventional charity, reconstruction, or even lobbyism, political advocacy can be practiced with relatively modest funds by highly motivated groups.

This chapter is not meant to be a comprehensive history of Jewish philanthropy and advocacy; nor can it do justice to specific campaigns. Neither does it deal with the material deliverables of transnational philanthropy, like soup kitchens, education, healthcare, small loans, or relief packages. Rather, it specifically assesses the Soviet Jewry movement in the United States and Israel, and to a lesser extent in the United Kingdom. In this way, the movement for Soviet Jewry will be a kind of test for the role of money in transnational intercession. The second section of the chapter will place this movement into wider theoretical and historical contexts by offering an overview of the intersections of Jewish philanthropy with informal diplomacy in the modern era, particularly the work of western Jews on behalf of their coreligionists in the East. In doing so, this part of the chapter probes how activists in the West tried to push—through financial and political means—otherwise resistant regimes to ease anti-Jewish pressures. By assessing these efforts vis-à-vis the non-Jewish landscape of philanthropy and advocacy, I make horizontal comparisons similar to those made by Derek Penslar, who elsewhere in this volume compares the contours of support for struggles of national liberation in the twentieth century.

The Campaign for Soviet Jewry: Continuity or Change?

For many Jewish communal activists and leaders today, the defining experience of their political lives was the Soviet Jewry movement, whatever the level of their personal engagement. Beyond their experiences, study of this movement reveals not just peculiarities of the time but also general lines of Jewish transnational activism throughout the many decades before it came of age in the late 1960s. The movement did not appear spontaneously. Rather, it had many antecedents (some of which will be discussed later in the chapter) and grew from modest beginnings in the 1950s.[3]

It should be said at the outset that the Soviet Jewry movement departed significantly from some lines of continuity. The mass activism in the Jewish worlds that emerged during these years in the Americas, Europe, and Australia—thanks to the Soviet Jewry movement—focused more on advocacy than on material aid. Most of these activists correctly understood that almost all Soviet Jews enjoyed relative economic stability and were not, as a rule, facing imminent assault by the state.[4] Consequently, perhaps for the first time in more than a century of activism, Jewish advocacy and philanthropy dealt only marginally with the delivery of physical resources and relief. When working on behalf of Soviet Jews from the 1960s onward, these activists focused on politics.

The democratizing movement was simultaneously a reaction against the image of the older generation's failure to respond to the Holocaust-era crisis in Europe and the means by which a younger generation of activists could achieve in their own minds a measure of moral redemption. Thereby, a curious dichotomy characterized the Soviet and the foreign arms of this movement. From one side, this was a political campaign waged in the midst of the Cold War, wherein Soviet Jews and western activists tried to influence the Soviet regime. But these attempts, successful or not, did not always accord with desires of the activists' home governments, whose policies often prioritized the normalization of relations with the Kremlin. From another side, the many branches of the Soviet Jewry movement embodied a generational upheaval, with radicalized young people breaking with the more conservative, and purportedly more passive, behavior of their elders.

Three challenges have overshadowed existing scholarship on this story. The first has been a near universal preference to examine the Soviet, American, and Israeli branches of the movement separately.[5] Farther afield, scholarship with regard to the British, French, Canadian, Australian, and other contexts of the movement is extremely limited.[6] A second challenge is a tendency to interpret the histories of these movements as a triumph of "good" over "evil." The scholarly question should *not* be whether—as nearly all of the existing studies insist—the Soviet Jewry movement starting in the 1960s brought the "happy end" of mass exodus from the Soviet Union starting in the late 1980s.[7] One pole of such arguments credits the movement with helping to topple the Iron Curtain. This interpretation has enjoyed greater currency among Jewish writers; non-Jewish scholars usually do not count the movement among the causes for the disintegration of the Soviet Union.[8] A third challenge facing scholarship has been the inaccessibility of pertinent archival collections; to date, these materials in the Anglo-Saxon world, and even more so in the former Soviet Union, remain underused.

Some facets of this history have nonetheless been resolved in the existing studies. Among these are the mechanisms of the movement inside the Soviet Union, written largely by former activists. This memoir literature describes what ideas sparked action among young Soviet Jews, how the domestic movement grew, the nature of its goals and tactics, the technical means by which more than 250,000 Jews left the Soviet Union between 1968 and 1987, and how the thousands of those refused exit visas to Israel (the "refuseniks") endured Soviet repression. The existing scholarship has also illuminated the relationship between refuseniks and the general dissident movement in the Soviet Union from the Brezhnev era onward.[9] Likewise, existing studies describe what motivated activists in the United States, many of whose leaders had participated in the civil rights movement.[10] Existing histories also are enlightening about relationships between refuseniks and American activists. This interaction was not always harmonious; as late as March 1987, for example, activists in the Soviet Union and the United States argued over the movement's priorities.[11]

Israel's involvement in the movement has similarly been written from the self-laudatory vantage point of former government officials. But even a cursory examination of primary source materials suggests that the reception of this support among refuseniks was ambivalent,[12] and, as shall be seen, so were relations between the Israeli government and parts of the Soviet Jewry advocacy movement in North America. In truth, the impact of advocacy and matériel from abroad on the Jewish movement in the Soviet Union is still uncertain, even regarding an issue as seemingly clear-cut as the aid packages delivered from the West.[13]

We already know much about the campaign in the United States, which has been written mostly by former activists or based on interviews of small sets of them. These studies chart the metamorphosis of the movement from a quiet approach practiced by the postwar generation of so-called establishment organizations, led by Nahum Goldmann, to more aggressive practices, starting in the mid-1960s, of a younger cadre of self-titled "grassroots" activists, as reflected in groups like the Students' Struggle for Soviet Jewry and the Union of Councils for Soviet Jewry.[14] In the process, these studies tend to dwell on the divisions between the "establishment" and the "grassroots." In the context of the Soviet Jewry movement starting in the late 1960s, the newer organizations identified the "establishment" (embodied by organizations like the National Council for Soviet Jewry) mainly in generational terms. Most former activists and scholars agree that the movement reached its apogee at the mass demonstration for Soviet Jewry in Washington, D.C., in December 1987, during a visit of General Secretary Mikhail Gorbachev. It must also be remembered that the major agreements in 1988 and 1989 allowing for the formal renewal of organized Jewish life in the Soviet Union were signed between Soviet officials and representatives of the World Jewish Congress and the Jewish Agency for Israel, both symbols of the Jewish "establishment."

The Soviet Jewry movement underwent a rapid process of fragmentation and democratization from the late 1960s into the early 1970s. For example, foundational documents of the Union of Councils for Soviet Jewry (UCSJ) sought to create a distinct organizational culture and action model that would set it apart from the older organs of the movement.[15] In an unexpected twist, its antiestablishment orientation generated tensions with the Israeli government, which the UCSJ and other "ground-up" groups believed meddled in the Soviet Jewry movement in the United States.[16] Nevertheless, the grassroots organizations—among them the UCSJ—found themselves over time adopting institutional structures similar to "establishment" organizations, like the National Council for Soviet Jewry, which they maligned. Moreover, grassroots organizations (barring a radical fringe) eventually advocated similar policies and coordinated some activities with establishment groups. As a last example of the blurring of "establishment" versus "antiestablishment" lines, the Greater New York Conference on Soviet Jewry—among the more effective organizations in the whole movement—belied any simple categorization because of its multigenerational and multiclass membership rolls, led by people who could not easily be labeled "ins" or "outs."

Most scholarly attempts to assess the movement's ability to coerce Soviet authorities have relied heavily on three sources. The first is the memoir of Petrus Buwalda, a Dutch diplomat in the Soviet Union, based almost entirely on his interaction with *Israeli*, and not *Soviet*, officials.[17] The second source is an annotated collection of Soviet-era archival documents. While extremely important in its own right, this volume presents a set of selective materials and thus cannot be considered definitive.[18] The third source is an intriguing memoir of the longtime Soviet ambassador to Washington, Anatoly Dobrynin. A close reading strongly suggests that, from the viewpoint of the Kremlin, the public campaign in the West for Soviet Jewry—including the Jackson-Vanik Amendment (to be discussed shortly)—indeed dealt a blow to the ongoing process of détente, but did little to widen the gates for Jewish emigration from the Soviet Union.[19] On the contrary, one may reasonably conclude from Dobrynin's book that the very public face of the campaign (and its more violent fringe) perhaps closed the gates of Jewish emigration more than they would have otherwise been during the 1970s.[20]

Notwithstanding such limitations, newer scholarship has distanced itself from oft-repeated arguments in older works that the movement saved Soviet Jewry from a Holocaust-type fate at the hands of the Kremlin. Rather, the newer publications admit that the majority of Jews during the final decades of the Soviet Union remained relatively secure by *Soviet* criteria, despite myriad pressures arising from the general decline in the country's overall standards of living.[21] For the large majority of Soviet Jews, as for their non-Jewish neighbors, change came with the socioeconomic and political upheavals that occurred throughout eastern Europe during the late 1980s. Thereafter, the political breakup of the Soviet bloc, coupled with the sharp decline in standards of living that a centralized, albeit highly dysfunctional, economy had produced, brought great challenges to all of its citizens.

What still awaits definitive scholarship? Inside the Soviet Union, we need to know more about how the movement influenced the real "Jews of Silence"—those millions of Soviet Jews who did *not* apply for exit visas before 1989, or those who preferred to emigrate to lands other than Israel, or those who remained in the former Soviet Union long after the gates had opened wide in the late 1980s.[22] In addition, we still are far from understanding the place of the Soviet Jewry movement in the context of Cold War politics and how, if at all, the various arms of the movement influenced states.[23] For example, tape recordings from the Nixon White House released in 2010 affirmed that neither the movement in the United States, nor pleas from Israel, moved President Nixon or his national security advisor, Henry Kissinger, toward intervention with the Kremlin on behalf of Soviet Jews. Rather, as Kissinger callously remarked to Nixon in May 1973 after meeting with Israeli Prime Minister Golda Meir, "The emigration of Jews from the Soviet Union is not an objective of American foreign policy, . . . And if they put Jews into gas chambers in the Soviet Union, it is not an American concern. Maybe a humanitarian concern."[24] Although an op-ed in from Kissinger in the *New York Times* nearly forty years later attempted to correct the unpleasant implications arising from this observation, the fact remains that at the time of the events, the Nixon administration remained mostly unmoved by issues of human rights when dealing with foreign policy or, more specifically, by the advocacy campaign for Soviet Jewry.[25]

A Closer Look: The Jackson-Vanik and Stevenson Amendments

The existing historiography on the movement often elevates the Jackson-Vanik Amendment (Section 402) to the Trade (Export Administration) Act of 1974 as the centerpiece of the global advocacy movement. With the benefit of hindsight, what does the amendment's history suggest?[26] During the three years before its enactment in January 1975, the amendment generated frenzied political activity in Washington, the Kremlin, and in the Soviet Jewry movement. As is often the case, members of Congress who voted in favor of the bill (including Senator Henry Jackson himself), or the movement as a whole, had many motivations.[27] Here, it is important to remember that Senator Jackson, Congressman Charles Vanik, and a small group of congressional staffers—not American-Jewish organizations—initiated the amendment. No less important for our assessment is that powerful actors promoted the bill for reasons having little to do with Jews; early on, the AFL-CIO gave its support, seeing the bill as a means to deter Soviet competition to American exports on world markets. Economics, therefore, did have a role in the amendment but not always in the usual ways.

It is possible, but far from certain, that the threat of congressional passage of the amendment helped convince the Soviets in April 1973 to suspend their recently instituted education (diploma) tax on emigration, which had drawn considerable ire from abroad during the brief time it had been enforced.[28] Indeed, the amendment applied pressure on illiberal states with nonmarket economies (namely, the Soviet Union) to allow freer emigration. But none of the existing scholarly studies provides proof that Jackson-Vanik, in combination with the even more restrictive (Adlai) Stevenson Amendment,[29] forced the Soviets to open the gates of Jewish emigration any wider than they would have done otherwise from 1973 onward, when the Congress commenced debates on these bills.[30]

Further consideration shows that the Soviet education tax was mostly an ill-conceived attempt to compensate the country for the loss of highly trained (Jewish) individuals who wished to leave. According to Moscow's thinking, these ungrateful Jews had benefited from state-sponsored university training. The tax indeed appeared exorbitantly high—all but unreachable for an average Soviet citizen. But, in principle, the idea that educated workers recompense the state if they migrated before "repaying" their debt to society through labor was not specifically Soviet. Around the same time, President Nixon's chief domestic policy advisor commented that the State of California had considered requiring an exit fee from anyone who received their medical education from a public university and subsequently intended to leave the state.[31] When seen from this angle, the Jackson-Vanik Amendment seems to be no less a product of considerations around labor migration than an upshot of outright repression or Cold War politics.

What did the Jackson-Vanik and Stevenson Amendments accomplish? They surely carried a seemingly weighty and unprecedented "stick" on behalf of Jewish (and other) emigration and catapulted this issue, as well as human rights as a whole, high onto the political agenda in the United States.[32] But electoral and other pressures in Washington prevented Congress from delivering the amendments' promised "carrot" to the Soviets as they eased emigration limits later in the decade; for their part, the Jewish advocacy organizations had difficulty formulating a uniform approach to easing trade restrictions on the Soviet Union in return for greater flows of Jewish emigrants.[33]

From its beginnings, the Jackson-Vanik and Stevenson Amendments did not enjoy consensus in the Jewish community.[34] During the congressional debates, they did draw support from Soviet Jewry activists with national notoriety.[35] But important figures in business, academia, and government warned in advance about the probability of Soviet circumvention of, or backlash against, the proposed amendments.[36] By the time of the public debate in 1979 around easing trade restrictions, an array of academics, business leaders, and government officials, even Senator Stevenson himself, believed that strict application of the amendments was counterproductive for the cause of emigration.[37] The Soviets, however, did not wait for this reevaluation. Calculating that the amendments emptied the Trade Act of most of its potential, the Soviets unilaterally abrogated it in December 1974 (and thereby suspended repayment of their outstanding debt from the wartime Lend-Lease program).

This series of events echoed the outcome of Jacob Schiff's strategy vis-à-vis the Russian Empire in the early twentieth century. Schiff—the undeclared leader of American Jewry and a frequent intercessor on behalf of Russian Jews—tried to orchestrate the denial of international bank credits to a financially strapped Russian treasury during the Russo-Japanese War. He believed that this pecuniary lever—firmly applied by all major lenders in North America and Europe against Russia teetering on the verge of bankruptcy—could coerce the reversal of the tsar's anti-Semitic policies and force the protection of Russia's Jews from recurring cycles of pogroms. In short, Schiff's campaign failed because he did not get full cooperation from his banking peers in Europe.[38]

The Jackson-Vanik and Stevenson Amendments contained a similar flaw. When the United States denied trade, bank credits, grain shipments, access to advanced technology, and Most Favored Nation status to the Soviet Union and thereafter refused to ease restrictions even when the Kremlin widened the gates for Jewish emigration, the Soviet Union acquired what it needed from Europe, Japan, Canada, and Argentina.[39] From the mid-1970s onward, in fact, when its oil revenues rose dramatically, the Soviet Union became less dependent on economic cooperation with Washington.[40] Adlai Stevenson concluded in 1989 that the linkage of human rights (including Jewish emigration) to international trade policy was "conceptually flawed," "counterproductive in operation" as a tool in diplomacy, and did not cause an increase in emigration.[41] Perhaps no less telling, the Canadian government never adopted similar legislation linking trade with the Soviet Union to human rights, even though "Canadian [Soviet Jewry] activists always looked to the Jackson-Vanik Amendment . . . as a model to encourage the Canadian government to adopt the concept of linkage."[42] As was the case in Jacob Schiff's efforts in 1904–1905, a lack of consensus in the West and the realities of the international market limited the force of financial leverage on the Soviet state in the cause of Jewish issues.

Judging the success or shortcomings of the Jackson-Vanik and Stevenson Amendments requires subtle measurements. Their enactment, despite opposition from the Nixon and Ford administrations (and inconsistent messages from Israel's representatives in the United States),[43] demonstrated a kind of "soft" American Jewish political power, to borrow a term from Henry Feingold.[44] That being said, the benefits of this power were illusory for Soviet Jews; in 1974–1975 the number of exit visas from the Soviet Union declined, thereby delaying by years the emigration of those denied.[45] We must also ask to what degree Soviet Jews really benefited by becoming a sort of pawn in the conduct of the Cold War.[46] Given the tensions around the emergent policy of détente, Jewish and non-Jewish activists and observers at the time expressed concerns about Jews appearing too hard or too soft on the Soviets, while Jewish leaders cautioned against the dangers of the movement becoming part of a more general anti-Soviet campaign.[47] Hence, any tactic chosen by activists to assist Soviet Jewry probably carried risks.

Hindsight allows for reassessment. For one, we know that the ascent of Mikhail Gorbachev in Moscow and of Ronald Reagan in Washington and the eventual growth of trust between them probably facilitated mass emigration more than any other factor. Neither Jewish activism nor amendments to the Trade Act brought General Secretary Gorbachev or President Reagan to power. Nevertheless, both believed that expanded emigration was a good (and relatively painless) sign that the Soviet Union could be trusted to uphold its international obligations, including the most recent commitment to protect human rights contained in the so-called Third Basket of the international treaty signed in Helsinki in 1975. The Helsinki Final Act and Accords dealt mostly with finalizing the borders of eastern Europe following the World War II. This part ("basket") of the agreement was seen as a compromise by the Soviets around civil rights, particularly for Jews.

Opening the gates was also a comparatively easy way for Gorbachev to demonstrate to his own people and to the world that he meant to implement reform in the Soviet Union.[48] Throughout most of the 1980s, the Reagan administration generally avoided engaging in confrontational politics about human rights with the Soviet Union; instead, it prioritized geopolitical issues. Moreover, as the director of the Office of Soviet Affairs at the U.S. State

Department (Marc R. Parris) noted, the administration "[followed] the lead of the Jewish community" regarding modification of the Jackson-Vanik Amendment.[49] Fast-forwarding to 1989 and the start of the mass emigration that accompanied the disintegration of the Soviet bloc, the board of governors of the National Council for Soviet Jewry recommended the temporary waiver of Jackson-Vanik; it was suspended in 1991. Based on the evidence, therefore, it seems reasonable to argue that while the Soviet Jewry movement achieved some of its goals, the exodus of Jews from the crumbling Soviet Union awaited the profound changes that occurred in eastern Europe during the second half of the 1980s and that this exodus had only slight, if any, connection to the plight of the refuseniks and the transnational efforts for their freedom during the preceding decades.

The U.S. government finally repealed the Jackson-Vanik Amendment in December 2012, even though its Cold War rationale had changed profoundly with the coming of perestroika in the second half of the 1980s. Then as now, Jackson-Vanik did not apply to any other human right and was never (re)applied to the Russian Federation—which, since 1991, has permitted free movement of its citizens and maintains a mostly market economy. The amendment's mere existence on the books until late 2012, however, aroused hostility toward the United States among Russian statesmen and lawmakers.[50] Until its annulment, Jackson-Vanik also caused considerable friction between the American business community and the Obama administration.[51]

Another Look: Israel in the Transnational Network

The Soviet Jewry movement diverged from older patterns of transnational activism in an important way: for the first time a sovereign state (Israel) planned to take part, if not lead, such a campaign. But, overall, did the creation of Israel in 1948 greatly alter the chances of success or failure in transnational intercession on behalf of endangered Jewish communities? Israel's government has not, in fact, displaced earlier forms of cross-border philanthropy or advocacy. While many reasons underlie this state of affairs, it is important to note that Israel has not superseded most existing agendas (or programs) of transnational philanthropies nor has it often been an axis for unified global Jewish philanthropic action.

Viewed through the lens of the Soviet Jewry movement, the centrality of Israel's role is still contentious. Despite declarations from some former government officials, we do not yet understand to what extent Israel influenced the campaign in the diaspora and in the Soviet Union.[52] Continuing debate around the "dropout" phenomenon—a term applied by Israelis to those Soviet Jews who chose to emigrate to the West during the second half of the 1970s despite having been allowed to leave the Soviet Union by virtue of visas to Israel—constitutes only one part of this tension.[53] In brief, Israel insisted that all emigrants from the Soviet Union arrive at its shores, whereas many activists in the West promoted "the right to choose"; among refuseniks still trapped at the time in the Soviet Union, this issue triggered stress, including ambivalence about the Jackson-Vanik Amendment.[54] For many activists in the West, the aim was to allow Soviet Jews to be more Jewish and more free, wherever they might choose to go. Even among dedicated activists and Israeli officials opinions differed.[55] This controversy still burns today among many activists.[56] There is no small measure of historic irony that the sudden Soviet reduction of emigration in the early 1980s may have saved the Jewish world from a major confrontation over the "dropouts."[57]

Contrary to recollections of former activists, the campaign in Israel lacked cohesion, much as it did in the diaspora. On one side, a semi-secret government agency, Nativ, tried to orchestrate action in the Soviet Union and in the Jewish communities of the West. The scholarship on Nativ, while sizeable, has been limited by the near absence of its archival record or pertinent documents from its Soviet adversaries.[58] It is clear from the available materials, however, that frictions abounded between Nativ and activists in the West.[59] If Israel exercised any kind of authority over the movement in the West, this probably occurred only briefly after the Six-Day War, when Jewish communities and others viewed Israel with great admiration.[60]

On another side of Israeli activism, grassroots and semi-official public campaigns have only just become subjects for scholarly research. These groups, which evolved gradually from the 1920s, eventually drew more public attention by the 1970s. Their membership rolls were never large, but evidently did have some impact on Israeli policy.[61] On yet another side, the Israeli government started speaking out for Soviet Jewry in 1969, departing from its practice of quieter diplomacy before and afterwards.

Israel's precarious position in a Cold War conflict zone presented its statesmen with unique challenges when formulating policy on Soviet Jewry. Israel's adversarial neighbors, many of whom were clients or allies of the Soviet Union, wanted the flow of Soviet Jews to cease. For its part, Israel was firmly situated in the Western side of the conflict, yet usually preferred not to antagonize the Kremlin for fear of possible repercussions for Soviet Jews.

Further complicating matters was that the Soviet Jews did not have a clear, long-term political patron in Israel who consistently delivered on promises made to domestic advocacy groups. While perhaps disappointing, this is a typical byproduct of Israel's political system whenever there is no powerful political constituency for specific issues.[62]

The Soviet Jewry movement also had important results for relations between Israel and parts of American-Jewish leadership. Starting in the 1960s, the movement accelerated a trend among American Jews to shift their focus away from Israel and toward their own communities. One scholar concluded, for example, that American-Jewish leaders at this time "came to see their 'Jewish interests' as differing from those of the Israelis."[63] The "dropout" controversy only widened that gap.[64] Any judgments regarding this issue should, however, take into account the fact that American Jewry rarely united in its entirety in support of Israel before (or after) the advent of the Soviet Jewry movement.

Assessing the Movement: Successes and Failures

Equivocations aside, several key points hold true about the global campaign for Soviet Jewry. First and foremost, even if the post-Stalin Soviet Union rarely employed lethal terror against its own population, the refuseniks mustered immense courage when confronting an unpredictable state. Most of them were risking the comfortable lives they had—comfortable, that is, by Soviet standards—when they openly stood up to a regime with a tradition of repression and no consistent policy toward those who requested to emigrate or renew organized Jewish life. These struggles affected not just Soviet and Western Jews: the emigration of more than two million Russian-speaking Jews has had enormous implications for the whole Jewish world since the early 1970s, at the very least by profoundly changing the demographic composition of communities on four continents.

Transnationalism figured as a second major feature of the movement, institutionalized through a series of world congresses begun in Brussels in 1971. The movement in the West put Soviet Jewry in the international public spotlight—no simple achievement given that this issue had to compete for attention with many crises around the globe and paradigm shifts in international diplomacy, not the least of which was budding détente with the Soviet Union, President Nixon's "opening" of China, and the complexities of the Vietnam War. All the same, this transnational Jewish network was more aspirational than real for most of the period leading to the mass exodus of Soviet Jews during the twilight years of the Soviet Union; the various groups and agencies never constituted more than a minority of Jews in their home communities, and institutional competition plagued attempts at full coordination.[65]

Did the American movement move presidents to action? No evidence has emerged to date proving this point with regard to the Johnson, Nixon, and Ford administrations. On the contrary, the fragmentation and interorganizational competition among arms of the movement in the United States seem to have allowed successive administrations at times to "divide and deflect."[66] Thus, the White House and the State Department met separately with delegations from multiple advocacy groups, giving each the impression of special access to the halls of power but in reality delivering very little. This was, evidently, a relatively painless substitute for real action when administrations preferred not to antagonize the Kremlin on behalf of Soviet Jewry. As stated earlier, if organizational unity ever arrived among American Jews during the campaign, it probably did so only during preparations for the mass rally in Washington in December 1987.[67]

What else can explain why the Kremlin opened, and then closed, the gates of Jewish emigration during the 1970s, despite the absence of financial pressure? Was it the influence of their commitments to human rights under the Third Basket of the Helsinki Final Acts and Accords of 1975?[68] The Kremlin adopted these international agreements to resolve outstanding territorial and other issues with the West. Seen in this light, the Third Basket was mostly an afterthought on their part. There is no evidence that any of the subsequent strategies of Soviet dissident groups had any effect on Soviet emigration policy before perestroika. Rather, rates of emigration rose to unprecedented heights during the late 1970s, then plummeted drastically in the early 1980s due to other developments as recurrent winds from the Cold War replaced détente following the Soviet invasion of Afghanistan.[69]

If we are to believe one of the persistent arguments in the scholarship, the Soviet regime feared the refuseniks because they threatened the unity of the Soviet Union. Taken to its end, this argument meant that allowing more Jewish emigration would unleash a "domino effect" in which all of the disgruntled minority peoples in the Soviet Union might demand the right to leave.[70] This argument is unconvincing for anyone with even a cursory knowledge of the final decades of the Soviet empire, when the major nationalist movements that accelerated its disintegration did *not* seek mass exodus from the Soviet Union. Rather, the Ukrainian, Lithuanian, and other national movements of constituent peoples in the Soviet Union demanded territorial sovereignty or, at the very least, true national autonomy.[71]

Can the advocacy movement be credited for the forthright stance taken on the Soviet Jewry issue by the Reagan administration? The record suggests that the relative activism of the Reagan presidency arose not in response to the American Jewish movement. Rather, the Soviet Jewry issue was for Reagan (as for his fellow "Cold Warrior," Senator Henry Jackson) a tool with which to bludgeon Soviet leaders; the administration may have listened to the leaders of the Soviet Jewry movement, but Washington's goals must be understood in the context of the Cold War's denouement. The movement did, however, gain important ground in terms of legal and material support for Soviet Jews who arrived in the United States when George Shultz became secretary of state in 1982.[72]

Transnational Activism: A Longue Durée View

We will now position the campaign for Soviet Jewry into a wider examination of cross-border intercession, continuing from approximately the place where Abigail Green's chapter in this volume completes its journey. As a diasporic people living for nearly two millennia in often hostile political environments spread over immense space, Jews have had an extraordinary need for transnational aid and intercession. Episodes of such aid have been numerous, starting as early as the return from the Babylonian exile, when diaspora communities supported their brethren in reestablishing Jewish life in the Holy Land. Traditions of cross-border contacts and mutual aid have endured since then as part of the Jewish religious ethos and group identity; until the mid-1800s, however, this aid was mainly reactive. Only later did Jewish philanthropy go on the "offensive." With the adoption of organizational structures and a preference for programs designed to productivize their co-religionists abroad, philanthropists no longer just responded to crises or atrocities. Instead, they promoted interventions and reconstructive projects.

This transnational activism has spurred changes in modern Jewish politics, economy, and society. The process began with the intervention of Adolphe Crémieux and Moses Montefiore in the Ottoman Empire during the Damascus Affair of 1840, during which these "great" men from western Europe mobilized tools of modernity, like the popular press, to intercede on behalf of Jews facing premodern blood libels.[73] Subsequent campaigns leading up to the Soviet Jewry movement—more than a century later—pursued many goals; these ranged from the provision of charity, to rescue from repression, vocational training, agricultural settlement, the orderly absorption of immigrants arriving in the West, and the advancement of Zionism and ultimately resulted in the building of the State of Israel. Until the Soviet Jewry movement, all of these efforts necessitated the collection of major resources from wealthy individuals and communities in the West and their distribution abroad. At times, the campaigns also required the dispatch of expertise from the West to needy Jews across borders.

Transnational activism as an agent for change at home had additional effects. Starting in the late 1880s, as increasing numbers of Jews in Europe and the Americas mobilized for their coreligionists in the East, international activism had the unanticipated affect of democratizing the organizations that these new players were manning and creating. Consequently, the very activation of transnational intercessions put this growing cohort at loggerheads with older generations of leaders over the control of Jewish politics. The increased participation of women in Jewish organizational life occurred within the democratizing process. This component of transnational activism had gone nearly unnoticed until recently in existing scholarship, despite the fact that significant transnational women's groups emerged around the turn of the twentieth century; instead, most scholarly attention was turned toward "great" Rothschilds, d'Hirschs, and Warburgs, who created major philanthropic organizations in the United States and Europe.[74] Women's groups included wholly independent philanthropies like Hadassah or women's branches of existing *landsmanshaften* (associations for the promotion of connections to one's homeland).[75] With increasing frequency into the 1970s, women comprised significant proportions of the largest and most dynamic Jewish advocacy groups in the West. Some of the new leaders had risen through the ranks of traditional philanthropies, while others were newcomers to Jewish organizational life. Some of the new faces were described as "housewives who came out of nowhere."[76] In the United Kingdom and Canada, the activity of the "35s" organization on behalf of Soviet Jewry signaled with a roar the arrival of women into the mainstream of Jewish organizational life.[77]

Jewish activism has conformed in part to international patterns of philanthropy and informal diplomacy. At the local and national levels, it bears similarities to Christian and Muslim trends: it provided charity first as a religious duty, then moved toward more secular values of noblesse oblige among "great" men and their foundations, then experimented during the interwar period with ideas of reconstruction and social engineering, and then, most recently, has gravitated toward "venture philanthropy." Intervention on behalf of embattled coreligionists was not unique to Jews. Communities of faith, ethnic groups, and loosely aligned collections of stake-holders have mobilized to aid their coreligionists, fellow nationals, or fellow mankind at least as long as Jews have done so. Moreover, Jews and non-Jewish ethnic groups have formed cross-border commercial and welfare networks since at least the early modern period.[78] The practice of Jewish and non-Jewish philanthropy migrated across the Atlantic during the nineteenth century together with general population shifts.[79] Similarities between Jewish and non-Jewish activism should not be overstated, however. At its most basic level, Judaism has never idealized or demonized poverty; instead, it views poverty as a remediable misfortune. Moreover, Jews have also directed their charitable actions toward their non-Jewish neighbors, whereas Christian charities rarely aided Jews.[80]

Phases and Trends of Activism

Medieval and early modern contacts between Jewish communities across borders in the "old" and "new" worlds grew slowly from traditional values of charity, whereas modern Jewish transnational philanthropy proliferated rapidly in three stages. The first was individual intercession, which survived the ruin of the First World War but never again enjoyed its prewar status given the collapse of the financial leverage many of these men had enjoyed in Europe until 1914. Consequently, the passage to the second stage also marked the shift of the center of Jewish transnational activism from Europe to North America, which was completed as a result of the Holocaust.

The second stage featured a transition to organized philanthropy, pioneered by the creation of the Alliance Israélite Universelle in 1860. Like some *shtadlanim*, the Alliance acted on a global scale. It, along with splinter European organizations, mobilized action on behalf of East European and Ottoman Jews starting in the 1870s.[81] Some *shtadlanim*, among them Jacob Schiff, lent their talents to more democratized forms of philanthropy and advocacy, even if they were not always comfortable with the more inclusive nature of these new organizations.[82] The Holocaust surely changed conditions for transnational aid, but important trends continued nonetheless during this second stage. Hence, while it is true that the deliverables of transnational philanthropy shifted by the mid-1950s from material aid to political advocacy after the physical crisis of Europe's displaced persons had receded, the principle of cross-border aid remained nearly constant. It should be kept in mind, however, that transnational aid could still require a mobilization of huge sums even at the end of the twentieth century, as witnessed by the colossal funds mustered for the resettlement of post-Soviet and Ethiopian Jewry in Israel.

"Ground-up" mobilizations, begun haltingly during the interwar period and strengthening markedly during in the 1960s, are the centerpiece of the third stage in the evolution of Jewish philanthropic activism in the West. If in previous generations elite groups typically led campaigns,[83] socially diverse men and women from the heights of Jewish communal service as well as from the "grassroots" headed the newer mobilizations.

Cross-border delivery of aid among Jews has exhibited institutional qualities from even before its first modern stage—at least as early as the mid-seventeenth century—when Jews in Western Europe and the "New World" organized to deliver humanitarian aid to target communities in the Ottoman Empire, eastern Europe, and the Land of Israel.[84] Throughout periodic changes in the sites of rescue, relief, and reconstruction, there has been a consistent chain of transnational intercession. Also, since the appearance of Sephardic trans-Atlantic networks in the early modern period, business interests and personages have overlapped with Jewish transnational intercession and philanthropy. Finally, Jewish transnational activism has been relatively secular when compared to such efforts launched by other religious communities.

Philanthropic aid and the practice of an informal transnational diplomacy merged in the Jewish world around the eighteenth century, in parallel with the rapid modernization of communications. With the strengthening of absolutism in eastern Europe, Jewish communities found themselves confronting states that periodically chose to victimize Jews while deconstructing their traditional support networks. Moreover, modern print culture made it possible for the perpetrators to spread anti-Jewish libels. But these same media also allowed the defenders of Jewish interests abroad to respond to crises in new ways. At this intersection of acute need and new technologies, a sort of transnational "third sector" emerged as a central feature of Jewish life, wherein *shtadlanim*—and eventually organizations—in the West mobilized to defend the interests of coreligionists in the East. In such cases, the delivery of philanthropic material aid took a second seat to political advocacy, which often found its greatest expression in media campaigns. At times of crisis, Jews faced politically or ideologically motivated repressions that were more immediate than a physical threat. Mobilization for Soviet Jewry may have been a relatively recent exemplar of this type of intercession but earlier examples abound: the transnational campaign of 1911–1913 to rescue Mendl Beilis from a blood-libel accusation in Kiev stands out as one of these.[85]

Modernity influenced the practice of transnational intercession in another way. Herein, the spread of nationalist ideologies in Europe influenced the formation of Jewish philanthropies and other communal bodies. The whirlwinds of European nationalism forced individuals and groups of activists to wrestle with dilemmas of identity that pitted their patriotism against their moral obligation to embattled brethren abroad.[86] This challenge for activists in Paris, Berlin, and London at times had dire consequences, as became clear for those eastern European Jews caught in the battlegrounds of the First World War, when their well-meaning coreligionists in Germany found themselves on the other side of the wartime divide.[87] These sorts of dilemmas have contributed to a Jewish style and experience of transnational intervention, very often developed under less-than-perfect conditions.

One must, however, beware of triumphalism when assessing such endeavors. Jewish intercession had its disappointments, even when bolstered by the force of international law. For example, Lucien Wolf and the Alliance Israélite Universelle failed during the 1920s to force Poland and Romania to repatriate their Jewish citizens who had been displaced during the First World War.[88] And obviously, attempts at intercession did not result in the large-scale rescue of European Jews from the horrors of Fascism.

Some authors have argued that transnational Jewish philanthropic mobilizations promoted liberalization in those illiberal societies where they intervened. Indeed, some intercessors in the nineteenth and early twentieth centuries employed lofty rhetoric at home to conform to domestic notions of a "civilizing mission."[89] But actions by Jewish transnational philanthropic and advocacy groups have almost always focused on more earthly assistance for their target communities. Secondly, philanthropic work helped to solidify (or even establish) leadership status within one's own Jewish community. Moreover, transnational philanthropy, when properly applied, could at once relieve a distant crisis while helping to ensure that its political or material solution would not cause undue class-based stress in one's home surroundings. For example, during the campaign for the relief of Jewish refugees stranded at Memel (Klaipeda) in the late 1860s, the German *shtadlan* Ludwig Philippson proposed that his fellow *German* Jews help to relieve the suffering of their *Russian* coreligionists by resettling them *in America*.[90] This fit trends among non-Jews in Philippson's time and later, when wealthy philanthropists marshaled resources to protect themselves against the arrival of masses of poor eastern Europeans at their borders.[91] Recognition of this sort of class-consciousness among architects and patrons of modern transnational philanthropy should not detract from the greater good that they strove to achieve.[92]

Conclusion: Economic and Political Contexts

Modern transnational Jewish philanthropy and advocacy are a type of nonstate politics. From the nineteenth century, the ability to put pressure on illiberal regimes has derived in great part from relative affluence in the West, willingly applied toward the betterment of Jewish life elsewhere. Properly mobilized, financial strength and electoral weight among western Jewish communities at times had a deep impact; transnational intercession often succeeded in making the rights and wellbeing of coreligionists abroad a priority for governments not naturally inclined to make it one.

But have contemporary shifts in the international system made moot what Jewish activists learned when dealing with tsars, commissars, sultans, or other "old" world political figures? Indeed, change always follows wars, treaties, and the rise and fall of empires, including the political landscape in eastern Europe after 1991. But a common thread of Jewish experience—transnational activism—has outlasted political tides since the 1880s. At times, this activity focused on raising the funds necessary for the long-distance delivery of matériel. But no less frequently, expressly political outcomes were the goal.

Transnationalism has helped democratize the modern Jewish world and has engaged over time fairly effectively (albeit in different ways) with autocratic, socialist, and quasi-democratic regimes. The spillover effects from transnational philanthropy have included a greater role for women in the Jewish organizational world. All this occurred despite huge financial gaps in traditional Jewish communities where prominent and wealthy men held power. By engendering inclusion and a sense of solidarity among multiple layers of Jewish society, transnational activism may have eventually resulted in mass action, even when, as in the Soviet Jewish movement, some of the mobilizations could have been characterized at first more by fragmentation than unity.[93] Campaigns by transnational activists have thereby tended to capitalize on the strengths of Jewish communities while minimizing their weaknesses.

How did the Soviet Jewry campaign in the West measure up to earlier mobilizations? At one level, it is still unclear whether the movement influenced the Kremlin any more than Western intercessors influenced authorities in Russia or Romania a century earlier. At another level, however, the direct deliverables to refuseniks from this campaign were probably enough; moral and material support, together with the knowledge that they were not alone against the Soviet regime, may have been no less important than political "highlights" like the Jackson-Vanik Amendment that are difficult to measure in terms of actual gains.

At yet another level, the movement served as a defining agent in the process of democratization, challenging the traditional elite communal leadership with energetic, young leaders. In the United States, Britain, and Israel, democratized grassroots movements saw it as their mission to push and shame existing communal and political structures toward greater activism for Soviet Jewry. In the United States and Britain, this meant moving older organizations toward more assertive policies. In Israel, this meant moving the state. We may never know with certainty whether these efforts actually pushed the Kremlin to "open the gates." We do know that the democratization of Jewish organizational life, accelerated by the Soviet Jewry movement, had important long-term results in the diaspora.

The movement underscored some newfound realities of Jewish transnationalism since 1948, when a sovereign state began to practice trans-border intercession aside existing non-state activists who lived in other nations. Surprisingly or not, the work of the Israeli government in this realm did not seem to reduce the energies of Jewish activists in the West. At times their goals coincided with Israel's; at times they did not.

As in earlier generations of activism, the campaign for Soviet Jewry mobilized language that fit discourses and political environments at home. In the mid-nineteenth century, this meant that European intercessors framed their efforts to free imprisoned Jews in Damascus in the rhetoric of humanitarianism.[94] In the 1920s, this meant framing the fundraising campaign in the United States for organized Jewish agricultural settlement in the Soviet Union in terms of Soviet Jews "going to the land" in southern Ukraine as if they were American homesteaders.[95] During the 1970s, this meant prioritizing the human (or civil) rights aspect of the Soviet Jewry campaign instead of the

Zionist motives of most refuseniks. By focusing their message on human rights, the activists at once pushed Washington toward a more energetic stance on Soviet Jewry and outflanked Moscow's contention that the treatment of Soviet Jews was a purely domestic issue. This does not mean—as some authors and activists claim—that advocacy for Soviet Jews sparked the disintegration of the Soviet Union. It did mean, however, that for two decades the Soviet Jewry issue rose far higher on the international political agenda than it otherwise would have.[96]

My study of the Soviet Jewry campaign also highlights a dividing line between the two models of transnational philanthropy practiced in the modern period: physical aid and political advocacy. The former depended upon the willingness of diaspora communities and governments to put economic resources in the hands of needy individuals; the latter grew from the willingness of organizations and individuals to mobilize (mainly) human resources for a focused political goal. While no doubt the daily lives of many refuseniks became more tolerable by virtue of aid packages received from western brethren, and millions of Soviet and post-Soviet Jewish emigrants to Israel and the West benefited from resettlement packages funded in great part through philanthropic networks, political advocacy characterized the Soviet Jewry campaign. This had often been the case in earlier mobilizations, including those examined in Abigail Green's chapter, as well as in the case of the Beilis ritual murder trial, mentioned earlier. The Soviet Jewry campaign stands, however, in stark contrast to the case examined by Derek Penslar, where the main contribution of diaspora communities to Israel in 1948 came in the form of massive economic infusions for the war effort and the development of civilian infrastructure.

Activism on behalf of Soviet Jewry from the 1960s until the 1980s reflects a greater truth about the much longer history of modern Jewish transnational intercession outlined in this chapter: the success or failure of a specific transnational campaign must not be judged solely by what it did, or did not, achieve for the target community. Rather, a campaign must also be assessed for the effects it had on the mobilized community that launched the effort.

Chapter 11

Anxieties of Distinctiveness: Walter Sombart's *The Jews and Modern Capitalism* and the Politics of Jewish Economic History

Adam Sutcliffe

The relationship between capitalism and the Jews does not lend itself to easy discussion. The association of Jews with commercial and financial power has long been a stock trope of anti-Semitic stereotyping, and both Jewish community leaders and scholars of Jewish history have generally been careful not to lend any sustenance to the conspiracy theories and ripples of *ressentiment* into which this topic readily plays. The financial crisis of autumn 2008, featuring the highly ethnically marked fall of Bernie Madoff as its most dramatic sideshow, perhaps reinvigorated old stereotypes, and certainly reinvigorated Jewish anxieties about them.[1] In recent years a sequence of important and excellent books have appeared by Derek Penslar, Jonathan Karp, and Jerry Muller, which together signal a renewed willingness by historians to engage with the importance of economics and economic relations in the Jewish past. All three of these studies, however, focus on debates, representations, and perceptions relating to the place of Jews in economic life, rather than the more sensitive topic of underlying economic realities. All three scholars also very appropriately note the shadow cast over their subject by the central calamity of the twentieth century.[2] The depiction of the Jews as parasitical capitalists featured prominently in the prelude to their genocide, and the field of Jewish economic history remains haunted by this fact. Careful microstudies and cautious qualifications abound; ambitious syntheses and broad generalizations are very rare.[3]

A century ago, the question of the economic significance of Jews was subject to no such caution or constraint. This was particularly the case in Germany, where the leading luminaries of the emerging interdisciplinary field of sociology focused much attention in the first decade of the twentieth century on the role of particular religious and cultural groups in the emergence and development of capitalism. The two major studies to emerge from this debate have had very different scholarly fates. Max Weber's *The Protestant Ethic and the Spirit of Capitalism* (1905) continues to inspire animated discussion and further research more than a century after its publication, and it is a core text in historical sociology.[4] Weber's famous ascription of a key role in the rise of capitalism to a "Protestant ethic" of industriousness and thrift is certainly much contested, but it is by no means a discredited thesis. The *Protestant Ethic* was strongly influenced by Werner Sombart's work earlier in the decade on capitalism, and it in turn stimulated a direct response from Sombart: his *The Jews and Modern Capitalism*, first published in Leipzig in 1911 as *Die Juden und das Wirtschaftsleben* and appearing in English translation two years later. Sombart was explicit about his debt to Weber. "Max Weber's researches are responsible for this book," he declared, while arguing that the traits Weber had identified with the most austere strains of Protestantism more correctly belonged to Judaism—indeed, that "Puritanism *is* Judaism."[5] Sombart's text, in marked contrast to Weber's, has acquired an aura of infamy. Read today, if at all, largely as an artifact in the history of anti-Semitism, the recoil from *The Jews and Modern Capitalism* is arguably largely responsible for Sombart's broader disappearance from the sociological canon.[6]

The reasons for this, in the light of the fate of German Jewry, scarcely require explication. Although the attitudinal stance toward the Jews suggested by Sombart's study was, as I shall argue below, not as straightforwardly hostile as many critics have assumed, his arguments were eagerly taken up by avowed anti-Semites such as Theodor Fritsch, who did not have to labor much to recast his arguments in a more trenchantly polemical form.[7] Sombart's own ideological outlook was fluid, subtle, and somewhat elusive. The son of a Protestant parliamentary deputy and Saxon estate owner, he sought to mark his distance from his father's patrician perspective but was clearly formatively influenced by his landowning values and concerns. While Sombart was a prominent socialist in his youth, a quasi-nationalist strain is nonetheless present in some of his early work. In old age he accommodated himself without difficulty to the rise of Nazism. He accepted public honors on the occasion of his seventy-fifth birthday in 1938 and had made no clear attempt to distance himself from the Nazi regime by the time of his death in May 1941.[8] The extermination taking place by then makes it impossible for us to read the arguments put forward in *The Jews and Modern Capitalism* in the same unencumbered spirit with which we can still approach Weber's thesis. Yet, even if Sombart had died younger, escaping the taint of his final decade, his characterization of Jews as archetypal capitalists would nonetheless be burdened with tragic overfamiliarity.[9]

Why, then, is Sombart's study worth a centennial reconsideration?[10] I would suggest two reasons. First, a reading of *The Jews and Modern Capitalism* in the context of the early twentieth-century debates to which it contributed illuminates an intellectual world in which racial difference was considered in terms very different from our own. The methodological premises underlying Sombart's research were widely shared among the social scientists of late Imperial Germany. In focusing directly on Jewish economic acumen, Sombart broached a subject that was delicate in the context of academic sociology, but that had been hanging heavily in the air for some time because of the widespread public interest in racial science not only on the German Right but also in other circles, including many Jews. The most intense controversy stirred by Sombart's book, indeed, was within the Jewish world. The assimilationist establishment of the German Jewish community attacked the book as anti-Semitic, but many Zionists celebrated it. A careful reconstruction of the formative influences and immediate impact of *The Jews and Modern Capitalism* thus reminds us of the complex and varied lineages in both German and Jewish thought of the notion of Jewish economic distinction.

The second reason to pay some attention to Sombart can be simply stated: he was not altogether wrong. Jews have indeed been, in many different environments, a disproportionately commercial minority, and there is no clear reason for or consensus about why this is the case. The argument that Jewish concentration in finance follows from their exclusion from so many other livelihoods is, according to Niall Ferguson, only the "least unsatisfactory" explanation.[11] The field of Jewish economic history would lose its cohesion as a transhistorical endeavor, and comparative volumes such as this one their essential meaningfulness, without some recognition of the persistent overrepresentation of Jews in commerce. The repeated repudiation of this perception of Jews cannot sustain much scholarly interest or impact, and is surely also an unwarrantedly defensive and anxious response to whatever links might exist today between the diffusion of anti-Semitism and the scholarly circulation of this stereotype. *The Jews and Modern Capitalism* is certainly ridden with errors and contains no insights that will greatly startle those who read it today. Nonetheless, if we are to think boldly about the *longue durée* continuities and connections in Jewish economic history, then we must acknowledge that we are picking up a challenge that was first and most comprehensively addressed by Sombart and that has for the most part been awkwardly evaded over the intervening century.

* * *

Scholars of Jewish history have tended to regard *The Jews and Modern Capitalism* as an anomalous product of late Wilhemine sociology, of a profoundly different quality not only from Weber's work, but also from that of their peers Georg Simmel and Ferdinand Tönnies. This reading, however, leaves us with a puzzle. According to David Landes, Sombart's book "should have been dismissed out of hand as a pseudo-scholarly hoax," while Paul Mendes-Flohr has confessed to finding the level of serious interest it attracted "somewhat baffling."[12] While Sombart's book certainly stirred considerable controversy and drew some sharp criticism, it was received cordially by his colleagues, and there is no sign that it in any way damaged his professional reputation or destabilized his position at the helm of his discipline. To make sense of this reception, we need to locate Sombart's work in its early twentieth-century context, and consider it not as an outlier but rather as expressive of many of the key concerns of his scholarly community. In contrast with Jeffrey Herf's reading of Sombart as part of a particular Weimar tradition of "reactionary modernism," advancing its own vision of technological modernization while repudiating the "Jewish" spirit of abstracted commercial capitalism, Kevin Repp has situated him within the context of a wider "anti-political" mood of deep ambivalence toward modernity that pervaded reformist circles in late Imperial Germany.[13] Sombart's thinking is notably mobile, passing through a number of distinct phases over the course of his long career. This mobility, far from reflecting some personal eccentricity or instability, is best seen as a product of Sombart's wide professional engagement and his openness to shifts in prevalent intellectual influences. The effect is to heighten rather than diminish both his representativeness and his impact as, according to his biographer

Friedrich Lenger, "perhaps the most influential German social scientist of the first third of the twentieth century."[14]

Sombart's antipathy toward capitalism was certainly typical of German intellectuals of his generation. Throughout his career, from his early socialism, through his turn around the turn of the century to a communitarian "voluntarism" influenced by Tönnies's nostalgic view of *Gemeinschaft*, to the increasing influence on him of Nietzschean ethics starting around 1910, he remained a critic of capitalism. Sombart's broadly pessimistic view of bourgeois society as sterile and banal and his persistent search for ways to protect the human values that he saw as threatened by the encroachments of modernity were also characteristic of sociological thought in Wilhemine Germany.[15] Equally typical of the values of his professional cohort was his understanding of the emergent discipline of sociology as both a scientific and a practical subject, oriented toward the search for solutions to the socioeconomic problems facing the nation-state. By 1899 Sombart had emerged, alongside Weber, as a leading figure in Germany's most important policy research institution, the Verein für Sozialpolitik (Social Policy Association), through which he engaged vigorously with contemporary issues of national economic productivity and social stability.[16] It was in this professional context that Sombart composed his magnum opus, the two-volume *Der Moderne Kapitalismus* (Modern Capitalism, 1902), a work that played a key role in popularizing the word "capitalism" and in shaping sociological debate over the following decade.

In *Der Moderne Kapitalismus* Sombart developed a careful analysis of the triumph of capitalist industry over earlier forms of production, placing great emphasis on the rise of a new "spirit" (*Geist*) of economic calculation, preoccupied with monetary instruments of valuation and exchange and driven no longer by simple satisfaction of needs' but by the "acquisitive principle." The influence of Marx is clear, and the work also clearly bears the imprint of Simmel's recent *Philosophy of Money* (1900). Sombart makes very little direct reference to Simmel in his study, but this is much more likely a symptom of rivalry rather than a reflection of any lack of interest in this pioneering investigation into the psychological and social aspects of the place of money in modern society by a fellow student of Sombart's doctoral advisor, Gustav Schmoller.[17] Weber's *Protestant Ethic*, three years later, in turn built on Sombart's analysis of the capitalist "spirit," associating it specifically with Protestant asceticism—to which Sombart's later work on the Jews, as we have noted, was in part an explicit rejoinder. All three thinkers, then, were engaged in close debate with each other and also in constructive critique of the work of Marx.[18] Sombart turned his attention to the Jewish role in capitalism as a step in this wider collective attempt to analyze sociologically the cultural and psychic aspects of the monetization of modern life.

The association of Jews with capitalism was, of course, a deeply familiar notion in the intellectual tradition of these thinkers, inherited from Marx's *On the Jewish Question* (1844) and embellished by Wilhelm Roscher (1817–1894), one of the founding thinkers of the German school of historical political economy.[19] The connection was first introduced to this particular debate, in passing, by Simmel, who was himself ethnically Jewish and encountered some professional hostility because of this, his own and his father's baptism notwithstanding.[20] The Jews became a "stranger people," Simmel wrote in his *Philosophy of Money*, because of their dispersed, "stranger" status; this had led them to adopt a distinct mentality, more focused on formal and rational monetary transactions than on creative production.[21] Sombart showed little interest in Jews in his *Der Moderne Capitalismus*, but did devote a few pages to them in his next book, *Die Deutsche Volkswirtschaft im 19. Jahrhundert* (*The German National Economy in the Nineteenth Century*, 1903), where for the first time he linked their racial characteristics to their economic success.[22]

The study of racial or ethnic differences, and particularly differences internal to Germany—most notably concerning Jews—was in general broached extremely gingerly by German sociologists in this period, as Michal Bodemann has recently shown.[23] This was not because of a lack of interest in racial matters, but rather because of a collective concern to establish the "scientific" credentials of the discipline and to maintain a distance from the passionate partisanship readily stirred by this topic. A strong commitment to value-free objectivity and scientific method was enshrined in the statues of the Deutsche Gesellschaft für Soziologie (German Sociological Association), founded in 1909 under the collective leadership of Sombart, Weber, Simmel, and Tönnies. With both racial biology and the "Jewish question" attracting much attention in Germany at this time, these topics could not be ignored by the organization. A paper by the leading racial biologist Alfred Ploetz was discussed at its first conference (*Soziologentag*) in 1910, while the issue of whether to discuss the Jewish "nationality question" at its second conference in 1912 exposed sharp disagreements in the organization's leadership. Weber regarded both racial theory and Sombart's recently published *Jews and Modern Capitalism* as insufficiently scientific, but argued, alongside

Sombart, that sociologists should address this topic. However, the more professionally purist view of Tönnies and Simmel prevailed, and German sociology remained institutionally aloof from the racial and national debates that most powerfully animated the public sphere in the years leading up to the First World War.[24]

Given the contrasting reception histories of Weber and Sombart, it is significant to note the common ground between these two men on this issue, in opposition to most of their prominent colleagues. While both Weber and Sombart were deeply committed to value neutrality in social science, they also believed it was important for sociologists to engage with influential schools of thought and currents of public debate. Weber also developed his respectful scholarly interaction with Sombart's work on the Judaic origins of capitalism, despite Sombart's own apparent loss of interest in the subject after 1913. Weber devoted a chapter to "Judaism and Capitalism" in his posthumously published *Economy and Society* (1925), and also developed his view of the Jews as a "pariah people" in his *Ancient Judaism* (1917–1919).[25] In both texts Weber sustained his disagreement with Sombart, insisting that Puritans, not Jews, were key to the advent of industrial capitalism. However, Weber also placed great emphasis on the asceticism and rationalism of the Jews and on the importance of these characteristics to their success in moneylending and their particular contribution to the "disenchantment of the world." Sombart's emphasis on the Jewish "rationalization of life," and in particular of sexuality, is more belabored, but is in essence the same argument.[26] Both men, while suppressing their evaluative perspectives beneath their ardent commitment to methodological value neutrality, also shared the same unmistakably cleft view of this phenomenon, irrespective of which religion was primarily responsible for it. Although they admired the cultural achievement of human self-discipline, they ascribed to it a fateful significance in ushering in the cold instrumentalism of modernity. In their core characterization and signification of Judaism, the two men were essentially in accord.[27]

The contextual significance of *The Jews and Modern Capitalism*, then, lies not so much in its content as in the boldness with which it broke through the barriers of diffidence and status consciousness that separated professional sociology from the wider discourse on Jews and Judaism in late Imperial Germany. The theme of Jewish ethnic distinctiveness was an uncomfortable one for many educated liberals, and particularly for prominent Jewish academics such as Franz Oppenheimer, who was the most vocal critic of racial theory within the German Sociological Association.[28] However, the subject was one of fascination not only for anti-Semites, but also, increasingly, among Jews. Sombart's broaching of the subject attracted immediate Jewish attention: his few pages on the economic importance of the Jews in *The German Economy in the Nineteenth Century* were swiftly reprinted in *Ost und West*, an "illustrated monthly for modern Jewry."[29] When *The Jews and Modern Capitalism* appeared in 1911, it perfectly caught the wind of the concerns of the time. Since the early years of the century, as Mitchell Hart's recent work has shown, Zionist Jews in particular (with the participation of some non-Zionists also) had been laboring to establish a "Jewish social science" that would furnish a statistical basis on which the "Jewish question" could be addressed. Sombart drew heavily on the early output of this project in his book, which in turn owed much of its impact to the immense interest it stirred among those same pioneers of Jewish social science and their readership in the wider Zionist movement.[30]

Sombart also drew a great deal of his material from the more longstanding tradition of Jewish historical research, from the early works of *Wissenschaft des Judentums* scholarship to the surge of productivity in this field in the decades on either side of the turn of the century. The footnotes of *The Jews and Modern Capitalism* contain frequent citations to articles in the *Revue des Études Juives* (founded in 1880), the *Jewish Quarterly Review* (from 1889), the *Publications of the American Jewish Historical Society* (from 1893), and the *Transactions of the Jewish Historical Society of England* (from 1895), as well as to works by leading nineteenth-century Jewish historians such as Heinrich Graetz and Meyer Kayserling; Sombart also cites the greatest project of Jewish scholarly synthesis in this period, the twelve-volume *Jewish Encyclopedia* published in New York between 1901 and 1906, which he praises highly. Most of his sources are Jewish, and some of his most inflated claims for the economic importance of the Jews reflect the prevalent preoccupations and perspectives of recent Jewish research. Sombart makes much, for example, of the Jewish role in the discovery of America, writing that "It is as though the New World came into the horizon by their aid and for them alone, as though Columbus and the rest were but managing directors for Israel."[31] An egregiously preposterous claim, to be sure—but one that Sombart based on the effusively celebratory literature on the Jewish contribution to the colonization of America that had emerged as part of the enthusiastic American Jewish commemorations of the 400th anniversary of Columbus's discovery and the 250th anniversary, in 1904, of Jewish settlement in America. Citing several of these works, Sombart commented in his next sentence that "It is in this light that Jews, proud of their past, now regard the story of that discovery, as set forth in the latest researches."[32]

Sombart's argument that Judaism promoted the "rationalization of family life" was likewise expounded with support from recent Jewish research. He included a table detailing the markedly lower frequency of illegitimate births among Jews than among Christians in Germany and Russia, which he drew from an article published only the previous year (1910) in the *Zeitschrift für Demographie und Statistik der Juden* (Journal for Jewish Statistics and Demography).[33] This new journal, published since 1905 by Arthur Ruppin's Berlin-based Bureau für jüdische Statistik (Bureau for Jewish Statistics), was the leading mouthpiece of the new Jewish social science, and it was of inestimable value to Sombart. Ruppin's aim, according to Mitchell Hart, was "to demonstrate scientifically the national, ethnic, and/or racial identity of Jewry, and thereby to offer empirical support to Jewish nationalist claims."[34] In the *Zeitschrift* Sombart found a treasure trove of articles surveying the racial and cultural distinctiveness of contemporary Jewry, written from a perspective of collective pride and self-assertion and with a methodological commitment to scientific rigor. It seems reasonable to assume that Sombart did not just raid this material to support his preconceived ideas, but that the *Zeitschrift* significantly both influenced and enabled *The Jews and Modern Capitalism.* In this journal he discovered an articulate seam of research on the distinctiveness of the Jews which shared his own professional scruples and idiom, had only become available since his first brief foray into Jewish economic history in 1903, and was not equivalently available for any other ethnic or religious group. It would be surprising, and contrary to Sombart's commitment to the authority of empirical social science research, for him not to have been impressed and persuaded by this vigorous marshaling of statistical data in support of Jewish socioeconomic distinctiveness.

The nature of the reciprocal intellectual relationship requires no speculation. The first generation of Jewish social scientists responded with great enthusiasm to Sombart's work. Arthur Ruppin, the driving force behind this movement and later the early architect of Jewish settlement in Palestine, was delighted by it, noting in his diary that Sombart was an "apostle" for his own *Die Juden der Gegenwart* (The Jews of Today).[35] This book, which Ruppin promoted as "the first scientific exposition of Zionism," was first published in 1904, but in 1911 he rushed out a revised version, eager to incorporate as swiftly as possible the reinforcements that Sombart provided for his argument.[36] *The Jews and Modern Capitalism* authoritatively brought together a large body of historical and statistical information that was eminently usable for Ruppin, but the deeper significance of Sombart's work for him was the imprimatur it bestowed on his own research: a leading sociologist had now finally endorsed his racial approach to the "Jewish question." Race was a key analytical category throughout Ruppin's career, crucially underpinning his Zionist politics.[37] Sombart's book enabled him and other Zionists to assert precisely what those in the leadership of the German Sociological Association who opposed addressing these topics had feared. Racial science, they could now claim, was not a marginal field of questionable rigor, but was fully respectable, having been firmly embraced by one of the leading sociologists of the day.

Sombart acquired celebrity status in the German Jewish community even before his book appeared. The lecture series he delivered on Jews and capitalism in Berlin in 1909 attracted a sell-out audience, including, according to reports in the Jewish press, "the elite of Berlin Jewry," whose response to his arguments was largely enthusiastically positive. (In the anti-Semitic press, in contrast, the lectures were criticized as "a hymn to the Jews.")[38] Responses to the book itself were more mixed and complicated, exposing and intensifying divisions in the German Jewish community. Tensions between Zionists and assimilationists, already running high, were brought to the fore by Sombart's study, which immediately became a highly charged focus for this conflict. The community establishment was generally strongly critical of the book. In his review, Franz Oppenheimer, for example, sharply critiqued Sombart's endorsement of the "racial chauvinism" espoused by radical Zionists and anti-Semites alike, regarding it as "making life for . . . cultured Jews unbearable."[39] Over the winter of 1911–1912, Sombart embarked on a fresh lecture tour, which prompted boycott calls from the prominent community organization dedicated to opposing anti-Semitism, the Centralverein. Younger Zionists, however, avidly attended these lectures. Serious intra-Jewish violence erupted during at least one of these meetings, and polemical divisions hardened, with some Zionists defending Sombart passionately and accusing the Centralverein of falsely painting them as Jewish anti-Semites.[40]

Sombart swiftly published these lectures in pamphlet form as *Die Zukunft der Juden* (The Future of the Jews, 1912), in which he offered his most explicit engagement with the politics of European Jewry. The liberal press, he here claimed, avoided discussion of the "Jewish problem": his aim was, therefore, to address it in open public debate.[41] The Jews in eastern Europe, he argued, faced real hardship, the solution to which was mass migration to another region.[42] This implicit endorsement of Zionism was not, however, without important caveats. If all western European Jews moved to Palestine, he observed, economic disaster would befall everybody else, comparable to the impact on France of the departure of the Huguenots.[43] He offered, however, no reassuring alternative to the Zionist option. Jewish assimilation was, and would probably remain, a failure because of the "differences of blood" between Jews and those of "'Aryan' races," and although anti-Semitism, defined as non-Jewish antipathy toward Jews, would always endure, this at least need not always be accompanied by the persecution or mistreatment of Jews.[44] This bluntly uneasy vision of the Jewish future readily appears to twenty-first century readers as slippery anti-Semitism thinly veiled as half-hearted Zionism. However, such an assessment does not take proper account of the charged dynamics of the debate on the "Jewish question" in the years just before the First World War, a debate in which Sombart sought to position himself as a somewhat aloof pacifier rather than as a direct participant. Certainly he enjoyed the public attention that his foray into this hotly disputed terrain brought him. He was, though, careful to maintain a scholarly distance from the explicitly political positions of his admirers and detractors. It was primarily among Jews—as well as among avowed anti-Semites—that the issue of Jewish racial and cultural difference raised intense passions. Sombart's sometimes gnomic utterances on the future of the Jews did not so much drive these internecine debates as provide a screen onto which they were projected and magnified.

The febrile intellectual environment in which Sombart's work was received and his own professorially restrained posture in the eye of the storm that he generated are highlighted by his contribution to a volume of short essays by both non-Jews and Jews edited by the editor and popular novelist (and Jewish convert to Protestantism) Artur Landsberger and published in 1912 under the title *Judentaufen* (Jewish Baptism). For this work, contributors were asked to address the likely outcome for all parties if Jewish assimilation, Zionism, or neither of these achieved their goals, and the relative desirability of these possible futures. Landsberger was fascinated by *The Jews and Modern Capitalism*, which, he wrote, might one day be recognized as the "beginning of a solution to the Jewish problem."[45] *Judentaufen* was presented as a commentary on Sombart, was published with his support, and begins, following Landsberger's introduction, with Sombart's own contribution. However, in this essay Sombart revealed himself to be somewhat impatient with the subjective and evaluative impetus behind the volume. He did not offer any direct response to Landsberger's questions, instead insisting that his own work was a "scientific" study of the Jewish question, in which all value judgments were set aside as absolutely irrelevant.[46] The higher status that Sombart's work conferred on sociobiological racial theories and their application to the "Jewish question" certainly breathed strength into these already highly active discourses. Having breached the barrier separating academic sociology from this charged political terrain, however, Sombart took pains to remind his readers that this demarcation was nonetheless crucial and that he was firmly on the "scientific" side of the divide.

Sombart set his analysis of Judaism within a wider interpretive context in his next major book, *Der Bourgeois* (1913), swiftly translated into English as *The Quintessence of Capitalism* (1915). Arguably Sombart's most incisive work, the historical and psychological portrait it draws of the modern businessman struck Thomas Mann as so acute that he immodestly speculated that his own acclaimed novel chronicling a nineteenth-century North German merchant family, *Buddenbrooks* (1901), might have been a formative influence on it.[47] Only about ten of the more than 350 pages of *Der Bourgeois* focus on Jews, and these generally summarize the core ideas of *The Jews and Modern Capitalism*. However, on this broader canvas Sombart both attenuates and heightens his argument for the Jews' distinctive role in the development of capitalism. The aptitude for capitalism, he claims, was unevenly distributed among the peoples of Europe, with three particular groups "over-inclined" to it: the Florentines, the Lowland Scots, and the Jews. At times Sombart strongly emphasizes the unity of this perhaps surprising list, even asserting that "Florentine, Scotchman, and Jew are interchangeable terms."[48] However, elsewhere he ascribes particular weight to the Jews' role in the emergence of capitalism, arguing that their *Fremdenrecht*—the distinction they came to draw in their business ethics between dealings among themselves and dealings with non-Jews—enabled them to be the first to unleash a fully competitive commercial spirit, which by the eighteenth century overpowered "the restraining influence of Christian ethics."[49] "The influence of Jewish ethics," he writes, was not the only factor shaping "the characteristics of modern man," though "that influence was not by any means slight." In summary he states that "The Jews were the catalytic substance in the rise of modern capitalism."[50]

Der Bourgeois ends on an ominously prophetic note. Sombart observes that the growth of capitalism is unsustainable and that its long-term compatibility with democratic civilization is uncertain.[51] In the light of the militaristic patriotism that he eagerly embraced the following year, to say nothing of his accommodation to Nazism in the 1930s, it is easy to see why this passage has been interpreted as evidence that Sombart had already adopted a "proto-fascist mentality" twenty years before Hitler's triumph.[52] However, Sombart's mood reflected the anxious pessimism that pervaded his late Wilhemine intellectual milieu and reached a crescendo in the years leading up to 1914. The First World War was enthusiastically seized upon as a welcome opportunity for collective purgation, revivification, and integration by many constituencies across Germany and beyond—including, not least, German Jews, who were able to reestablish cross-communal harmony through their united commitment to the war effort.[53] Sombart's own adaptation to the new wartime atmosphere was particularly vigorous. His *Händler und Helden* (Merchants and Heroes, 1915) is a brazen piece of anti-English propaganda, reworking the argument of *Der Bourgeois* to cast the Germans as the entrepreneurial heroes of the early stage of capitalism and the English as the traders that rose to dominance in capitalism's later, ruthlessly competitive phase.[54] The ease with which Sombart was able to replace the Jews with the English as the quintessentially mercantile race in his ethnic schema of history exposes the impressionable superficiality of his thinking. It also suggests that he was less preoccupied with the Jewish commercial nexus than many critics have assumed. In the Weimar period he neglected the "Jewish question" altogether, returning to it only two decades later in a brief, elliptical, and highly problematic chapter of his *Deutscher Sozialismus* (1934), translated into English as *A New Social Philosophy* (1937) and written from a position of avowed sympathy with National Socialism.[55]

* * *

Most recent Anglophone historians have swiftly dismissed *The Jews and Modern Capitalism* as a shoddy, pseudo-scholarly outpouring of anti-Semitism—"a rhapsody of sophistic effusions"; an "execrable . . . study"; a work providing "a scholarly patina for what was already one of the most frequent motifs of anti-Semites."[56] Sociologists, conscious of the foundational significance of Sombart for their discipline and more tolerant of theory-driven generalizations, have tended to assess his work more patiently, while also predominantly approaching this book through the prism of its place in the history of anti-Semitism.[57] Sombart is today most strongly associated with the trafficking of the stereotype of the Jewish arch-capitalist, and this facet of his work has largely overshadowed his broader analysis of the historical sociology of capitalism. Ironically, while some of his most admired and ambitious writings, such as his pioneering *Der Moderne Capitalismus*, have never been translated into English, only *The Jews and Modern Capitalism*—regarded both at the time of its publication and by more recent historians of sociology as one of his minor works—has, despite or more probably because of its excoriation; remained almost continuously in print. This text was most recently reissued in the 1980s with a thorough and insightful scholarly introduction.[58]

Sombart's reception in Britain and America was not always so hostile. The publication of *The Jews and Modern Capitalism*, along with the rapid appearance of Mordecai Epstein's translation two years later in 1913, stimulated considerable debate on both sides of the Atlantic. The *Jewish Chronicle* gave the book an effusive review, describing its scientific analysis of the importance of the economic impact of Jews as "a magnificent tribute to the Jewish character," of "monumental" authority for non-Jews, and for Jews a book that "will open the eyes of many a cynical coreligionist to the beauties of his own religion."[59] While, as in the Germanic world, Sombart's work divided opinion among Anglophone Jews, the initial consensus on *The Jews and Modern Capitalism* among American Jewish historians was unhesitatingly admiring. In recognition of the book's significance, its author was honored with a corresponding membership to the American Jewish Historical Society.[60] As late as 1937, an admiring study of Sombart was published by Mortin Plotnik, then a political scientist at Columbia University and later a benefactor of the Hebrew University. Plotnik lauded Sombart as "the mind of the century" and as the originator of a *Verstehende* approach to economics (though he briefly noted with horror Sombart's recent transformation, in his *Deutscher Sozialismus*, into an apologist for Nazism).[61] However, the Second World War marks a sharp watershed in Sombart's scholarly reputation. The one later synthetic work that emphasizes the importance of commerce in Jewish history in a way that bears some affinities with Sombart's approach—Ellis Rivkin's *The Shaping of Jewish History* (1971)—explicitly disavows any Sombartian influence, while the one modern attempt empathetically to reconstruct and develop the debate between Sombart and Weber on Judaism has emerged outside the Anglophone world, by the French sociologist Freddy Raphaël.[62]

The Jews and Modern Capitalism is certainly marred by factual errors and methodological tendentiousness. Blundering into the field of idiomatic

Yiddish, Sombart makes much of the supposed ubiquity of the word *tachlis* as evidence of the teleological worldview of the Jews; reading Glikl of Hameln with a single-minded focus on his own preoccupations, he counts 609 mentions of money in her memoir.[63] He reiterates the claim that the Jews invented the bill of exchange—a myth that first surfaced in print in a mid-seventeenth-century French manual of commercial law and soon became widely accepted. Scholars now know that these credit instruments were first used by Italian merchants in the fourteenth century and similarly know that the widespread seventeenth- and eighteenth-century perception of the importance of the Sephardim in long-distance trade was somewhat exaggerated. Sombart here echoed the many earlier inflated assertions of the commercial innovation and prowess of the Sephardim made by British writers on political economy such as Joseph Addison, John Toland, and Adam Smith and by Montesquieu and the *Encyclopédie*, as well as by Jews seeking to advance persuasive tolerationist arguments, such as Simone Luzzatto and Menasseh ben Israel.[64] The unreliability of *The Jews and Modern Capitalism* here, then, cannot fairly be ascribed to the personal scholarly sloppiness of its author. Sombart drew together a vast amount of secondary material on the economic history of the Jews, and his specific claims were mostly based either on longstanding consensus beliefs, for example regarding the economic acumen of the Sephardim, or on the recent research of Jewish social science. There is undoubtedly much to fault in Sombart's research. However, when assessed according to the standards and assumptions of its time and the theory-driven synthetic norms of his sociological discipline, his book is conventionally if not even in some respects impressively professional and does not warrant the anachronistic condemnation of many recent scholars.

It is also simplistic to interpret Sombart's study as straightforwardly anti-Semitic. It is undoubtedly the case that a steoreotypical view of Jews and Judaism animates his book and that these stereotypes closely overlapped with, and gave sustenance to, the stock imagery of early twentieth-century populist anti-Semitism. However, as we have seen, his characterization of Jews as particularly adept capitalists drew on and reflected a much wider span of opinion among Jews as well as non-Jews. Sombart did not evince any particular warmth toward Judaism, commenting gruffly in *Judentaufen* that he "considerably preferred" German to Jewish culture.[65] However, his personal relations with Jews seem to have been far from frosty. The memoirs of his son, Nicolaus, recount his parents' vigorous socializing with many of their Jewish neighbors in the affluent Berlin enclave of Grunewald, until, in 1938, these regular visitors to the Sombart family home suddenly migrated to the United States or London and were no longer mentioned.[66] Over the course of his career, Sombart had many Jewish associates and students, from whom there is some testimony to the lack of any evident hostility or prejudice in his private relationships. Indeed, no less a figure than Salo Baron made a point of putting on record Sombart's willingness to write letters of recommendation for Jewish students of his who were forced to leave Nazi Germany.[67]

More significantly, the evaluative tone of *The Jews and Modern Capitalism* is itself ambiguous. Sombart was a critic of capitalism, and so his ascription to the Jews of a key role in this economic system was in this overarching context certainly not complimentary. However, he nonetheless intermittently appeared to admire the intellectual prowess, single-minded focus, and family-oriented sobriety of the Jews and unambiguously cast them as exerting a hugely disproportionate impact on human history. Statements such as "Israel passes over Europe like the sun: at its coming new life bursts forth; at its going all falls into decay" were readily cited by those who saw Sombart as a friend of the Jews, whether they were his Jewish admirers or anti-Semites such as Theodor Fritsch, who were fiercely critical of what they regarded as an errant streak of philo-Semitism in his work.[68] *The Jews and Modern Capitalism* was indeed, as Derek Penslar has noted, a "protean" work, open and immediately subject to many contrasting interpretations.[69] This was in large measure due to Sombart's own strenuous efforts to adhere to the sociological standards of value neutrality to which he, no less than Weber, was so deeply committed. Although Sombart sought to eschew any evaluative inflection in his study, it was almost impossible for readers in the charged environment of late Wilhemine Germany, and nearly as difficult for more recent readers, not to ascribe one to him.

Early scholarly engagements with Sombart tried to meet him on objective social-scientific terrain. Several Jewish scholars of Jewish economic history reviewed his book respectfully, while Moses Hoffmann, an Orthodox rabbi who had recently completed a doctorate on medieval economic history, swiftly wrote a book-length response, taking Sombart to task for his exaggerations and particularly for his portrayal of Judaism itself as intrinsically economistic, while nonetheless concurring with him on many points.[70] Jacob Katz's passing engagement with Sombart in his *Tradition and Crisis* (first published in Hebrew in 1958) is in a broadly similar vein, acknowledging the legitimacy of high-level sociological generalizations about Jewish capitalism, but rejecting essentializing claims for some timeless affinity between capitalism and Jewish life and religion. The prominence of Jews as early modern financiers in the development of state capitalism was above all due, Katz argued, to the "historical accident" of their early concentration in commerce, though this was compounded by the usefulness of their international ties, their political vulnerability, and the self-reinforcing stereotype of their business acumen. Sombart was entirely wrong to see unrestrained competition, for example, as an intrinsic trait of Jewish economic activity. On the contrary, Katz emphasized, there were sophisticated mechanisms internal to Jewish society—the only domain over which Jewish norms could hold sway—for managing and restraining competition.[71] More recent work by Mordechai Levin has further attempted to refute Sombart's characterization of Judaism by demonstrating the noneconomic value system expounded by authoritative religious sources such as *musar* literature.[72]

In recent decades, however, there has been little historiographical discussion of Sombart and a broad retreat from the *longue durée* approach to Jewish economic history that he exemplified. The small body of work in this field still strongly influenced by Marx, which on occasion includes a nod to Sombart, is a partial exception to this trend.[73] Beyond this school, one of the few historians to follow Sombart in recognizing a "Jewish ethic" at work in Jewish economic behavior, attributed not only to contingent factors but also in part to religious influences such as the more positive attitude to commercial activity in the Talmud when compared to Christian texts, is Werner Mosse, whose detailed studies of the nineteenth- and early twentieth-century German Jewish economic elite stand in contrast to the general tendency among historians to avoid dwelling on the dynamics of Jewish financial success, in that particular place and time above all.[74] For the early modern period, Jonathan Israel has provided an integrated Jewish history largely driven by commerce and has revisited aspects of Jewish economic distinctiveness that have been too delicate for most postwar historians to address, such as the sheltered experience and advantageous impact of the Thirty Years' War for German Jewry.[75] Focusing more recently on the vitally important role of Sephardic and converso Jews in the commercial networks of the early modern Atlantic, Israel has argued that the Sephardim were international "cross-cultural brokers" par excellence from the mid-sixteenth to the mid-eighteenth century, possessing a cultural malleability and a geographical reach unmatched by any other trading diaspora in this period.[76] However, Jewish economic history remains for the most part a somewhat hesitant field, more comfortable with microstudies and the deconstruction of stereotypes than with ambitious synthesis or theorization.

In a characteristically incisive essay, Natalie Zemon Davis has pinpointed both the importance and the central limitation of Sombart's approach to the study of religion and capitalism. She rightly identifies him, together with Weber, as a key pioneer of the study of the role of religion and culture in shaping economic behavior and economic change. However, their highly influential framing of these questions, was, she argues, flawed by the narrowness of their "one-path model" of modernization.[77] Reading Glikl of Hameln's memoirs alongside Jacob Emden's contemporaneous biography recording the piety and moderation of his father, the rabbi Zevi Hirsch Ashkenazi, Davis shows that Jewish attitudes to money were much more complicated and varied than Sombart suggests, even within the single, highly mercantile environment of seventeenth-century Hamburg. "Understanding those differences," she concludes, "is the business of the historian."[78] The nuanced exploration and interpretation of such particularities has certainly been the immense strength of history influenced by the discipline's "anthropological turn," of which Davis has been a leading exponent. However, continuities, recurrences, and connections in history demand our attention no less than differences and particularities. Historians should certainly aspire to be much more attuned to internal dissonances and individual or local distinctions in Jewish commercial culture than Sombart was. This should not, though, blot out our recognition of the countervailing strength of his theoretical ambition and synthetic drive. A meaningfully integrated approach to Jewish economic history is impossible unless we restore to some extent the methodological legitimacy of this goal.

Jewish history has become a field particularly averse to "grand theory." This is partly a natural disciplinary reaction to the heavy over-determination to which Jews have been subjected in the past and the role this has played in genocidal anti-Semitism. Christian, Marxist, and nationalist theories of history (including Zionism) have imbued and continue to imbue the Jewish past and the Jewish future with pregnant significance. The work of many Jewish historians writing today is shaped by a concern to diffuse these narratives by challenging the stereotypes associated with them and advancing alternative ways of thinking about Jewish history that emphasize diversity, individual agency, and comparability with the experiences of other ethnic groups. This scholarship has indubitably been of immense value in displacing entrenched stereotypes and providing a much richer and more nuanced understanding of Jewish history. However, micro-specialization and diversification has come at the expense of the exploration of long-term connections and continuities. Without sustained attention to these, the field risks a loss of the analytical language that binds the study of Jewish history together and connects it to other terrains of inquiry.

The serious study of economic history demands a particularly hard-nosed attention to the often uncomfortable realities of the workings of money and power. Without this, lingering evasions and embarrassments inevitably fester and readily mutate into awkward taboos, hostile stereotypes, or conspiracy theories. The "ethnic turn," as Eli Lederhendler has argued in the context of modern American Jewish history (and modern American history more broadly), has reflected a shift of scholarly interest toward subjective and elective aspects of personal identity and away from attention to the importance of labor and economic activity within a social framework of class.[79] It is not so long ago that the class-based analysis of Jewish history was not only intellectually vibrant but also a major influence on Zionist ideology and praxis.[80] However, the political shifts of the past few decades have led that particular analytical tradition into an impasse. Socialist Zionism has since the middle of the last century had to negotiate the increasingly embarrassing dependence on Sombartian thinking: its call for the transformatory normalization of Jewish economic activity was inescapably predicated on an acceptance of Sombart's historical diagnosis of the Jews as particularly associated with capitalism. Other modes of engagement with the politics of Jewish commerce have not sat easily with the image anxieties and counter-stereotypical reflexes that have so strongly inflected recent historiography on the Jews. In many ways, this is legitimate grounds for relief: economics is at last no longer necessarily the lens through which Jewish–non-Jewish relations are primarily viewed and interpreted. However, economics still matters, and although the connections between religion and capitalism perceived by both Sombart and Weber were in many ways reductive and problematic, their research is not without merit or insight, and the field of inquiry they opened up remains worthy of serious attention.[81]

The boldest and most innovative recent work in Jewish history has been willing to embrace sweeping generalizations about Jews, commerce, and history. Yuri Slezkine's analysis of the twentieth century as "the Jewish century," in which majority populations, hitherto primarily agrarian, hurriedly sought to imitate the mercurial flexibility, mobility, and entrepreneurialism of the Jews, offers an excellent example of the stimulating power of ambitious and uninhibited synthetic argument.[82] Slezkine's work leaves plenty for specialists to quibble over and has provoked unease among those who feel that publicly emphasizing certain forms of Jewish distinctiveness, particularly in relation to money, is simplistic, vulgar, or dangerously close to the stock themes of anti-Semitism. Whether or not these general fears are still warranted, it is surely time for the field of Jewish economic history to escape from their shadow. Without a license to generalize, historians will always struggle to be interesting; and without a willingness to overcome the constraints on discussion of the particularities of Jewish commerce, this field will remain mired in a repetitious discourse of disavowal. The road toward a more ambitious, integrated, frank and challenging approach to Jewish economic history is signaled by a return to big questions about the relationships among commerce, culture, and power across the broad sweep of Jewish history—questions first raised and systematically explored, for all his flaws, by Werner Sombart.

Notes

Introduction

1. Daron Acemoglu and James A. Robinson, *Why Nations Fail: The Origins of Power, Prosperity and Poverty* (New York: Crown Business, 2012); Francesco Boldizzoni, *The Poverty of Clio: Resurrecting Economic History* (Princeton, N.J.: Princeton University Press, 2011); On the question of Jews and the economy, see Gideon Reuveni and Sarah Wobick-Segev, eds., *The Economy in Jewish History: New Perspectives on the Interrelationship Between Ethnicity and Economic Life* (New York: Berghahn Books, 2011); Rebecca Kobrin, ed., *Chosen Capital: The Jewish Encounter with American Capitalism* (New Brunswick, N.J.: Rutgers University Press, 2012); and Jerry Muller, *Capitalism and the Jews* (Princeton, N.J.: Princeton University Press, 2010).

2. This insight was first developed by Marx in the mid-nineteenth century. Karl Marx, "The Eighteenth Brumaire of Louis Napoleon," in *The Marx-Engels Reader*, ed. R. Tucker (New York: Norton, 1978), 595.

3. Jonathan Karp, "Can Economic History Date the Inception of Jewish Modernity?," in Reuveni and Wobick-Segev, eds., *The Economy in Jewish History*, 23.

4. Karl Marx, "Zur Judenfrage," *Deutsch-Französische Jahrbücher* (February 1844). For English versions, see Karl Marx, "On the Jewish Question," in *The Marx-Engels Reader*, ed. R. Tucker, 26–46; Werner Sombart, *The Jews and Modern Capitalism*, trans. M. Epstein (Glencoe, Ill.: Free Press, 1951).

5. See most recently, Muller, *Capitalism and the Jews*, 32–45, 53–60.

6. This group will be discussed in more detail below.

7. The essay by Adam Sutcliffe in this volume is the only one to examine Sombart's theory in depth, and it is he who expresses the need to reconsider the importance of the grand theory.

8. The historiographical discussion that follows is by no means intended to be a comprehensive survey, but rather to point out what the authors see as some of the major trends and most important works written in the field over the last century.

9. Leopold Zunz, *Etwas über die rabbinische Literatur* (Berlin: In der Maurerschen Buchhandkung, 1818), 24. For further discussion of this essay, see Gideon Reuveni,

"Prolegomena to an Economic Turn in Jewish History," in Reuveni and Wobick-Segev, *The Economy in Jewish History*, 2.

10. On Schiper, see Jacob Litman, *The Economic Role of Jews in Medieval Poland: The Contribution of Yitzhak Schipper* (Lanham, Md.: University Press of America, 1984).

11. Ignacy Schiper, quoted in Raphael Mahler, "Yitzhak Schipper (1884–1943)," in idem, *Historiker un vegveizer* (Tel Aviv: Farlag Israel Bukh, 1967), 260. For a slightly different translation see Litman, *The Economic Role of Jews in Medieval Poland*, 247.

12. On interwar Jewish historiography in Poland, see Artur Eisenbach, "Jewish Historiography in Interwar Poland," in *The Jews of Poland Between Two World Wars*, ed. I. Gutman (Hanover, N.H.: University Press of New England, 1989), 453–93; Natalia Aleksiun, "Narratives Under Siege: Polish-Jewish Relations and Jewish Historical Writings in Interwar Poland," in *Antisemitism Worldwide 2003–2004*, ed. Dina Porat and Roni Stauber (Tel Aviv: Tel Aviv University, 2005), 29–50.

13. Emanuel Ringelblum, *Projekty i próby przewarstwowienia Żydów w epoce stanisławowskiej*. Offprint from *Sprawy Narodowościowe* 8 (1934). Raphael Mahler, *Yidn in amolikn poyln in likht fun tsifern* (Warsaw: Yidish bukh, 1958). Mahler also went on to publish an important statistical study of interwar Polish Jewry, giving much detail about economic structure; see Raphael Mahler, *Yehudei Polin bein shtei milhamot `olam* (Tel Aviv: Dvir, 1968).

14. Much work remains to be done on the groups of Jewish historians writing Marxist history in the Soviet Union in the 1920s. In the meantime, see Avraham Greenbaum, *Jewish Scholarship and Scholarly Institutions in Soviet Russia, 1918–1953* (Jerusalem: Hebrew University, 1978). Also see Deborah Yalen, "Red kasrilevke: Soviet Ethnographies of Economic Transformation in the Soviet Shtetl, 1917–1939" (Ph.D. diss., University of California–Berkeley, 2007).

15. Gershon Hundert, "The Role of the Jews in Commerce in Early Modern Poland-Lithuania," *Journal of European Economic History* 16 (1987): 245–57.

16. On Mahler, see the entry in *YIVO Encyclopedia of Jews in Eastern Europe*, ed. G. Hundert, 2008. http://www.yivoencyclopedia.org/article.aspx/Mahler_Raphael.

17. For the English version, see Raphael Mahler, *Hasidism and the Jewish Enlightenment: Their Confrontation in Galicia and Poland in the First Half of the Nineteenth Century*, trans. E. Orenstein, A. Klein, and J. Machlowitz Klein (Philadelphia: Jewish Publication Society, 1985).

18. On the attitude to Mahler of a leading figure in the Jerusalem School, Shmuel Ettinger, see Jacob Barnai, *Shmuel Ettinger: Historion, moreh, ve-ʻish tsibur* (Jerusalem: Merkaz Zalman Shazar, 2011). Interestingly enough, Ettinger had written a pathbreaking study of his own on Jewish economic history as part of his doctorate on the history of the Jews of Ukraine before 1648. The section was published as a separate article, but Ettiger never followed it up with another study in the field. Shmuel Ettinger, "Helkam shel ha-yehudim be-kolonizatsiyah shel Ukra'inah (1569–1648)," *Zion* 21 (1956): 107–42.

19. Ben-Zion Dinur, "Reshitah shel ha-hasidut ve-yesodoteihah ha-sotsi'aliyim ve-ha-meshihiyim," in idem, *Bemifnei hadorot* (Jerusalem: Mossad Bialik, 1955), 83–227; Chone Shmeruk, "Mashma'utah ha-hevratit shel ha-shehitah ha-hasidit," *Zion* 20 (1955): 47–72; idem, "Ha-hasidut ve-`iskei ha-hakhirot," *Zion* 35 (1970): 182–92.

20. On "pariah capitalism," see Daniel Gutwein, "Kapitalizm, pariah kapitalizm u-mi'ut: Temurot ba-teoriyah ha-yehudit shel Marx `al reka ha-diyun be-ma'afyanei ha-kalkalah ha-yehudit," in *Dat ve-kalkalah—yahasei gomlin: Shay le-Ya'akov Katz bi-mle'ot lo tish`im shana*, ed. M. Ben-Sasson (Jerusalem: Merkaz Zalman Shazar, 1995), 65–76; idem, "Ha-yahas bein ha-yehudim ve-ha-kapitalizm be-tfisato shel Marx: Mi-Sombart le-Weber," *Zion* 55 (1990): 419–47.

21. Selma Stern, *The Court Jew* (Philadelphia: Jewish Publication Society, 1950).

22. Hannah Arendt, *The Origins of Totalitarianism* (New York: Harcourt, Brace and Co., 1951), 11–28.

23. Heinrich Schnee, *Die Hoffinanz und der moderne Staat: Geschichte und System der Hoffaktoren an deutschen Fürstenhöfen im Zeitalter des Absolutismus*, 6 vols. (Berlin: Duncker & Humblot, 1953–67).

24. Bernard Weinryb's review was published in the *Journal of Economic History* 18, no. 2 (1958): 234–36. Another German professor who published on Jewish economic history during and after the Nazi period was Herman Kellenbenz. His work did not stir up the same hostility as Schnee's. See Herman Kellenbenz, *Sephardim an der unteren Elbe. Ihre wirtschaftliche und politische Bedeutung vom Ende des 16. bis zum Beginn des 18. Jahrhunderts* (Wiesbaden: Steiner, 1958).

25. The situation behind the iron curtain was, however, different. In People's Poland, there was a small group of dedicated Polish Jewish historians who continued to write on the economic aspects of Polish Jewish history. Due to the exigencies of state censorship, their work was written along strictly Marxist lines and tended to be highly empirical and archive-based. Prominent in the group were Jakub Goldberg, Janina Morgensztern, Maurycy Horn, and Anatol Leszczyński. Of these, only Goldberg left Poland for the West, settling in Israel in 1968. He continued to write on economic history in his new home. He also encouraged those graduate students with whom he worked to take on economic themes in their research. See Adam Teller and Magda Teter, "Introduction: Borders and Boundaries in the Historiography of the Jews in the Polish-Lithuanian Commonwealth," *Polin* 22 (2010): 25–33; Adam Teller, "Polish-Jewish Relations: Historical Research and Social Significance: On the Legacy of Jacob Goldberg," *Studia Judaica* 15, nos. 1–2 [29–39] (2012): 27–47.

26. Jonathan Israel, *European Jewry in the Age of Mercantilism, 1550–1750* (Oxford: Oxford University Press, 1985).

27. David Engel, "Crisis and Lachrymosity: On Salo Baron, Neobaronianism, and the Study of Modern European Jewish History," *Jewish History* 20, nos. 3–4 (December 2006): 243–64; Robert Liberles, *Salo Wittamayer Baron: Architect of Jewish History* (New York: New York University Press, 1995).

28. Liberles, *Salo Wittamayer Baron*, 168.

29. Salo Wittmayer Baron, "Ghetto and Emancipation: Shall We Revise the Traditional View?," *Menorah Journal* 14 (1928): 515–26; idem, "Modern Capitalism and the Jewish Fate," *Menorah Journal* 30 (1942): 116–38.

30. Salo Wittmayer Baron, "Ghetto and Emancipation: Shall We Revise the Traditional View?" *Menorah Journal* 14 (June 1928): 515–26.

31. For more on Simon Kuznets, see Moses Abramovitz, "Simon Kuznets, 1901–1985," *Journal of Economic History* 46, no. 1 (1986): 241–46; Vibha Kapuria-Foreman and Mark Perelman, "An Economic Historian's Economist: Remembering Simon Kuznets, 1901–1985," *Economic Journal* 105 (November 1995): 1524–47.

32. E. Glen Weyl, "Introduction: Simon Kuznets, Cautious Empiricist of the Eastern European Jewish Diaspora," in *Jewish Economies*, ed. Stephanie Lo and E. Glen Weyl (New Brunswick, N.J.: Transaction Publishers, 2012).

33. Ibid., xxiv–xxv.

34. Kapuria-Foreman and Perlman "An Economic Historian's Economist," 1526, 1529.

35. See in particular Simon Kuznets's "Economic Structure and Life of the Jews," in *The Jews: Their History, Culture and Religion*, vol. 2, ed. Louis Finkelstein (New York: Harper and Brothers, 1960), 1597–1661.

36. Jonathan Frankel, "Introduction to Arcadius Kahan," in *Essays in Jewish Social and Economic History*, ed. Roger Weiss (Chicago: University of Chicago Press, 1986), xii.

37. There is a robust literature on the places Jews have occupied in the social hierarchy of the United States and how that relates to larger theories on market structure in the United States. For examples, see these pioneering essays of Barry R. Chiswick: "The Occupational Attainment and Earnings of American Jewry, 1890 to 1990," *Contemporary Jewry* 20 (1999): 68–98; "The Skills and Economic Status of American Jewry," in *Terms of Survival: The Jewish World Since 1945*, ed. Robert S. Wistrich (London: Routledge, 1995), 115–29; "The Occupational Attainment of American Jewry, 1900–2000," *Contemporary Jewry* 27 (2007): 80–111.

38. Kahan, *Essays in Jewish Economic and Social History*; Simon Kuznets, "Immigration of Russian Jews to the United States: Background and Structure," *Perspectives in American History* 9 (1975): 35–124; Calvin Goldscheider and Alan S. Zuckerman, *The Transformation of the Jews* (Chicago: University of Chicago Press, 1984); Marshall Sklare, ed., *America's Jews* (New York: Random House, 1971).

39. In a different way, this can also be seen in Fritz Stern's classic biography of Gerson von Bleichröder, banker to Otto von Bismarck, *Gold and Iron: Bismarck, Bleichröder, and the Building of the German Empire* (New York: Knopf, 1979). This is a study of the relationship between the two men, based on the economic services that Bleichröder gave his master. Yet while it describes in detail the banker's economic activities, the book's focus is clearly on the social and political aspects of the story and what they can tell us about relations between Germans and Jews in the second half of the nineteenth century.

40. The one notable exception is Barry Chiswick, who continued to explore Jews' place in the economy throughout this era. See Barry R. Chiswick, "The Post-War Economy of American Jews," in "A New Jewry? America Since the Second World War,

1948–1968," ed. Peter Y. Medding, *Studies in Contemporary Jewry* 8 (1992): 85–101, as well as those articles referred to in n. 36, above.

41. The shift from seeing Jews as an ethnic minority to part of the dominant racial majority ("white") was part of a larger shift in how ethnic difference was dealt with in the academy. On this general topic, see Mary C. Waters, *Ethnic Options: Choosing Identities in America* (Berkeley: University of California Press, 1990); Matthew Frye Jacobsen, *Roots Too: White Ethnic Revival in Post-Civil Rights America* (Cambridge, Mass.: Harvard University Press, 2006). For work that specifically addresses how Jews became "white," see Karen Brodkin, *How Jews Became White Folks and What that Says About Race in America* (New Brunswick, N.J.: Rutgers University Press, 1998); Eric Goldstein, *The Price of Whiteness: Jews, Race and American Identity* (Princeton, N.J.: Princeton University Press, 2008). For the problem with this erasure of Jewish difference in the writing of American Jewish economic history, see David Hollinger, "Rich, Powerful, and Smart: Jewish Overrepresentation Should Be Explained Rather than Mystified or Avoided," *Jewish Quarterly Review* 94, no. 4 (Fall 2004): 595–602.

42. Israel, *European Jewry in the Age of Mercantilism.*

43. Derek Jonathan Penslar, *Shylock's Children: Economics and Jewish Identity in Modern Europe* (Berkeley: University of California Press, 2001).

44. Ibid., 262.

45. Jonathan Karp, *The Politics of Jewish Commerce: Economic Thought and Emancipation in Europe, 1638–1848* (Cambridge: Cambridge University Press, 2008).

46. Muller, *Capitalism and the Jews.*

47. Eli Lederhendler, *Jewish Immigrants and American Capitalism, 1880–1920: From Caste to Class* (Cambridge: Cambridge University Press, 2009).

48. In fact, the notes to many of the studies in Rebecca Kobrin's edited volume, *Chosen Capital: The Jewish Encounter with American Capitalism* (New Brunswick, N.J.: Rutgers University Press, 2012), bear witness to the existence of a number of economic studies of Jewish immigrant experience in the United States written as early as the 1990s.

49. Reuveni, "Prolegomena to an Economic Turn in Jewish History," 8.

50. Jonathan Israel, *Diasporas within a Diaspora: Jews, Crypto-Jews, and the World Maritime Empires (1540–1740)* (Leiden: Brill, 2002).

51. See, e.g., Jessica V. Roitman, *The Same but Different: Inter-Cultural Trade and the Sephardim, 1559–1640* (Leiden: Brill, 2011).

52. Sarah Abrevaya Stein, *Plumes: Ostrich Feathers, Jews, and a Lost World of Global Commerce* (New Haven, Conn.: Yale University Press, 2008).

53. Avner Greif, *Institutions and the Path to the Modern Economy: Lessons from Medieval Trade* (Cambridge: Cambridge University Press, 2006). Since the publication of his study, historians have returned to this field, bringing a much less heavily theoretical approach, and sometimes disputing his findings. See Jessica Goldberg, *Trade and Institutions in the Medieval Mediterranean: The Geniza Merchants and Their Business World* (Cambridge: Cambridge Unversity Press, 2012); Phillip Ackerman-Lieberman,

The Business of Identity: Jews, Muslims, and Economic Life in Medieval Egypt (Stanford, Calif.: Stanford University Press, 2014).

54. In historical terms, Greif's work relied heavily on the massive studies of Professor Shlomo Dov Goitein, whose work on the world of the Cairo Geniza documents from decades earlier dealt very intensively with economic history. See Shlomo Dov Goitein, *A Mediterranean Society: The Jewish Communities of the Arab World as Portrayed in the Documents of the Cairo Geniza*, 6 vols. (Princeton, N.J.: Princeton University Press, 1967–1985); Volume 1 is dedicated to economic issues.

55. The best introduction to his work is probably still Douglass North, *Structure and Change in Economic History* (New York: Norton, 1981). See also idem, *Institutions, Institutional Change and Economic Performance* (Cambridge: Cambridge University Press, 1990); Ronald Coase, "The New Institutional Economics," *American Economic Review* 88, no. 2 (1998): 72–75; Oliver E. Williamson, "The New Institutional Economics: Taking Stock, Looking Ahead," *Journal of Economic Literature* 38, no. 3 (2000): 595–613.

56. Adam Teller, *Kesef, koah ve-hashpa'ah: Ha-yehudim be-'ahuzot bet Radzhivil be-Lita' ba-me'ah ha-18* (Jerusalem: Merkaz Zalman Shazar, 2005). This monograph is slated to appear in English translation in 2015. In its embrace of economic theory, Teller's work represents a break with studies in the field that preceded his, including Moshe Rosman, *The Lords' Jews: Magnate-Jewish Relations in the Polish Lithuanian Commonwealth during the Eighteenth Century* (Cambridge, Mass.: Harvard University Press, 1990); Gershon Hundert, *The Jews in a Polish Private Town: The Case of Opatów in the Eighteenth Century* (Baltimore: Johns Hopkins University Press, 1992).

57. Francesca Trivellato, *The Familiarity of Strangers: The Sephardic Diaspora, Livorno, and Cross-Cultural Trade in the Early Modern Period* (New Haven, Conn.: Yale University Press, 2009).

58. For another, recent example of this, see Maristella Botticini and Zvi Eckstein, *The Chosen Few: How Education Shaped Jewish History, 70–1492* (Princeton, N.J.: Princeton University Press, 2011).

59. Penslar, *Shylock's Children*, 3.

60. First published as Werner Sombart, *Die Juden und das Wirtschaftsleben* (Leipzig: Duncker & Humblot, 1911).

Chapter 1. Licenses, Cartels, and Kehila

1. For bibliographic details on this document, see n. 95. On the term *keri'a*, see n. 26.

2. Shakespeare, *The Merchant of Venice*, 3.3.26–29; see also 4.1.101–2 and 3.2. 278–79.

3. For survey treatments, see Michele Luzzati, "Ruolo e funzioni dei banchi ebraici dell'Italia centro-settentrionale nei secoli XV e XVI," in *Banchi pubblici, banchi privati e monti di pietà nell'Europa preindustriale: Amministrazione, tecniche operative e ruoli economici; Atti del convegno, Genova, 1–6 ottobre 1990* (Genoa: Società ligure di storia patria, 1991), 733–49; and Luzzati, "Banchi e insediamenti ebraici nell'Italia centro-settentrionale fra tardo Medioevo e inizi dell'Età moderna," in *Gli ebrei in Italia*, ed. Corrado Vivanti, vol. 11 of *Storia d'Italia: Annali* (Turin: Giulio Einaudi, 1996),

173–235. Still useful is Léon Poliakov, *Les banchieri juifs et le saint-siège du XIIIe au XVIIe siècle* (Paris: S.E.V.P.E.N., 1976; the English translation by Miriam Kochan, *Jewish Bankers and the Holy See from the Thirteenth to the Seventeenth Century* [London: Routledge and Kegan Paul, 1977], is incomplete, omitting most of the footnotes and all the appendices). A major revision in our understanding of the markets for Jewish loans, especially in fifteenth-century Tuscany, is offered by Maristella Botticini, "A Tale of 'Benevolent' Governments: Private Credit Markets, Public Finance, and the Role of Jewish Lenders in Medieval and Renaissance Italy," *Journal of Economic History* 60, no. 1 (March 2000): 164–89.

4. For an example of such a claim to immunity made by bankers in Bologna at roughly the same time, see Bernard Cooperman, "Political Discourse in a Kabbalistic Register: Isaac de Lattes' Plea for Stronger Communal Government," in *Be'erot Yitzhak: Studies in Memory of Isadore Twersky*, ed. Jay M. Harris (Cambridge, Mass.: Harvard University Press, 2005), 47–68, 79*–93*.

5. There are many studies of the history of Rome's Jewish community over the centuries. Shlomo Simonsohn provides an overview of both primary sources and secondary literature in "The Pope's Jews: A. Rome," in *Apostolic See and the Jews: History*, Studies and Texts 109 (Toronto: Pontifical Institute of Medieval Studies, 1991), 402–23.

6. See n. 36.

7. Responsa of Isaac de Lattes, Österreichischen Nationalbibliothek (Vienna), Cod. Heb. 24; Institute for Microfilmed Hebrew Manuscripts at the Jewish National Library in Jerusalem, 1303. In the descriptive catalog by Arthur Zacharias Schwarz, *Die hebräischen Handschriften der Nationalbibliothek in Wien* (Leipzig: K. W. Hiersemann, 1925), the manuscript is listed as Hebrew 80. Mordekhai Tzvi [Max Hermann] Friedländer produced a partial edition of de Lattes's *She'elot u-Teshuvot* (Vienna: I. Knöpflmacher, 1860).

8. Roman archives contain almost endless material that could easily provide a lifetime of work to any scholar dedicated to tracing the Jewish financial sector over the years. For example, the Fondo Banchieri ebrei (Archivio di Stato di Roma at EUR) alone contains 88 volumes of notarized records dating from 1585 to 1684. I have limited myself to the Hebrew-language notarial records commonly referred to as *Notai ebrei* and preserved in the Archivio Storico Capitolino, Rome, Sezione III. Documents are cited by F. (*filza*), l. (*libro*), and fol. (*folio*). Where the notarial register is not paginated, I have placed my folio references in brackets. Unfortunately, volumes for the period October 1543–August 1548 are no longer extant. It is a pleasure to thank the staff of the Archivio Capitolino, and in particular Anna Maria La Pica and Nicola Immediato, for assistance that often went well beyond what a researcher should reasonably expect. Kenneth Stow prepared annotated summaries (*regesta*) for 2,005 of the Hebrew documents through late January 1557; *Jews in Rome* (Leiden: Brill, 1995 and 1997). Although I have been guided throughout by his listing, I have checked each document in the original, and there have inevitably been many points at which we disagree over the details or substance of inividual documents. Rather than encumbering this chapter with specifics, I

have simply noted the number assigned by Stow to each document so that readers can easily compare our readings and interpretations.

Dates in this chapter have been calculated according to the Julian calendar through the tables provided in Natan Fried, ed., *Luah le-Sheshet Alafim Shana: Luah Hashva'a la-Minyanim ha-Shonim mi-Bri'at ha-Olam ad Sof ha-Elef ha-Shishi* (Jerusalem: Mosad ha-Rav Kuk, 1975–76), based on the work of A. S. Akaviah. Occasionally the day of the week provided in the notarial text differs from the one calculated in the *Luah*. I believe that this is because events held at night might be referred to by the Christian day of the week but the Hebrew day of the month, and the two calendars differ for the hours between sunset and midnight. For example, F. 11, l. 4, fol. 23v (Stow, *Jews in Rome*, §486) records a meeting that took place on "Sunday, 3 Marheshvan, [5]301." In that year, however, Sunday fell on 2 Marheshvan. If the meeting was held Sunday night after sunset, it would have been considered 3 Marheshvan in the Hebrew calendar. The corresponding Julian date was Sunday, October 3, 1540. (For at least one case where this reconstruction seems not to apply, see n. 83.)

9. Anna Esposito, "Credito, Ebrei, Monte di Pietà a Roma tra Quattro e Cinquecento," *Roma Moderna e Contemporanea* 10 (2002): 559–82.

10. Ibid., 563–64; Anna Esposito, "Prestatori ebrei a Marino alla fine del quattrocento: Nuove testimonianze," *Rassegna Mensile di Israel* 67 (2001): 265–74.

11. The charter of 1473 issued by Pope Sixtus IV for Isaac, Abraham, and their partners quashed the proceedings against their illegal operation; Shlomo Simonsohn, *Apostolic See and the Jews* (Toronto: Pontifical Institute of Mediaeval Studies, 1988–91), §967, 1206–8.

12. *Motuproprio* of Pope Leo X in Simonsohn, *Apostolic See and the Jews*, §1292 (September 14, 1521), 1618–21: "vocatis Hebreis in dicta Urbe fenus exercentibus, litterasque predictas patentes habentibus, easdem litteras . . . mutes, innoves et confirmes, numerumque feneratorum competentem, . . . dummodo ultra XX computatis banchis sociorum suorum a te tolerandis in dicta Urbe, non teneantur" (1619). Although supervision over Roman Jews fell normally to the office of the papal *vicario*, control over the Jewish bankers was a jealously guarded right of the *camerlengo*; see, for example, ibid., §§1401–2 (March 8 and April 12, 1529), 1749, and §2038 (June 25, 1541), 2225–26. The first *capitoli* issued by the *camerlengo* Francesco Armellino seem not to have survived; the renewal issued by his successor, Agostino Spinola, in 1534 was published by Esposito, "Credito, Ebrei, Monte di Pietà," 576–78.

13. The license renewal of 1534 specifically states that no additional tax could be required of the bankers beyond what the community already paid. However, the same document mentions an annual fee of one hundred *ducati d'oro* paid directly to the *camerlengo*. The text also refers to "la taxa de li mutuanti che haranno a pagar annuatim" to be assigned or apportioned each year by the bankers' elected leaders. Whether this refers to how the fee of one hundred ducats was divided or to some separate membership fee paid to the cartel itself, it is significant that government officials could step in to regulate the process; Esposito, "Credito, Ebrei, Monte di Pietà," 577–78.

14. The *motuproprio* of 1521 complains that the moneylenders already operating in Rome under individual licenses are taking an "immoral" rate "beyond what the Holy Mother Church commonly tolerates—namely one giulio or leo for each ducat per month," a rate that (assuming that we are dealing in moneys of account) amounted to 10 percent per month. From 1521 the rate could not exceed half that (twenty quattrini per ducat equivalent, assuming four quattrini per baiocco and one hundred baiocchi per ducat, to 5 percent per month or 60 percent per annum). For rates later, see n. 87. For a brief overview of changing moneys of account and values of coinage in papal Rome in the period, see Jean Delumeau, "Problèmes monétaires et hausse des prix," in *Rome au XVIe siècle* (Paris: Hachette, 1957), pt. 3, chap. 1, 159–82; for greater detail, see Delumeau, *Vie économique et sociale de Rome dans la seconde moitié du XVIe siècle* (Paris: Éditions E. de Boccard, 1959), 2:655–88.

15. I intentionally use the modern term "cartel" rather than "guild" since there is no indication that the group served any other purposes than monopolistic ones. Emmanuel Rodocanachi, whose pioneering study *Les corporations ouvrières à Rome depuis la chute de l'empire romain* (Paris: A. Picard et fils, 1894) provided detailed descriptions of the organizations of many city guilds, commented that "no people ever possessed the instinct, taste, and genius of association to a higher degree than the people of Rome" (v).

16. On the day-to-day operation of the banks, see Poliakov, *Banchieri juifs*, chap. 6. Poliakov (309–28) provides a French translation of the seventeenth-century parody "The Book of the Laws of the Lender and Borrower," based on the text published by Abraham N. Z. Roth as "Sefer Hilkhot Malve ve-Love ha-Meyuhas be-Ta'ut le Zecharia Pulyese [i.e., Pugliese]," *Hebrew Union College Annual* 26 (1955): Hebrew section, 39–74. Although the text is humorous in its intent, it does give us a sense of how the banks functioned and how they were physically arranged.

17. The terminology seems to have been flexible. *Brurim* here would probably be best translated as "elected" rather than as "arbitrators," the most common use for the term in Hebrew legal literature. The 1534 renewal of the license refers at one point to "deputati da li sopradetti doi soperiori" and "lor fattore infra mensem," suggesting that each month one of the two served as "*parnas* of the month" and that for at least one of their tasks they "deputized" others; Esposito, "Credito, Ebrei, Monte di Pietà," 578.

18. The relation between partnerships in banks and voting rights in the cartel remains to be clarified.

19. This is from the notarized Hebrew record of the election of two officers held on June 11, 1536; *Notai Ebrei*, F. 11, l. 3, fol. [95v—last unnumbered page], a rough draft, and F. 11, l. 1, fol. [17v], a clean copy of the same document; Stow, *Jews in Rome*, §§28 and 80.

20. Esposito, "Credito, Ebrei, Monte di Pietà," 578–79. Esposito mentions four charters of renewal in the sixteenth century (1534, 1552, 1561, and 1589), of which she reproduces the first two. Note that these were notarized by a Christian notary and then submitted to the papal authorities.

21. Simonsohn, *Apostolic See and the Jews*, 1620: "omnibus et singulis raby, magistris Hebreorum . . . ut omnes et singulas excommunicationes contra Hebreos feneratores

huiusmodi, seu eorum aliquem, dicta de causa impositas et forsitan imponendas, removeant, irritent, aboleant et penitus deleant."

22. I stress that this shift antedated the introduction of the ghetto, which was, it seems to me, as much a response to as a cause of major changes in the patterns of Jewish settlement and organization in Italy. For a different approach, see Stefanie Siegmund, *The Medici State and the Ghetto of Florence: The Construction of an Early Modern Jewish Community* (Stanford, Calif.: Stanford University Press, 2005), who argues that ghettoization in Florence and, by extension, Jewish communal structure there derived from the needs of the early modern state.

23. For Mantua, see Shlomo Simonsohn, *History of the Jews in the Duchy of Mantua* (Jerusalem: Kiryath Sefer, 1997), 318–24 and 505–17 (highlighted in Robert Bonfil, *Jewish Life in Renaissance Italy* [Berkeley: University of California Press, 1994], 192–93). For Bologna, see Bernard Cooperman, "Theorizing Jewish Self-Government in Early Modern Italy," in *Una Manna Buona per Mantova: Man Tov le-Man Tovah; Studi in onore di Vittore Colorni per il suo 92° compleanno,* ed. Mauro Perani (Florence: Olschki, 2004), 365–80.

24. On the institution generally, see Louis Isaac Rabinowitz, *The* Ḥerem Hayyishub: *A Contribution to the Medieval Economic History of the Jews* (London: E. Goldston, 1945). For the *hazaka* and banking, see Bernard Cooperman, "A Rivalry of Bankers: Responsa Concerning Banking Rights in Pisa in 1547," in *Studies in Medieval Jewish History and Literature*, vol. 2, ed. I. Twersky (Cambridge, Mass.: Harvard University Press, 1984), 41–81. As for the *hazaka* applied to residential property, Amedeo Tagliacozzo assumes that it was linked to ghettoization; "Lo 'jus di gazagà' nell'ordinamento giuridico italiano," in *Scritti in memoria di Umberto Nahon—Saggi sull'Ebraismo Italiano*, ed. Roberto Bonfil, Daniel Carpi, Maria Modena Mayer, Giorgio Romano, and Gisueppe B. Sermoneta (Jerusalem: Fondazioni Sally Mayer and Raffaele Cantoni, 1978), 240–55. I hope to investigate this further in a separate study.

25. Bernard Cooperman, "Ethnicity and Institution Building Among Jews in Early Modern Rome," *AJS Review* 30 (2006): 119–45.

26. The term is evidenced in Rome at least as early as November 13, 1511 (Anna Esposito, *Un'altra Roma: Minoranze nazionali e comunità ebraiche tra Medioevo e Rinascimento* [Rome: Il Calamo, 1995], 270): Aragonese Jews discuss the "tre della cheria," the three whom their group elected each year to represent them on the council. The term derives from the Hebrew for "calling" and might therefore be translated "convocation."

27. Simonsohn, *Apostolic See and the Jews*, §1179, pp. 1482–83.

28. This terminology is adopted, for example, in the prologue (and papal response) to the constitution of 1524 that I shall discuss later; Houghton Library, Harvard University, MS Ital 141 (hereafter cited as Houghton MS Ital 141), fols. 1v–2v and 18v.

29. A document published by Attilio Milano, "I capitoli di Daniel da Pisa e la comunità di Roma," *Rassegna Mensile di Israel* 10 (1935–36): 324–38 and 409–426, mentions ten synagogues in 1524 (338), although in 326 n. 1, Milano mentions a possible eleventh.

Of the synagogues, perhaps half were organized specifically along "ethnic" lines for immigrant groups that maintained the liturgical traditions of their homelands.

30. For a summary of the evolution of Jewish self-government in Rome, see Cooperman, "Ethnicity and Institution Building among Jews in Early Modern Rome," especially 136–41, based heavily on the many archival studies of Anna Esposito. In the documents the local (i.e., non-*oltramontani*) Jews are variously referred to as Romani, Romaneschi, or Italiani. To avoid confusion, I have adopted the last of these terms (Italiani) to refer to Jews from central and north central Italy who traced their origins to the medieval Roman community and followed its liturgical traditions (*minhag roma*). I use the term "Roman" to refer to all Jews physically living in the city, whatever their origins and liturgical tradition.

31. For the date, see Milano, "Capitoli di Daniel da Pisa," 335, doc. 3.

32. None of the da Pisas appear as members on the various lists of cartel members. Daniel's brother Salomon later acquired a license, but so far as I have been able to determine, that was only after 1527. See below.

33. Simonsohn, *Apostolic See and the Jews*, §1327; confirmation dated December 12, 1524.

34. The communal *capitoli* of 1524 were brought to historians' attention in 1893 by two scholars: D. Castelli, "Notizia di un documento sulla storia degli Ebrei a Roma," *Archivio Storico Italiano*, ser. 5, 11 (1893): 398–407; and Abraham Berliner, *Geschichte der Juden in Rom* (Frankfurt am Main: J. Kaufmann, 1893), vol. 2, pt. 1, 88–95. Attilio Milano published large portions of the text in "Capitoli di Daniel da Pisa" from a manuscript that is unfortunately not currently available to scholars. I hope to present a detailed textual analysis at some point in the future.

35. What Paul Rieger wrote more than a century ago is unfortunately still true: "Concerning the inner life of the the community, we are still very poorly informed"; Hermann Vogelstein and Paul Rieger, *Geschichte der Juden in Rom* (Berlin: Mayer and Müller, 1895–96), 2:127. I rely on his numbers for the size of the council before 1524.

36. Houghton MS Ital 141: "Capitoli ordinationi statuti et informatione," as well as the brief of Clement VII addressed to "Universitati hebraeorum tam Romanorum quam ultramontanorum seu forentium in alma urbe nostra" (December 12, 1524). My thanks go to Mr. James Capobianco at the Houghton Library, who helped secure a copy of this manuscript for me. The manuscript (22 leaves; 23 cm.), formerly in the collection of Michael M. Zagayski, appears to be a clean copy prepared from the text intended for submission to the papal authorities for approval. I hope to offer a critical edition once I have had a chance to examine the manuscript published by Milano.

37. Curiously, there were only eighteen bankers at the meeting, divided equally into lists of Italiani and *oltramontani*. The *banchieri Italiani Romani* were M[aestr]o Servidio di Fioreno, Diodato di Nola, M.o Rafaello da Ferrara, Sabbatuccio di Tivoli, Rafaello di Camerino, Guiglelmo Sacerdoto, M.o Abraamo di Civitaducale, Salamone Charenita, and Dattilo da Rignano. The *oltramontani* were M.o Isaach Zarfati, M.o Moise Abudaram, Isaach Usiglio, Joseph el Tordose, Joseph Aven Pesat, Leone Gattegno,

Jacob Levi, Isaach de Himano, and Salamone Bergantino; Houghton MS Ital 141, fols. 1v–2r. This even division suggests that the banking licenses were assigned equally between the two communities.

38. Houghton MS Ital 141, fol. 1r–v.

39. Nicolò Tommaseo and Bernardo Bellini, *Dizionario della lingua italiana* (Turin: Unione Tipografico-Editrice, 1865), s.v. *artieri*.

40. In particular, the terms for "middle-level" and for "artisan" are used in contradictory senses. Milano, "Capitoli di Daniel da Pisa," 330, describes the second group as "heads of family, 'all very rich, notable and worthy'" (*ricchissimi tutti, signalati e degni*), and the third group as "from the broad Jewish population, that is, middle-level people, but all men of intelligence and prudence" (*dalla moltitudine ebrea, cioè uomini mediocri, ma tutti uomini di intelletto e di prudenza*). On 337 the second group is "rich" or "very rich," while the third group is middle-level (*mezzani*), and then the second group is made up of artisans (*artegiani*), while the third is middle-level.

41. "Tutti huomini che pagano le date nell'università di Roma"; ibid., 337, citing what Milano labels document 6.

42. Ibid., "Capitoli di Daniel da Pisa," 337, and Houghton MS Ital 141, fol. 2v.

43. Houghton MS Ital 141, fols. 1v–2v. So far as I am aware, there is no similar distinction by wealth or profession in the election process for Roman communal officials; cf. Emmanuel Rodocanachi, *Institutions communales de Rome sous la Papauté* (Paris: A. Picard, 1901).

44. Esposito, "Credito, Ebrei, Monte di pietà," 576 ff. Similar arrangements were implicit in the 1554 renewal, although the language is not quite so explicit.

45. Simonsohn, *Apostolic See and the Jews*, 1620.

46. On Isaac de Lattes, see Cooperman, "Political Discourse in a Kabbalistic Register"; and Bernard Cooperman, "Organizing Knowledge for the Jewish Market: An Editor/Printer in Sixteenth-Century Rome," in *Perspectives on the Hebraic Book: The Myron M. Weinstein Memorial Lectures at the Library of Congress*, ed. Peggy K. Pearlstein (Washington, D.C.: Library of Congress, 2012), 79–129. To the studies cited there, add Simon Schwarzfuchs, "Rabbi Isaac Joshua ben Immanuel of Lattes and the Jews of the Apostolic States," in *Gli ebrei nello Stato pontificio fino al Ghetto (1555)*, Italia judaica 6 (Rome: Ministero per i Beni Culturali e Ambientali, Ufficio Centrale per i Beni Archivistici, 1998), 66–79.

47. De Lattes, Responsa, fol. 47r–v, §31 in Schwarz, *Hebräischen Handschriften der Nationalbibliothek in Wien*, but not included in Friedländer's partial edition. De Lattes seems unsure about the date of the case. At the start he says that the matter had come before him in [5]302 (i.e., 1541–42), but then he signs his opinion with the date [5]301 (i.e., 1540–41). The exact dates are provided in *Notai ebrei*, F. 11, l. 3, fol. [24v]; Stow, *Jews in Rome*, §352, and the follow-up documents cited below.

48. The notary (see n. 47) refers to the two men as "*parnasim* of the committee of the twenty" and then, somewhat awkwardly, to Goioso as "of the *keri'a*."

49. This is the only mention I have yet seen that de Lattes was a medical doctor.

50. "I hereby attest that I have freed and given up my place et c[eter]a and presumptive right, and promise never at any time to take advantage of, nor cause [anyone else] to take advantage of the said place. Moreover, I renounce it from this moment and cede it to the said twenty [bankers' guild]." My thanks to Professor Sandra Debenedetti Stow for explaining the Roman dialectical term "da mo."

51. David da Sicilia may indeed have been an unusually and unreasonably litigious individual; Stow places him in several other lawsuits. For example, Stow says that in 1536 David refused to abide by an agreement reached between the French and Castilian congregations in Rome because he was not informed of the initial selection of arbiters (*Notai ebrei*, F. 11, l. 1, fol. 81r, Tuesday and Wednesday, January 4–5, 1536; Stow, *Jews in Rome*, §122). Striking is the terminology of the arbitration agreement on May 24, 1551, to resolve a dispute over the leasehold on the house in which David ben Shabbetai lived (*Notai ebrei*, F. 7, l. 1, fol. 86v; Stow, *Jews in Rome*, §1125): in addition to the usual agreement to abide by the arbiter's judgment, David was also enjoined from addressing "contentious words" (*devarim raviyim*—the reading is a little doubtful) toward the house owner. It should be noted, however, that in neither of these cases is the identity of the litigant certain. In the earlier text, only the given name David appears; in the later, the litigant is identified as David ben Shabbetai, but there is no reference to origins in Sicily. The name David ben Shabbetai was hardly unique in Rome at the time: a "Davit qd. Sabati Rogilla siculus macellarius" is mentioned by Anna Esposito and Micaela Procaccia, "La 'schola siculorum de Urbe': La fine della storia?," in *Gli ebrei in Sicilia sino all'espulsione del 1492: Atti del V convegno internazionale, Palermo, 15–19 giugno 1992*, Italia judaica 5 (Rome: Ministero per i Beni Culturali e Ambientali, Ufficio Centrale per i Beni Archivistici, 1995), 419n30, unfortunately without an indication of the date; and a David di Sabato di Mozzone enters into a business partnership in May 1538 (Stow, *Jews in Rome*, §287). For yet another altercation involving Magister David da Sicilia, see Simonsohn, *Apostolic See and the Jews*, §1749, June 11, 1535.

52. *Notai ebrei*, F. 11, l. 4, fol. 10r; mentioned in Stow, *Jews in Rome*, §355.

53. For the trial's start, see n. 47; for the continuation, *Notai ebrei* F. 11, l. 4, fols. 9r–10r, drawn up on 17 Adar II (Friday, March 7, 1539); Stow, *Jews in Rome*, §355.

54. Although the notary refers to Gershom with the exalted honorific "*ha-mefo'ar*" (*il magnifico*), it would seem that he had not been especially successful at business. He had repeatedly petitioned the courts for protection from his creditors. Simonsohn, *Apostolic See and the Jews*, §§1400 (January 20, 1529; six-month moratorium), 1500 (September 19, 1530; three-month moratorium); 1524 (May 12, 1531; two-month moratorium), 1650 (March 19, 1534; payment plan worked out), and 1652 (April 1534; two-month moratorium).

55. *Notai ebrei*, F. 11, l. 3, fol. [26r]; Stow, *Jews in Rome*, §360.

56. *Notai ebrei*, F. 11, l. 3, fol. [27r]; Stow, *Jews in Rome*, §365.

57. On 1534, see the section "Jewish Bankers in Rome" earlier in this chapter, along with n. 20. On 1540, see *Notai ebrei*, F. 11, l. 4, fol. 23v (Stow, *Jews in Rome*, §486). Yo'av does not appear in the 1536 list of bankers (see n. 19).

58. *Notai ebrei*, F. 11, l. 3, fol. [27v]; Stow, *Jews in Rome*, §366. The number of giulii seems to have been overwritten; forty was corrected to fifty. Yo'av's offer was witnessed by Yo'av da Pavoncello and Yehuda Cohen. Different witnesses (Israel [?] and Mordechai da Benafri [?]) attest to David's refusal on a line inserted between the original offer and the separate record of a marriage contract that was written below it.

59. On the Sicilian Jews and their slow transfer to Rome, see Esposito and Procaccia, "'Schola siculorum de Urbe,'" 411–22, as well as Anna Esposito, "La 'schola siculorum de Urbe,'" an appendix to her larger treatment of "Le 'comunità' ebraiche prima del sacco: Problemi di identificazione," in *Un'altra Roma*, 280–91; Esposito, "Ebrei siciliani a Roma tra Quattro e Cinquecento," in *Hebraica hereditas: Studi in onore di Cesare Colafemmina*, ed. G. Lacerenza (Naples: Università degli Studi di Napoli L'Orientale, 2005), 59–66; and Ariel Toaff, "Gli ebrei siciliani in Italia dopo l'espulsione: Storia di un'integratzone mancata," in *Gli ebrei in Sicilia sino all'espulsione del 1492*, 390. For an overview and bibliographical references to hard-to-find local historical studies of Jewish communities in Lazio (including Tivoli), see N. Pavoncello, "Le comunità ebraiche laziale prima del bando di Pio V," in *Rinascimento nel Lazio*, ed. Renato Lefevre, Lunario romano 9 (1980) (Rome: Gruppo Culturale di Roma e del Lazio, 1979), 47–77.

60. In the original agreement to arbitrate, David's father is identified as Sabbetai da Tivoli, and so he appears in a Hebrew notarial document filed by his son; see n. 55. For Sabbatuccio di Tivoli in the constitutional process of 1524, see n. 37. Although Sabbatuccio was Sicilian, he is listed among the Italiani bankers, rather than the *oltramontani*; on this practice, see Esposito and Procaccia, "Schola siculorum de Urbe," 421.

61. Sarfati's fate is famously recounted by Joannis Piero Valeriano, *De literatorum infelicitate* (Venice, 1620), 19–20 (conveniently available at several sites online in the 1647 Amsterdam edition, 30 ff.). See also Vogelstein and Rieger, *Geschichte der Juden in Rom*, 2:83–84; Umberto Cassuto, *Gli ebrei a Firenze* (Florence: Olschki, 1918), 346–48; and the many other citations in Dan Almagor, "Yosef ben Shmu'el Tsarfati: Bibliografiya Mu'eret [in Hebrew]," *Italia* 12 (1996): 53–113 [Hebrew]. Sarfati was not among the original licensees; at that time he may have been in Istanbul trying to recover the money that had been stolen by a family retainer when his father died. Nor does his name appear among the bankers listed in the constitutional document of 1524 even though he was by then back in Rome. (His personal and family privileges were renewed by Pope Clement VII on February 25 of that year; Simonsohn, *Apostolic See and the Jews*, §1313; cf. Simonsohn's note to §1513. David Reubeni remembered that Sarfati had served as his translator before Pope Clement VII in 1524, although he noted somewhat resentfully that Sarfati seemed to spend the bulk of the interview pushing his own pesonal affairs; A. Z. Aescoly, *Sipur David ha-Re'uveni* [Jerusalem: Mosad Bialik, 1940], 58.) Presumably, Sarfati bought a banking license between 1524 and 1527. As we shall see later, the claim to a license made by Sarfati's estate was recognized in 1540; Simonsohn, *Apostolic See and the Jews*, §1959.

62. Simonsohn, *Apostolic See and the Jews*, §2739. Raphael da Mirandola is likely the M.o Raffaelo da Ferrara mentioned as one of the bankers in 1524; see n. 37. Mirandola is about twenty-five miles east of Ferrara.

63. Simonsohn, *Apostolic See and the Jews*, §1527. The earliest documentation I have found of Sabbatuccio's demise is dated March 7, 1539; *Notai ebrei*, F. 11, l. 4, fol. 9a; Stow, *Jews in Rome*, §355.

64. Simonsohn, *Apostolic See and the Jews*, §1711, March 5, 1535. From the synopsis, it is impossible to determine whether David da Sicilia targeted da Pisa as *parnas* of the bankers or on the grounds that the latter had usurped specifically his family's license. Da Pisa was not one of the bankers in 1524.

65. Ibid., §1714, March 15, 1535.

66. On April 24, 1542—that is, after losing the suit that is my concern—Rabbi David Sabbatucci was found guilty of defrauding the papal chamber in connection with the payment of the vigesima tax. He agreed to a settlement; ibid., §2138. On April 17, 1544, he and his son Laudadio were enjoined from using household or other property from the dowry brought by Laudadio's wife in order to pay off fines or debts they owed personally; ibid., §2391. On September 13, 1553, Laudadio and his family obtained a two-year moneylending license in Piperno; ibid., §3173.

67. *Notai ebrei*, F. 11, l. 3, fols. [45v–46r]; Stow, *Jews in Rome*, §403.

68. *Notai ebrei*, F. 11. l. 3, fols. [47v–48r]; Stow, *Jews in Rome*, §405. Interestingly, a few nonbankers seem to have joined in on this document.

69. Simonsohn, *Apostolic See and the Jews*, §1959; see n. 61.

70. See n. 62.

71. Elia Corcos, who began lending in June 1536 (Stow, *Jews in Rome*, §28), received a special license on October 26, 1543; Simonsohn, *Apostolic See and the Jews*, §2308. Salamone da Pisa, who was a member of the cartel and was sued by David da Sicilia in 1539, received a special license on November 23, 1551; ibid., §3042.

72. On this issue, see Menahem Elon, *Ha-Mishpat ha-Ivri: Toldotav, Mekorotav, Ekronotav*, 2nd expanded ed. (Jerusalem: Magnes Press, 1978), 13–17 and "Index," s.v. *erka'ot shel goyim*.

73. Asher Gulack, *Otsar ha-Shetarot ha-Nehugim be-Yisrael* (Jerusalem: Defus Ha-Poalim, 1926), 272.

74. *Notai ebrei*, F. 11, l. 4, fol. 10v; Stow, *Jews in Rome*, §356.

75. *Notai ebrei*, F. 11, l. 4, fols. 34v–35r; Stow, *Jews in Rome*, §§510, 507, 511

76. *Notai ebrei*, F. 11, l. 3, fol. [44v]; Stow, *Jews in Rome*, §398.

77. Indeed, even Rabbi de Lattes, when he came to Rome, was fleeing from his angry ex-wife, Chiarita di Monteos, who was suing him in a non-Jewish court over a divorce settlement. That lady had no qualms about sending a relative, Jacob di Monteos, to sue de Lattes before the papal governor in Rome. Despite pressure from the community, that suit was actually brought, as can be seen from the index to the volume of records for 1539 of the *Notai Capitolini* in the Archivio di Stato di Roma (although the

trial record itself has been lost through the ravages of time). See also *Notai ebrei*, F. 11, l. 3, fol. [36]r–v; Stow, *Jews in Rome*, §379. In his *Theater of Acculturation: The Roman Ghetto in the Sixteenth Century* (Seattle: University of Washington Press, 2001), 108–21, Stow takes a very different approach to the social function and emotional valence of the notarial acts.

78. My point here is to highlight the paradox of the Jewish notarial system, not to ignore the fact that Jews also made regular use of the services of Christian notaries. Indeed, notarial records by Christians are occasionally to be found in the copy books of Jewish notaries, either to confirm what had already been recorded in Hebrew or, very rarely, as independent witnesses to a transaction. It seems that Jews turned to Jewish notaries especially when they wanted a document that answered the needs of halakhic jurisprudence.

79. See *Statuta almae urbis Romae* (Rome, 1580), I.151, p. 66. Professor Simona Feci of the University of Palermo, whom I thank for this reference, informs me that similar provisions are also to be found in earlier versions of the statute dating from the Trecento, 1494, and 1521–23. For similar voiding of commercial transactions and contracts entered into by young people under Jewish law, see Elon, *Ha-Mishpat ha-Ivri*, 480 ff. and n. 182; and Menahem Elon, "The Sources and Nature of Jewish Law and Its Application in the State of Israel," pt. 4, *Israel Law Review* 4 (1969): 122, and the sources cited there. Apparently the practice among Italian rabbis was to accept such contracts as binding. For cases of bankers sending a son who was, from the Christian point of view, still a minor to close up a partnership, see De Lattes, Responsa, fols. 57r–59r, November 8, 1541 (Schwarz, *Hebräischen Handschriften*, §37); and fols. 59r–60r (undated) (Schwarz, §38).

80. That David was still a young man is also suggested by his rabbinic title *haver*; see n. 82.

81. *Notai ebrei*, F. 11, l. 3, fols. [45v–46r]; Stow, *Jews in Rome*, §403; above, n. 67.

82. On the title *haver* as compared to "rabbi" in Renaissance Italy and on the relevance of age to the title, see Re'uven [Robert] Bonfil, *Ha-Rabanut be-Italya bi-Tefkufat ha-Renesans* (Jerusalem: Magnes Press, 1979), 27–28, 41–42, 62–63, and the documents on 216 and 235 ff; and idem, *Jewish Life in Renaissance Italy*, 137, citing Elia Levita's Hebrew dictionary, *Sefer Tishbi* (Isna, 1541), s.v. "haver," 107–8: "a man with rabbinical credentials who does not yet have the right to issue decisions in legal matters and is not yet called 'Moreniu ha-Rav.'" The title depended not only on the scholar's abilities but also on his age (usually between eighteen and forty) and even on marital status. David was already married on February 12, 1537; on his wife, Laura (לאבורה), see *Notai ebrei*, F. 11, l. 2, fol. [89v]; Stow, *Jews in Rome*, §140.

83. For the case in which David da Siclia was appointed and then disqualified, see *Notai ebrei*, F. 11, l. 2, fol. [82v] (Stow, *Jews in Rome*, §283). For other cases in which he served as an arbiter between 1538 and 1542, see *Notai ebrei*, F. 11, l. 3, fol. [57r], Monday, October 27, 1539 (Stow, *Jews in Rome*, §421), where David signs as *eved nirtsa* (a pierced-ear slave, implying that he was totally committed to serving his clients; cf. Exod. 21:6); *Notai Ebrei*, F. 11, l. 3, fol. [57v], Sunday, November 9, 1539 (Stow, *Jews in Rome*,

§424); Notai ebrei, F. 11, l. 3, fol. [59r] (Stow, Jews in Rome, §427), Wednesday, November 26, 1539, where David is called maskil and haver while the other arbiter is called only maskil; and Notai ebrei, F. 11, l. 3, fol. [61v–62r], December 16, 1539 (Stow, Jews in Rome, §429–30). Only in a document of [Saturday night?], July 22 (9 Av!), 1542, is David finally mentioned with the title "rabbi"; Notai ebrei, F. 2, l. 1, fol. [27r] (Stow, Jews in Rome, §701). The use of the rabbinical title for him already in the spring of 1539 (Stow, Jews in Rome, §§365 and 366) was presumably simply a courtesy.

84. For example, David tried to cite halakhic procedural rules regarding the point up to which litigants had the right to withdraw their testimony.

85. On the *monti di pietà* and the Jewish loan banks as contemporaneous approaches to providing credit for the poor, see Attilio Milano, "Considerazioni sulla lotta dei Monti di Pietà contro il prestito ebraico," in *Scritti in Memoria di Sally Mayer (1875–1953): Saggi sull'Ebraismo Italiano* (Jerusalem: 1956), 199–223. On the continuing debate in Rome over the legitimacy of Jewish loan banking, see Kenneth Stow, "The Good of the Church, the Good of the State: The Popes and Jewish Money," in *Christianity and Judaism*, ed. Diana Wood, Studies in Church History 29 (Oxford: Blackwell for the Ecclesiastical History Society, 1992), 237–52.

86. Although the papal bull establishing the Monte is dated September 9, the institution seems to have begun its work several months earlier. See Federico Arcelli, *Il Sacro Monte di Pietà di Roma nel XVI secolo (1539–1584)* (Naples: Editoriale Scientifica, 2001), 11n9; and the revised English version, *Banking and Charity in Sixteenth-Century Italy: The Holy Monte di Pietà of Rome (1539–84)* (Leicestershire: Upfront Publishing, 2003), 91n2.

87. On the rate allowed the Jews, see n. 14. The rate allowed the bankers in 1534 was identical to that granted in 1521: twenty *quattrini vecchi* for each *ducato d'oro* per month.

88. Barbara Wisch, "Violent Passions: Plays, Pawnbrokers, and the Jews of Rome, 1539," in *Beholding Violence in Medieval and Early Modern Europe*, ed. Allie Terry-Fritsch and Erin Felicia Labbie (Farnham, U.K.: Ashgate, 2012), 197–214. I thank Professor Wisch for sending me the chapter in advance of its publication.

89. Simonsohn, *Apostolic See and the Jews*, §1858; Moses Gayli was fined 100 scudi for illegal lending, although 80 scudi were ultimately forgiven; May 10, 1538.

90. *Notai ebrei*, F. 11. l. 4, fol. 23v; Stow, *Jews in Rome*, §486. On the date of this meeting, see n. 7.

91. In 1552 new bankers could charge 0.5 grosso (i.e., 2.5 baiocchi) per scudo, a rate of 2.5 percent per month (Esposito, "Credito, Ebrei, Monte di Pietà," 579; but compare the rate mentioned in n. 96). Obviously, the lower rate would have made their loans more attractive to customers. That they did not put the "old lenders" out of business indicates that there must have been some other sort of limit on their business—perhaps a regulation limiting the amount of any loan or a limit on the total amount of capital they could make available. The new lenders were subjected to the same business rules as their established competitors; Simonsohn, *Apostolic See and the Jews*, §3106; and Esposito, "Credito, Ebrei, Monte di Pietà," 579–80.

92. *Notai ebrei*, F. 11, l. 4, fol. 40r–v; Stow, *Jews in Rome*, §525.

93. In Bologna *yehide ha-kahal* were loan bankers who were exempt from the control of the communal council and had therefore to be cajoled (rather than ordered) to participate in a special tax; Cooperman, "Political Discourse in a Kabbalistic Register," 49.

94. The relation between this twenty-one-member *va'ad* and the twenty-member group previously mentioned remains to be clarified.

95. *Notai ebrei*, F. 2, l. 1, fols. 41v–45r, October 7–8, 1542; Stow, *Jews in Rome*, §735. The importance of the case is indicated by the number of times the texts were rewritten by the notary to make sure that there was a clear copy.

96. On July 19, 1544, Moise Levi, a physician of Salonica, was granted one of the twenty "new" licenses because he helped the papacy reduce the monthly rate charged by old lenders from 20 to 16 quattrini and that by the new lenders to 10 quattrini; Simonsohn, *Apostolic See and the Jews*, §2436.

Chapter 2. Contraband for the Catholic King

1. Archivo Histórico Nacional, Madrid (henceforth cited as AHN), Inq., lib. 1145, fol. 45v, declaration of Juan Márquez.

2. Fray Francisco de Torrejoncillo, *Centinela contra judíos, puesta en la torre de la Iglesia de Dios* (Madrid: Julián de Paredes, 1674; rev. ed. Madrid: Joseph Fernández de Buendía, 1676), 188: "Como humo perece [in later editions: parece] el que vendiò en la vida tantos humos: Assi, pues, auian tambien de morir todos los Iudios, que desuanecidos pretenden los mejores lugares, sillas, y oficios, para consiguientemente ahumar à los pobrecitos del mundo, y ahogarlos con sus humos." A merely metaphorical meaning is given to this sentence by François Soyer, *Popularizing Anti-Semitism in Early Modern Spain and its Empire: Francisco de Torrejoncillo and the* Centinela contra judíos *(1674)* (Leiden: Brill, 2014), 77, 251–52.

3. Sander L. Gilman, "Smoking Jews on the Frontier: On the Relationship Between Jews and Tobacco, from the 17th Century to the Present," in *Jewish Frontiers: Essays on Bodies, Histories, and Identities*, ed. Sander L. Gilman (New York: Palgrave Macmillan, 2003), 96.

4. Whereas Vicente da Costa Matos was still dominated by the usurer stereotype in 1622, José Pellicer gave a long list of monopolies allegedly invented by Jews in 1640; *Comercio impedido. Primera proposición: Si es util a la monarquia de España el comercio abierto con Francia y Olanda, y sus aliados, assi en el tiempo presente de guerra como en el de paz. Segunda proposición: Si conviene castigar conforme a los vandos y leyes destos Reynos a los que huuieren incurrido en ellos, ó indultarlos* (n.p.: n.n., 1640), fol. 11v.

5. In spite of his biased treatment of the question, Arthur W. Madsen, *The State as Manufacturer and Trader: An Examination Based on the Commercial, Industrial and Fiscal Results Obtained from Government Tobacco Monopolies* (London: Fisher Unwin, 1916), still gives the most comprehensive collection of data on the control of tobacco by the modern state; newer studies from which I will quote here concentrate on particular countries.

6. Sarah Abrevaya Stein, *Plumes: Ostrich Feathers, Jews, and a Lost World of Global Commerce* (New Haven, Conn.: Yale University Press, 2008), 12.

7. Mary Norton, *Sacred Gifts, Profane Pleasures: A History of Tobacco and Chocolate in the Atlantic World* (Ithaca, N.Y.: Cornell University Press, 2008), 211–12.

8. Sabino Lizama Fernandez, "Administración y administradores de la renta del tabaco en la segunda mitad del siglo XVII en Castilla," in *Tabaco y Economía en el siglo XVIII*, ed. Agustín González Enciso and Rafael Torres Sánchez (Pamplona: EUNSA, 1990), 299–318.

9. Julio Caro Baroja, *Los judíos en la España moderna y contemporánea* (Madrid: Istmo, 1978), 3:27; Rafael de Lera García, "La última gran persecución inquisitorial contra el criptojudaísmo: El tribunal de Cuenca 1718–1725," *Sefarad* 47, no. 1 (1987): 104; Michael Alpert, *Criptojudaísmo e Inquisición en los siglos XVII y XVIII* (Barcelona: Ariel, 2001), 174–75; Juan Ignacio Pulido Serrano, *Los conversos en España y Portugal* (Madrid: Arco Libros, 2003), 72.

10. Francisco Comín Comín and Pablo Martín Acaña, *Tabacalera y el estanco del tabaco en España, 1636–1998* (Madrid: Fundación Tabacalera, 1999).

11. Jacob Price, *France and the Chesapeake: A History of the French Tobacco Monopoly, 1674–1971, and of Its Relationship to the British and American Tobacco Trade*, 2 vols. (Ann Arbor: University of Michigan Press, 1973); Marc and Muriel Vigié, *L'herbe à Nicot: Amateurs de tabac, fermiers généraux et contrebandiers sous l'Ancien Régime* (Paris: Fayard, 1989), 217.

12. Carmen Sanz Ayán, *Los banqueros de Carlos II* (Valladolid: Universidad, 1989), 361–63; Maria Fernanda Guimarães and António Júlio Andrade, "Percursos de Gaspar Lopes Pereira e Francisco Lopes Pereira, dois cristãos-novos de Mogadouro," *Cadernos de Estudos Sefarditas* 5 (2005): 253–97.

13. Wilhelm Stiede, "Das Tabakmonopol in Mecklenburg-Schwerin," *Jahresbericht des Vereins für Mecklenburgische Geschichte und Altertumskunde* 75 (1910): 170–71.

14. Peer Schmidt, "Crédit vient de *credere*: Les commerçants séfarades et le tabac dans l'économie atlantique (XVIIe–XVIIIe siècles)," in *Des marchands entre deux mondes: Pratiques et représentations en Espagne et en Amérique (XVe–XVIIIe siècles)*, ed. Béatrice Pérez, Sonia V. Rose, and Jean-Pierre Clément (Paris: PUPS, 2007), 60.

15. Uwe Liszkowski, "'Politökonomie des Wodkas': Die jüdische Schenke im polnischen Feudalismus," in *Jüdische Welten in Osteuropa*, ed. Annelore Engel-Braunschmidt and Eckhard Hübner (Frankfurt: Peter Lang, 2005), 141–53.

16. Between 1627 and 1647, Portuguese army contractors (*asentistas*) assured a constant proportion of 27 percent of the kingdom's credits, which afterwards dropped to 8 percent. The role they assumed in state finance remained always secondary to that of their Italian counterparts. See the statistics supplied by Carlos Álvarez Nogal, *Los banqueros de Felipe IV y los metales preciosos americanos (1621–1665)* (Madrid: Banco de España, 1997), 23, 27, 35. The Portuguese fared much better in the field of foreign payments; see James C. Boyajian, *Portuguese Bankers at the Court of Spain, 1626–1650* (New Brunswick, N.J.: Rutgers University Press, 1983), 173.

17. Bernardo López Belinchón, *Honra, Libertad y Hacienda: Hombres de negocios y judíos sefardíes* (Madrid: Universidad de Alcalá, 2001), 173–74.

18. James C. Boyajian, "The New Christians Reconsidered: Evidence from Lisbon's Portuguese Bankers, 1497–1647," *Studia Rosenthaliana* 13 (1979): 129–56.

19. Markus Schreiber, *Marranen in Madrid 1600–1670* (Stuttgart: Franz Steiner Verlag, 1994), 48–49.

20. Carmen Sanz Ayán, "Presencia y fortuna de los hombres de negocios genoveses durante la crisis hispana de 1640," *Hispania* 65, no. 1 (2005): 91–114, and quoting the president of the Council of Finance who in 1647 declared the Portuguese "most pernicious and hostile" and recommended their expulsion from treasury positions and from Castile itself (112).

21. See the statistics supplied by Jean-Pierre Dedieu, "Les quatre temps de l'Inquisition," in *L'Inquisition espagnole*, ed. Bartolomé Bennassar (Paris: Hachette, 1979), 21.

22. *Avisos de D. Jerónimo de Barrionuevo (1654–1658)*, ed. Antonio Paz y Mélia (Madrid: M. Tello, 1892), 1:48; Sanz Ayán, *Los Banqueros*, 164.

23. Boyajian, *Portuguese Bankers*, 175–76. There were not more cases of bankruptcy among them than among their Italian rivals; Sanz Ayán, "Presencia y fortuna," 97.

24. Sanz Ayán, *Los Banqueros*, 337.

25. Henry Kamen, *La Inquisición española* (Barcelona: Editorial Crítica, 1985), 297–98; Schreiber, *Marranen in Madrid*, 360–66; López Belinchón, *Honra*, 393.

26. September 15, and October 23, 1655, quoted by Norton, *Sacred Gifts*, 209.

27. Schreiber, *Marranen in Madrid*, 175–79, 315. On the conditions of his lease, see the anonymous leaflet *Arrendamiento que se hace a Diego Gomez de Salazar de la renta del estanco del Tabaco de los Reinos de Castilla y Leon, por tiempo de 10 años a partir de 1656* (Madrid: n.p., 1656?).

28. Maurits A. Ebben, "Un triángulo imposible: La Corona española, el Santo Oficio y los banqueros portugueses, 1627–1655," *Hispania* 53 (184): 541–56.

29. Antonio Domínguez Ortiz, "España ante la Paz de los Pireneos," *Hispania* 77 (1959); repr. in Domínguez Ortiz, *Crisis y decadencia de la España de las Austrias*, 155–93 (Barcelona: Ariel, 1969), 184–85.

30. Sanz Ayán, *Los Banqueros*, 160, 168.

31. Carlos Álvarez Nogal, *El crédito de la Monarquía Hispánica en el reinado de Felipe IV* (Valladolid: Junta de Castilla y León, 1997), 336–40.

32. Felipe Ruiz Martín, *Las finanzas de la Monarquía Hispánica en tiempos de Felipe IV (1621–1665)* (Madrid: Real Academia de la Historia, 1990), 102–11.

33. José Ignacio Andrés Ucendo, "Una visión general de la fiscalidad castellana en el siglo XVII," in *La declinación de la Monarquía Hispánica en el siglo XVII*, ed. Francisco José Aranda Pérez (Cuenca: Universidad de Castilla–La Mancha, 2004), 359–75, see 366.

34. Norton, *Sacred Gifts*, 213.

35. Santiago de Luxán and Óscar Bergasa, "La institucionalización del modelo tabaquero español, 1580–1636: La creación del estanco del tabaco en España," *Vegueta* 7 (2003): 148; cf. José Manuel Rodríguez Gordillo, *La creación del estanco del tabaco en España* (Madrid: Fundación Altadis, 2002), 83–158; Norton, *Sacred Gifts*, 212.

36. In Portugal, where the monopoly started around the same time, it replaced the declining Indian commerce; see Carl A. Hanson, "Monopoly and Contraband in the Portuguese Tobacco Trade, 1624–1702," *Luso-Brazilian Review* 19 (1982): 151.

37. Laura Nater, "Colonial Tobacco: Key Commodity of the Spanish Empire, 1500–1800," in *From Silver to Cocaine: Latin American Commodity Chains and the Building of the World Economy, 1500–2000*, ed. Stephen Topik, Carlos Marichal, and Zephyr Frank (Durham, N.C.: Duke University Press, 2006), 105. See also Agustín González Enciso, "Tabaco *vs.* metales: el tabaco como elemento de una hacienda imperial," in *O sistema atlântico do tabaco ibérico: complementaridades e diferenças (séculos XVII-XIX)*, ed. Rafael Chambouleyron and Karl-Heinz Arens (Belém: Azaí, 2014), 1–14.

38. AHN, Inq., lib. 1131, fols. 339r–v, 343r, 345r, letters of Andrês Nunes Belmonte. His interrogations are collected in AHN, Inq., lib. 1129, fols. 593–674.

39. Luxán and Bergasa, "La institucionalización del modelo tabaquero," 143.

40. Ella M. Koen and Wilhelmina C. Pieterse, "Notarial Records Relating to the Portuguese Jews in Amsterdam up to 1639," *Studia Rosenthaliana* 33, no. 1 (1999): 81–82; no. 3457, 34; no. 1 (2000): 87–88; no. 3544, 35; nos. 1–2 (2001): 67; no. 3546, 78; no. 3589, 79; no. 3593, 88; no. 3631; Norton, *Sacred Gifts*, 212.

41. López Belinchón, *Honra*, 87–90. Virginia tobacco was shipped to Spain in significant quantities only from 1668 onwards; see José Manuel Rodríguez Gordillo, "La influencia del tabaco de virginia en la configuración del mercado español en la segunda mitad del siglo XVII," in *O sistema atlântico do tabaco ibérico*, 40–60.

42. López Belinchón, *Honra*, 102–4.

43. On this category, see Natalia Muchnik, "Des intrus en pays d'Inquisition: Présence et activités des juifs dans l'Espagne du XVIIe siècle," *Revue des Études Juives* 164, nos. 1–2 (2005): 119–56.

44. Yosef Kaplan, "The Travels of Portuguese Jews from Amsterdam to the 'Lands of Idolatry' (1644–1724)," in *Jews and Conversos*, ed. Yosef Kaplan (Jerusalem: Magnes Press, 1985), 197–224; idem, "Ha-ma'avak neged ha-shivah le'Iberyah ba-pezurah ha-sefaradit" [in Hebrew], *Zion* 64 (1999), 65–100; idem, "El vínculo prohibido: las relaciones de la 'nación sefardí' occidental con Iberia en el siglo XVII," in *Encuentros y desencuentros: Spanish Jewish Cultural Interaction Throughout History*, ed. Carlos Carrete Parrondo, Marcelo Dascal, Francisco Márquez Villanueva, and Ángel Sáenz Badillos (Tel Aviv: University Publishing Projects, 2000), 39–50; idem, "Amsterdam, the Forbidden Lands, and the Dynamics of the Sephardi Diaspora," in *The Dutch Intersection: The Jews, and the Netherlands in Modern History*, ed. Yosef Kaplan (Leiden: Brill, 2008), 33–62.

45. Kaplan, "Dynamics," 43, 45, 50.

46. Kaplan, "Travels," 210, 213–14; idem, "Struggle," 94.

47. Cecil Roth, "Abraham Nunez Bernal et autres martyrs contemporains de l'Inquisition," *Revue des Études Juives* 100bis (1936): 38–51; Miriam Bodian, *Dying in the Law of Moses: Crypto-Jewish Martyrdom in the Iberian World* (Bloomington: University of Indiana Press, 2007), 193–94.

48. Interrogations of this kind can be found in two different archival collections of the Spanish National Archives: first, in the trial records of the Toledo Inquisition (AHN, Inq., legs. 1–500), source of the studies by Julio Caro Baroja and David L. Graizbord, and second, in the prosecutors' records (AHN, Inq., libs. 1101–48), on which I have based most of my investigations. The trial the Toledo Inquisition conducted in absentia against the major merchant of Bayonne, Diogo Rodrigues Cardoso (AHN, Inq. leg. 177, no. 11), includes interrogations with twenty-seven travelers from the years 1641–78. Most of these witnesses were arrested in the years 1658–62. See Caro Baroja, *Los judíos*, 2:145–59, and the list in David L. Graizbord, *Souls in Dispute: Converso Identities in Iberia and the Jewish Diaspora, 1580–1700* (Philadelphia: University of Pennsylvania Press, 2004), 181–82.

49. Graizbord, *Souls in Dispute*, 103.

50. Kaplan, "Travels," 204.

51. In 1661, Francisco Rodrigues Lopes accounted for his expatriation to France with novelesque storytelling; see AHN, Inq., lib. 1129, fols. 193v–195r.

52. Graizbord, *Souls in Dispute*, 87–89, 139–69, 175.

53. AHN, Inq., lib. 1129, fol. 385r–v, in a letter by Manuel Alvares Flores, dated February 19, 1650: "Dizen los de aqua que lleuan intento se no tubieren otro remedio para poder uiuir en espanha, de aprezentarse em la santa inquisision lo qual hazen por cumplimento e para quedaren seguros robando el mundo no dando cumplise alguno en sus confissiones de los muchos que ai en espanha eso remedean con dar los judios de fransia a la buelta mesclan dalgunos catolicos asi de espanha como de fransia o en estando llenos se uienen a olanda ou jtalia a las sinagogas como uemos todos los dias."

54. When he was imprisoned in 1664, the León tax collector Fernando Gomes Dias tried to make the Inquisitors believe that he had forgotten the exact name of his place of origin in Portugal (later in his trial he remembered that it was Vilaflor, which he himself describes as a "hotbed of heretics"), and that he had never dared to communicate about Judaism with anybody in Spain. In exchange, he denounced in detail the Jewish life of the Portuguese in France; AHN, Inq., leg. 177, no. 11, fols. 43r, 44r.

55. Kaplan, "Vínculo," 39–41; idem, "Dynamics," 33–34. The author stresses "the general economic interest of the [Portuguese Jewish] Nation" as the background of these travels ("Dynamics," 56). In his earlier studies, he envisioned a different hypothesis: at least some of the travelers were "marginal people, who lived alongside the community but did not take an active part in events within it" (Kaplan, "Travels," 211), the flexibility of this group having posed "one of the greatest threats to the integrity of the communities" (idem, "Wayward New Christians and Stubborn New Jews: The Shaping of a Jewish Identity," *Jewish History* 8, nos. 1–2 [1994]: 27).

56. Henry Méchoulan, "Présence de l'Espagne dans la pensée juive à Amsterdam au temps de Spinoza," *Les Nouveaux Cahiers* 62 (1980): 26–31; idem, *Hispanidad y judaísmo en tiempos de Espinoza: Edición de "La Certeza del Camino" de Abraham Pereyra (Amsterdam, 1666)* (Salamanca: Universidad, 1987), 33–48; idem, "1492 dans la mémoire des Juifs d'Amsterdam au XVIIe siècle," in *Mémoire et fidélité séfarades*, ed. Albert Bensoussan (Rennes: Presses Universitaires de Rennes, 1993), 121–28; Gérard Nahon, "Yshak de Acosta et David Silveyra: Mémoire rabbinique, memoire politique de l'Espagne, Bayonne, 1722–1790," in *Mémoires juives d'Espagne et du Portugal*, ed. Esther Benbassa (Paris: Publisud, 1996), 145–69; Yosef Kaplan, "Una diáspora en exilio: Actitudes hacia España entre los Sefardíes de la Edad Moderna," in *Marginados y minorías sociales en la España moderna y otros estudios sobre Extremadura*, ed. Felipe Lorenzana de la Puente and Francisco J. Mateos Ascacíbar (Llerena, Spain: Sociedad Extremeña de Historia, 2005), 9–25.

57. López Belinchón, *Honra*, 278–79. Even authors committed to the representation of a prejudiced and persecuting society do not document any direct verbal or physical agression; see Michèle Escamilla Colin, *Crimes et Chatiments dans l'Espagne inquisitoriale: Essai de typologie délictive et punitive sous le dernier Habsbourg et le premier Bourbon* (Paris: Berg International, 1992), 1:266–72; Juan Ignacio Pulido Serrano, *Injurias a Cristo: Religión, política y antijudaísmo en el siglo XVII (Análisis de las corrientes antijudías durante la Edad Moderna)* (Alcalá, Spain: Universidad de Alcalá, 2002), 310–11.

58. Quoted by Schreiber, *Marranen in Madrid*, 397–98.

59. I. S. Révah, *Spinoza et le dr Juan de Prado* (Paris: Mouton, 1959), 33, 68; Kaplan, "Dynamics," 53.

60. I do not exclude from this generalization my own *Jüdisch-christliches Doppelleben im Barock: Zur Biographie des Kaufmanns und Dichters Antonio Enríquez Gómez* (Frankfurt: Peter Lang, 1994), 54.

61. Jean de Jaurgain and Raymond Ritter, *La Maison de Gramont, 1040–1967*, pref. Duke of Lévis Mirepoix, 2 vols. (Lourdes: Les Amis du musée pyrénéen, 1968). On one of these conflicts, see Carsten L. Wilke, "Le rapport d'un espion du Saint-Office sur sa mission auprès des crypto-juifs de Saint-Jean-de-Luz (1611)," *Sigila* 16 (2006): 127–41.

62. AHN, Inq., lib. 1131, fol. 363r, letter of Andrês Nunes Belmonte.

63. Alpert, *Criptojudaísmo e Inquisición*, 96.

64. Gérard Nahon, "Inscriptions funéraires hébraïques et juives à Bidache, Labastide-Clairence (Basses-Pyrénées) et Peyrehorade (Landes): Rapport de mission," 3rd part, *Revue des études juives* 128 (1969): 353–54; Claudine Laborde, "La communauté juive de Peyrehorade aux XVIIe, XVIIIe et XIXe siècles," *Bulletin de la Société de Borda* 111 (1986): 285–86.

65. Anne Zink, "Communautés et corps social: Les juifs à Saint-Esprit-lès-Bayonne du XVIIe au début du XIXe siècle," in *Les Étrangers dans la ville: Minorités et espace urbain du bas Moyen Age à l'époque moderne*, ed. Jacques Bottin and Donatella Calabi (Paris: Éditions de la Maison des Sciences de l'Homme, 1999), 313–28.

66. I. S. Révah, "Les Marranes," *Revue des études juives* 118 (1959–60): 66; see also Gérard Nahon, "From New Christians to the Jewish Nation in France," in *Moreshet Sepharad: The Sephardi Legacy*, ed. Haim Beinart (Jerusalem: Magnes Press, 1992), 2:341: "The Jewish Nation acted as the sentry of Judaism posted at the exit from the Iberian Peninsula."

67. Jonathan I. Israel, "Crypto-Judaism in 17th-Century France: An Economic and Religious Bridge between the Hispanic World and the Sephardic Diaspora," in idem, *Diasporas within a Diaspora: Jews and the World Maritime Empires (1540–1740)* (Leiden: Brill, 2002), 245–68; idem, "El comercio de los judíos sefardíes de Amsterdam con los conversos de Madrid a través del suroeste francés," in *Familia, religión y negocio: El sefardismo en las relaciones entre el mundo hispánico y los Países Bajos en la Edad Moderna*, ed. Jaime Contreras, Bernardo J. García García, and Ignacio Pulido (Madrid: Fundación Carlos de Amberes, 2003), 373–90.

68. Pellicer, *Comercio impedido*, fol. 8r.

69. Graizbord, *Souls in Dispute*, 79–80.

70. AHN, Inq., lib. 1105, fol. 309r, his own declaration; Graizbord, *Souls in Dispute*, 80.

71. Graizbord, *Souls in Dispute*, 87.

72. Israel, "Crypto-Judaism in 17th century France," 252; idem, "El comercio de los judíos sefardíes," 375, 378. Israel is at a loss to explain the survival and expansion of the border communities after the Franco-Spanish peace of 1659; see "Crypto-Judaism in 17th century France," 265; idem, "El comercio de los judíos sefardíes," 387–88.

73. Michel Morineau, "Bayonne et Saint-Jean-de-Luz, relais du commerce néerlandais vers l'Espagne au début du XVIIe siècle," *Actes du Congrès national des sociétés savantes: Section d'Histoire moderne et contemporaine* 94 (1971): 2:324–25.

74. Anne Zink, "Bayonne, arrivées et départs au XVIIe siècle," in *1492, l'expulsion des juifs d'Espagne*, ed. Roland Goetschel (Paris: Maisonneuve et Larose, 1996), 40.

75. Anne Zink, "Une niche juridique: L'installation des Juifs à Saint-Esprit-lès-Bayonne au XVIIe siècle," *Annales—Histoire, Sciences Sociales* 49, no. 3 (1994): 659.

76. Zink, "Bayonne," 46: "Le véritable essor de Saint-Esprit date de la reprise qui accompagne la fin de la guerre."

77. After conceding numerous import licenses for French goods, the crown revoked them all in September 1657; Ángel Alloza Aparicio, *Europa en el mercado español: mercaderes, represalias y contrabando en el siglo XVII* (Salamanca: Junta de Castilla y León, 2006), 209.

78. Anne Zink, "Juifs d'eau douce et juifs de mer: Le rôle économique des juifs de Saint-Esprit-lès-Bayonne au XVIIe siècle," in *Il ruolo economico delle minoranze in Europa. Secc. XIII–XVIII*, ed. Simonetta Cavaciocchi (Florence: Le Monnier, 2000), 209–18. Zink supposes that the Southern French, Castilian, and Atlantic markets were targeted by specialized sub-networks inside the local Portuguese community: "Les deux axes se rencontrent a Bayonne où les juifs des rivières et des chemins venus

de Castille et de Navarre cohabitent avec les juifs de mer, lusitaniens" (216). This thesis would merit further study. Meanwhile, research on individual Portuguese merchants has shown their astonishing variety of commercial pursuits; see Jacques Blamont, *Le Lion et le moucheron: Histoire des marranes de Toulouse* (Paris: Éditions Odile Jacob, 2000).

79. Jonathan Israel, "Spain and the Dutch Sephardim, 1609–1660," *Studia Rosenthaliana* 12, nos. 1–2 (1978): 1–61, repr. in idem, *Empires and Entrepôts: The Dutch, the Spanish Monarchy and the Jews, 1585–1713* (London: Hambledon Press, 1990), 410.

80. Manuel Herrero Sánchez, "La política de embargos y el contrabando de productos de lujo en Madrid (1635–1673): Sociedad cortesana y dependencia de los mercados internacionales," *Hispania* 59, no. 1 (1999): 188.

81. Alloza Aparicio, *Europa en el mercado español*, 138.

82. Sanz Ayán, *Los Banqueros*, 166.

83. Carsten L. Wilke, "Un judaïsme clandestin en France au XVIIe siècle: Un rite au rythme de l'imprimerie," in *Transmission et passages en monde juif*, ed. Esther Benbassa (Paris: Publisud, 1997), 305–9.

84. AHN, Inq., lib. 1145, fol. 31r–v, declaration of João Marques.

85. He is still mentioned in 1673; Blamont, *Le Lion*, 52. His tombstone is preserved, but the date has become illegible; Jacob Henry Léon, *Histoire des juifs de Bayonne* (Paris: Durlacher, 1893), 209–10.

86. Kaplan, "Wayward," 31–33.

87. Leon, *Histoire*, 20: "défendant de les rechercher . . . en leur vie"; Gérard Nahon, ed., *Les "Nations" juives portugaises du Sud-Ouest de la France (1684–1791): Documents* (Paris: Fundação Calouste Gulbenkian, 1981), 32–35; Zink, "Niche," 645; idem, "L'émergence de Saint-Esprit-lès-Bayonne: La place d'une ville nouvelle dans l'espace juif à l'époque moderne," *Archives Juives* 37, no. 1 (2004): 21; idem, "Bayonne," 45.

88. AHN, Inq., leg. 177, no. 11, fol. 138r, declaration of Francisco Paz Ferreira.

89. Pellicer, *Comercio impedido*, fol. 11r.

90. David Willemse, *Un portugués entre los castellanos: El primer proceso inquisitorial contra Gonzalo Baez de Paiba, 1654–1657* (Paris: Fundação Calouste Gulbenkian, 1974). On Vaz Martins, see Caro Baroja, *Los judíos*, 2:153; Schreiber, *Marranen in Madrid*, 154.

91. Elvira Pérez Ferreiro, "Crónica de un exilio forzado: la emigracion clandestina de judeoconversos españoles como respuesta al incremento de la presión inquisitorial a mediados del siglo XVII," *Hispania* 64, 2, no. 217 (2004): 543–70.

92. AHN, Inq., lib. 1105, fols. 316v–23r, declaration of Joseph Sanches: "Nonbres de las mugeres que estan en peñaorada y tienen sus mari[dos] en españa."

93. Statistics based on a survey of the society's registers in Stadtsarchief Amsterdam, PA 334, nos. 1141–44.

94. Pellicer, *Comercio impedido*, fols. 3v, 5v, 7v.

95. AHN, Inq., lib. 1105, fol. 301v, declaration of Joseph Sanches.

96. See the route description by Francisco Rodrigues Lopes, tobacconist of Granada, AHN, Inq., lib. 1129, fol. 194v.

97. The two young brothers Francisco and António Rodrigues Idanha, in company of one muleteer from Pamplona, left Saint-Esprit on March 30 or 31, 1651, and arrived in Madrid on April 7 or 8; see AHN, Inq., lib. 1124, fol. 108v.

98. The small Pyrenean kingdom of Navarre had monopolized tobacco trade in 1652; however, transports from France remained free of charge until 1713. See Mario García Zúñiga, "El estanco del tabaco en Navarra durante el Antiguo Regimen," in *VIII Congreso de la Asocoacion Espanola de Historia Economica, sesion B2: El tabaco en la historia economica* (Santiago de Compostela, 2005), http://www.usc.es/es/congresos/histec05/b2.jsp.

99. AHN, Inq., lib. 1116, fol. 40, declaration of João Gomes Flores, 1652.

100. AHN, Inq., leg. 177, no. 11, end, declaration of Gaspar Isidro de Velasco on December 19, 1671.

101. AHN, Inq., lib. 1105, fol. 392v, declaration of João Soares de Azevedo.

102. In the 1630s, a woman from Madrid called Doña Elvira was known as "a veteran in the business"; AHN, Inq., lib. 1105, fol. 324r, declaration of Joseph Sanches. Her inn located in Caballero de Gracia Street was denounced in an anonymous letter published in I. S. Révah, *Antonio Enríquez Gómez, un écrivain marrane (v. 1600–1663)*, ed. Carsten L. Wilke, pref. Gérard Nahon (Paris: Chandeigne, 2003), 510. The landlady of the Mesón de la Condesa in Toledo, nicknamed "the Countess," had the reputation of knowing and faithfully keeping the Jewish smugglers' secrets; AHN, Inq., lib. 1112, fols. 79v, 100r, declaration of João Lopes de Morais.

103. AHN, Inq., lib. 1112, fol. 160v, declaration of Vasco Fernandes Valentim, 1650, on an encounter in the Mesón de la Cabeza del Oso at Medina de Ríoseco.

104. Wilke, *Jüdisch-christliches Doppelleben*, 138, quotation on 356; López Belinchón, *Honra*, 89, 115; Révah, *Antonio Enríquez Gómez*, 607.

105. Jesús Antonio Cid, "Judaizantes y carreteros para un hombre de letras," in *Homenaje a Julio Caro Baroja*, ed. Antonio Carreira (Madrid: Centro de Investigaciones Sociológicas, 1978), 275.

106. AHN, Inq., lib. 1107, fol. 76r, declaration of Matías Rodrigues Cardoso, alias Isac Gabai, on August 20, 1635.

107. The Inquisition opened a trial against Fernandes in 1655; see AHN, Inq., leg. 189, no. 10, and Inq., lib. 1125, fols. 494–540; Schreiber, *Marranen in Madrid*, 263; Natalia Muchnik, *De paroles et de gestes: Constructions marranes en terre d'Inquisition* (Paris: EHESS, 2014), 188.

108. AHN, Inq., lib. 1105, fol. 309v, his own declaration.

109. AHN, Inq., lib. 1124, fol. 8r, declarations of Gonçalo Correa, 1659.

110. Gérard Nahon, "Les rapports des communautés judéo-portugaises de France avec celle d'Amsterdam au XVIIe et au XVIIIe siècle," *Studia Rosenthaliana* 10 (1976): 37–78, 175–88.

111. Carsten L. Wilke, *Histoire des Juifs portugais* (Paris: Chandeigne, 2007), 188.

112. See the declarations by Gonçalo Correa, May 5, 1659, about Saint-Esprit and by Francisco de Paz Ferreira, February 2, 1651, about Bordeaux; AHN, Inq., lib. 1124, fol. 5v; Wilke, "Un judaïsme clandestin en France," 300.

113. AHN, Inq., lib. 1103, fol. 11r, declaration of António da Costa de Paz.

114. AHN, Inq., leg. 177, no. 11, fol. 52v, his own declaration.

115. Graizbord, *Souls in Dispute*, 141.

116. AHN, Inq., lib. 1103, fols. 7r, 8r, declaration of António da Costa de Paz.

117. Schreiber, *Marranen in Madrid*, 237.

118. AHN, Inq., lib. 1124, fols. 87r–91r, 108v–9v, declarations of Francisco Rodrigues Idanha.

119. AHN, Inq., lib. 1129, fol. 192–218.

120. Cid, "Judaizantes," 274.

121. AHN, Inq., lib. 1105, fols. 316v, 318v, declarations of Joseph Sanches.

122. AHN, Inq., lib. 1129, fol. 475v, declaration of Martim Gonçalves, 1661.

123. AHN, Inq., lib. 1129, fol. 252v, declaration of Fernão Henriques da Veiga, 1661; lib. 1139, fol. 275r.

124. AHN, Inq., lib. 1129, fols. 633v, 647v, declarations of Joseph Garcia de Leão.

125. AHN, Inq., lib. 1129, fols. 470–500.

126. AHN, Inq., lib. 1129, fol. 607r–v, declarations of Joseph Garcia de Leão.

127. Schreiber, *Marranen in Madrid*, 356–57.

128. AHN, Inq., lib. 1131, fols. 307–8, letter of Andrês Nunes Belmonte; Schreiber, *Marranen in Madrid*, 265–66; Pérez Ferreiro, "Crónica," 567.

129. See AHN, Inq., leg. 4000–4022, mentioned in a manuscript note in the research papers of I. S. Révah; Paris, Alliance Israélite Universelle, Archives, AP 39, box 19.

130. AHN, Inq., leg. 4000, letter by Juan Negrete to Francisco Lopes Capadose, February 19, 1653: "Y si en su negoçio de vmd no obro como quisiera no es defecto de mi boluntad sino el no poder mas, porque el tienpo es terrible y los hebreos estan descahidos y vmd no ha gustado de hazer lo que he aconsejado, Jacob soliçita licençia para hir a esa corte yo lo deseo ynfinito porque vmd se ajuste con el." On the trials against Francisco Lopes Capadose, see Caro Baroja, *Los judíos*, 2:103–4; Schreiber, *Marranen in Madrid*, 88–90.

131. AHN, Inq., lib. 1129, fols. 612v, 630r, declarations of Joseph Garcia de Leão.

132. AHN, Inq., lib. 1129, fol. 632r–v; lib. 1139, fol. 193r; Schreiber, *Marranen in Madrid*, 315.

133. This aspect has been studied by Pilar Huerga Criado, *En la raya de Portugal: Solidaridad y tensiones en la comunidad judeoconversa* (Salamanca: Universidad de Salamanca, 1994), 191–96.

134. Francesca Trivellato, *The Familiarity of Strangers: The Sephardic Diaspora, Livorno, and Cross-Cultural Trade in the Early Modern Period* (New Haven, Conn.: Yale University Press, 2009), 181.

135. Wilke, *Juifs portugais*, 162; Trivellato, *Familiarity of Strangers*, 145–46, quotation from 144. Interaction across ethnic lines is highlighted in similar terms by Jessica V.

Roitman, *The Same but Different? Inter-Cultural Trade and the Sephardim, 1595–1640* (Leiden: Brill, 2011), 272.

136. AHN, Inq., lib. 1129, fol. 619r, declaration of Joseph Garcia de Leão, 1661.

137. Sanz Ayán metions them under different names; see *Los Banqueros*, 339, 348 (*agente*), 360 (*administrador*), 365 (*brazo semiindependiente*), 375 (*correspondiente*).

138. Pellicer, *Comercio impedido*, fol. 14v.

139. Wilke, "Un judaïsme clandestin en France," 310.

140. AHN, Inq., lib. 1129, fol. 179r, declaration of Manuel de Meza: "En françia traen las mangas de la camisa descubiertas y las mangas de los jubones abiertas."

141. During the peace negotiations of 1659, a nephew of the affluent Passarinho brothers called Carlos de Andrade lent money to Spanish noblemen in Paris and then returned to Spain via Bordeaux and Bayonne. He wore a "vestido a la françesa con vna vngarina de terçiopelo negro" (AHN, Inq., lib. 1129, fol. 606v, declarations of Joseph Garcia de Leão). In Bayonne, he was the first Jew of Saint-Esprit who shaved his head and wore a wig; see ibid., fol. 117r–v, declaration of António da Cunha: "Cauello rubio, y quando paso por Burdeos benia rapado y traia cabellera postiça larga."

142. The young informer Manuel (Isaac) Rodrigues, also called Manuelillo, arrived in Mardrid from Biarritz in November 1632, "vestido a la françessa," as is stated at the beginning of the interrogations held with him; AHN, Inq., lib. 1105, fol. 475r (olim 433).

143. Pellicer, *Comercio impedido*, fol. 10r.

144. AHN, Inq., lib. 1124, fols. 108v, 109v, declarations of Francisco Rodrigues Idanha.

145. AHN, Inq., lib. 1129, fol. 633v, declarations of Joseph Garcia de Leão.

146. AHN, Inq., lib. 1103, fol. 14r, declarations of António da Costa de Paz; Inq., lib. 1112, fols. 95v–96r, declaration of João de Morais.

147. Norton, *Sacred Gifts*, 217–18.

148. AHN, Inq., lib. 1129, fols. 629v–30r, declaration of Joseph Garcia de Leão. See also Caro Baroja, *Los judíos*, 2:152–53.

149. AHN, Inq., leg. 162, no. 1, fols. 109r–10r, his own declaration.

150. AHN, Inq., leg. 162, no. 1, fols. 78v, 82r, 94v–96r, 103r.

151. AHN, Inq., lib. 1124, fol. 99r–v, declaration of Francisco Rodrigues Idanha.

152. Kaplan, "Wayward," 32–33.

153. Brian Pullan, "A Ship with Two Rudders: 'Righetto Marrano' and the Inquisition in Venice," *Historical Journal* 20 (1977): 44.

154. Francisco Rodrigues Lopes was circumcised and renamed Jacob one year before he crossed the border, according to his own confession; AHN, Inq., lib. 1129, fol. 200v. See also the case reported by Caro Baroja, *Los judíos*, 2:155. The London Jewish community in 1727 or 1728 made it a principle that new arrivals from Spain and Portugal had to be circumcised before they were allowed to travel back there; Kaplan, "Wayward," 38 (n.d.).

155. J. L. Cardozo de Bethencourt, "Bio-bibliographie juive" in *Archives municipales de Bordeaux*, ms. 79 S 2, fol. 604r.

156. Charles H. Parker, ed., *Global Interactions in the Early Modern Age, 1400–1800* (Cambridge: Cambridge University Press, 2010).

157. Wilke, "Un judaïsme clandestin," 306.

158. Révah, *Antonio Enríquez Gómez*, 399, 579.

159. Caro Baroja, *Los judíos*, 2:42, 51–54, 57. Bernardo López Belinchón reports anti-Portuguese polemic with approval; see especially the conclusion of his article " 'Sacar la sustancia al Reino': Comercio, contrabando y conversos portugueses, 1621–1640," *Hispania* 61, 3, no. 209 (2001): 1017–50; and idem, *Honra*, 304–10.

160. Daviken Studnicki-Gizbert, "Revisiting 1640, or, How the Party of Commercial Expansion Lost to the Party of Political Conservation in Spain's Atlantic Empire, 1620–1650," in *The Atlantic Economy During the Seventeenth and Eighteenth Centuries*, ed. Peter A. Coclanis (Columbia: University of South Carolina Press, 1999), 152–85; idem, *A Nation upon the Ocean Sea: Portugal's Atlantic Diaspora and the Crisis of the Spanish Empire, 1492–1640* (New York: Oxford University Press, 2007), 39, 180.

161. Most of the money raised by the Portuguese taxmen served to throw back the invasion of their compatriots in the Spanish Extremadura; Sanz Ayán, *Los Banqueros*, 167.

162. Nicolas Broens, *Monarquía y capital mercantil: Felipe IV y las redes comerciales portuguesas (1627–1635)* (Madrid: Ediciones de la Universidad Autónoma de Madrid, 1989), 70: "Simbiosis, antes deseada por la Corona, con las redes comerciales extraterritoriales"; Schreiber, *Marranen in Madrid*, 337–41, chapter titled "Zusammenarbeit zwischen Staat und 'Nation' "; Maurits A. Ebben, *Zilver, brood en kogels voor de koning: Kredietverlening door Portugese bankiers aan de Spaanse kroon, 1621–1665* (Leiden: Rijksuniversiteit, 1996), 22: "samenwerking tussen staat en particuliere ondernemers."

163. Kaplan, "Vínculo," 47.

164. See the chapter on "The Expanding Leviathan," in Norton, *Sacred Gifts*, 223–28.

Chapter 3. Daily Business or an Affair of Consequence?

1. David S. Landes, *Dynasties: Fortunes and Misfortunes of the World's Great Family Businesses* (New York: Viking, 2006), ix–xvii.

2. Abner Cohen, "Cultural Strategies in the Organization of Trading Diasporas," in *The Development of Indigenous Trade and Markets in West Africa*, ed. Claude Meillassoux (Oxford: Oxford University Press, 1971), 266; Philip D. Curtin, *Cross-Cultural Trade in World History* (Cambridge: Cambridge University Press, 1984), 7.

3. Francesca Trivellato, *The Familiarity of Strangers: The Sephardic Diaspora, Livorno, and Cross-Cultural Trade in the Early Modern Period* (New Haven, Conn.: Yale University Press, 2009), 273.

4. Sebouh David Aslanian, *From the Indian Ocean to the Mediterranean: The Global Trade Networks of Armenian Merchants from New Julfa* (Berkeley: University of California Press, 2011), 167–68.

5. Michael Davern, "Social Networks and Economic Sociology: A Proposed Research Agenda for a More Complete Social Science," *American Journal of Economics and Sociology* 56, no. 3 (1997): 287–302.

6. Aslanian, *From the Indian Ocean*, 219–20, 224–25, 228; Jonathan I. Israel, *European Jewry in the Age of Mercantilism, 1550–1750*, 3rd ed. (Oxford: Littman Library of Jewish Civilization, 1998), 198–201, 203–5.

7. Mark Steele, "Bankruptcy and Insolvency: Bank Failure and Its Control in Preindustrial Europe," *Banchi pubblici, banchi privati e monti di pietà nell' Europa preindustriale* 31, no. 15 (1991): 186.

8. Erich Landsteiner, "Editorial: Bankrott," *Österreichische Zeitschrift für Geschichtswissenschaft* 19, no. 3 (2008): 5–8; Thomas Max Safley, "Bankruptcy: Family and Finance in Early Modern Augsburg," *Journal of European Economic History* 29, no. 1 (2000): 55, 73–74.

9. For France, see Pierre Claude Reynard, "The Language of Failure: Bankruptcy in Eighteenth-Century France," *Journal of European Economic History* 30, no. 2 (2001): 357.

10. "Bankerot" in *Oekonomische Encyclopaedie, oder allgemeines System der Staats- Stadt- Haus- und Landwirthschaft*, ed. Johann Georg Krünitz (Berlin: Pauli, 1774), 3:515–19, http://www.kruenitz1.uni-trier.de/xxx/b/kb00287.htm.

11. Jürgen Schneider, "Messen, Banken und Börsen (15.–18. Jahrhundert)," *Banchi pubblici, banchi privati e monti di pietà nell' Europa preindustriale* 31, no. 1 (1990): 146, 168. See also Carl Günther Ludovici, *Grundriß eines vollständigen Kaufmanns-Systems, nebst den Anfangsgründen der Handlungswissenschaft, und angehängter kurzer Geschichte der Handlung zu Wasser und zu Lande. Zweyte vermehrte und verbesserte Auflage* (Leipzig: Bernhard Christoph Breitkopf und Sohn, 1768), 2:1790.

12. Schneider, "Messen, Banken und Börsen," 150–51.

13. On the introduction of the joint liability rule, see Herman van der Wee, "Monetary, Credit, and Banking Systems," in *The Cambridge Economic History of Europe*, ed. M. M. Postan and H. J. Habakkuk (Cambridge: Cambridge University Press, 1977), 325–27; Veronica Aoki Santarosa, "Financing Long-Distance Trade Without Banks: The Joint Liability Rule and Bills of Exchange in Eighteenth-Century France" (Ph.D. diss., Yale University, 2012).

14. Robert Beachy, "Bankruptcy and Social Death: The Influence of Credit-Based Commerce on Cultural and Political Values," *Zeitsprünge. Forschungen zur Frühen Neuzeit* 4, no. 4 (2000): 328–30, 333, 339–40.

15. Gotthold Ephraim Lessing, *G. E. Lessings schrifften* (Berlin: C. F. Voss, 1753), 1:220–22.

16. Lessing was familiar with the case, having served as an interpreter during the trial.

17. "Acta die Einschränkung der Anzahl der Juden und deren Gewerbes in der Residenz-Stadt, Dresden, ingleichen für letztere publicirte Juden-Ordnung betr., Ao. 1763" (Sächsisches Hauptstaatsarchiv Dresden [henceforth cited as SHstA], 10026 Ge-

heimes Kabinett, Loc. 581/2), 9, 14; "Korrespondenz mit dem Residenten Hecht, 1753–1771" (Geheimes Preußisches Staatsarchiv Berlin [henceforth cited as GStA], I. HA, Rep. 50, no. 28, Fasz 75), n.p.

18. On the financial and commercial connections between Amsterdam, Hamburg, and Prussia, see Isabel Schnabel and Hyun Song Shin, "Liquidity and Contagion: The Crisis of 1763," *Journal of the European Economic Association* 2, no. 6 (2004): 929–68.

19. "Juden Acta betreffend die jährlich einzureichenden Juden Tabellen, 1748–1759" (Stadtarchiv Frankfurt/Oder, Abteilung I, VII, 107), 325v–26. His marriage with Hendele took place in Frankfurt/Oder but is mentioned in "D. T. P. Ondertrouwen" (Stadsarchief Amsterdam), mf. 741, 420.

20. "Metryka Koronna, 1764–1780, KK 18 (mf. A-6083)" (Archiwum Główne Akt Dawnych Warsaw [henceforth cited as AGAD]), 171.

21. "D. T. P. Ondertrouwen," mf. 739, 402, mf. 741, 420.

22. Wilhelm Mangold, *Voltaires Rechtsstreit mit dem Königlichen Schutzjuden Hirschel 1751: Prozeßakten des Königlich-Preußischen Hausarchivs* (Berlin: Ernst Frensdorff, 1905), iv–xxxvii. See also "Juden Sachen betr. u.a. Memoire des Juden Hirschel wider Mr. de Voltaire" (SHstA Dresden, 10026 Geheimes Kabinett, Loc. 1391/1), n.p.

23. Quoted from Mangold, *Voltaires Rechtsstreit mit dem Königlichen Schutzjuden Hirschel*, 10.

24. Ibid., 41.

25. Originally, Berlin papers were not allowed to publish on the trial, but papers in Hamburg could not be restricted. Eventually, the information became public in Berlin as well. Ibid., xxvi.

26. Chava Turniansky, ed., *Glikl: Zikhronot, 1691–1719* (Jerusalem: Merkaz Zalman Shazar le-toldot Yisrael, 2006), 394–410, 538–41.

27. Ibid., 30, 52–54, 60–64, 130, 354–56, 370–72. Natalie Zemon Davis, *Women on the Margins: Three Seventeenth-Century Lives* (Cambridge, Mass.: Harvard University Press, 1995), 34–35. See also Natalie Zemon Davis, "Religion and Capitalism Once Again? Jewish Merchant Culture in the Seventeenth Century," in *Trading Cultures: The Worlds of Western Merchants. Essays on Authority, Objectivity, and Evidence*, ed. Jeremy Adelman and Stephen Aron (Turnhout, Belgium: Brepols, 2001), 75–77.

28. Josef Seligmann, ed., *Aron Isaks Sjelfbiografi. Efter Författarens Handskrift* (Stockholm: Isaac Marcus' Boktr.- Aktiebolag, 1897), 2, 5.

29. Ibid., 15.

30. Mark Wischnitzer, ed., *Zikhronot R. Dov mi-Bolihov* (Berlin: Hotsa'at Kelal, 1922), 27, 53.

31. Ibid., 94, 96. See also Israel Bartal, "Dow M' Bolechow—Pamiętnikarz czasów kryzysu sejmu czterech ziem w XVIII stuleciu," in *Żydzi w Dawnej Rzeczypospolitej. Materiały z konferencji "Autonomia Żydów w Rzeczypospolitej Szlacheckiej," Międzywydziałowy Zakład Historii i Kultury Żydów w Polsce, Uniwersytet Jagielloński 22–26 IX 1986*, ed. Andrzej Link-Lenczowski (Warsaw: Zakład Narodowy Im. Ossolińskich, 1991), 83.

32. Wischnitzer, *Zikhronot*, 52, 55, 110.

33. For an example of how public as well as private texts concerning merchants in early modern England sought to establish trust, see Ceri Sullivan, *The Rhetoric of Credit: Merchants in Early Modern Writing* (Madison, N.J.: Fairleigh Dickinson University Press and Associated University Presses, 2002), 11, 19, 23, 43–44.

34. Turniansky, *Glikl: Zikhronot*, 408, 394–410. Glikl regularly integrated the classic formula "because of our many sins" into her narrative and the description of individuals. Davis, *Women on the Margins*, 44–45.

35. See especially Glikl's stories about Moses Helmstedt and R. Juda in Turniansky, *Glikl: Zikhronot*, 208–14, 220–22, 290–96.

36. "Acta betr. den Prozeß zwischen dem Juden Barend Simon/ Amsterdam und seinem Sohn Isaac Simons hierselbst, 1754–1759" (GStA Berlin, I. HA, Rep. 9 [Allgemeine Verwaltung], Y2, Fasz. 123), n.p.

37. "[File regarding the trial of Berend and Isaac Symons]" (GStA Berlin, I. HA, Rep. 49, Lit. K, 1759–1769, Paket no. 16213), 815v–18. The brothers were regular visitors at the Leipzig fair until 1750, but they do not appear in the list of Jewish visitors after 1751, while Isaac Symons is listed in 1753 and 1754. "Judenverzeichnisse 1726–1742" (SHstA Dresden, 10024 Geheimer Rat [Geheimes Archiv], Loc. 9482/4); "Judenverzeichnisse 1742–1764" (SHstA Dresden, 10024 Geheimer Rat [Geheimes Archiv], Loc. 9482/3).

38. Moshe Rosman, "The Role of Non-Jewish Authorities in Resolving Conflicts Within Jewish Communities in the Early Modern Period," *Jewish Political Studies Review* 12, nos. 3–4 (2000): 53–65.

39. On communal cohesion as a crucial element of early modern Jewish culture, see David Ruderman, *Early Modern Jewry: A New Cultural History* (Princeton, N.J.: Princeton University Press, 2010), 57–98.

40. In 1730, the Jewish civil jurisdiction was limited to ceremonial matters; the Revised General Code of 1750 allowed for the jurisdiction of civil cases by arbitration. Andreas Gotzmann, *Jüdische Autonomie in der Frühen Neuzeit: Recht und Gemeinschaft im deutschen Judentum* (Göttingen: Wallstein, 2008), 86–89.

41. An exchange of letters regarding the case between Moses Mendelssohn and Leo Hartog (Zvi Hirsch), secretary of the Berlin Jewish community, can be found in Moses Mendelssohn, *Gesammelte Schriften, Jubiläumsausgabe, vol. 20, 2: Briefwechsel (1761–1785)* (Stuttgart: Friedrich Frommann Verlag—Günther Holzboog, 1994), 135–48.

42. Steven M. Lowenstein, *The Berlin Jewish Community: Enlightenment, Family, and Crisis, 1770–1830* (New York: Oxford University Press, 1994), 21.

43. On the importance of institutions and the distinction between informal and formal institutions, see Douglass Cecil North, *Institutions, Institutional Change, and Economic Performance* (Cambridge: Cambridge University Press, 1990), 4, 46–47. Trust remained crucial to networks and their business operations despite the increasing regulation of trade by institutions and international law. David Sunderland, *Social Capital, Trust and the Industrial Revolution, 1780–1880* (London: Routledge, 2007), 205.

44. Gunnar Dahl, *Trade, Trust, and Networks: Commercial Culture in Late Medieval Italy* (Lund: Nordic Academic Press, 1998), 17.

45. "Resolution für den Schutzjuden Israel Jacob aus Flatow wegen Wechsel Process" (GStA Berlin, I. HA, Rep. 7B, no. 30, Fasz. 70), n.p.

46. See, for example, "Simon Symons und Levin Pincus Schlesinger wegen ihrer in Pohlen ausstehenden Wechsel und andere Forderungen," (GStA Berlin, I. HA, Geheimer Rat, Rep. 9 [Polen], no. 28-7C), n.p.

47. See note 13.

48. For a more detailed analysis of about four hundred bills of exchange from Amsterdam, see Cornelia Aust, "Commercial Cosmopolitans: Networks of Jewish Merchants Between Amsterdam and Warsaw, 1750–1820" (Ph.D. diss., University of Pennsylvania, 2010) 208–33. For a printed collection of notarized protests, see Geoffrey Hampson, ed., *Southampton Notarial Protest Books, 1756–1810* (Southampton, U.K.: Southampton University Press, 1973); see also Santarosa, "Financing Long-Distance Trade Without Banks," 13, 28.

49. Steele suggests that the interest of creditors in forcing bankruptcy was always closely linked "with the general economic milieu and with the form of legal arrangements for insolvent firms." Steele, "Bankruptcy and Insolvency," 184.

50. "Literae Moratoriae Infideli Wolffgang Moses Heymann ad Spatium Sex Mensium dantur" (AGAD Warsaw, Metryka Koronna, Księgi Kancelarskie 39 [mf. 6130]), 297–98; "Prorogatio Literarum Moratoriarum Infideli Wolffgang Moses Heymann" (AGAD Warsaw, Metryka Koronna, Księga Kancelarskie 56 [mf. 6130]), 131–33; Maurycy Horn, *Regesty dokumentów i ekscerpty z Metryki Koronnej do historii Żydów w Polsce, 1697–1795* (Warsaw: Zakład Narodowy im. Ossolińskich, 1984), vol. 2/1 no. 204, 208, 221, 223; vol. 2/2, no. 321. In general, it was a common phenomenon that insolvent firms or merchants had been important creditors to the government. On moratoria as a major policy option in early modern Europe, see also Steele, "Bankruptcy and Insolvency," 194, 201.

51. Ignacy Schiper, *Dzieje handlu żydowskiego na ziemiach polskich* (Warsaw: Druk. Narodowa, 1937; repr. Cracow: Krajowa Agencja Wydawnicza, 1990), 330.

52. "Acta betr. des Creditwesen des Juden Hirsch Markiewicz" (GStA Berlin, I. HA, Rep. 7C, No. 32a, Fasz 42), n.p.

53. Barbara Grochulska, "Echos de la faillite des banques de Varsovie," *Annales historiques de la Révolution Française* 53, no. 4 (1981): 529–40.

54. "Acta betreffend Gesuch des Schutzjuden Abraham Hirschel zur Konzession zur Anlegung einer Battist- und Kammertuch-Fabrik, 1754" (GStA Berlin, II. HA, GD, Abr. 25 Fabrik-Department, Tit. 240, no. 134a), 14.

55. "Sache: Jacobin wegen intendirten Mordts an der Generalin von Doecum intus verh. Simons" (GStA Berlin, I. HA, Rep. 49, Lit. H, 1755–1759 [Packet: 16164]), 330–85.

56. "Acta betr. den Prozeß zwischen dem Juden Barend Simon/ Amsterdam und seinem Sohn Isaac Simons hierselbst, 1754–1759" (GStA Berlin, I. HA, Rep. 9, Y2, Fasz. 123), n.p.

57. The estate was conveniently situated on the direct travel route between Warsaw and Dresden. The case attests to Hirschel's close relationship with Brühl, who more or less ran the Saxon state during the reign of August III. The mulberries served for the rearing of silkworms, the saffron for the dying of cloth. Hirschel's enterprise in Pförten eventually failed, and the entire estate was burned down in 1758 in the course of the Seven Years' War. Walter Fellmann, *Heinrich Graf Brühl: Ein Lebens- und Zeitbild* (Leipzig: Koehler & Amelang, 1989), 169–71.

58. "Acta betr. den Prozeß zwischen dem Juden Barend Simon/Amsterdam und seinem Sohn Isaac Simons hierselbst, 1754–1759" (GStA Berlin, I. HA, Rep. 9, Y2, Fasz. 123), n.p. See also "Interzession für die Juden Benjamin und Samuel Simon in Berlin wegen ihrer Forderung an den sich in Dresden aufhaltenden Juden Abraham Hirschel, Okt. 1755–Nov. 1755" (GStA Berlin, I. HA, Rep. 41, no. 2502), n.p.

59. "Acta betr. den Prozeß zwischen dem Juden Barend Simon/Amsterdam und seinem Sohn Isaac Simons hierselbst, 1754–1759," n.p. Apparently, there were also court cases that involved Hirschel in Leipzig, but unfortunately the records of the commercial court in Leipzig do not exist anymore.

60. Ibid.

61. "[File regarding the trial of Berend and Isaac Symons]" (GStA Berlin, I. HA, Rep. 49, Lit. K, 1759–1769, Paket no. 16213), 817v–18.

62. Ibid., 322.

63. "Acta die Einschränckung der Anzahl der Juden und deren Gewerbes in der Residenz-Stadt Dresden, auch die von selbigen zu entrichtende Personen-Steuer Ao. 1775" (SHstA Dresden, 10026 Geheimes Kabinett, Loc. 581/3), 39v–40, 104v–5.

64. Ibid. (Loc. 581/2), 134; ibid. (Loc. 581/3), 76v–77, 103.

Chapter 4. Jewish Quarters

1. While Jews in the tsarist empire proper were confined to a Pale of Settlement, Jews in the other Polish partitions (Prussian Poland, Galicia, and the Kingdom of Poland) always lived "beyond the Pale." Compare Benjamin Nathans, *Beyond the Pale: The Jewish Encounter with Late Imperial Russia* (Berkeley: University of California, 2002).

2. In this chapter, the "Christian merchants" who appear in the sources seem to be Polish Catholics, to judge by their surnames. Although recent scholarship on the early modern period emphasizes the diversity of Christian merchants, who included Scots, Italians, and ethnic Germans, only the latter appear to have retained a significant degree of ethnic and religious distinctiveness by the nineteenth century.

3. This privilege accompanied the incorporation of the Mazowia District into the Polish Crown lands under King Sigismund I. See Emanuel Ringelblum, *Żydzi w Warszawie. Od czasów najdawniejszych do ostatniego wygnania w r. 1527* (Warszawa: n.p., 1932). A revised picture is offered by Hanna Węgrzynek, who argues for a large Jewish presence in Warsaw prior to their formal readmittance in "Illegal Immigrants: The Jews of Warsaw, 1527–1792," in *Warsaw. The Jewish Metropolis: Studies in Honor of*

Professor Antony Polonsky's 70th Birthday, ed. Glenn Dynner and Francois Guesnet (London: Brill Academic Publishers, 2015).

4. Eleonora Bergman, "The *Rewir* or Jewish District and the *Eyruv*," *Studia Judaica* 5, no. 1 (2002): 87; Archiwum Główne Akt Dawnych (henceforth cited as AGAD), Komisji Rządowej Spraw Wewnętrznych (henceforth cited as KRSW) 188, fols. 227–42; KRSW 202, pp. 172–73. For an extensive study of Poznań, a legal "town within a town," see Adam Teller, *Hayim betsavata: harova hayehudi shel poznan bamahatsitharishonah shel hame'ah ha-17* (Jerusalem: 2003).

5. See, for example, Gershon Hundert, *Jews in Poland-Lithuania: A Genealogy of Modernity* (Berkeley: University of California Press, 2004), 30. On the popular misconception and construction of a ghetto myth in the nineteenth century, see Max Weinreich, "The Reality of Jewishness Versus the Ghetto Myth: The Sociolinguistic Roots of Yiddish," in *Never Say Die! A Thousand Years of Yiddish in Jewish Life and Letters*, ed. Joshua A. Fishman (The Hague: Mouton, 1981). This residential integration was true even of Warsaw, where Jewish residence was technically illegal until 1802, but where, before that date, the Jewish community may have been larger than that of any other European city. See Wegrzyenk, "Illegal Immigrants."

6. Prussia did away with *de non tolerandis Judaeis* privileges, which had often become a dead letter, while Austria left the issue vague.

7. In issuing that decree, Frederick August had been responding to complaints from the Warsaw municipality about noblemen who allowed Jews to rent apartments in "the most profitable neighborhoods and best houses," often transforming the lower levels of those houses into stores while residing on the upper floors. See Eleonora Bergman, *"Nie masz bóżnicy powszechnej": Synagogi i domy modlitwy w Warszawie od końca XVIII do początku XIX wieku* (Warsaw: 2007), 58. The original decree is no longer extant, but it is reprinted in Tsar Alexander's July 10, 1821, decree, published in *Dziennik Praw* 7:155, n.a.

8. AGAD, Rada Ministów Księstwa Warszawskiego 165, pp. 14–24. For more details, see Glenn Dynner, *Yankel's Tavern: Jews, Liquor and Life in the Kingdom of Poland* (New York: Oxford University Press, 2013), chap. 3. Part of the confusion over the Warsaw legislation among historians derives from differing definitions of the *rewir*. According to Henryk Bartoszewicz, Frederick August's 1809 decree did not demarcate borders in a specific part of the city and was thus not properly a *rewir*. Eleonora Bergman defines *rewir* more capaciously, considering the restricted streets mentioned there as inversely forming the first *rewir*. See Henryk Bartoszewicz, "Projekty rewirów dla ludności żydowskiej w miastach mazowieckich 1807–1830," *Rocznik Mazowiecki* 18 (2006): 104–20; and Eleonora Bergman, *"Nie masz bóżnicy powszechnej,"* 53.

9. Rada Ministrów Księstwa Warszawskiego 165, pp. 28–32.

10. Bina Garncarska-Kadary, *Ḥelḳam shel ha-Yehudim be-hitpatḥut ha-ta aśiyah shel Ṿarshah ba-shanim 1816/20–1914* (Tel Aviv: bha-Makhon le-ḥeḳer ha-tefutsot, 1985), 48.

11. Adam Wein, "Żydzi poza rewirem żydowskim w Warszawie (1809–1862)," *Biuletyn ŻIH* 41 (1962): 45–70.

12. KRSW 188, fols. 93–96, pp. 33–34 (Wschowa); Akta Rady Ministrów Księstwa Warszawskiego 165, pp. 46–78 (Płock); p. 95 (Maków); p. 100 (Przasnysza). The municipality of Dochodów was more candid, deeming a Jewish quarter necessary for "profitable trade and similar practical considerations." KRSW 4394, pp. 100–103.

13. Although the specifically delineated Jewish quarters in Wschowy, Płock, Maków, and Przasnysza predated Warsaw's Jewish quarter (before 1813, there were only "excluded streets"), each decree establishing Jewish quarters in those towns refers to the Warsaw 1809 policy as its model.

14. AGAD, Akta Kancerlaria Senatora Nowosilcowa 206, pp. 14–18. The same delegation made a similar request of the Grand Duke Constantine, who was military commander of the new kingdom. See ibid., 25.

15. Ibid., pp. 103–4.

16. Artur Eisenbach, *The Emancipation of the Jews in Poland, 1780–1870*, ed. Antony Polonsky (London: Blackwell, 1988), 218.

17. Eisenbach, ibid., dates the decree as May 7, 1822; however, this must be a reiteration of the July 10, 1821 decree.

18. Decree issued on July 10, 1821, and published in *Dziennik Praw*, 7:155–73. As justification, Alexander cited concerns about the over-concentration of Jews in the capital articulated in the 1809 decree. At the same time, Alexander permitted Jews to purchase empty lots for the construction of stone houses on any street not deemed restricted, thereby departing slightly from the 1809 decree, which permitted such purchases on restricted streets. The tsar's apparent ignorance of the "Jewish City" decree is implied in an investigation into Jewish legal status in Warsaw from around 1816, which mentions only the 1809 restricted streets decree. See Akta Kancelaria Senatora Nowosilcowa 206, p. 90.

19. Garncarska-Kadary, *Ḥelḳam shel ha-Yehudim*, 38–40.

20. The policy that Nathans terms "selective integration" with respect to the tsarist empire proper in the late 1850s was thus long preceded by a similar process in the Kingdom of Poland. See Nathans, *Beyond the Pale*, 45–79. On exempted families in Warsaw, see Wein, "Żydzi poza rewirem żydowskim w Warszawie (1809–1862)." Only two Jewish families were permitted to live on each restricted street. On 1842, see KRSW 5752. The 131 families mentioned there consisted of a total of 705 people. By 1842, 47 out of Warsaw's 223 streets were "restricted." Over half of those streets—27—contained Jewish enterprises.

21. KRSW 188, fols. 96–97; Protokoły Rady Administracyjnej Królestwa Polskiego (PRAKP), vols. 11–16. It should be noted that a Jewish quarter was also established in the tsarist empire proper, in Vilna. A copy of the decree in Yiddish and Polish, expelling Jews from houses, stores, and market stalls on five principal streets, is found in the Dubnow Papers in the YIVO (Institute for Jewish Research) archive, New York, RG 87, folder 940, 2:23.

22. Compasses were established in fifteen of forty such royal towns; in one out of thirty such clergy-owned towns; and in eight of twenty such noble-owned towns.

23. A map of Zakroczym reveals that the town's Sabbath/festival boundary (*eruv*) lay well outside the designated Jewish quarter. The *eruv* was disputed by the Bishop of Płock, who feared that local Catholics might vandalize those portions that lay too close to a church or were fastened to poles originally used for altars, which might in turn cause Jews to profane the sacrament in revenge. AGAD, Centralne Władze Wyznaniowe 1410, pp. 67–69; Bergman, "The *Rewir* or Jewish District," 91. The following towns planned and mapped Jewish quarters during this period but did not enforce them: Augustów, Biała Podlaska, Bolimów, Chorzele, Ciechanów, Czyżew, Janowo, Kielce, Krasnystaw, Kuczbork, Łosice, Płońsk, Węgrów, Wyszków, and Wyszogród. In addition, the towns Wschowa and Maków do not seem to have been able to reinstate their Jewish quarters after 1821. See Maria Łodynska-Kosinska, ed., *Katalog rysunków architektonicznych z Akt Komisji Rządowej Spraw Wewnętrznych w Archiwum Głównym Akt Dawnych w Warszawie* (Warsaw: PWN, 1974). On the successful Jewish resistance to their implementation in Ciechanów, see Bartoszewicz, "Pojekty rewirów," 113; and Janusz Szczepański, *Społeczność żydowska Mazowsza w XIX–XX wieku* (Pułtusk: WSH, 2005), 53.

24. KRSW 188, fols. 223–26. See also fol. 98; and KRSW 6632, p. 68. These statistics, compiled by the "Zarządzający Wydziałem Administracyjnym Radca Stanu Biernacki," confirm the low end of Bergman's estimate that Jewish quarters existed in 12 to 15 percent of towns in the kingdom. "The *Rewir* or Jewish District," 86.

25. The number of Jews residing in towns with formal Jewish quarters was 83,915; another 70,694 Jews lived in towns with *de non tolerandis Judaeus* or clergy-owned towns with residential restrictions. See KRSW 6632, p. 68.

26. Montefiore—St. Petersburg archives (Sergei's batch), 1946, Privy Councilor Turkul' document 14, pp. 226–65, trans. Svetlana Rukhelman. Many thanks to Abigail Green for sharing these documents with me.

27. During a failed attempt to establish a Jewish quarter in the town of Chorzele, for example, it became clear that four houses around the perimeter of the market square (*rynek*) and two houses on other principal streets were owned by Jews, and that thirty-seven additional houses had Jewish occupants. How would it be possible to find Christians with the financial means to occupy these houses, local officials wondered? Faced with the prospect of empty houses all over town, they concluded that the wealthiest Jews would have to be exempted. See KRSW 4287, pp. 63–68.

28. These towns lay within three miles of one of those borders. Decree issued on May 29, 1834, published in *Dziennik Praw* 16. A list of those towns is provided in KRSW 188, which, however, states the date of the decree as 1836. See also KRSW 6632, p. 64.

29. Mahler, *Hasidism and the Jewish Enlightenment: Their Confrontation in Galicia and Poland in the First Half of the Nineteenth Century*, trans. Eugene Orenstein, Aaron Klein, and Jenny Machlowitz Klein (Philadelphia: Jewish Publication Society, 1985), 184–86.

30. I address the importance of periodizing and contextualizing the East European Jewish economic crisis in *Yankel's Tavern*, chap. 5.

31. Azriel Natan Frenk, "Di tzel iden un zeyre basheftigongen in di shtet un derfer fun Kenigreikh Poylin in 1843-tn yahr," *Bleter far idishe demografye, statistik un ekonomik* 3 (1923): 184–93.

32. Garncarska-Kadary, *Ḥelḳam shel ha-Yehudim*, 65–77, 88, 95. In 1907, at the peak of Jewish involvement in Warsaw industry, Jews constituted a full 74.8 percent of the city's factory workers. Ibid., 118. By World War I, over half of all factory workers in Warsaw resided in the western (i.e., "Jewish") section of Warsaw. Ibid., 114.

33. For the residential segregation period (pre-1860), it should be noted that Garncarska-Kadary focuses on only a small group of Jewish plutocrats who managed the transition from private banking and army purveying to the financing of factories and railroads, while examining the wider Jewish population only during the later period of accelerated industrialization and unrestricted Jewish residence. But her overarching claim that residential restrictions did not prove overwhelmingly destructive to Jewish economic endeavor seems right.

34. See, for example, Zelig Salinger's petition from 1834, in KRSW 5914, pp. 5–6; and Staniław Brunner's petition, in ibid., pp. 8–9.

35. KRSW 5911, fols. 54–56, 75–76.

36. KRSW 5914, pp. 1–4.

37. For example, Szprynca Salberg was "a widow bereft of a husband and, what is more, a mother of 3 children." KRSW 5914, pp. 10–13. For other examples, see ibid., pp. 90–91; KRSW 6704, pp. 55, 74, 133, 149, 174, 177. The higher incidence of working Jewish women is only verifiable anecdotally at this point, though I am currently investigating this important topic.

38. KRSW 5914, pp. 51–61. For examples, see Dynner, *Yankel's Tavern*, chap. 3.

39. KRSW 5914, pp. 15–16.

40. KRSW 6704, pp. 77–80, 89, 152–59, 258. See Dynner, *Yankel's Tavern*, chap. 3.

41. KRSW 5914, pp. 116–20. For more detail, see Dynner, *Yankel's Tavern*, 91.

42. KRSW 5914, pp. 218, 263–65.

43. Ibid., pp. 164–65.

44. KRSW 5910, fols. 195–96.

45. KRSW 5911, fols. 80–81. Charczewski's request was rejected. Ibid., fols. 82–83.

46. KRSW 5914, p. 19. A similar petition from this period was submitted by the Warsaw Christian resident Jozef Kowiecki.

47. KRSW 5910, fol. 246–47.

48. A Jewish delegation approached Nowosilcov as early as April 15, 1813, while he was still vice president of the Supreme Council of the former Duchy of Warsaw, and presented him with a memo protesting an impending closure of Jewish-run taverns, accompanied by a bribe and promise of more to come. On July 28, 1814, Warsaw Jewish lay leaders Michał Ettinger, Wolf-Michał Cohn, and Sachna Neuding presented Tsar Alexander I himself with a lengthy and detailed protest against planned tavern closures. Dawid Kandel, "Nowosilcow a Żydzi," *Biblioteka Warszawska*, vol. 3 (1911): 142; A. N. Frenk, "Mehiat mekhirat mashkim," *Ha-Tzefirah* 179 (August 21, 1921); Szymon

Askenazy, "Z dziejów Żydów polskich w dobie Księstwa Warszawskiego," *Kwartalnik poświęcony badania przeszłości Żydów w Polsce* 1, no. 1 (1912): 8–9.

49. Akta Kancerlaira Sentaora Nowosilcowa 206, pp. 14–16. The same delegation made a similar request of the Grand Duke Constantine, who was military commander of the new kingdom. See ibid., 25.

50. Ibid., 28–29. He informed Zajączek that the Jews had approached him about residential restrictions and that he thought it best to delay their implementation until the tsar weighed in on the matter. Ibid., 103.

51. KRSW 6628, p. 212. The decree is from August 11, 1810.

52. See Dynner, "Hasidism and Habitat: Managing the Jewish-Christian Encounter in the Kingdom of Poland," in *Holy Dissent: Jewish and Christian Mystics in Eastern Europe*, ed. Glenn Dynner (Detroit: Wayne State University Press, 2011), 117, table 2. On urban Hasidic enclaves in the nineteenth century, see Yehezkel Kotik, *Meine Zikhroynes* (Warsaw: 1913), 78; Ya'akov Milkh, *Oytobiagrafishe skitzen* (New York: 1946), 81–82.

53. Elazar Tahlgrin, *Tohahat musar: Ha-sefer Tehilim* (Warsaw: 1854), fols. 18, 2b–4a, 28b–29. His criticisms of Hasidism begin on fol. 10b. On the "clothing decrees," see Dynner, "The Garment of Torah: The Clothing Decrees and the Warsaw Career of the Gerer Rebbe," in *Warsaw, the Jewish Metropolis*, ed. Dynner and Guesnet. We may estimate the date of Tahlgrin's social critique by its approbation by the Chief Rabbi of Warsaw, Hayyim Dawidzsohn, dated 1848. Tahlgrin was an admirer of rabbinic celebrities like Akiba Eiger and the former Chief Rabbi of Warsaw, Shlomo Zalman Lifshitz, and himself a descendent of a line of distinguished rabbis (although "in all the seven years [he] lived in Warsaw, no one ever heard [him] boast about this"). Yet he refers glowingly to Moses Mendelssohn's German translation of the Bible and criticizes Jewish linguistic norms.

54. Ibid., fols. 16–17.

55. Jan Glucksberg (attr.), *Rzut oka na obecny stan Izraelitów w Polsce* (Warsaw: 1831), 5–6. The earlier French version is published in full in Eisenbach, "Memoriał o położeniu ludności żydówskiej w dobie konstytucyjnej Królestwa Kongresowego," *Teki archiwalne* (1989), 177–215.

56. Glucksberg, *Rzut oka,* 49.

57. KRSW 6600, fols. 229–43. For more detail, see Dynner, *Yankel's Tavern,* 99.

58. *Jutrzenka* 2 (1862): 241–42.

59. Garncarska-Kadary, *Ḥelḳam shel ha-Yehudim,* 44.

60. Eleonora Bergman emphasizes the aesthetic rationale. See *"Nie masz bóżnicy powszechnej,"* 58–60.

61. Mahler, *Hasidism and the Jewish Enlightenment*, 180; KRSW 6632, p. 67. See also Artur Eisenbach, "Mobilność terytorialna ludności Żydowskiej w Królestwie Polskim," *Społeceństwo królestwa polskiego* (5 vols.) vol. 2, ed., Witold Kula and Janina Leskiewiczowa (Warsaw: PWN, 1966), 207–21.

62. KRSW 6600, fol. 296.

63. KRSW 187, fol. 175.

64. KRSW 188, fols. 86–90; KRSW 6632, p. 67.

65. See Eisenbach, *The Emancipation of the Jews in Poland*, 264.

66. KRSW 202, pp. 166–79. Bergman's statistics for Warsaw Jewry do not include 1845; however, they show only 41,000 Jews living in Warsaw by 1856. See *"Nie masz bóżnicy powszechnej,"* 15, table 1.

67. KRSW 202, pp. 166–79.

68. On Montefiore's humanitarian ventures in Russia and Poland, see Abigail Green, *Moses Montefiore: Jewish Liberator, Imperial Hero* (Cambridge, Mass.: Belknap Press of Harvard University Press, 2010), 174–98; and Israel Bartal and David Assaf, "Shtadlanut ve-ortodoksiyah: tzaddikei Polin be-mifgash im ha-zmanim ha-hadashim," in *Tzaddikim ve-anshe ma'aseh: Mehkarim be-hasidut Polin*, ed. Rachel Elior, Yisrael Bartal, and Chone Shmeruk (Jerusalem: Mosad Bialik, 1994), 65–90.

69. AGAD KRSW 188, fols. 86–89, 101–4.

70. Ibid., pp. 6–32.

71. KRSW/KRPiS 1849, p. 328.

72. Jean Czynski, *An Enquiry into the Political Condition of the Polish Jews, Considered in Relation to the General Interests of Europe* (London: n.p., 1834), 18.

73. Antoni Ostrowski, *Pomysły o potrzebie reformy towarzyskiéy w ogolności, a mianowiciéy, co do Izraelitów w Polszcze / przez założyciela miasta Tomaszowa Mazowieckiego* (Paris: Gisserni and Pinard, 1834), 45.

74. KRSW 188, fol. 100; Wein, "Żydzi poza rewirem," 65.

75. Montefiore—St. Petersburg archives, 6–32.

76. AGAD, KRSW 6643, fols. 10–11. See also my forthcoming "The Garment of Torah."

77. Turkul' rephrased the four original rationales as follows: "(1) To prevent an excessive accumulation of inhabitants in cities, and the frequent fires that result from it; (2) to avert the spread of disease and contagion; (3) to limit in some measure the ability of the Jews to engage in all kinds of roguery and fraud at the expense of the Christians, to avert the spread of drunkenness among the lowest class of the Christian population, and to prevent an excessive rise in the prices of vital goods; and (4) to promote the beautification and cleanliness of the cities." Montefiore—St. Petersburg archives (Sergei's batch), Privy Councillor Turkul', document 14, pp. 226–65.

78. Ibid.

79. Ibid.

80. KRSW 6600, fols. 331–43.

81. KRSW 6600, pp. 72–76.

82. Eisenbach, *Emancipation of the Jews of Poland*, 394–95.

83. For a good summary of this process, see Michael Jerry Ochs, "St. Petersburg and the Jews of Russian Poland, 1862–1905" (Ph.D. diss., Harvard University, 1986), 20–24.

84. Examples of this include Yuri Slezkine, *The Jewish Century* (Princeton, N.J.: Princeton University Press, 2004); David Hollinger, "Rich, Powerful and Smart: Jewish

Overrepresentation Should Be Explained Rather than Avoided or Mystified," *Jewish Quarterly Review* 94, no. 4 (2004): 595–602; and Natalie Zemon Davis, "Religion and Capitalism Once Again? Jewish Merchant Culture in the Seventeenth Century," *Representations* 59 (1997): 56–84.

85. Artur Eisenbach, for example, dismisses officials' claims about Jewish economic distinctiveness as mere prejudice, and decries residential restrictions as "inconsistent with the declarations of the government on the necessity of integrating the Jews into the population of the country." Eisenbach, *The Emancipation of the Jews in Poland*, 177.

86. Sarah Abrevaya Stein, *Plumes: Ostrich Feathers, Jews, and a Lost World of Global Commerce* (New Haven, Conn.: Yale University Press, 2008), 10–15.

87. Francesca Trivallato, *The Familiarity of Strangers: The Sephardic Diaspora, Livorno, and Cross-Cultural Trade in the Early Modern Period* (New Haven, Conn.: Yale University Press, 2009), 45, 51–53. Trivallato finds, more specifically, that western Sephardic merchants differed from Christian merchants in their preference for endogamous marriage, large dowries for financing business ventures, and general, informal family partnerships. See ibid., 132–52. On partnerships with non-Jews, see especially ibid., 145.

88. Robert Johnston, *Travels Through Part of the Russian Empire and the Country of Poland* (New York: David Longworth, 1816), 382; J. T. James, *Journal of a Tour in Germany, Sweden, Russia, Poland during the Years 1813–1814* (London: John Murray, 1827), 358.

89. Johnston, *Travels*, 381–82.

90. Józef Gołuchowski [Klemens Przezor], *Kwestya reformy Żydów* (Lipsk: Księgarnia, Zagraniczna, 1854), 37.

91. Jewish urbanization is frequently overdetermined, and is a subject in dire need of reexamination. On Eisenbach's manipulation of demographic data, see my article "Legal Fictions: The Survival of Rural Jewish Tavernkeeping in the Kingdom of Poland," *Jewish Social Studies: History, Culture, Society* n.s. 16, no. 2 (Winter 2010): 63n100. Garncarska-Kadary attempts to explain away reverses in Jewish urbanization by referring to Jewish census dodging, which was, however, an ever-present phenomenon. In addition, the proportion of Jews in Warsaw remained virtually unchanged (around 32 percent) during the *second* half of the nineteenth century; while the rate of Christian population growth in the city surpassed the Jewish rate in that period. See *Ḥelḳam shel ha-Yehudim*, 25–27, including tables 3 and 4.

92. Garncarska-Kadary, *Ḥelḳam shel ha-Yehudim*, 22, table 2.

93. Ibid., 63, 118, table 17.

94. Moshe Rosman, "The History of Jewish Women in Early Modern Poland," *Polin* 18 (2008): 25–56. For the women-as-enabler image, see Iris Parush, *Reading Jewish Women: Marginality and Modernization in Nineteenth-Century Eastern European Jewish Society* (Hannover, N.H.: Brandeis University Press, 2004); and Daniel Boyarin, *Unheroic Conduct: The Rise of Heterosexuality and the Invention of the Jewish Man* (Berkeley: University of California, 1997), chap. 1.

95. Dynner, "Legal Fictions," and *Yankel's Tavern*, esp. chap. 2. Maristella Botticini and Zvi Eckstein argue that education was the key to Jewish economic success; however, they seem to miss the critical role of Jewish women, who did not have the benefits of formal education, in Jewish household economies. Maristella Botticini and Zvi Eckstein, *The Chosen Few: How Education Shaped Jewish History, 70–1492* (Princeton, N.J.: Princeton University Press, 2012).

96. Hayim Hillel Ben Sasson, *Hagut ṿe-hanhagah: Hashḳefotehem ha-ḥevratiyot shel Yehude Polin be-shilhe yeme ha-benayim* (Jerusalem: Mosad Bialik, 1959).

Chapter 5. From Moses to Moses

1. Madeline House, Graham Storey, and Kathleen Tillotson, eds., *The Letters of Charles Dickens* (Oxford: Clarendon Press, 1974), 3:610.

2. *London Times*, October 27, 1843, 4, October 28, 1843, 7, in Sheila Blackburn, *A Fair Day's Wages for a Fair Day's Work?* (London: Ashgate, 2007), 17–20. See also Sarah Levitt, *Victorians Unbuttoned* (London: Allen & Unwin, 1986), 16, 181, 186; and Robert Wechsler, "The Jewish Garment Trade in East London 1875–1914: A Study in Conditions and Responses" (Ph.D. diss., Columbia University, 1979), 41–42.

3. For a detailed discussion of these broader processes, see Adam D. Mendelsohn, *The Rag Race: How Jews Sewed their Way to Success in America and the British Empire* (New York: New York University Press, 2015).

4. For a useful summary of Jewish involvement in international commerce, see Harold Pollins, *Economic History of the Jews in England* (Rutherford, N.J.: Farleigh Dickinson University Press, 1982), 43–54. On trade with India, see Gedalia Yogev, *Diamonds and Coral: Anglo-Dutch Jews and Eighteenth-Century Trade* (New York: Holmes & Meier, 1978), 124–80, 253–74. On trade with the Maghreb, see Daniel J. Schroeter, *The Sultan's Jews: Morocco and the Sephardi World* (Stanford, Calif.: Stanford University Press, 2002), 71–87. On the Caribbean trade, see Stephen Fortune, *Merchants and Jews: The Struggle for British West Indian Commerce, 1650–1750* (Gainesville: University of Florida Press, 1984), 73–77, 94–98, 130–50; and Eli Faber, *Jews, Slaves, and the Slave Trade* (New York: New York University Press, 1998), 22–43. On the Levantine trade, see Eliezer Bashan, "Contacts Between Jews in Smyrna and the Levant Company of London in the Seventeenth and Eighteenth Centuries," *Jewish Historical Studies* 29 (1986): 53–73, and Todd Endelman, *The Jews of Georgian England, 1714–1830* (Ann Arbor: University of Michigan Press, 1999), 24. On the Mediterranean trade, see T. M. Benady, "The Role of Jews in the British Colonies of the Western Mediterranean," *Jewish Historical Studies* 33 (1994): 48, 52. Jews were also involved in the export of fabric produced in Lancashire to the Ottoman Empire, South America, West Africa, and Europe. See Bill Williams, *The Making of Manchester Jewry, 1740–1875* (Manchester, U.K.: Manchester University Press, 1985), 81, 83, 87; Todd Endelman, "German-Jewish Settlement in Victorian England," in *Second Chance: Two Centuries of German-Speaking Jews in the United Kingdom*, ed. Werner Mosse (Tübingen: Mohr Siebeck, 1991). For the extent of textile exports, see Robert Ross, *Clothing: A Global History* (Cambridge,

U.K.: Polity, 2008), 71; D. A. Farnie, *The English Cotton Industry and the World Market, 1815–1896* (Oxford: Oxford University Press, 1979), 86.

5. On their business activities, see Louis Herrman, *A History of the Jews of South Africa* (Johannesburg: SAJBD, 1935), 123–26; Lawrence Green, *At Daybreak for the Isles* (Cape Town: H. B. Timmins, 1950), 80–82; Israel Abrahams, *The Birth of a Community* (Cape Town: Cape Town Hebrew Congregation, 1955), 32–33; Louis Hotz, "Contributions to Economic Development," in *The Jews in South Africa: A History*, ed. Gustav Saron and Louis Hotz (Cape Town: Oxford University Press, 1955), 352. On guano export, see Edward Napier, *Excursions in South Africa*, vol. 1 (London: William Shoberl, 1849), 324–25; E. Littell, *The Living Age* (Boston: Waite, Peirce & Company, 1847), 12:173–74. For their provenance in London, see Albert Hyamson, *The Sephardim of England* (London: Methuen & Co., 1951), 294, 314, 336, 397. On their charitable giving, see London *Jewish Chronicle* (hereafter cited as *JC*), December 25, 1846, July 7, 1854, December 12, 1862, January 13, 1865.

6. For Melbourne, see *JC*, December 12, 1862; *Reports of Cases Argued and Determined in the English Court of Common Law, Volume C* (Philadelphia: T. & J. W. Johnson & Co., 1871), 516–23; Henry Turner, *A History of the Colony of Victoria* (London: Longman, Green, & Co., 1904), 94; *Victoria Government Gazette* (Melbourne: Government Printer, 1861), 24; *The South African Jewish Year Book* (Johannesburg: South African Jewish Historical Society, 1929), 240; Lazarus Goldman, *The Jews in Victoria in the Nineteenth Century* (Melbourne: L. M. Goldman, 1954), 131, 147–48, 164.

7. J. S. Levi and G. F. J Bergman, *Australian Genesis: Jewish Convicts and Settlers, 1788–1850* (London: Hale, 1974), 199; Goldman, *Jews in Victoria*, 141.

8. He was joined in Sydney by his nephew Jacob Levi Montefiore of Bridgetown, Barbados, in 1837. See *Jewish World*, January 30 and February 2, 1885; Levi and Bergman, *Australian Genesis*, 175.

9. See Levi and Bergman, *Australian Genesis*, 76, 196–201, 213–14, 297.

10. On international trade networks involving hawkers and peddlers in medieval and early modern Europe, see Linda Woodbridge, "The Peddler and the Pawn," in *Rogues and Early Modern English Culture*, ed. Craig Dionne and Steve Mentz (Ann Arbor: University of Michigan Press, 2004), 149–51; Laurence Fontaine, *History of Peddlers in Europe* (Durham, N.C.: Duke University Press, 1996), 8–49. On Jewish hawkers selling sponges, see Henry Mayhew, *London Labour and the London Poor* (London: Griffin, Bohn, & Company, 1861), 1:442–43. On the sale of oranges and lemons, see ibid., 61, 79, 81, 86–89. The peddling of lemons declined as the citrus became a profitable commodity, the result of the passage of a law that required foreign-bound ships to be provided with lemon juice; ibid., 89. On the supply of sponges from Smyrna, Rhodes, Beirut, and Greece, see James McCoan, *Our New Protectorate: Turkey in Asia* (London: Chapman and Hall, 1879), 82, 115, 118–20; John McCulloch, *A Dictionary, Geographical, Statistical, and Historical* (London: Longmans, Green, & Co., 1851), 968. On Jewish involvement in the wholesale of these products by the 1850s, see Mayhew, *London Labour*, 2:118. On Jewish involvement in the sponge trade, see Jonathan Frankel, *The Da-*

mascus Affair: "Ritual Murder," Politics, and the Jews in 1840 (Cambridge: Cambridge University Press, 1997), 70; Pollins, *Economic History*, 107. On the North African Jewish trading network that supplied ostrich feathers to London, see Sarah Abrevaya Stein, "Mediterranean Jewries and Global Commerce in the Modern Period: On the Trail of the Jewish Feather Trade," *Jewish Social Studies: History, Culture, Society* 13, no. 2, (2007): 1–39. On secondhand garments, see Joseph Nightingale, *London and Middlesex* (London: Longman, 1815), 3:134; John Wallis, *Wallis's Guide to London* (London: Sherwood, Neely, and Jones, 1814), 347.

11. See Adam Mendelsohn, "Tongue Ties: Religion, Culture and Commerce in the Making of the Anglophone Jewish Diaspora, 1840–1870" (Ph.D. diss., Brandeis University, 2008), 17–48. Neither of the two best recent reevaluations of Anglo-Jewish history—Todd Endelman's *The Jews of Britain, 1650 to 2000* (Berkeley: University of California Press, 2002); and David Feldman's *Englishmen and Jews* (New Haven, Conn.: Yale University Press, 1994)—makes any reference to South Africa, Jamaica, or Australia in its index. The latter discusses the importance of empire—but only in the period following 1880.

12. See Sarah Abrevaya Stein, *Plumes: Ostrich Feathers, Jews, and a Lost World of Global Commerce* (New Haven, Conn.: Yale University Press, 2008).

13. See John Mills, *The British Jews* (London: Houlston and Stoneman, 1853), 264. John Weale made the identical assessment in *The Pictorial Handbook of London* (London: Henry G. Bohn, 1854), 533.

14. Elias has received some attention from historians. See Andrew Godley, "Moses, Elias (1783–1868)," *Oxford Dictionary of National Biography* (Oxford: Oxford University Press, 2004); Stanley Chapman, "The Innovating Entrepreneurs in the British Ready-Made Clothing Industry," *Textile History* 24 (1993); idem, "The 'Revolution' in Ready-Made Clothing, 1840–1860," *London Journal* 29, no. 1 (2004): 44–61.

15. *Godwin's Emigrants Guide to Van Diemen's Land* (London: Sherwood, Jones, 1823).

16. For one such extensive list of recommended items of clothing, see *Sidney's Emigrant's Journal*, December 7, 1848, 78, February 22, 1849, 165.

17. For the eligibility requirements established by the emigration commissioners for assisted passages to the Cape and Australia, see *Sidney's Emigrant's Journal*, January 25, 1849, 130, June 28, 1849, 309.

18. Margaret Maynard, *Fashioned from Penury: Dress as Cultural Practice in Colonial Australia* (New York: Cambridge University Press, 1994), 139–40; Chapman, "Innovating Entrepreneurs," 6; Levitt, *Victorians Unbuttoned*, 77. For their advertisements aimed at emigrants, see *Sidney's Emigrant's Journal*, December 28, 1848, 104, January 11, 1849, 120. For prices of different immigration outfits, see *The Library of Elegance* (London: E. Moses & Son, 1852), 22.

19. Quoted in Chapman, "Ready-Made Clothing," 45–46.

20. Weale, *Pictorial Handbook of London*, 533; Chapman, "Innovating Entrepreneurs," 16. For contemporary criticism of their use of gas lighting and other marketing

techniques, see Lynda Neal, *Victorian Babylon: People, Streets and Images in Nineteenth-Century London* (New Haven, Conn.: Yale University Press, 2000), 89; Beth Harris, "All That Glitters Is Not Gold: The Show-Shop and the Victorian Seamstress," in *Famine and Fashion: Needlewomen in the Nineteenth Century*, ed. Beth Harris (Burlington, Vt.: Ashgate, 2005), 123; George Sala, *Gaslight and Daylight, with Some London Scenes They Shine Upon* (London: Chapman and Hall, 1859), 257–58. The store was also praised in poetry: see William Thackeray, *Ballads and Songs* (New York: Scribner, 1906), 116–19.

21. E. Moses and Son, *The Growth of an Important Branch of British Industry* (London: 1860), 8; *The Dressing Room Companion or Guide to the Glass* (London: E. Moses & Son, 1848), 24; *The Library of Elegance*, 25. For the Moses's innovations within the clothing business, see E. Moses and Son, *The Growth of an Important Branch of British Industry*, 4–7; Chapman, "Ready-Made Clothing," 46–52, 57–58; Chapman, "Innovating Entrepreneurs," 5–25; Weale, *Pictorial Handbook of London*, 533–34.

22. *Times*, July 3, 1841, 8, May 13, 1842, 11.

23. *Illustrated London News*, October 22, 1842. For contemporary praise of their advertising techniques, see William Smith, *Advertise: How? When? Where?* (London: Routledge, Warne, and Routledge, 1861), 36.

24. On their advertising in Dickens, see Bernard Darwin, ed., *The Dickens Advertiser: A Collection of the Advertisements in the Original Parts of Novels by Charles Dickens* (New York: Macmillan, 1930), 140–55.

25. Dave Hollett, *Fast Passage to Australia* (London: Fairplay, 1986), 31.

26. See *Punch* 14 (1848): 127.

27. *Quarterly Review* 97 (1855): 212.

28. See Parliamentary Papers, Great Britain, Parliament, House of Commons, 1847, vol. 9 (reports, vol. 5), cmd. 666, 1847, "Reports from the Select Committee on Sunday Trading," q. 462.

29. David Richardson, *The Anglo-Indian Passage Homeward and Outward* (London: James Madden, 1849), 202–3; James Barber, *The Overland Guide* (London: Wm. H. Allen, 1850); *The Library of Elegance*, 6.

30. *The Merchant Shippers of London, Liverpool, Manchester, Birmingham, Bristol, and Hull* (London: Straker & Sons, 1868, 1878).

31. Mills, *The British Jews*, 264. Weale made a similar assessment in *The Pictorial Handbook of London*, 533. The Moses family was also connected by marriage with the Hyam, Hart, and Levy clans, all leading clothing manufacturers and retailers.

32. Henry's eldest son and business partner, Edward, was married to Isaac Moses's eldest child, Julia.

33. In 1806, an average agricultural laborer could expect to earn around £40 a year, a teacher around £43, and a skilled builder £55. Estimates of the current equivalent value of historic currency are notoriously difficult. Here amounts have been calculated according to the historic standard of living using MeasuringWorth. http://www.measuringworth.com/uscompare/relativevalue.php. For average annual salaries, see

http://privatewww.essex.ac.uk/~alan/family/N-Money.html. Insurance records for Samuel Moses for 1779, 1794, 1802, and letters of administration from the London Commissary Court, May 1806, in the private collection of George Rigal.

34. Guildhall Library, Records of the Sun Fire Office, MS 11936/457/879744; MS 11936/479/966353; MS 11936/506/1045585; MS 11936/555/1250004; MS 11936/517/1098528; MS 11936/563/1031882; *Proceedings of the Old Bailey*, October 30, 1816, 35; April, 16, 1817, 42; March 1835, 144.

35. There is evidence of his growing prosperity in the early 1820s, when he worked as a slop-seller in Houndsditch. He also acted as a landlord to several artisans, leasing and owning several houses (including five in Rosemary Lane), which were insured for the substantial sum of £1,700 in 1822. By the end of the decade, he had bought additional property. In 1829, his house was valued at £350, his possessions (including musical instruments) at £100, and the contents of his warehouse at £900. By contrast, the contents of his house were valued at £150 and his stock at £150 in 1814. In 1836, the stock at his warehouse in Tower Hill was valued at £1,300. Henry's primary business premise was in Houndsditch as late as 1833. See Guildhall Library, Records of the Sun Fire Office, MS 11936/490/995647; MS 11936/489/989191; MS 11936/514/1074086; MS 11936/479/66353; MS 11936/457/879744; MS 11936/517/1084440; MS 11936/517/1098528; MS 11936/524/1113792; MS 11936/557/34829. For the importance of his investment in property see *JC*, April 1, 1884.

36. See John Levi, *These Are the Names* (Carlton: Melbourne University Press, 2006), 370.

37. Lawrence Nathan, "Thirty-Eight Presidents," *Australian Jewish Historical Society* 9, no. 7 (1984): 487–501; Peter and Ann Elias, eds., *A Few from Afar: Jewish Lives in Tasmania from 1804* (Hobart: Hobart Hebrew Congregation, 2003), 232; Lawrence Nathan, *As Old as Auckland: The History of L. D. Nathan & Co. Ltd and of the David Nathan Family, 1840–1980* (Auckland: L. D. Nathan, 1984), 17–19, 53–54, 62, 125, 146; William Kelly, *Life in Victoria* (London: Chapman and Hall, 1859), 1:147; Goldman, *Jews in Victoria*; Levi and Bergman, *Australian Genesis*, 213, 249, 268, 295; *Official Descriptive and Illustrated Catalogue of the Great Exhibition*, part 4: Colonies-Foreign States (London: Spicer Brothers and W. Clowes, 1851), 990–91; Chapman, "Innovating Entrepreneurs," 10.

38. Insurance records reveal a significant jump in his insured property in the 1830s. For evidence of his sales to clothiers in England, see *The Draper and Clothier* (London: Houlston and Wright, 1860), 1:45.

39. Guildhall Library, Records of the Sun Fire Office, MS 11936/557/1234829; *Furniture Gazette*, October 11, 1879, 246; *Proceedings of the Central Criminal Court*, August 23, 1841, 16, February 3, 1845, 78, October 27, 1845, 109–10, May 5, 1861, 13; 1851 Census, HO 107/1532 175; National Archives; Pamela Sharpe, "'Cheapness and Economy': Manufacturing and Retailing Ready-Made Clothing in London and Essex 1830–50," *Textile History* 26, no. 2 (1995): 207.

40. Mayhew complained that prison labor undercut the wages of free workers and pinned the blame on Jewish manufacturers: "the prisoners engaged in executing large

contracts for Houndsditch Jews, and thus rendering honesty and virtue more and more hard to be carried on in connection with industry at the east end of the Metropolis." Henry Mayhew and John Binny, *The Criminal Prisons of London* (London: Griffin, Bohn, 1862), 195, 254, quotation on 476.

41. Chapman, "Innovating Entrepreneurs," 23.

42. For trends within the clothing business, see Chapman, "Ready-Made Clothing," 46–49; Chapman, "Innovating Entrepreneurs," 23.

43. Robert Montgomery Martin, *The British Colonies: Their History, Extent, Condition and Resources*, vol. 4 (London: London Printing and Publishing, 1851), 6; *Official Descriptive and Illustrated Catalogue of the Great Exhibition*, 1991. He was identified in the 1850 census as a colonial merchant.

44. On the paucity of credit in the colonies, see Kirsten McKenzie, *Scandal in the Colonies: Sydney and Cape Town, 1820–1850* (Melbourne: Melbourne University Press, 2005), 84–86.

45. On credit in Montreal, see Gerald Tulchinsky, "'Said to Be a Very Honest Jew': The R. G. Dun Credit Reports and Jewish Business Activity in Mid-19th Century Montreal," *Urban History Review* 18, no. 3 (1990): 200–209; Gerald Tulchinsky, *Taking Root: The Origins of the Canadian Jewish Community* (Hanover, N.H.: Brandeis University Press, 1993), 61–81. On Jews and access to credit in America, see Rowena Olegario, "'That Mysterious People': Jewish Merchants, Transparency, and Community in Mid-Nineteenth Century America," *Business History Review* 73, no. 2 (June 1999): 161–89; Stephen Mostov, "Dun and Bradstreet Reports as a Source of Jewish Economic History: Cincinnati, 1840–1875," *American Jewish History* 72, no. 3 (1983): 333–53; Elliott Ashkenazi, *The Business of Jews in Louisiana, 1840–1875* (Tuscaloosa: University of Alabama Press, 1988), 23–24, 93–100, 151–53; William Toll, *The Making of an Ethnic Middle Class: Portland Jewry over Four Generations* (Albany: State University of New York Press, 1982), 12–13, 17–18; David Gerber, "Cutting Out Shylock: Elite Anti-Semitism and the Quest for Moral Order in the Mid-Nineteenth-Century American Marketplace," in *Anti-Semitism in American History*, ed. David Gerber (Urbana: University of Illinois Press, 1987), 211–25.

46. On Jews as retail clothiers in Melbourne, see Hilary Rubinstein, *The Jews in Victoria, 1835–1985* (Sydney: Allen & Unwin, 1986), 8–9; Levi and Bergman, *Australian Genesis*, 296–97.

47. *Port Phillip Herald*, December 2, 1842, December 19, 1843; *JC*, July 30, 1897; Williams, *Manchester Jewry*, 321–23; Pollins, *Economic History of the Jews*, 98–101; Rodney Benjamin, "David Benjamin of Launceston, Melbourne and Bayswater (London), 1815–1893," in *A Few from Afar*, 61–62.

48. Levi, *These Are the Names*, 86.

49. See Hobart *Courier*, February 22, 1853, 1; Melbourne *Argus*, February 12, 1856, 7, February 20, 1856, 2, March 19, 1856, 2, April 8, 1856, 8; Kelly, *Life in Victoria*, 2: 341, 1:147. The firm appears to have reentered the Australian market—without a local store—only in the mid-1860s.

50. On the expense of clothing in Canada, see *Sidney's Emigrant's Journal*, November 23, 1848, 59.

51. General Railroad Celebration Committee, Montreal in 1856: A Sketch Prepared for the Celebration of the Opening of the Grand Trunk Railway of Canada (Montreal: John Lovell, 1856), 46; Gerald Tulchinsky, *The River Barons* (Toronto: University of Toronto Press, 1977), 219–20; idem, *Canada's Jews* (Toronto: University of Toronto Press, 2008), 43–44; idem, *Taking Root*, 70; idem, "'Said to Be a Very Honest Jew,'" 206.

52. He returned to London in December 1858, living close to Regents Park. His funeral in October of 1873 was attended by the chief rabbi, Moses Montefiore, and two hundred others. See *JC*, October 16, 1873; Elias, *A Few from Afar*, 31; Levi, *These Are the Names*, 568–69, 571–72; Levi and Bergman, *Australian Genesis*, 268.

53. He lived at 6 Finsbury Circus in Shoreditch until at least 1860, before moving to the West End in 1870. For his East End properties, see Frederick Pollock, *The Law Reports: Chancery Division*, vol. 1 (London: William Clowes and Son, 1902), 100–103; *Medical Times & Gazette*, October 15, 1859, 394; Pre-Registration Deeds of Title, LBL/DALS/12/8, Lambeth Archives Department, London; *JC*, December 10, 1875, 597A.

54. Wechsler, "Jewish Garment Trade," 89–91.

55. *Furniture Gazette*, October 11, 1879, 246; Nathan, *As Old as Auckland*, 126.

56. Quoted in Chaim Bermant, *The Cousinhood* (New York: Macmillan, 1972), 361.

57. Several other leading Jewish families in the clothing trade followed suit. Moses Hyam, son of one of Henry's major rivals, changed his name by deed poll in 1872 to Montague Halford. The children of Samuel Jacob Moses took the name Walford. Abraham Lyon Moses, proprietor of the firm Moses, Levy & Co. changed their name to Merton.

58. *Medical Times & Gazette*, October 15, 1859, 394; Lambeth Archives Department, LBL/DALS/12/8; Mews, *The Law Journal Reports for the Year 1902*, 69: 102; Chapman, "Innovating Entrepreneurs," 14; Last Will and Testament of Henry Moses, dated March 23, 1873; photocopy in the possession of George Rigal. For the relative scale of the family fortune, see William Rubinstein, "Jewish Top Wealth-Holders in Britain, 1809–1909," *Jewish Historical Studies* 37 (2001): 142, 151.

59. A third brother, David Moses, shared Henry's extraordinary success.

60. *Proceedings of the Old Bailey*, May 11, 1826, 52; Guildhall Library, MS 11936/464/899316; Last Will and Testament of Jacob Moses, dated March 20, 1845; photocopy in the possession of George Rigal.

61. *Proceedings of the Old Bailey*, October 28, 1807, 31, May 31, 1827, 57, October 18, 1832, 90, February 3, 1840, 30; Guildhall Library, Records of the Sun Fire Office, MS 11936/536/1154989, MS 11936/537/1148723.

62. Levi, *These Are the Names*, 553–54, 556–57; Levi and Bergman, *Australian Genesis*, 249–50, 295, 312.

63. "The Life of Jacob Frankel," *Australian Jewish Historical Society Journal* 13, no. 3 (1996): 401; Last Will and Testament of Moses Moses, dated March 20, 1845; photocopy in the possession of George Rigal. Levi, *These Are the Names*, 556–57, Levi and Bergman, *Australian Genesis*, 249–50, 295, 312.

64. Andrew Godley and Nancy L. Green have done pioneering work that compares the Jewish economic experience in England and the United States. See Andrew Godley, *Jewish Immigrant Entrepreneurship in New York and London 1880–1914: Enterprise and Culture* (Basingstoke, U.K.: Palgrave, 2001), and Nancy L. Green, *Ready-to-Wear and Ready-to-Work: A Century of Industry and Immigrants in Paris and New York* (Durham, N.C.: Duke University Press, 1997).

Chapter 6. Brokering a Rock 'n' Roll International

1. Michael Billig, *Rock 'n' Roll Jews* (Nottingham, U.K.: Five Leaves, 2000); Ken Emerson, *Always Magic in the Air: The Bomp and Brilliance of the Brill Building Era* (New York: Penguin, 2006).

2. See, for instance, Jon Stratton, *Jews, Race and Popular Music* (Surrey, U.K.: Ashgate, 2009); Ben Sidran, *There Was a Fire: Jews, Music and the American Dream* (Brooklyn, N.Y.: Nardis, 2012); Seth Rogovoy, *Bob Dylan: Prophet, Mystic, Poet* (New York: Scribner, 2009); Jonathan Karp, "Killing Tin Pan Alley: Bob Dylan and the (Jewish) American Songbook," *Guilt and Pleasure* 6 (Winter 2007): 51–55; David Kaufman, *Jewhooing the Sixties: American Celebrity and Jewish Identity* (Waltham, Mass.: Brandeis University Press, 2012).

3. A point affirmed by John Broven's masterful and encyclopedic *Record Makers and Breakers: Voices of Independent Rock 'n' Roll Pioneers* (Urbana: University of Illinois Press, 2009), ebook, 9–10; see also Jonathan Karp, "Blacks, Jews and the Business of Race Music, 1945–1955," in *Chosen Capital: The Jewish Encounter with American Capitalism*, ed. Rebecca Kobrin (New Brunswick, N.J.: Rutgers University Press, 2012), 141–67; Sidran, *There Was a Fire*, 137–55.

4. A number of black labels emerged in Los Angeles, dating back to Sunshine Records in the 1920s and later including the labels Dootone, Recorded in Hollywood, Exclusive, and Swing Time. Examples elsewhere include Merritt Records in Kansas City, Duke/Peacock Records in Houston, VeeJay in Chicago, and Atlas and Red Robin in New York. Many more short-lived labels were created in a number of major American cities.

5. These labels were often interdependent; for instance, Sam Phillips's Sun records had local distribution deals with the Bihari Brothers' Modern Records in Los Angeles (which also had important business relationships with Imperial Records in New Orleans) and with Chess Records in Chicago.

6. There is currently no comprehensive study of American popular entertainment explored in terms of an array of allied Jewish businesses or businesses in which Jews were highly overrepresented. For a suggestive approach, see Neil Gabler, *An Empire of Their Own: How Jews Invented Hollywood* (New York: Anchor, 1989).

7. The literature here is vast and controversial. Among the most important conceptual treatments, see Simon Kuznetz, *Jewish Economies*, 2 vols., ed. Stephanie Lo and E. Glen Weyl (New Brunswick, N.J.: Transaction, 2012), and Jerry Z. Muller, *Capitalism and the Jews* (Princeton, N.J.: Princeton University Press, 2011). On medieval Jewish

economic life, superseding all previous overviews, see Michael Toch, *The Economic History of European Jews: Late Antiquity and Early Middle Ages* (Leiden: Brill, 2013). A recent important addition to scholarship on the origins of medieval Jewish commerce and urbanism is Maristella Botticini and Zvi Eckstein, *The Chosen Few: How Education Shaped Jewish History, 70–1492* (Princeton, N.J.: Princeton University Press, 2012). Derek Penslar's *Shylock's Children: Economics and Jewish Identity in Modern Europe* (Berkeley: University of California Press, 2001) remains a touchstone of the field as a whole.

8. See M. J. Rosman, *The Lord's Jews: Magnate-Jewish Relations in the Polish-Lithuanian Commonwealth During the Eighteenth Century* (Cambridge, Mass.: Harvard University Press, 1992); Adam Teller, *Money, Power, and Influence: The Jews on the Radziwill Estates in 18th-Century Lithuania* [in Hebrew] (Jerusalem: Merkaz Zalman Shazar, 2005); Glenn Dynner, *Yankl's Tavern: Jews, Liquor, and Life in the Kingdom of Poland* (New York: Oxford University Press, 2014).

9. See the classic work of Thomas Kessner, *The Golden Door: Italian and Jewish Immigrant Mobility in New York City, 1880–1915* (New York: Oxford University Press, 1977). The view has recently been challenged by Eli Lederhendler, *Jewish Immigrants and American Capitalism: From Caste to Class* (New York: Cambridge University Press, 2009).

10. Kenneth Kantor, *The Jews on Tin Pan Alley: The Jewish Contribution to American Popular Music, 1830–1940* (New York: Ktav, 1982); Jack Gottlieb, *Funny, It Doesn't Sound Jewish: How Yiddish Melodies Influenced Tin Pan Alley, Broadway and Hollywood* (Albany: State University of New York Press, 2004), 110. Isaac Goldberg's 1930 *Tin Pan Alley: A Chronicle of American Popular Music* (New York: F. Ungar, 1961) remains useful.

11. David Suisman, *Selling Sounds: The Commercial Revolution in American Music* (Cambridge, Mass.: Harvard University Press, 2009).

12. Goldberg, *Tin Pan Alley*; Jonathan Karp, "Of Maestros and Minstrels: American Jewish Composers Between Black Vernacular and European Art Music," in *The Art of Being Jewish*, ed. Barbara Kirshenblatt-Gimblett and Jonathan Karp (Philadelphia: University of Pennsylvania Press, 2007), 57–77.

13. Foster Hirsch, *The Boys from Syracuse: The Shuberts' Theatrical Empire* (Carbondale: Southern Illinois University Press, 1998); Frank Rose, *The Agency: William Morris and the Hidden History of Show Business* (New York: Harper, 1996).

14. Andre Millard, *America on Record: A History of Recorded Sound* (New York: Columbia University Press, 2005), 159–60.

15. Russel and David Sanjek, *Pennies from Heaven: The American Popular Music Business in the Twentieth Century* (New York: Da Capo Press, 1996).

16. Rebee Garofalo, "Crossing Over: From Black Rhythm and Blues to White Rock 'n' Roll," in *Rhythm and Business: The Political Economy of Black Music*, ed. Norman Kelley (New York: Akashic Books, 2002), 113–17; Karp, "Blacks, Jews and the Business of Race Music."

17. James N. Gregory, *The Southern Diaspora: How the Great Migrations of Black and White Southerners Transformed America* (Chapel Hill: University of North Carolina Press, 2005); Isabel Wilkerson, *The Warmth of Other Suns: The Epic Story of America's Great Migration* (New York: Vintage, 2010).

18. Jon Hartley Fox, *The King of Queen City: The Story of King Records* (Urbana: University of Illinois Press, 2009), 9–21; Bar Biszick-Lockwood, *Restless Giant: The Life and Times of Jean Aberbach and Hill and Range Songs* (Urbana: University of Illinois Press, 2010).

19. See Karp, "Blacks, Jews, and the Business of Race Music."

20. Quoted in Jerry Leiber and Mike Stoller, *Hound Dog: The Leiber and Stoller Autobiography* (New York: Simon & Schuster, 2009), 36.

21. Rick Kennedy and Randy McNult, *Little Labels—Big Sound: Small Record Companies and the Rise of American Music* (Bloomington: Indiana University Press, 1999), passim.

22. Michael Siegel, "The Great Blues Migration," Schomburg Center for Research on Black Culture, New York Public Library (Rutger's Cartography, 2005), http://www.inmotionaame.org/gallery/detail.cfm?migration=8&topic=10&id=8_007M&type=map.

23. Historians have yet to give serious attention to the business links between New York Jews and those of other American commercial centers, not to mention small and medium towns. On the business life of small-town Jews, see Lee Shai Weissbach, *Jewish Life in Small Town America* (New Haven, Conn.: Yale University Press, 2005); and Ewa Morawska, *Insecure Prosperity: Industrial Life in Small Town America, 1890–1940* (Princeton, N.J.: Princeton University Press, 1996). A raft of histories have been produced on Jews in other individual American cities, such as Chicago, Cleveland, and Los Angeles.

24. See Deborah Dash Moore, *To the Golden Cities: Pursuing the American Dream in Los Angeles and Miami* (New York: The Free Press, 1994).

25. Johnny Otis, *Upside Your Head! Rhythm and Blues on Central Avenue* (Hanover, N.H.: Wesleyan University Press, 1993); On Jewish Los Angeles, see Moore, *To the Golden Cities*.

26. On Jews in the scrap business, see Jonathan Z. S. Pollack, "Success from Scrap and Second-Hand Goods," in *Chosen Capital*, ed. Kobrin, 93–112; on Jews and the American liquor industry, see Marni Davis, *Jews and Booze: Becoming American in the Age of Prohibition* (New York: New York University Press, 2012). Suggestive remarks about Jews and dry goods can be found in Stephen J. Whitfield, "The Missing Piece: Jewish Shopkeepers in the American South," *AJS Perspectives* (Fall 2009): 28–33.

27. Quoted in Kennedy and McNult, *Little Labels*, 61.

28. D. K. Peney, ed., "Syd Nathan's King Records," http://history-of-rock.com/king_records.htm.

29. Nadine Cohodas, *Spinning Blues into Gold: The Chess Brothers and the Legendary Chess Records* (New York: St. Martin's Press, 2000).

30. Broven, *Record Makers and Breakers*, 40–52.

31. Tommy James, with Martin Fitzpatrick, *Me, the Mob, and the Music: One Helluva Ride with Tommy James and the Shondells* (New York: Scribner, 2010).

32. Quoted in Charles Shaar Murray, *Boogie Man: The Adventures of John Lee Hooker* (New York: St. Martin's Press, 2000), 136.

33. Quoted in Galen Gart and Roy C. Ames, *Duke/Peacock Records: An Illustrated History with Discography* (Milford, N.H.: Big Nickel, 1990), 94. The preceding paragraphs borrows heavily from my "Blacks, Jews and the Business of Race Music," 160–61.

34. Quoted in Benjamin Filene, *Romancing the Folk: Public Memory and American Roots Music* (Chapel Hill: University of North Carolina Press, 2000), 90.

35. Bruce Boyd Raeburn, *New Orleans Style and the Writing of American Jazz History* (Ann Arbor: University of Michigan Press, 2009), chap. 1; Dan Morgenstern, "Recording Jazz," in *The Oxford Companion to Recorded Jazz*, ed. Bill Kirschener (New York: Oxford University Press, 2000).

36. Jerry Wexler, *Rhythm and the Blues: A Life in American Music* (New York: Knopf, 1993), 91.

37. Quoted in Kennedy and McNult, *Little Labels*, 63–64.

38. Chuck Berry, *The Autobiography* (New York: Harmony, 1987), 100.

39. Gilbert Millstein, "Profiles: For Kicks—I," *New Yorker*, March 9, 1946, 30–42; See also the memoir of Gabler's nephew, Billy Crystal, *700 Sundays* (New York: Time-Warner, 2005), 31–37.

40. John Chilton, *Let the Good Times Roll: The Story of Louis Jordan and His Music* (London: Quartet, 1992); Arnold Shaw, *Honkers and Shouters: The Golden Years of Rhythm and Blues* (New York: Macmillan, 1978), 64.

41. Quoted in Emerson, *Always Magic in the Air*, 64.

42. *Expresso Bongo* (1959), DVD, directed by Val Guest (New York: Kino Video, 2001).

43. As Andrew Loog Oldham, former manager of the Rolling Stones, recalled in his memoir, "*Expresso Bongo*'s run in the West End signaled a coming of age for the new music, the new style, the new hustle. Even better, it owed very little to its Yank progenitors; it was Brit to the core." Andrew Loog Oldham, *Stoned* (New York: St. Martin's Press, 2000), 30.

44. Milton R. Rackmil, "Pioneers' Dream Becomes Reality with Decca Family," *Billboard*, August 28, 1954.

45. Broven, *Record Makers and Breakers*, 397–414.

46. Gordon Thompson, *Please Please Me: Sixties British Pop, Inside Out* (Oxford: Oxford University Press, 2008), 44.

47. *Billboard*, June 19, 1954. Andrew Blake, *The Land Without Music: Music, Culture and Society in Twentieth-Century Britain* (Manchester, U.K.: Manchester University Press, 1997), 91.

48. Blake, *The Land Without Music*, 76–124.

49. Wolf Mankowitz, *Make Me an Offer, Expresso Bongo, and Other Stories* (London: Hutchinson, 1961), 148.

50. Andrew Godley, *Jewish Entrepreneurship in New York and London, 1880–1914* (Houndmills, U.K.: Palgrave, 2001), 21.

51. See Irving Berlin's impressions of the London music publishing scene, which he visited in 1910, in Laurence Bergreen, *As Thousands Cheer: The Life of Irving Berlin* (New York: Viking, 1990), 53–54. In London, Berlin met Bert Feldman, who began as a London agent for American Tin Pan Alley publishers but eventually created a major British publishing house of his own.

52. Harold Pollins, *Economic History of the Jews of England* (Rutherford, N.J.: Fairleigh Dickenson University Press, 1982), 213, 216.

53. Quoted in ibid., 195.

54. Mansel G. Blackford, *The Rise of Modern Business: Great Britain, the United States, Germany, Japan, and China*, 3rd ed. (Chapel Hill: University of North Carolina Press, 2008), chap. 6. With some exceptions, chain stores took off in Britain only in the late 1960s. See Sean Glynn and Alan Booth, *Modern Britain: An Economic and Social History* (London: Routledge, 1996).

55. Garofalo, "Crossing Over," 118–19; Thompson, *Please Please Me*, 24.

56. Adrian Johns, *Death of a Pirate: British Radio and the Making of the Information Age* (New York: Norton, 2011), 48–51, 147.

57. Bergreen, *As Thousands Cheer*, 53.

58. David Roper, *Bart! The Unauthorized Life and Times* (London: Pavilion, 1994), 19.

59. Johnny Rogan, *Starmakers and Svengalis* (London: Futura Books, 1989), 41.

60. Quoted in Debbie Geller, *In My Life: The Brian Epstein Story* (New York: St. Martins, 2000), 57. Author Jonathan Gould claims that "homosexuality was virtually the norm among British pop managers of the period." Jonathan Gould, *Can't Buy Me Love: The Beatles, Britain and America* (New York: Three Rivers Press, 2007), 116.

61. Rogan, *Starmakers and Svengalis*, 36–37.

62. Oldham described Harvey as "the actor who would tower in my youthful imagination as a paragon of accomplishment and style" and *Expresso Bongo* as a kind of pop manager's Bible. See Oldham, *Stoned*, 12.

63. Don Arden, *Mr. Big: Ozzy, Sharon and My Life as the Godfather of Rock* (London: Robson, 2004), 12.

64. Millard, *America on Record*, 254.

65. Arden, *Mr. Big*, 58–59.

66. Brian Southall, with Rubert Perry, *Northern Songs: The True Story of the Beatles Song Publishing Empire* (London: Omnibus, 2006).

67. Biszick-Lockwood, *Restless Giant*.

68. Simon Garfield, *Expensive Habits: The Dark Side of the Music Industry* (London: Faber & Faber, 1986), 42.

69. Biszick-Lockwood, *Restless Giant*, 202.

70. "Kasner and Bron Split," *Billboard*, August 30, 1952.

71. Quoted in Ray Davies, *X-Ray: The Unauthorized Autobiography* (Woodstock, N.Y.: Overlook, 1994), 179–81.

72. Arden, *Mr. Big*, 51–97.

73. Rogan, *Starmakers and Svengalis*, 42.

74. Southall, *Northern Songs.*

75. Geller, *In My Life*, 47.

76. Gould, *Can't Buy Me Love*, 197

77. Oldham, *Stoned*, 117.

78. Rogan, *Starmakers and Svengalis*, 398–99; Thompson, *Please, Please Me*, 98; Oldham, *Stoned*, 45, 169.

79. Oldham, *Stoned*, 30.

80. It is curious, however, that Capitol Records, an American company purchased by British EMI in 1955, initially refused to distribute Beatles records in the United States out of a disdain for rock 'n' roll music. Not only Capitol (which had right of first refusal) but CBS, Columbia, RCA, and Decca all declined to release the Beatles in the United States. Instead, the first American Beatles releases came out on two indie labels, the tiny Swan Records in Philadelphia and the more substantial but financially insolvent VeeJay Records, a Chicago label owned by an African American woman, Vivian Carter. See George Martin's comments in Geller, *In My Life*, 71.

81. On Grossman, see especially Fred Goodman, *The Mansion on the Hill: Dylan, Young, Geffen, Springsteen, and the Head-On Collision of Rock and Commerce* (New York: Vintage, 1998), 82–92.

82. Peter Guralnick, *Dream Boogie: The Triumph of Sam Cooke* (New York: Little, Brown and Company, 2005), 463–66.

83. Millard, *America on Record*, 233–34, 331.

84. In his split over management with the others, the beginning of the end for the Beatles, Paul chose to be managed by his brother-in-law, John Eastman, under the supervision of his father-in-law, Lee Eastman, a.k.a. Leopold Epstein, a Jewish music business attorney.

Chapter 7. The "West" and the Rest

1. "Eine schöne Erscheinung aus der neuern Zeit," *Allgemeine Zeitung des Judentums* 36, no. 7 (February 13, 1872): 119–22.

2. See the groundbreaking work by Aron Rodrigue, *French Jews, Turkish Jews: The Alliance Israélite Universelle and the Politics of Jewish Schooling in Turkey, 1860–1925* (Bloomington: Indiana University Press, 1990). See also Eli Bar-Chen, *Weder Asiaten noch Orientalen. Internationale jüdische Organisationen und die Europäisierung "rückständiger" Juden* (Berlin: Ergon Verlag, 2005).

3. See Abigail Green, "Nationalism and the 'Jewish International': Religious Internationalism in Europe and the Middle East, c. 1840–c. 1880," *Comparative Studies in Society and History* 50, no. 2 (April 2008): 535–58; Abigail Green, "Sir Moses Montefiore and the Making of the 'Jewish International,'" *Journal of Modern Jewish Studies* 7, no. 3 (November 2008): 287–307.

4. On Montefiore, see Abigail Green, *Moses Montefiore: Jewish Liberator, Imperial Hero* (Cambridge, Mass.: Harvard University Press, 2010). On Crémieux, see S. Posener, *Adolphe Crémieux, a Biography* (Philadelphia: Jewish Publication Society of America, 1940); Daniel Amson, *Adolphe Crémieux, l'oublié de la gloire* (Paris: Seuil, 1988).

5. On the origins of the Alliance Israélite, see Michael Graetz, *The Jews in Nineteenth-Century France: From the French Revolution to the Alliance Israélite Universelle*, trans. Jane Marie Todd (Stanford, Calif.: Stanford University Press, 1996); Lisa Moses Leff, *Sacred Bonds of Solidarity: The Rise of Jewish Internationalism in Nineteenth-Century France* (Stanford, Calif.: Stanford University Press, 2006).

6. See Lloyd P. Gartner, "Roumania, America, and World Jewry: Consul Peixotto in Bucharest, 1870–1876," *American Jewish Historical Quarterly* 58 (1968): 25–117; idem, "Documents on Roumanian Jewry, Consul Peixotto, and Jewish Diplomacy, 1870–1875," in *Salo Wittmayer Baron Jubilee Volume*, ed. Saul Liebermann and Arthur Hyman (Jerusalem: American Academy for Jewish Research, 1974), 1:467–90.

7. But see the core argument made in Leff, *Sacred Bonds of Solidarity.*

8. Jonathan Israel, *European Jewry in the Age of Mercantilism, 1550–1750*, 3rd ed. (Oxford, U.K.: Littman Library of Jewish Civilization, 1998), chap. 1. Still, note the formation of parallel diasporas in this period, as discussed in Jonathan Ray, "New Approaches to the Jewish Diaspora: The Sephardim as a Sub-Ethnic Group," *Jewish Social Studies* 15, no. 1 (Fall 2008): 10–31; Joseph Davis, "The Reception of the Shulḥan 'Arukh and the Formation of Ashkenazic Jewish Identity," *AJS Review* 26, no. 2 (2002): 251–76.

9. On diaspora support for the Yishuv, see Jacob Barnai, *The Jews in Palestine in the Eighteenth Century Under the Patronage of the Istanbul Committee of Officials for Palestine*, trans. Naomi Goldblum (Tuscaloosa: University of Alabama Press, 1992), esp. part 3. Matthias B. Lehmann is currently working on a new overview of this subject. See Matthias B. Lehmann, *Emissaries from the Holy Land: The Sephardic Diaspora and the Practice of Pan-Judaism in the Eighteenth Century* (Stanford, Calif.: Stanford University Press, 2014). On the Moroccan dimension, see Shalom Bar Asher, "The Jews of North Africa and the Land of Israel in the Eighteenth and Nineteenth Centuries: The Reversal in Attitude Toward Aliyah (Immigration to the Land) from 1770 to 1860," in *The Land of Israel: Jewish Perspectives*, ed. Lawrence A. Hoffmann (Notre Dame, Ind.: University of Notre Dame Press, 1986), 303–4.

10. Matthias B. Lehmann, "Rethinking Sephardi Identity: Jews and Other Jews in Ottoman Palestine," *Jewish Social Studies* 15, no. 1 (Fall 2008): 84.

11. Adam Teller, "The Shape of the Jewish World: Economic, Social and Cultural Aspects of the Ashkenazic Refugee Crisis in the Mid-17th Century" (unpublished seminar paper). My thanks to Adam for letting me see this paper.

12. Jacob Katz, *Tradition and Crisis: Jewish Society at the End of the Middle Ages* (New York: New York University Press, 1993), 97.

13. See Andrée Aelion Brooks, *The Woman Who Defied Kings: The Life and Times of Doña Gracia Nasi—a Jewish Leader During the Renaissance* (St. Paul, Minn.: Paragon

House, 2002); and Cecil Roth, *Doña Gracia of the House of Nasi* (Philadelphia: Jewish Publication Society of America, 1977).

14. Jonathan Israel, *European Jewry in the Age of Mercantilism, 1550–1750*, 3rd ed. (Oxford, U.K.: Littman library of Jewish Civilization, 1998), 168–69.

15. Jonathan Irvine Israel, *Diasporas Within a Diaspora: Jews, Crypto-Jews and the World Maritime Empires (1540–1740)* (Leiden: Brill, 2002), chap. 12, esp. 398–413.

16. Ibid., 400.

17. Brooks, *Woman Who Defied Kings*, chap. 18.

18. On *shtadlanut*, see François Guesnet, "Die Politik der 'Fürsprache'—Vormoderne jüdische Interessenvertretung," in *Synchrone Welten: Zeitenräume jüdischer Geschichte*, ed. Dan Diner (Göttingen: Vandenhoeck & Ruprecht, 2005), 67–92; François Guesnet, "Politik der Vormoderne—Shtadlanut am Vorabend der polnischen Teilungen," *Jahrbuch des Simon-Dubnow Instituts* 1, no. 2002 (2002): 235–55. Guesnet is currently preparing a book-length study of Shtadlanut.

19. See Baruch Mevorach, "Die Interventionsbestrebungen in Europa zur Verhinderung der Vertreibung der Juden aus Böhmen und Mähren, 1744–1745," *Jahrbuch des Instituts für Deutsche Geschichte* 9 (1980): 15–81; François Guesnet, "Textures of Intercession—Rescue Efforts for the Jews of Prague, 1744–1748," *Simon Dubnow Institute Yearbook* 4 (2005): 355–75.

20. On the dotar, see Miriam Bodian, *Hebrews of the Portuguese Nation: Conversos and Community in Early Modern Amsterdam* (Bloomington: Indiana University Press, 1997), 134–41.

21. Matthias B. Lehmann, "Levantinos and Other Jews: Reading H. Y. D. Azulai's Travel Diary," *Jewish Social Studies* n.s. 13, no. 3 (Summer 2007): 1–34.

22. See for instance Abigail Green, "The British Empire and the Jews: An Imperialism of Human Rights?" *Past & Present* 199 (May 2008): 175–205; Eli Bar-Chen, *Weder Asiaten noch Orientalen*; Leff, *Sacred Bonds of Solidarity.*

23. Jonathan Frankel, "Jewish Politics and the Press: The 'Reception' of the Alliance Israélite Universelle," *Jewish History* 14 (2000): 30. More generally on the Jewish press, see the rest of this special issue of *Jewish History* 14. See also Sarah Abrevaya Stein, *Making Jews Modern: The Yiddish and Ladino Press in the Russian and Ottoman Empires* (Bloomington: Indiana University Press, 2004); David Cesarani, *The Jewish Chronicle and Anglo-Jewry, 1841–1991* (Cambridge: Cambridge University Press, 1994).

24. Adam Mendelsohn, "Tongue Ties: The Emergence of an Anglophone Jewish Diaspora in the Mid-Nineteenth Century," *American Jewish History* 93, no. 2 (June 2007): 177–209.

25. "Smyrna," *Voice of Jacob*, July 8, 1842, 166.

26. This distinction is not universally applicable. See Warren F. Ilchman, Stanley N. Katz, and Edward L. Queen II, eds., *Philanthropy in the World's Traditions* (Bloomington: Indiana University Press, 1998).

27. "Florenz, 14. August [Zeitungsnachrichten/ Italien]," *Allgemeine Zeitung des Judentums* 24, no. 36 (September 4, 1860): 535–36.

28. Treasurer of the Damascus Mission to A. J. Jones, August 8, 1842, Arthur Sebag-Montefiore Archive, Oxford Centre for Hebrew and Jewish Studies.

29. On the Ashkenazi immigrants of the 1830s, see Sherman Lieber, *Mystics and Missionaries: The Jews in Palestine 1799–1840* (Salt Lake City: University of Utah Press, 1992), chap. 10.

30. Khayim Abr. Gagin—with six other Portuguese names. R. Moshe Rivlin—accompanied by six German signatures, also Israel Drucker, Jerusalem, 9 Sivan 5604—received by Montefiore, July 2, 1844, Montefiore List of Letters, 1844–51, Mocatta 8, Mocatta Library, University College London (UCL), Letter No. 27.

31. Israel Drucker and Israel Moshe Khazan, Jerusalem, 17 Ab 5604—letter received by Montefiore September 12, 1844. "Montefiore List of Letters, 1844–51," Letter No. 73.

32. On the importance of the Crimean War as a turning point, see Green, *Montefiore*, chap. 11.

33. On the Hausdorf campaign, see Green, *Montefiore*, 321–22.

34. Toledano, Joseph, President; Moses Parrento, VP; Aaron Abensue, Secretary & 6 Other Members, Tangier, to Sir Moses Montefiore, recorded in minutes of a meeting held February 26, 1861, minute books of the Board of Deputies of British Jews, London Metropolitan Archives, Acc/3121/A/009 (ff.124–138).

35. For more detail, see M. Mitchell Serels, *A History of the Jews of Tangier in the Nineteenth and Twentieth Centuries* (New York: Sepher-Hermon Press, 1991), chap. 3.

36. For more detail on this campaign in Britain and France, see Green, *Montefiore*, 288–92.

37. Jeffrey Maynard, "HaMagid Persian famine donation lists from Lithuania, 1871–1872," JewishGen, http://www.jewishgen.org/databases/Lithuania/Magid72.htm.

38. See David Sorkin, "Montefiore and the Politics of Emancipation," *Jewish Review of Books* (Summer 2010): 23–25.

39. See Fritz Stern, *Gold and Iron: Bismarck, Bleichröder and the Building of the German Empire* (Harmondsworth, U.K.: Penguin, 1977), esp. chap. 14.

40. This argument is further elaborated in Abigail Green, "Intervening in the Jewish Question, 1840–1878," in *Humanitarian Intervention: A History*, ed. Brendan Simms and David Trim (Cambridge: Cambridge University Press, 2011). For longer term implications of this development, see Carole Fink, *Defending the Rights of Others: The Great Powers, the Jews, and International Minority Protection, 1878–1938* (Cambridge: Cambridge University Press, 2004).

41. See for instance Chaim Bermant, *The Cousinhood* (New York: Macmillan, 1971).

42. This argument was compellingly made by Eli Lederhendler, *The Road to Modern Jewish Politics: Political Tradition and Political Reconstruction in the Jewish Community of Tsarist Russia* (Oxford: Oxford University Press, 1989).

43. See for instance, Mark Levene, *War, Jews and the New Europe: The Diplomacy of Lucien Wolf, 1914–1919* (London: Littman Library of Jewish Civilization, 1992).

44. "Affaire de Damas," *Univers*, October 8, 1840.

45. *Univers*, October 23, 24, 25 (1858?) and October 15, 16, 1858. Cited after Nathalie Isser, *Antisemitism During the French Second Empire* (New York: Peter Lang, 1991), 34, 49.

46. Karl Anton von Hohenzollern-Sigmaringen to Prince Carol, March 22, 1868, in *Aus dem Leben König Karls von Rumänien. Aufzeichnungen eines Augenzeugen*, (Stuttgart: J. G. Cotta, 1894), 1:260.

47. Letter received 9/21 May 1868, in ibid., 267.

48. Louis Loewe, ed., *Diaries of Sir Moses and Lady Montefiore, Comprising Their Life and Work as Recorded in Their Diaries from 1812 to 1883* (London: Griffith Farran Okedan & Welsh, 1890), 2:294.

49. On Brafman, see John Doyle Klier, *Imperial Russia's Jewish Question, 1855–1881* (Cambridge: Cambridge University Press, 1995), 262–83.

50. Ludwig Philippson, "Ueber die Alliance Israélite Universelle," *Allgemeine Zeitung des Judentums* 24, no. 38 (September 18, 1860): 557–59. More generally, see Frankel, "Jewish Politics and the Press."

Chapter 8. Rebels Without a Patron State

Many thanks to Ben Shakinovsky for research assistance and to Noa Schonmann and Ian Lustick for their comments on earlier versions of this article.

1. Alf Andrew Heggoy, *Insurgency and Counterinsurgency in Algeria* (Bloomington: Indiana University Press, 1972), 115.

2. Sharon B. Stichter, "Workers, Trade Unions, and the Mau-Mau Rebellion," *Canadian Journal of African Studies* 9 (1975): 26; Robert Edgerton, *Mau Mau: An African Crucible* (New York: The Free Press, 1989), 52.

3. Christopher Goscha, *Vietnam: Un état né de la guerre, 1945–1954* (Paris: Armand Colin, 2011), 304.

4. Richard and Joan Brace, *Ordeal in Algeria* (Princeton, N.J.: D. Van Nostrand, 1960), 172–73; Irwin Wall, *France, the United States and the Algerian War* (Berkeley: University of California Press, 2001), 226.

5. Christopher Lew, *The Third Chinese Revolutionary Civil War, 1945–49* (London: Routledge, 2009), 136.

6. Heggoy, *Insurgency and Counterinsurgency*, 116–17.

7. Goscha, *Vietnam*, 114, 116, 122, 286.

8. Ibid., 96, 115.

9. Ibid., 301.

10. Marie-Pierre Ulloa, *Francis Jeanson: A Dissident Intellectual from the French Resistance to the Algerian War*, trans. Jane Marie Todd (Stanford, Calif.: Stanford University Press, 2007), 158.

11. Douglas Woodwell, "The 'Troubles' in Northern Ireland: Civil Conflict in an Economically Well-Developed State," in *Understanding Civil War*, ed. Paul Collier and Nicholas Sambanis (Washington, D.C.: World Bank Publications, 2005), 170–71.

12. *Report of [sic] American Committee for Relief in Ireland* (New York, 1922), 42–44.

13. Peter Hart, *The I.R.A. at War, 1916-1923* (New York: Oxford University Press, 2003), 179–92.

14. Ibid., 177.

15. Woodwell, "The 'Troubles' in Northern Ireland," 171.

16. Charles Tilly, "War Making and State Making as Organized Crime," in *Bringing the State Back In*, ed. Peter Evans, Dietrich Rueschemeyer, and Theda Skocpol (Cambridge: Cambridge University Press, 1985), 169–87.

17. Orlando Figes, *Peasant Russia, Civil War: The Volga Countryside in Revolution (1917-1921)* (Oxford: Clarendon Press, 1989), 246–67.

18. Suzanne Pepper, *Civil War in China: The Political Struggle, 1945–1949* (Berkeley: University of California Press, 1978), 244–47, 307–11.

19. Heggoy, *Insurgency and Counterinsurgency*, 119–29.

20. Goscha, *Vietnam*, 101.

21. Caroline Elkins, *Britain's Gulag: The Brutal End of Empire in Kenya* (London: Jonathan Cape, 2005); David Anderson, *Histories of the Hanged: Britain's Dirty War in Kenya and the End of Empire* (London: Phoenix, 2005).

22. Issa Khalaf, *Politics in Palestine: Arab Factionalism and Social Disintegration, 1939–1948* (Albany: State University of New York Press, 1991); Joshua Landis, "Syria in the 1948 Palestine War: Fighting King Abdullah's Greater Syria Plan," in *Rewriting the Palestine War: 1948 and the History of the Arab-Israeli Conflict*, ed. Eugene Rogan and Avi Shlaim (Cambridge: Cambridge University Press, 2001), 178–205; Benny Morris, *1948: A History of the First Arab-Israeli War* (New Haven, Conn.: Yale University Press, 2008), 84–85, 88–93; Ronen Yitzhak, "Fauzi al-Qawuqji and the Arab Liberation Army in the 1948 War: Toward the Attainment of King `Abdallah's Political Ambitions in Palestine," *Comparative Studies of South Asia, Africa and the Middle East* 28 (2008): 459–66.

23. Moshe Naor, "Israel's 1948 War of Independence as a Total War," *Journal of Contemporary History* 43, no. 2 (2008): 241–57. Thanks to both Dr. Naor and David Tal for their insights on these issues.

24. Yitzhak Greenberg, "Financing the War of Independence," *Studies in Zionism* 9, no. 1 (1988): 63–80; Haim Barkai, "Ha-'alut ha-realit shel milhemet ha-'atsma`ut," in *Milhemet ha-atsma'ut 1948–1949: Diyun mehudash*, ed. Alon Kadish (Tel Aviv: Ministry of Defense, 2004), 2:759–91; Moshe Naor, "From Voluntary Funds to National Loans: The Financing of Israel's 1948 War Effort," *Israel Studies* 11 (2006): 62–82.

25. Rafael Rosenzweig, *The Economic Consequences of Zionism* (Leiden: Brill, 1997), 135–36.

26. For conflicting accounts about the Sonneborn Institute's key players, see Bernard Postal and Henry W. Levy, *And the Hills Shouted for Joy: The Day Israel Was Born* (Philadelphia: Jewish Publication Society, 1973), 133–44; and Robert St. John, *Ben-Gurion* (London: Jarrolds, 1959), 92. The archival document with the actual list of

attendees at the meeting is reproduced in appendix B of Doron Almog, *Ha-rekhesh ba-artsot ha-berit, 1945–1949* (Tel Aviv: Ministry of Defense, 1987).

27. Ricky-Dale Calhoun tartly terms the operation "a highly effective criminal conspiracy" in his article "Arming David: The Haganah's Illegal Arms Procurement Network in the United States, 1945–1949," *Journal of Palestine Studies* 36 (2007): 31.

28. Travis's handwritten memoir, dated April 1994, is preserved in the William Breman Jewish Heritage Museum in Atlanta. The memoir, which breathlessly narrates the founding and activities of the Sonneborn group, is particularly interesting for its description of a host of secondary Zionist activists in the southeastern United States who raised money and acquired munitions and equipment to be sent to Palestine. On Shapiro, see the online *Encyclopedia of Cleveland History*, http://ech.cwru.edu/ech-cgi/article.pl?id=SEZ.

29. For Sonneborn, see his father's and his obituaries in the *New York Times*, September 20, 1940, and June 4, 1986, respectively; and Gilbert Sandler, *Jewish Baltimore: A Family Album* (Baltimore: Johns Hopkins University Press, 2000), 84, 169. For Rosenbloom, see the oral history by Alex Lowenthal, transcribed in 1978 by Selma Berkman, Pittsburgh Jewish Federation archives (many thanks to Professor Barbara Burstin of the University of Pittsburgh for this information); the *Pittsburgh Post-Gazette*, May 19, 1970; and Rosenbloom's obituaries in the *Pittsburgh Jewish Chronicle*, April 5, 1973, 1, 21, 31; and the *New York Times*, April 2, 1973. For Sylk, see Murray Friedman, ed., *Philadelphia Jewish Life, 1940–1985* (Ardmore, Pa.: Seth Press, 1986), 68. For Lowenthal and Lown, see their obituaries in the *New York Times*, January 12, 1990, and November 3, 1976, respectively. Fligelman is mentioned briefly in *Time*, August 17, 1953, in an article on the founding of the Brandeis Camp Institute. For Broad, see his obituary in the *Miami Herald*, November 9, 2001, and Deborah Dash Moore, *To the Golden Cities: Pursuing the American Jewish Dream in Miami and Los Angeles* (New York: The Free Press, 1994), 45, 52, 159–61.

30. The first book-length study of the Sonneborn group's activity was Leonard Slater's journalistic, riveting, and, if read judiciously, useful account, *The Pledge* (New York: Simon and Schuster, 1970). Almog's *Ha-rekhesh ba-artsot ha-berit, 1945–1949* is slim but packed with information about the relation between the Sonneborn group and the Haganah's American operatives, as is Amitzur Ilan, *The Origin of the Arab-Israeli Arms Race: Arms, Embargo, Military Power and Decision in the 1948 Palestine War* (New York: New York University Press, 1996). The most important recent monograph on the subject is Doron Rozen, *Be-ikhvot ha-otsar ha-amerika'i: Pe'ilut ha-haganah ba-artsot ha-berit, 1945–1949* (Tel Aviv: Ministry of Defense, 2008). The statistic about Jewish involvement in the United States trucking industry appears in Slater, *The Pledge*, 187; and in Almog, *Rekhesh*, 46.

31. Almog, *Rekhesh*, 37–38, 41; Rozen, *Be-ikhvot ha-otsar ha-amerika`i*, 131, 135, 137, 343–44, 351.

32. Rozen, *Be-ikhvot ha-otsar ha-amerika`i*, 138.

33. Ibid., 75–76, 90, 99–109, 344–46, 351–53.

34. Almog, *Rekhesh*, 106–7. Schwimmer stayed in Israel after the war and founded Israel Aircraft Industries, which became the pillar of Israel's military and civilian aerospace industry. See Anthony David, *Ha-shamayim hem ha-gvul: Al Shvimmer, mekayem ha-ta'asiyah ha-avirit* (Tel Aviv: Schocken, 2008).

35. Slater, *The Pledge*, 71, 181, 192, 319–21; Almog, *Rekhesh*, 102, 114.

36. Interview by Slater in *The Pledge*, 321.

37. Slater, ibid., 123–24, attributes this quotation to a "gentleman from Philadelphia," speaking at a meeting of Sonneborn activists at the Waldorf Astoria hotel in New York in October of 1947.

38. Almog, *Rekhesh*, 56.

39. Robert Rockaway, *But He Was Good to His Mother: The Lives and Crimes of Jewish Gangsters* (Jerusalem: Geffen, 2000), 246–53.

40. Ilan, *The Origin of the Arab-Israeli Arms Race*, 89, 172.

41. Rozen, *Be-ikhvot ha-otsar ha-amerika`i*, 133, 138.

42. Ibid., 309; Samuel Halperin, *The Political World of American Zionism* (Detroit: Wayne State University Press, 1961), appendix 4.

43. Samuel Halperin, "Ideology or Philanthropy? The Politics of Zionist Fund-Raising," *Western Political Quarterly* 13, no. 4 (1960): 969–70.

44. Deborah Dash Moore, "Bonding Images: Miami Jews and the Campaign for Israel Bonds," in *Envisioning Israel: The Changing Ideals and Images of American Jews*, ed. Alon Gal (Jerusalem: Magnes University Press, 1996), 258; Rozen, *Be-ikhvot ha-otsar ha-amerika`i*, 309, 314, 322–23.

45. This estimate is offered in Barkai, "Ha-'alut ha-realit shel milhemet ha-'atsma`ut," 779.

46. Halperin, "Ideology or Philantropy?," 969.

47. Ibid., 966.

48. Greenberg, "Financing," 74; Ilan, *Origins*, 153, 181–200, 224; Rozen, *Be-ikhvot ha-otsar ha-amerika`i*, 322.

49. Benny Gshur, "Mitnadvim mi-tsafon amerika bi-milhemet ha-shihrur" (Ph.D. diss., Hebrew University of Jerusalem, 2009), chap. 2. Many thanks to Dr. Gshur for allowing me to read the manuscript.

50. There is a vast body of published writing on the Machal, much of it the memoirs of participants or celebratory accounts by amateur historians, for example, Henry Katzer, *South Africa's 800: The Story of South African Volunteers in Israel's War of Birth*, rev. ed. (Israel: Machal Museum, 2003). For a reliable overview, see Yaakov Markovitzky, *Machal: Overseas Volunteers in Israel's War of Independence* (Tel Aviv: World Machal, 2003). For a more thorough account that is both scholarly and riveting, see David Bercuson, *The Secret Army* (New York: Stein and Day, 1983).

51. See the sober analysis of the limited role of air power in the 1948 war in Ilan, *The Origin of the Arab-Israeli Arms Race*, 5–6, 107–8, 172.

52. Morris, *1948, A History of the First Arab-Israeli War*, 227–29.

53. Gshur, "Mitnadvim mi-tsafon amerika bi-milhemet ha-shihrur," chap. 3.

54. Ibid.

55. Derek J. Penslar, *Shylock's Children: Economics and Jewish Identity in Modern Europe* (Berkeley: Univeristy of California Press, 2001), chap. 5.

56. United States Memorial Holocaust Museum, *Holocaust Encyclopedia*, q.v. "American Jewish Joint Distribution Committee and Refugee Aid," http://www.ushmm.org/wlc/en/article.php?ModuleId=10005367.

Chapter 9. Orthodoxy Through Diamonds

1. In this sense, this discussion follows the lines of Sarah Stein's article "'Falling into Feathers': Jews and the Trans-Atlantic Ostrich Feather Trade," which "grapples with ethnicity as a powerful force in the shaping of commodity networks and, conversely, with the notion that particular commercial networks had an impact on the identity formation of their participants." Sarah A. Stein, "'Falling into Feathers': Jews and the Trans-Atlantic Ostrich Feather Trade," *Journal of Modern History* 79 (December 2007): 777.

2. Hilde Greefs, "Sociabiliteit: Informele netwerken van de zakenelite in Antwerpen, 1796–1830," *De Achttiende Eeuw* 39, no. 2 (2007): 63–64, 67–68. See also M. Casson, "Entrepreneurial Networks in International Business," *Business and Economic History* 26 (1997): 813; A. Etzione and P. R. Lawrence, eds., *Socio-Economics: Towards a New Synthesis* (Armonk, N.Y.: M. E. Sharpe, 1991); J. Brown and M. B. Rose, eds., *Entrepreneurship, Networks and Modern Business* (Manchester, U.K.: Manchester University Press, 1993); M. Granovetter, "The Strength of Weak Ties," *American Journal of Sociology* 78 (May 1973): 1360–80.

3. Sarah A. Stein, *Plumes: Ostrich Feathers, Jews, and a Lost World of Global Commerce* (New Haven, Conn.: Yale University Press, 2008); Sarah A. Stein, "'Falling into Feathers,'" 811; Francesca Trivellato, *The Familiarity of Strangers: The Sephardic Diaspora, Livorno, and Cross-Cultural Trade in the Early Modern Period* (New Haven, Conn.: Yale University Press, 2009).

4. The Diamantcasino was founded in 1898; it would become, in 1904, the Beurs voor Diamanthandel (or Diamantbeurs). Many of its founders were Jews. Also in 1898, the Jewish diamond dealer Adolphe Adler founded the Diamantclub van Antwerpen. The other three exchanges were Fortunia (1910), the Vereniging voor Vrije Diamanthandel (1911), and the Antwerpse Diamantkring (1929). The least important exchange, Fortunia, no longer exists. The other four remain important diamond exchanges in the city. In 1936, these four exchanges partnered together as the Federatie der Belgische Diamantbeurzen, and joined the World Federation of Diamond Bourses. Eric Laureys, *Meesters van het diamant: De Belgische diamantsector tijdens het nazibewind* (Tielt, Belgium: Lannoo, 2005), 57–62, 131–32; World Federation of Diamond Bourses, "Listing Bourses," http://www.wfdb.com/.

5. Veerle Vanden Daelen, "In the Port City We Meet? Jewish Migration and Jewish Life in Antwerp, 1880–1914," paper presented at the conference on Jewish Migration to the Metropolises of Europe, 1848–1918: A Comparative Perspective, Vienna, December 11–13, 2009 (publication forthcoming).

6. Lieven Saerens, *Vreemdelingen in een wereldstad: Een geschiedenis van Antwerpen en zijn joodse bevolking (1880–1944)* (Tielt, Belgium: Lannoo, 2000), 10, 15, 201–2.

7. These figures are all estimates, as ethnicity and religion have never been officially registered in Belgium. Unlike in neighboring countries such as the Netherlands, Belgium's liberal constitution has never allowed for registration of ethnicity or religion. The only registrations available are a population survey of 1846 (which in fact violated the constitution) and the obligatory registrations taken during Germany's occupation of the country during World War II. The latter registrations cannot be considered complete, as many Jews had fled the country or did not comply with edicts to present themselves for registration. Thus, researchers have had no alternative but to work with estimates in order to describe evolutions in Jewish demographics. The approximate numbers, however, clearly show that Antwerp's Jewish population rose dramatically in the late nineteenth and first half of the twentieth centuries. Jean-Philippe Schreiber, *L'immigration juive en Belgique du moyen âge à la première guerre mondiale* (Brussels: Editions de l'Université de Bruxelles, 1996), 96–97; Veerle Vanden Daelen, *Laten we hun lied verder zingen: De heropbouw van de joodse gemeenschap in Antwerpen na de Tweede Wereldoorlog (1944–1960)* (Amsterdam: Aksant, 2008), 15, 27–34; Machsike Hadas, *Tourist Traveler Guide for the Jewish Visitor by Machsike Hadass Antwerp* (Antwerp: Machsike Hadass, 2001), 42.

8. Rudi Van Doorslaer, *Kinderen van het getto: Joodse revolutionairen in België, 1925–1940* (Antwerp: Baarn, 1996), 25–26.

9. Abraham Karlikow, "5715 (1954–1955): Belgium," *American Jewish Year Book* 57 (1956): 330–31; Jacques Gutwirth, "Hassidim de notre temps," *Les nouveaux cahiers* 7 (1966): 56–62.

10. Laureys, *Meesters van het diamant*, 58–62, 131–32; Martine Vermandere, *Adamastos: 100 jaar Algemene Diamantbewerkersbond van België* (Antwerp: AMSAB, 1995), 89–90.

11. This workforce number fell significantly after the city's liberation and would remain at about 15,000 until the early 1980s. Today the number is even smaller. Laureys, *Meesters van het diamant*, 23–24.

12. Veerle Vanden Daelen, "Negotiating the Return of the Diamond Sector and Its Jews: The Belgian Government During the Second World War and in the Immediate Post-war Period," in "Governments-in-Exile and the Jews During the Second World War," special issue, *Holocaust Studies* 18 (Autumn–Winter 2012): 231–60.

13. Laureys, *Meesters van het diamant*, 65–69.

14. Esther Kreitman, *Diamonds*, trans. Heather Valencia (London: David Paul, 2010), 77.

15. Ibid., 77, 143; Jacques Gutwirth, *Vie juive traditionnelle: Ethnologie d'une communauté hassidique* (Paris: Éditions de Minuit, 1970), 86, 95; Vanden Daelen, *Laten we hun lied verder zingen*, 87–90.

16. Alexander, Belz, Ger, Rab Chaïm Dovidl (Zanz), Sighet, Satmar, Tchortkov, and Wischnitz. Ephraim Schmidt, *Geschiedenis van de Joden in Antwerpen: In woord en*

beeld (Antwerp: De Vries Brouwers, 1994), 314–17; Central Archives for the History of the Jewish People, Claims Conference files (henceforth cited as CAHJP, CC-files), 1957, 1957/019, Tifereth Israel aan Claims Conference, June 6, 1957; Gutwirth, *Vie juive traditionnelle*, 29; n.a., *Der nayer binyen fun Beth Rakhel d'Satmar in Antverpn* (Antwerp: n.p., n.d.), 10.

17. Daniël Dratwa, *Répertoire des périodiques juifs parus en Belgique de 1841–1986* (Brussels: Institut de sociologie de Í Université libre de Bruxelles, 1987).

18. Vanden Daelen, *Laten we hun lied verder zingen*, 73–75; Laureys, *Meesters van het diamant*.

19. Trivellato, *The Familiarity of Strangers*.

20. National Archives of Belgium (Brussels), Archives of the Foreigners' Police, file 845.566 (R. Goldmuntz). Goldmuntz was a member of the Diamantclub and of the Diamantbeurs. The firm R. & L. Goldmuntz was a client of Forminière.

21. Jean-Philippe Schreiber, "Romi Benjamin Goldmuntz," in Jean-Philippe Schreiber *Dictionnaire biographique des Juifs en Belgique. Figures du judaïsme belge XIXe—XXe siècles*, ed. Jean-Philippe Schreiber (Brussels: De Boeck Université, 2002), 128–29.

22. National Archives of Belgium (Brussels), Archives of the Foreigners' Police, file 888.186 (G. Schamisso); Sylvain Brachfeld and Jean-Philippe Schreiber, "Gedalia ou Herman Schamisso," in Schreiber, *Dictionnaire biographique*, 306–7.

23. Laureys, *Meesters van het diamant*, 286–87, 308.

24. The British feared the Belgian government was not taking sufficient efforts and measures to ensure that London would remain the destination of rough diamonds from the Congo. In particular, there was acute concern that Forminière would eventually supply the United States directly with rough stones, bypassing the London intermediary. Therefore, the British were prepared to accept far-reaching accommodations for Belgium concerning import and export, transport, security, and insurance, as long as Belgium would secure these mutual interests as soon as possible. See confidential report, F. A. Mathias of the Diamond Advisory Committee, January 9, 1941, cited by Laureys, *Meesters van het diamant*, 291–92.

25. "The diamond industry is perhaps the most exemplary case of a capitalist sector that thrives on family ties, oral contacts, and extralegal adjudication." Trivellato, *The Familiarity of Strangers*, 278. Renée Rose Shield, *Diamond Stories: Enduring Change on 47th Street* (Ithaca, N.Y.: Cornell University Press, 2002).

26. Interview V. Vanden Daelen with Maurice Schamisso and family, January 7, 2009.

27. Ibid.

28. "My youngest sister . . . was a very clever girl; she was fluent in French and Flemish, and very good in English as well, even knew a bit of Russian. . . . My father, via Goldmuntz and all his friends, got her a job as secretary to l'Office Parlementaire. She was very popular, because she was quite able—and she was secretary at the embassy—and then another reason why she was popular, she said she was prepared to volunteer,

and to work free of charge, and of course all these politicians, who had no money at all, were pleased that some of their work or records could be typed free of charge." Ibid.

29. American Jewish Archives, World Jewish Congress files (collection 361) (henceforth cited as AJA, WJC files (coll. 361), H56/16, Belgium, 1944. The Belgian Jewish Committee (BJC) served to promote the return of the diamond diaspora, as evidenced in a letter from the BJC to the Belgian Jewish Representative Committee (BJRC) in New York: "The Antwerp diamond people here [in London] are also anxious as to their future prospects in Belgium and it is a great consolation to know that the Belgian Government have definitely decided to reinstate the diamond industry there as soon as possible and will use their best efforts in the speedy repatriation of all concerned." The letter is signed by the president and the treasurer, that is, Schamisso and Goldmuntz, respectively. Yad Vashem Archives, BJC, M22 1 correspondence BJC, letter BJC to BJRC, July 27, 1944.

30. Yad Vashem Archives, Belgian Jewish Committee (BJC), M22 3 Huysmans, copy of radio speech of March 29, 1944, sent to Romi Goldmuntz March 30, 1944; National Archives of Belgium (Brussels), Dossiers van het kabinet van de ministeries van Financiën en Defensie, Schatkist WO2 Londen, "Diamonds," Gutt to Spaak, July 13, 1942; Laureys, *Meesters van het diamant*, 300–308, 365–66, 374.

31. Ethel Blitz, quoted in Judith Tydor Baumel, "Kehillath Morya: Portrait of a Refugee Community in New York City, 1943–1987," in *Belgium and the Holocaust: Jews, Belgians, Germans*, ed. Dan Michman (Jerusalem: Yad Vashem, 1998), 499.

32. Ibid., "Kehillath Morya," 500–502.

33. Interview V. Vanden Daelen with Mr. and Mrs. M. Ratzersdorfer on November 9, 2003, New York.

34. Yad Vashem Archives, BJC, M22 3 Huysmans, copy of "They're Here to Stay," *New York World-Telegram*, November 8, 1943, from Huysmans (Belgian Parliamentary Office) to BJC (in answer to letter of December 1, 1943); M22 2 correspondence BJC, copy of New York report of November 17, 1943. Jewish refugee diamond dealers in London were not amused with the articles in the American press concerning the definite establishment of the diamond industry in the United States. The articles "had made a bad impression in Belgian governmental circles (. . . the result of the 'they are here to stay' article in particular had been very bad). Such things should at any price be avoided! People who do not have the intention to return ought to keep calm and think about the consequences of their publicity." AJA, WJC files (coll.361), H56/16, O. Strassberg (London) to L. Kubowitzki (New York), May 8, 1944. For further information on the Belgian government's attitude toward the return of the diamond sector, see Vanden Daelen, "Negotiating the Return of the Diamond Sector."

35. Vanden Daelen, "Negotiating the Return of the Diamond Sector"; Vanden Daelen, *Laten we hun lied verder zingen*, 77–78.

36. The BJC had obtained, shortly after its foundation, the guarantee of the Belgian government-in-exile that all Jews who had officially resided in Belgium would be able to return to the country after the war, Yad Vashem Archives, BJC, M22 5 and

7 Minutes BJC, Meeting March 7, 1944, February 7, 1944, and January 19, 1944; letter BJC to BJRC, June 8, 1944; Minutes, April 23, 1945, March 27, 1945, February 26, 1945; M22 2 correspondence BJC, copy of letter of Pierlot to Huysmans, February 1, 1944.

37. Laureys, *Meesters van het diamant*, 370–72.

38. See, for example, AJA, WJC files (coll. 361), H58/9, letter addressed by W. Eeckeleers to the editor of the Jewish Telegraphic Agency (London) of September 27, 1945, a copy of this letter was sent by O. Strassberg (BJC, London) to Kubowitzki (World Jewish Congress, New York) on October 8, 1945.

39. Yad Vashem Archives, BJC, M22 5 and 7 Minutes BJC, minutes of meeting held at the London Diamond Club, June 27, 1945.

40. Study Commission into the Fate of the Belgian Jewish Community's assets, which where plundered or surrendered or abandoned during the war 1940–1945 (Prime Minister's Office), *De bezittingen van de slachtoffers van de jodenvervolging in België: spoliatie—rechtsherstel—bevindingen van de Studiecommissie. Eindverslag* (Brussels: Prime Minister's Office, 2001), 464. The report of the Study Commission (*The Assets of the Victims of the Anti-Jewish Persecutions in Belgium: Looting, Re-establishment of Rights, Findings of the Study Commission. Final Report*) was published in Dutch and French. An English summary and further information is available online: http://www.combuysse.fgov.be/.

41. The Commission for the indemnification for the Belgian Jewish community's assets, which were plundered, surrendered or abandoned during the war 1940–1945, *Final report*, 2008, http://www.combuysse.fgov.be/en/index.html. For a history of the Hirsch company, see Véronique Pouillard, *Hirsch & Cie Bruxelles, 1869–1962* (Brussels: Éditions de l'Université de Bruxelles, 2000), 68–80. Confiscations of private property alone included 587,987.66 Belgian francs, numerous valuable artworks (especially paintings) and furniture pieces; reimbursements for these were not granted until the Restitution Commission had completed its work in 2007.

42. Vanden Daelen, *Laten we hun lied verder zingen*, 43–46.

43. Yad Vashem Archives, BJC, M22 5 and 7 Minutes BJC, meeting January 1, 1945; M22 1 correspondence BJC.

44. Reb Nusen Lustig collected funds for the Antwerp Jesode Hatora-Beth Jacob from among the Antwerp diamond dealers in New York. The school also received support from the Antwerp religious community and the local chevra kadischa, as well from Agudath Israel in London and from the CCI, which was sponsored by American Orthodoxy. The Tachkemoni School also received support from the Antwerp Jewish community, as well as from the Jewish Agency, and Rabbi Brodt held fundraising collections in New York. Vanden Daelen, *Laten we hun lied verder zingen*, 323–25, 329; private archives D. Klagsbald (Antwerp), report of CCI to Rabbi Porush, July 25, 1946; Yeshiva University Archives, Vaad Hatzala 1/1, 1/4 and 36/128 (support from Vaad Hahatzala via CCI); Sam Perl, ed., *100 jaar Jesode Hatora—Beth-Jacob 1895–1995* (Antwerp: De Vries-Brouwers, 1995), 26; Archives Shomre Hadas Antwerp, Collection "Verenigde Israëlitische Gemeenten" (VIG) (henceforth cited as Archives SH, VIG

coll.), for example A12, minutes VIG July 1, 1945 or A63, minutes chevra kadisha, August 22, 1946; n.a. "België: Tachkemoni—Antwerpen," *Nieuw Israëlietisch Weekblad* 78, no. 34 (August 8, 1947/22 Menachem 5707): 6; Central Zionist Archives, KH4/11378, E. Margelith (KH Brussels) to KH Jerusalem, February 24, 1954 (21 Adar I 5714); KKL5/17637, K. Lichtenstein (director KKL Brussels) to Arzi (KKL Jerusalem), January 30, 1951.

45. Vanden Daelen, *Laten we hun lied verder zingen*, 109, 115, 169; Andrée Katz, *75 jaar Centrale: Armoede en uitsluiting . . . een uitdaging!* (Antwerp: De Vries-Brouwers, 1995), 42.

46. Laura Hobson Faure and Veerle Vanden Daelen, "Imported from the United States? The American Jewish Welfare System in Post–World War II Europe: The Cases of Belgium and France, 1944–1960," in *Religious Perceptions of Poverty & Welfare Policy*, ed. Jonathan Cohen (Hebrew Union College Press, forthcoming). This article can be seen as a follow-up to Maud Mandel's seminal research into the influence of JDC activities in postwar France in "Philanthropy or Cultural Imperialism? The Impact of American Jewish Aid in Post-Holocaust France," *Jewish Social Studies* 9, no. 1 (Fall 2002): 53–94.

47. For a more detailed analysis of Jewish orphans and Jewish education in Antwerp after the World War II, see Vanden Daelen, *Laten we hun lied verder zingen*, 269–350.

48. The name of the Brussels main office was Aide aux Israélites Victimes de la Guerre (AIVG). The Antwerp section worked under the Dutch name of this organization and was called Hulp aan Israëlieten Slachtoffers van de Oorlog (HISO).

49. For example, Laura Margolis, Kate Mendel, and Beatrice Vulcan represented the JDC in Belgium in the immediate postwar period.

50. AJA, WJC files (coll. 361), D78/15, report to Dr. A. Leon Kubowitzki, Headquarters, New York, from Miss Sophie Perelman, Secretary, WJC Office, Brussels, July 6, 1945.

51. AJA, WJC files (coll. 361), D95/2, Belgian Jewish Representative Committee.

52. Baumel, "Kehillath Morya," 510–11; Interview V. Vanden Daelen with Mr. and Mrs. M. Ratzersdorfer on November 9, 2003, New York; private archives M. Ratzersdorfer (New York).

53. Archives SH, VIG coll., A12, management board minutes VIG, January 26, 1946.

54. AJA, WJC files (coll. 361), D78/15, report to Dr. A. Leon Kubowitzki, Headquarters, New York, from Miss Sophie Perelman, Secretary, WJC Office, Brussels, July 6, 1945: "We [WJC office Brussels] thank you [WJC] heartily for the promise of a million francs. . . . Inasmuch as Antwerp has so far been treated unfairly by the Child Care Committee, we shall probably place this sum at the disposal of the Antwerp Child Care Committee, so that it may be able to reopen the old orphanage." See, for example: "They [friends of the author in Antwerp] ask me to particularly stress the calamity being continued in the practice of supporting about 1,500 Jewish children in the hands of gentiles who *raise our own children to be rabid anti-semites. The alibi used to justify*

this practice is that there is no home available for these children." AJA, WJC files (coll. 361), D78/16, David Stein (New York) to Kubowitzky (WJC New York), December 3, 1945. This letter attests to the unrest within Antwerp's Jewish community, which reached a culmination point in February 1946. See also Archives Service Social Juif (Brussels), minutes AIVG, October 3, 1945.

55. Archives of the American Jewish Joint Distribution Committee, New York (henceforth cited as JDC-NY), coll. 45/54, file 149, Moses A. Leavitt (Joint New York) to Laura Margolis (Joint Brussels), July 27, 1945.

56. Jean-Philippe Schreiber, "Léon Kubowitzki," in Schreiber, *Dictionnaire biographique*, 204–5.

57. Alex Grobman, *Battling for Souls: The Vaad Hatzala Rescue Committee in Post-Holocaust Europe* (Jersey City, N.J.: KTAV Publishing House, 2004), 20. Grobman states in his introduction:

> As the primary American Jewish organization providing relief and rehabilitation to the Jews of Europe, the JDC came into conflict with other entities that it felt infringed on its territory, and perhaps hindered its work. The JDC and the World Jewish Congress (WJC), founded in 1936, for example, continually were at odds over who should administer aid to Jews. The differences were an outgrowth of their different world views. The WJC believed in the unity of the Jewish people throughout the world and sought to establish a political entity to represent world Jewry. The JDC rejected this view of nationalism and was disturbed that the WJC competed with it for funds.

Alex Grobman, *Rekindling the Flame: American Jewish Chaplains and the Survivors of European Jewry, 1944–1948* (Detroit: Wayne State University Press, 1993), 3; AJA, WJC files (coll. 361), D78/15, report to Dr. A. Leon Kubowitzki, Headquarters, New York, from Miss Sophie Perelman, Secretary, WJC Office, Brussels, July 6, 1945: "It is the aim of the Council to form a unified Child Care Committee under its aegis, but we are aware that this will be no easy matter"; H57/1, Sophie Perelman (WJC, Brussel) to A. Leon Kubowitzki (WJC, New York), January 21, 1946; Vanden Daelen, *Laten we hun lied verder zingen*, 276–78, 292–93.

58. AJA, WJC files (coll. 361), H57/2 (presumably Leon Kubowitzki) to Isaac Kubowitzki, October 16, 1945 (translated by author; original French text: "N'a-t-il pas encore été possible de mettre sur pied un Conseil anversois assez représentative pour impressionner les Anversois d'ici?").

59. Letterhead orphanage, Archives SH, VIG coll., A 38–39, letter orphanage to "Morijah," September 16, 1949. Further sources are JDC-NY, coll. 45/54, file 150, Joint-disco "outgoing cable Brussels" Joint-fund, January 22, 1946; AJA, WJC files (coll. 361), H57/2, Leon Kubowitzki (New York) to Isaac Kubowitzki (Brussels), November 21, 1945; AJA, WJC files (coll. 361), H57/1, "Problème des enfants juifs en Belgique—Tâche du Congrès Juif Mondial," January 21, 1946.

60. Vanden Daelen, *Laten we hun lied verder zingen*, 308–12, based on archival research in AJA, WJC files (coll. 361), C247/5, D78/17, G69/3, H57/2, H58/13, and 15, H59/7, H60/3, J11/5; CAHJP, CC-files, 1958, Comité Central Israélite); Archives of the American Jewish Joint Distribution Committee, Jerusalem (henceforth cited as JDC-I), box 178B179A, folder 10.

61. Vaad Hahatzala was founded in November 1939 to bring an alternative for Orthodox Jews for the JDC. Its collecting agency, Rescue Children, was founded in June 1946.

62. Yehuda Bauer, *American Jewry and the Holocaust: The American Jewish Joint Distribution Committee 1939–1945* (Detroit: Wayne State University Press, 1981), 127; Efraim Zuroff, *The Response of Orthodox Jewry in the United States to the Holocaust: The Activities of the Vaad ha-Hatzala Rescue Committee, 1939–1945* (New York: Michael Scharf Publication Trust of Yeshiva University Press, 2000), 36; Alex Grobman, *Battling for Souls*, 99–100, 103, 284, 289; Vanden Daelen, *Laten we hun lied verder zingen*, 291–92, 298–305; JDC-I, box 178B179A, folder 3, Agreement between the American Jewish Joint Distribution Committee and the Union of Orthodox Rabbis of the USA and Canada, July 29, 1947; Yeshiva University Archives, Collection Maurice Enright, box 1, folder 3, Agreement between American Jewish Joint Distribution Committee, Inc. and Rescue Children, Inc., January 1, 1948; Vaad Hatzala, 1/3, 13/4, and 22/9; private archives of the Rottenberg family in New Jersey (one of Jozef Rottenberg's sons).

63. Mandel, *Philanthropy or Cultural Imperialism?*, 64.

64. Vanden Daelen, *Laten we hun lied verder zingen*, 281–87, based on archival research in Agudath Israel-Archives, Coll. Michael G. Tress Des. Save-a-Child Foundation: Case histories, M. Swerdloff, Brussels, publicity date 1947–1949, Loc. I-22; Archives SH, VIG coll., A16, correspondence Morris Swerdloff and Herman Treisser (Agudath Israel Youth Council of America) with United Jewish Communities Antwerp, June 24, 1948, July 5, 1948; JDC-NY, coll. 45/64, file 3724; JDC-I, box 178A, folder 30, S. Ratzersdorfer (Centrale Antwerp) to L. Seidenman (Joint-Brussel), December 22, 1959. Also based on work by Hanne Hellemans, "'Zij die verloren zijn, zullen niet vergeten worden' (II Samuel 14:14): Pogingen tot herintegratie van de kinderen in de joodse gemeenschap na de Tweede Wereldoorlog. Een ideologisch debat" (master's thesis, University of Ghent, 2002), 54, 120, 123, 126, 129–31; idem, "Tot wie behoort de ziel van het kind? De herintegratie van kinderen in de joodse gemeenschap na de Tweede Wereldoorlog," *Bijdragen tot de Eigentijdse Geschiedenis/Cahiers d'Histoire du Temps Présent* 13–14 (2004): 200. Concerning the "children's question" in Belgium, see Hanne Hellemans, *Schimmen met een ster: Het bewogen verhaal van joodse ondergedoken kinderen tijdens de Tweede Wereldoorlog in België* (Antwerp: Manteau, 2007).

65. Vanden Daelen, *Laten we hun lied verder zingen*, 339–44.

66. Jacques Gutwirth, *La renaissance du Hassidisme: De 1945 à nos jours* (Paris: Odile Jacob, 2004), 28.

67. Edouard Robberechts, *Les Hassidim* (Turnhout, Belgium: Brepols, 1990), 270–75; Vanden Daelen, *Laten we hun lied verder zingen*, 197, 201–5; Gutwirth, *La renaissance*

du Hassidisme, 25; Archives SH, VIG coll. A30, VIG to chief rabbi of Belgium, Dr. S. Ullman, December 30, 1955; A32, VIG to chief rabbi of Belgium, Dr. S. Ullman, January 4, 1956; A33, rapport de la Communauté Synagogue Israélite Orthodoxe Machsike-Hadass, Exercice 1955.

68. Gutwirth, *La renaissance du Hassidisme,* 28–30, 35–36, 39.

69. Vanden Daelen, *Laten we hun lied verder zingen*, 204–5.

70. Ibid., 316, calculations based on Maxime Steinberg, *L'étoile et le fusil: La question juive, 1940–1942* (Brussels: Éditions Vie ouvrière, 1983), 67.

71. Ibid., based on [no author identified], "Van het Joint-front," *Centrale* 7, no. 26 (December 1959): 22; Sylvain Brachfeld, *Het joods onderwijs in België* (Antwerp: B'nai B'rith, 1966), 82.

72. CAHJP, CC-files, 3175, European schools, [second half of the 1950s]; Brachfeld, *Het joods onderwijs*, 82.

73. Machsike Hadas, *Tourist Traveler Guide*; Machsike Hadas, *Luach/Almanak der Israëlitische Orthodoxe Gemeente Antwerpen Machsike Hadas, 5769 (30 September 2008–18 September 2009)* (Antwerp: Machsike Hadas, 2008). For an overview of Jewish day schools and their dates of foundation, see Vanden Daelen, *Laten we hun lied verder zingen*, 316–17.

74. "Fun yidishn lebn in Belgye. Fun Antverpn: Algemeyne farzamlung fun 'Hiso,'" *Unzer Vort (Brisl),* March 11, 1949, 2; "Fun yidish-gezelshaftslebn in Antverpn: Farvos zenen di mitglider fun di linke tsienistishe parteyen aroysgetretn fun 'Hiso'?," *Unzer Vort (Brisl),* March 18, 1949, 5; Roger van Ransbeek, *50 jaar Centraal Beheer van Joodse Weldadigheid en Maatschappelijk Hulpbetoon (1920–1970)* (Antwerp: Centraal Beheer van Joodse Weldadigheid en Maatschappelijk Hulpbetoon, 1970), 78; Evelien Gans, *De kleine verschillen die het leven uitmaken. Een historische studie naar joodse sociaal-democraten en socialistisch-zionisten in Nederland* (Amsterdam: Vassallucci, 2002), 587; Evelyn Adunka, *Die vierte Gemeinde. Die Wiener Juden in der Zeit von 1945 bis heute* (Vienna: Philo Verlag, 2000), 18, 61, 64; Vanden Daelen, *Laten we hun lied verder zingen*, 114.

75. Baumel, "Kehillath Morya," 500, 516.

76. Centre Communautaire Laïc Juif David Susskind asbl [Secular *Jewish* Community Center], "David Susskind, une vie pour le peuple juif," December 9, 2009, http://www.cclj.be/article/22/794; for a documentary on David Susskind, see Willy Perelsztejn, director, *Sois un Mensch, mon fils!* (GSARA Production, 2007).

77. "These children did not have any Jewish background and it was therefore impossible to integrate them into the regular classes." CAHJP, CC-files, 1959, Mark Uveeler (Claims Conference) to Moses A. Leavitt (Joint-New York): Request from Yesode Hatorah-Beth Jacob Schools in Antwerp for a grant from the Conference Teachers' Reserve Fund, May 20, 1959. "[Fifty-six] pupils of newly arrived refugee families from Poland must receive intensive Jewish instruction, to be able to join the regular classes of the school." CAHJP, CC-files, 1959, 3076 Tachkemoni School, Antwerp. Vanden Daelen, *Laten we hun lied verder zingen*, 340–41.

78. For example, Goldmuntz, who remained one of the most important diamond dealers in Antwerp, was a major sponsor of Antwerp's Jewish communal life. The city's Jewish Community Center and one of its major synagogues are named for him. Herman Schamisso, and later on his son Maurice, always remained actively involved in the diamond trade and the community and held leading positions (including the presidency) in various communal institutions, such as the central Jewish social welfare office and the religious community.

79. Interviews V. Vanden Daelen with P. Kornfeld, Antwerp, March 3, 2009, and with M. Bloch, Antwerp, March 4, 2009.

80. *The Diamond's Business* (Zodiak, 2010), broadcast on Belgian public television Canvas (Terzake), August 23, 2010.

81. Trivellato, *The Familiarity of Strangers*, 10. Trivellato notes that the more "Jewish," or the more explicit the boundaries were between Jews and non-Jews in these commercial contacts, the easier such contacts were to establish (50). Also relevant here is the idea of "communitarian cosmopolitanism" resulting in a highly diverse and yet highly segregated society (73).

82. Stein, *Plumes*, 151.

83. Interview V. Vanden Daelen with P. Kornfeld, March 3, 2009, and with J. Mörsel, March 12, 2009, both in Antwerp.

84. Stein develops similar ideas concerning the ostrich feather trade in "'Falling into Feathers,'" 786–800.

85. Stein, *Plumes*, 152.

86. Gutwirth, *La renaissance du Hassidisme*, 28–31.

87. "'Es war wie im Himmel,' sagt Jackie Morsel, 'ze zwei Stunden am Tag arbeitete, hatte genug zum Leben und lernte den Rest des Tages Tora und Talmud. Wer mehr arbeitete, konnte etwas zurücklegen.'" T. Kühn, "Abgeschliffen," *Jüdische Allgemeine*, May 15, 2008, 3.

88. Duncan Bartlett, "Jews Lose Hold of Antwerp Diamond Trade," BBC News, Antwerp, September 18, 2008, http://news.bbc.co.uk/2/hi/europe/7619722.stm; Sharai Parnoese Toive (SPT is an organization which was established to improve the economic situation within the Jewish community of Antwerp by organizing customized training programs, job placement, career assistance, and guidance for new and established entrepreneurs), http://sptantwerpen.be/. Interview V. Vanden Daelen with P. Kornfeld, March 3, 2009; M. Schamisso and family, January 7, 2009; M. Bloch, March 4, 2009; J. Mörsel, March 12, 2009. Guido Joris, "Joodse entrepreneur krijgt prestigieuze 'enterprize award,'" *Joods Actueel* 22 (November 2008): 14–15.

Chapter 10. Faith Meets Politics and Resources

Research for this chapter was supported by the Israel Science Foundation (grant no. 462/05).

1. For the non-Jewish world, see Thomas Adam, ed., *Philanthropy, Patronage, and Civil Society: Experiences from Germany, Great Britain, and North America* (Bloomington:

Indiana University Press, 2004), 9; idem, "Transatlantic Trading: The Transfer of Philanthropic Models between European and North American Cities During the 19th and 20th Centuries," *Journal of Urban History* 28, no. 3 (2002): 345.

2. Other definitions exist. See, for example, Phiroshaw Camay and Anne J. Gordon, eds., *Advocacy in Southern Africa: Lessons for the Future* (Johannesburg: CORE, 1998), 4–5, 7.

3. Some of these are mentioned in the interview of Phil Baum, May 24, 1989, William E. Wiener Oral History Library of the American Jewish Committee, "Soviet Jewry Movement in America" (henceforth cited as AJC interviews), 1–13.

4. For data on economic life after 1945, see Mordechai Altshuler, *Soviet Jewry Since the Second World War: Population and Social Structure* (New York: Greenwood, 1987).

5. A first attempt to integrate multiple branches of the movement can be found in Gal Beckerman, *When They Come for Us We'll Be Gone: The Epic Struggle to Save Soviet Jewry* (New York: Houghton Mifflin, 2010). See also Laura Bialis's documentary film *Refusenik* (Los Angeles: Foundation for Documentary Projects, 2008).

6. For an overview of these branches of the movement, see Binyamin Pinkus, *Tehiya u-tkumah le'umit: Ha-tsionut veha-tnuah ha-tsionit be-Brit ha-moatsot, 1947–1987* (Sde Boker, Israel: Ben Gurion Heritage Center, 1993), 523–28.

7. For example, Fred A. Lazin, *"We Are Not One": American Jews, Israel and the Struggle for Soviet Jewry* (Ann Arbor: University of Michigan Press, 2009), 17–18.

8. For example, John Keep, *Last of the Empires: A History of the Soviet Union, 1945–1991* (Oxford: Oxford University Press, 1995), does not mention the movement.

9. Many of these issues are examined in Yaacov Ro'i, ed., *The Jewish Movement in the Soviet Union* (Baltimore: Johns Hopkins University Press, 2012).

10. One such figure was Morris Abram, already a nationally recognized civil rights lawyer when he became chairman of the American Council for Soviet Jewry (the predecessor of the National Council). Another was Rabbi Richard Hirsch, who was among the architects of the civil rights movement and founders of the Religious Action Center of Reform Judaism.

11. For example, see Beckerman, *When They Come for Us*, 514–15.

12. Stefani Hoffman, "Voices from the Inside: Jewish Activists' Memoirs, 1967–1989," in *The Jewish Movement in the Soviet Union*, ed. Ro'i, 247–48.

13. Michael Beizer, "How the Movement Was Funded," in *The Jewish Movement in the Soviet Union*, ed. Ro'i, 388–90. See also Sarah Fainberg, "Friends Abroad: How the Western Campaign for Soviet Jews Influenced Activists in the Soviet Union," in *The Jewish Movement in the Soviet Union*, ed. Ro'i, 406–18.

14. Early in the twentieth century, the Jewish "establishment" was understood to consist of German-speaking elites at the head of communal organizations like the American Jewish Committee.

15. For example, see American Jewish Historical Society (henceforth cited as AJHS), I-410a, Union of Councils of Soviet Jewry (henceforth cited as UCSJ), box 1, folder 1 (Rosenblum memo, May 2, 1968). As an important activist noted, similar trends char-

acterized the civil rights movement in the United States. See interview of Abraham Bayer, May 5, 1989, AJC interviews, 6.

16. AJHS, I-410a, UCSJ, box 1, folder 1 (Rosenblum to Baruch, March 13, 1970), (Yaroslavsky to Rosenblum, April 25, 1970), (Rosenblum mailing, April 27, 1970), (Rosenblum to Rabin, May 4, 1970): AJHS, William Korey Papers, P-903, box 11, folder SSSJ #3 (Birnbaum to Frumkin, July 39, 2008). For an Israeli perspective, see interview of Yoram Dinstein, November 28, 1989, AJC interviews, 4–10.

17. Petrus Buwalda, *They Did Not Dwell Alone: Jewish Emigration from the Soviet Union, 1967–1990* (Washington, D.C.: Woodrow Wilson Center, 1997). Buwalda served as the Dutch ambassador to Moscow from 1986 to 1990. The Dutch legation to the Soviet Union represented Israeli diplomatic interests from 1967 to 1990.

18. Boris Morozov, ed., *Documents on Soviet Jewish Emigration* (Portland, Ore.: Cass, 1999).

19. Noam Kochavi, "Insights Abandoned, Flexibility Lost: Kissinger, Soviet Jewish Emigration, and the Demise of Détente," *Diplomatic History* 29, no. 3 (2005): 503–7.

20. Anatoly Dobrynin, *In Confidence: Moscow's Ambassador to America's Six Cold War Presidents* (Seattle: University of Washington Press, 1995), 159, 268, 269, 336–37, 365, 368.

21. For a reassessment, see Samuel Barnai, "Social Trends Among Jews in the Post-Stalin Years," in *Revolution, Repression and Revival: the Soviet Jewish Experience*, ed. Yaacov Ro'i and Zvi Gitelman, 131–52 (Lanham, Md.: Rowman and Littlefield, 2007).

22. The reference here is to the best-selling book by Elie Wiesel, *The Jews of Silence: A Personal Report on Soviet Jewry* (New York: Holt, 1966). First published in French, translated into English and eprinted many times, Wiesel's book disseminated an iconic image in the West of a reemergent Jewish national identity and the Soviet repression it sparked.

23. For brief discussions of the international context, see Henry Feingold, *"Silent No More": Saving the Jews of Russia—The American Jewish Effort, 1967–1989* (Syracuse, N.Y.: Syracuse University Press, 2007), 109–10, 147–48.

24. Adam Nagourney, "In Tapes, Nixon Rails About Jews and Blacks," *New York Times*, December 10, 2010.

25. Henry A. Kissinger, "Putting the Nixon Tape in Context," *Washington Post*, December 26, 2010.

26. The amendment tied continued trade with the Soviet Union to a rise in emigration rates for Soviet Jews. It would deny Most Favored Nation Status if such rates were not achieved. For a detailed description of its legislation, see Paula Stern, *Water's Edge: Domestic Politics and the Making of American Foreign Policy* (Westport, Conn.: Greenwood, 1979).

27. For an interesting contrast, see "The Reminiscences of Jacob Javits," Ethnic Groups and American Foreign Policy project, Oral History Research Office, Columbia University (henceforth cited as Columbia interviews), 1977, 1; and "The Reminiscences of Richard Maass," Columbia interviews, 1977, 33–34. See also Feingold, *Silent*

No More, 142, 143; and National Archives and Records Administration (henceforth cited as NARA), RG 59, Subject Numeric Files, 1970–73, box 3109, folder "SOC 14, USSR, 1/1/70" (memorandum on Eilberg lecture, March 8, 1970).

28. Some authors contend that the Soviets suspended the tax because it had not deterred requests for emigration. See Laurie Salitan, *Politics and Nationality in Contemporary Soviet-Jewish Emigration, 1968–89* (New York: St. Martin's, 1992), 42–43. For details of the tax, see Nehemia Levanon, *Ha-kod: Nativ* (Tel Aviv: Am oved, 1995), 394.

29. The Stevenson Amendment to the Export-Import Ban Bill capped U.S. credits to the Soviet Union at $300 million over four years unless the Kremlin permitted higher emigration. It was repealed in April 1992.

30. When asked, Michael Gorbachev stated that Jackson-Vanik had no effect. See transcript of Charlie Rose interview of Michael Gorbachev and George Shultz, PBS, April 21, 2009, http://www.charlierose.com/view/interview/10246#frame_top. It is unclear whether Gorbachev's intent was to the years he served as General Secretary of the CPSU or during earlier periods. For emigration data, see Salitan, *Politics and Nationality*, 108–10; and Baruch Gur-Gurevitz, *Open Gates: The Inside Story of the Mass Aliya from the Soviet Union and Its Successor States* (Jerusalem: Jewish Agency, 1996), 277–85. Some believed that Jackson-Vanik may have even slowed Jewish emigration until 1978; see Avi Beker, "Superpower Relations and Jewish Identity in the Soviet Union," in *Jewish Culture and Identity in the Soviet Union*, ed. Yaacov Ro'i and Avi Beker (New York: New York University Press, 1991), 446; and Beckermman, *When They Come for Us*, 312, 396, 419. Edith Rogovin Frankel notes that the education tax was not rescinded and continued to be applied among some states in the former Soviet Union. See her "Behind the Scenes," in Ro'i, *The Jewish Movement in the Soviet Union*, 188–89.

31. NARA, Nixon White House Tapes, Oval Office, Tape 788, conversation #8, September 29, 1972. At the time, John Erlichman was President Nixon's chief domestic advisor.

32. Feingold, *Silent No More*, 116–17, 146–47.

33. Marshall Goldman, "Jackson-Vanik: A Dissent," in *A Second Exodus: The American Movement to Free Soviet Jews*, ed. Murray Friedman and Albert Chernin (Hanover, N.H.: UPNE, 1999), 115–23; Salitan, *Politics and Nationality*, 88–91. Compare the opinions expressed in AJHS, A-410a, UCSJ, box 1, folder 13 (Gordon to Perle, May 4, 1979), (Gordon to Vanik, May 4, 1979).

34. Stuart Altshuler, *From Exodus to Freedom: A History of the Soviet Jewry Movement* (Lanham, Md.: Rowman and Littlefield, 2005), 88–96, summarizes—from a "grassroots" vantage point—the position of the American Jewish "establishment" on this issue.

35. For example, see AJHS, I-410a, UCSJ, box 1, folder 6 (Morgenthau statement to Finance Committee, April 1974). Evidently, noted refuseniks had some input into the details of the Jackson-Vanik Amendment. See Pauline Peretz, *Le combat pour les Juifs soviétiques: Washington-Moscou-Jéruslaem, 1953–1989* (Paris: Armand Colin, 2006),

250; Philip Spiegel, *Triumph over Tyranny: The Heroic Campaigns That Saved 2,000,000 Soviet Jews* (New York: Devora, 2008), 70.

36. AJHS, I-410a, UCSJ, box 1, folder 5 (Spulber to Bergman, May 1, 1973); "The Reminiscences of Ambassador Sol M. Linowitz," Columbia interviews, 1977, 29–31; Beckerman, *When They Come for Us*, 456–58.

37. For a variety of views, see AJHS, A-410a, UCSJ, box 1, folder 11 (Georgetown University report on U.S.-Soviet trade and emigration, June 11, 1979). See also AJHS, A-410a, UCSJ, box 12, folder 6 (memorandum from Eizenstat and Gagné to Schapira, Singer, and Epstein, April 16, 1985); interview of Phil Baum, May 24, 1989, AJC interviews, 29–32.

38. Naomi W. Cohen, *Jacob H. Schiff: A Study in American Jewish Leadership* (Hanover, N.H.: Brandeis University Press, 1999), 135–36; Feingold, *Silent No More*, 10.

39. Beckerman, *When They Come for Us*, 419, notes that Brezhnev also hoped in 1979 that increased emigration rates would encourage the United States to approve the SALT II Treaty.

40. Buwalda, *They Did Not Dwell Alone*, 112.

41. Adlai E. Stevenson and Alton Frye, "Trading with the Communists," *Foreign Affairs* 68, no. 2 (1989): 54–60. President Reagan purportedly told Dobrynin in 1983 that the Jackson-Vanik Amendment had been a mistake; Dobrynin, *In Confidence*, 518.

42. Wendy Eisen, *Count Us In: The Struggle to Free Soviet Jews, A Canadian Perspective* (Toronto: Burgher Books, 1995), 179.

43. For examples, see Noam Kochavi, "Idealpolitik in Disguise: Israel, Jewish Emigration from the Soviet Union, and the Nixon Administration, 1969–1974," *International History Review* 29, no. 3 (2007): 550–72. See also Dina Zisserman-Brodsky, "The 'Jews of Silence'—the 'Jews of Hope'"—the 'Jews of Triumph': Revisiting Methodological Approaches to the Study of the Jewish Movement in the USSR," *Nationalities Papers* 33, no. 1 (March 2005): 133–34.

44. Feingold, *Silent No More*, 296; idem, *Jewish Power in America: Myth and Reality* (New Brunswick, N.J.: Transaction, 2009), 67. David Biale developed a similar analysis; see his *Jewish Power and Powerlessness in History* (New York: Schocken, 1986), 177–205. Also, while President Ford apparently supported the amendments (and signed Jackson-Vanik), most of his senior officials did not.

45. For one example, see Ari Volvovsky, "The Teaching and Studying of Hebrew," in *The Jewish Movement in the Soviet Union*, ed. Ro'i, 341. Feingold, *Silent No More*, 147, notes that, barring three years during the 1970s, Soviet emigration policy did not substantially change until perestroika.

46. Buwalda, *They Did Not Dwell Alone*, 109–10.

47. For example, see "The Reminiscences of Richard Maass," Columbia interviews, 1977, 36.

48. Transcript of Charlie Rose interview of Michael Gorbachev and George Shultz, PBS, April 21, 2009. See an affirmation of this opinion from a surprising source: "Interview of Rabbi Pinchas Teitz," October 26, 1989, AJC interviews, 24.

49. AJHS, A-410a, UCSJ, box 2, folder 11 (Geller to Tanenbaum, May 19, 1986), 3. Former Secretary of State George P. Shultz confirms this argument for Reagan's geopolitical focus, while adding other factors; see his "Epilogue: The United States in the Movement's Triumph," in *The Jewish Movement in the Soviet Union*, ed. Ro'i, 419–28.

50. For recent reconsiderations, see the conference proceedings contained in,"The Legacy and Consequences of Jackson-Vanik: Reassessing Human Rights in 21st Century Russia," Kennan Institute Occasional Paper #305, ed. F. Joseph Dresen and William E. Pomeranz (Washington, D.C.: Woodrow Wilson International Center, 2010); and "Jackson-Vanik After Russia's Accession to the WTO," *Kennan Institute Meeting Report* 29, no. 10 (2012). See also the editorials "A Costly Anachronism," *New York Times*, February 28, 2012, A24; "Trade Relations with Russia," *New York Times*, August 12, 2012, Sunday Review, 12; and, David M. Herszenhorn, "Russian Opposition Urges U.S. to End Cold War Trade Sanctions," *New York Times*, March 12, 2012.

51. Peter Baker, "In Trade Deal with Russia, U.S. Plans Sanctions for Human Rights Abuses," *New York Times*, July 18, 2012, p. A9.

52. For a rosy view, see Levanon, *Ha-kod: Nativ*, 382–88, 394–408.

53. For analyses, see Fred A. Lazin, *The Struggle for Soviet Jewry in American Politics: Israel Versus the American Jewish Establishment* (Lanham, Md.: Lexington, 2005), 79–178; Peretz, *Le combat*, 301–13; and, Steven F. Windmeuller, "The 'Noshrim' War: Dropping Out," in Friedman and Chernin, *A Second Exodus*, 161–72.

54. Zisserman-Brodsky, "Jews of Silence," 132; AJHS, I-410a, UCSJ, box 1, folder 10 (Manekofsky memo, November 25, 1978); Feingold, *Silent No More*, 115.

55. For examples, see "The Reminiscences of Rabbi Israel Miller," Columbia interviews, 1978, 22; interview of Phil Baum, May 24, 1989, AJC interviews, 24–25; interview of Eugene Gold, January 10, 1990, AJC interviews, 24; interview of Theodore Comet, April 4, 1989, AJC interviews, 16–21; interview of Richard Maass, March 13, 1989, AJC interviews, 4–5; interview of Seymour Reich, February 2, 1990, AJC interviews, 20–21; interview of Yoram Dinstein, November 28, 1989, AJC interviews, 36–39.

56. For example, see Yakov Kedmi, *Milhamot avudot: Edut ishit* (Tel Aviv: Matar, 2011), 174–75.

57. Lazin, " 'We Are Not One,' " 31.

58. To date, the archives of Nativ are mostly inaccessible to the public. For examples of monographs about Nativ written without the benefit of archival material, see Lazin, *The Struggle*, and Peretz, *Le combat*.

59. For example, see AJHS, I-410a, UCSJ, box 2, folder 4 (Sofios report #17, October 21, 1980).

60. This view is shared in the interview of Yoram Dinstein, November 28, 1989, AJC interviews, 9, 19–20.

61. For analysis of these campaigns, see Leonid Gershovitz, "Anahnu v'atem?: Ha-ma'avak ha-tsiburi b'yisrael leman shihrur v'aliyat yehudei Brit ha-moetsot' 1948–1989" (master's thesis, Hebrew University, 2010).

62. See an assessment from an Israeli "insider": Meir Rosenne interview, November 10, 1989, AJC interviews, p. 8, copy found in AJHS, William Korey Papers, P-903, box 8, folder "American Jewish Conference on Soviet Jewry," folder 8 (American Jewish Committee).

63. Lazin, "'We Are Not One,'" 29–30.

64. AJHS, I-410a, UCSJ, box 2, folder 3 (Manon to Prital, July 17, 1980), folder 4 (trip report to Soviet Union, September 17–October 6, 1980).

65. For firsthand accounts, see "The Reminiscences of Hyman Bookbinder," Columbia interviews, 1978; interview of David Geller, February 20, 1981, AJC interviews, 19–22; "The Reminiscences of Richard Maass," Columbia interviews, 1977, 4–5.

66. For examples, see AJHS, I-181, box 15, folder "Conference of Presidents" (Lowell to Miller, September 11, 1975), (Miller to Lowell, September 16, 1975), box 8, folder "Executive Committee Correspondence" (Sprayregen to Lowell and Goodman, October 29, 1974); NARA, Nixon Papers, WHCF, SMOF, Garment, box 116, file "Jewish matters, 1969–70/1" (Kissinger to Garment, September 27, 1969), 1; NARA, RG 59, Central Foreign Policy Files, 1967–1969, box 3112, folder "SOC 12-1 USSR, 1/1/68 (Katzenbach to Bohlen, May 27, 1968); NARA, RG 59, Central Foreign Policy Files, 1967–1969, box 3113, folder "SOC 14, USSR, 5/1/69" (memorandum of meeting with Bnai Brith, June 22, 1967); NARA, RG 59, Central Foreign Policy Files, 1967–1969, box 3113, folder "SOC 14, USSR, 1/1/68" (Read to Rostow, April 1, 1968), (Leddy to Under Secretary, March 28, 1968), (memorandum of meeting with ACF, March 26, 1968), (memorandum of meeting with AJCSJ, March 11, 1968); NARA, RG 59, Subject Numeric Files, 1970–1973, box 3110, folder "SOC 14, USSR, 1/1/71" (memorandum on meeting with ADL, January 29, 1971), (memorandum of meeting with AJCSJ, January 28, 1971), (Eliot to Kissinger, February 19, 1971); NARA, Nixon Papers, Staff, H. A. Kissinger Telecons, Chronological File, box 16 (conversation with Garment, September 21, 1972); NARA, Nixon, WHCF, Subject files, CO 158, box 70, folder "USSR, begin May 30, 1969" (Kissinger to Sloan, April 22, 1969); and Feingold, *Silent No More*, 122.

67. Feingold, *Silent No More*, 272–74, 310; interview of Morton Yarmon, April 14, 1989, AJC interviews.

68. My analysis differs from other authors. For example, see William Korey, "From Helsinki: A Salute to Human Rights," in Friedman and Chernin, *A Second Exodus*, 124–35.

69. Richard Schifter, "American Diplomacy, 1985–1989," in ibid., 137.

70. Beckerman, *When They Come for Us*, 534–35, restated this argument.

71. For descriptions, see Ben Fowkes, "The National Question in the Soviet Union Under Leonid Brezhnev: Policy and Response," in *Brezhnev Reconsidered*, ed. Edwin Bacon and Mark Sandle (Houndmills, U.K.: Palgrave, 2002), 68–89; Benjamin Pinkus, *Sofah shel tekufah: Yehudei Brit ha-moetsot b'eidan Gorbachev, 1985–1991* (Beer Sheva: Ben Gurion University, 1999), 27–40, 48–52, 355. Salitan, *Politics and Nationality*, 84–87, 91–97, 104–5, dispels a belief that foreign policy considerations circumscribed the Soviet Union's's emigration policy.

72. Lazin, "'We Are Not One,'" 10–11; Feingold, *Silent No More*, 242–43; transcript of Charlie Rose interview of Michael Gorbachev and George Shultz, PBS, April 21, 2009.

73. Jonathan Frankel, *The Damascus Affair: "Ritual Murder," Politics, and the Jews in 1840* (Cambridge: Cambridge University Press, 1997).

74. Some of these are described in Mary McCune, *The Whole Wide World Without Limits: International Relief, Gender Politics, and American Jewish Women, 1893–1930* (Detroit: Wayne State University Press, 2005).

75. Rebecca Kobrin, "Auxiliary or Artery? Rethinking Gender, Power and Philanthropy in the East European Jewish Immigrant Community," AJS Annual Convention, 2005; and idem, *Jewish Bialystok and Its Diaspora* (Bloomington: Indiana University Press, 2010), 155–61.

76. Altshuler, *From Exodus to Freedom*, 50.

77. Daphne Gerlis, *Those Wonderful Women in Black* (London: Minerva, 1996); Eisen, *Count Us In*.

78. For details, see Jonathan I. Israel, *Diaspora within a Diaspora: Jews, Crypto-Jews and the World Maritime Empires, 1540–1740* (Leiden: Brill, 2002).

79. Adam, *Philanthropy*, 3; idem "Transatlantic Trading," 328–29.

80. For an enduring overview, see Ephraim Frisch, *An Historical Survey of Jewish Philanthropy from the Earliest Times to the Nineteenth Century* (New York: Macmillan, 1924). See also Cohen, *Schiff*, 56.

81. Georges J. Weill, "The Alliance Israélite Universelle and the Emancipation of Jewish Communities in the Mediterranean," *Jewish Journal of Sociology* 24, no. 2 (1982): 117–34; Eli Bar-Chen, "Two Communities with a Sense of Mission: The Alliance Israélite Universelle and the Hilfsverein der Deutschen Juden," in *Jewish Emancipation Reconsidered: The French and German Models*, ed. Michael Brenner, Vicki Caron, and Uri R. Kaufman (Tübingen: Mohr Siebeck, 2003), 111–21; Andre Chouraqui, *L'Alliance israélite universelle et la renaissance juive contemporaine, 1860–1960* (Paris: Presses Universitaires de France, 1965).

82. Evyatar Friesel, "Jacob H. Schiff and the Leadership of the American Jewish Community," *Jewish Social Studies* 8, nos. 2–3 (2002): 61–72. For an example of early organized efforts, see Judith S. Goldstein, *The Politics of Ethnic Pressure: The American Jewish Committee Fight Against Immigration Restriction, 1906–1917* (New York: Garland, 1990).

83. Prominent leaders like Schiff, Felix Warburg, and Louis Marshall formed the American Jewish Joint Distribution Committee in 1914 for this purpose.

84. For later debates, see Gary J. Bass, *Freedom's Battle: The Origins of Humanitarian Intervention* (New York: Vintage, 2008).

85. For example, see Zosa Szajkowski, "The Impact of the Beilis Case on Central and Western Europe," *Proceedings of the American Academy for Jewish Research* 31 (1963): 197–218.

86. Discussed further in David Vital, "Diplomacy in the Jewish Interest," in *Jewish History: Essays in Honor of Chimen Abramsky*, ed. Ada Rapoport-Albert and Steven Zipperstein (London: Halban, 1988), 683–95.

87. Jonathan Frankel, *Crisis, Revolution and Russian Jews* (Cambridge: Cambridge University Press, 2009), 137–38.

88. Carole Fink, *Defending the Rights of Others: The Great Powers, the Jews, and International Minority Protection, 1878–1938* (Cambridge: Cambridge University Press, 2004), 283–92.

89. For example, see Lisa Moses Leff, *Sacred Bonds of Solidarity: The Rise of Jewish Internationalism in Nineteenth-Century France* (Stanford, Calif.: Stanford University Press, 2006), 157, 160, 190–91; and Fink, *Defending the Rights*, 9, 16–17, 362–63.

90. Yaakov Kelner, *Reshitoh shel tikhnun hevrati klal-yehudi: Ha-hitarvut ha-memusedet ba-metsukat yehudei Russya be-reshit shanot ha-70 shel ha-meah ha-19* (Jerusalem: Hebrew University, 1975), 9.

91. For a more recent expression of concerns about the influx of masses of Jewish immigrants into the United States, see AJHS, I-410a, UCSJ, box 1, folder 10 (Manekofsky memo, November 25, 1978).

92. For a classic overview of efforts at this time, see Mark Wischnitzer, *To Dwell in Safety: The Story of Jewish Migration Since 1800* (Philadelphia: Jewish Publication Society, 1948), 67–96.

93. The following sources highlight the contrast: AJHS, William Korey Papers, P-903, box 8, folder "AJCSJ 7" (American Jewish Congress, Minutes of Executive Committee, November 17, 1970); interview of Yoram Dinstein, November 28, 1989, AJC interviews, 27; and, author's interview of Rabbi Richard Hirsch, Jerusalem, April 29, 2012.

94. Abigail Green, *Moses Montefiore: Jewish Liberator, Imperial Hero* (Cambridge, Mass.: Harvard University Press, 2010), 140, 168–69.

95. Jonathan Dekel-Chen, *Farming the Red Land: Jewish Agricultural Colonization and Local Soviet Power* (New Haven, Conn.: Yale University Press, 2005), chap. 3.

96. This view is shared, in part, by Feingold, *Jewish Power in America*, 58; and by Yaacov Ro'i, "The Achievements of the Jewish Movement," in *The Jewish Movement in the Soviet Union*, ed. Ro'i, 113–16.

Chapter 11. Anxieties of Distinctiveness

1. One report commissioned during the crisis found that 31 percent of respondents placed some degree of blame for it on Jews in the financial industry. See "Attitudes Toward Jews in Seven European Countries," Anti-Defamation League report, February 2009, 16, posted at www.adl.org.

2. Jonathan Karp, *The Politics of Jewish Commerce: Economic Thought and Emancipation in Europe, 1638–1848* (Cambridge: Cambridge University Press, 2008), 268–69; Derek J. Penslar, *Shylock's Children: Economics and Jewish Identity in Modern Europe* (Berkeley: University of California Press, 2001), 256–62; Jerry Z. Muller, *Capitalism and the Jews* (Princeton, N.J.: Princeton University Press, 2010), 1–3.

3. An exception to this is the work of the Hungarian historian and sociologist Victor Karady, particularly his *The Jews of Europe in the Modern Era* (Budapest: CEU Press, 2004). This volume, originally published in Hungarian in 2000, offers a theoretically

sophisticated analysis of modern European history, with particular reference to eastern Europe, in which he links Jewish cultural and economic distinctiveness in ways silently reminiscent of Sombart's work. Tellingly, this book has been largely ignored by Anglophone scholars. For another impressive exception, see Jonathan Karp, "Economic History and Jewish Modernity—Ideological Versus Structural Change," *Simon Dubnow Institute Yearbook* 6 (2007): 249–66.

4. For a recent survey see William H. Swatos Jr., and Lutz Kaelber, eds., *The Protestant Ethic Turns 100: Essays on the Centenary of the Weber Thesis* (Boulder, Colo.: Paradigm Publishers, 2005).

5. Werner Sombart, *The Jews and Modern Capitalism*, trans. M. Epstein (London: Unwin, 1913; repr. New Brunswick, N.J.: Transaction, 1982), 191–92, 249.

6. Reiner Grundmann and Nico Stehr, "Why Is Werner Sombart Not Part of the Core of Classical Sociology?" *Journal of Classical Sociology* 1 (2001): 257–87.

7. Matthew Lange, *Antisemitic Elements in the Critique of Capitalism in German Culture, 1850–1933* (Bern: Peter Lang, 2007), 215–27.

8. Friedrich Lenger, *Werner Sombart, 1863–1941: Eine Biographie* (Munich: Beck, 1994), 384; Rolf Rieß, "Werner Sombart Under National Socialism: A First Approximation," in *Werner Sombart (1863–1941): Social Scientist; Volume 1: His Life and Work*, ed. Jürgen Backhaus (Marburg: Metropolis, 1996), 193–204. For the best summary of Sombart's intellectual trajectory in English, see Arthur Mitzman, *Sociology and Estrangement: Three Sociologists of Imperial Germany* (New Brunswick, N.J.: Transaction, 1973), 135–266.

9. In contrast, Lenger, *Sombart*, 385–87, argues for a "non-teleological" reappraisal of Sombart's career.

10. Although unmarked in America or Britain, one significant German volume was published in association with this centenary: Nicolas Berg, ed, *Kapitalismusdebatten um 1900—Über antisemitisierende Semantiken des Jüdischen* (Leipzig: Leipziger Universitätsverlag, 2011).

11. Niall Ferguson, *The House of Rothschild: Money's Prophets, 1798–1848* (New York: Viking, 1998), 41.

12. David Landes, "The Jewish Merchant—Typology and Stereotypology in Germany," *Leo Baeck Institute Yearbook* 19 (1974): 22; Paul Mendes-Flohr, "Werner Sombart's *The Jews and Modern Capitalism*: An Analysis of Its Ideological Premises," *Leo Baeck Institute Yearbook* 21 (1976): 93. See also Jerry Z. Muller, "Kapitalismus, Rationalisierung und die Juden—Zu Simmel, Weber und Sombart," in *Kapitalismusdebatten*, ed. Berg, 23–48.

13. Jeffrey Herf, *Reactionary Modernism: Technology, Culture and Politics in Weimar and the Third Reich* (Cambridge: Cambridge University Press, 1984), 130–51; Kevin Repp, *Reformers, Critics, and the Paths of German Modernity: Anti-Politics and the Search for Alternatives, 1890–1914* (Cambridge, Mass.: Harvard University Press, 2000), 148–214.

14. Lenger, *Sombart*, 9.

15. See Mitzman, *Sociology and Estrangement*, 3–36; Harry Liebersohn, *Fate and Utopia in German Sociology, 1870–1923* (Cambridge, Mass.: MIT Press, 1988), esp. 1–10.

16. Mitzman, *Sociology and Estrangement*, 137–61.

17. Sam Whimster, *Understanding Weber* (London: Routledge, 2007), 29–47; David Frisby, preface to Georg Simmel, *The Philosophy of Money*, 3rd ed. (London: Routledge, 2004), xlvii–xlix.

18. On this debate, see Martin Riesebrodt, "Dimensions of the *Protestant Ethic*," in *Protestant Ethic*, ed. Swatos and Kaelber, 23–51.

19. See Toni Oelsner, "The Place of the Jews in Economic History as Viewed by German Scholars—a Critical-Comparative Analysis," *Leo Baeck Institute Yearbook* 7 (1962): 183–212.

20. David F. Lindenfeld, *The Practical Imagination: The German Sciences of State in the Nineteenth Century* (Chicago: University of Chicago Press, 1997), 283–84.

21. Simmel, *Philosophy of Money*, 223–25. See Amos Morris-Reich, "The Beautiful Jew Is a Moneylender: Money and Individuality in Simmel's Rehabilitation of the 'Jew,'" *Theory, Culture and Society* 20 (2003): 127–42.

22. Werner Sombart, *Die deutsche Volkswirtschaft in neunzehnten Jahrhundert* (Berlin: Bondi, 1903), 114–16. On this text see Mitzman, *Sociology and Estrangement*, 194–206.

23. Y. Michal Bodemann, "Ethnos, Race and Nation: Werner Sombart, the Jews and Classical German Sociology," *Patterns of Prejudice* 44 (2010): 117–36.

24. Ibid., 119–23, 127–32; Liebersohn, *Fate and Utopia*, 109–20; Lenger, *Sombart*, 201–7.

25. Max Weber, *Economy and Society*, ed. Guenther Roth and Claus Wittich (Berkeley: University of California Press, 1978 [1925]), 611–23; idem, *Ancient Judaism*, trans. and ed. Hans H. Gerth and Don Martindale (New York: The Free Press, 1952 [1917–19]), 336–55.

26. Sombart, *Jews*, 222–33.

27. See Jack Barbalet, "Max Weber and Judaism: An Insight into the Protestant Ethic Methodology," *Max Weber Studies* 6 (2006): 51–67; idem, *Weber, Passions and Profits* (Cambridge: Cambridge University Press, 2008), 183–213; Colin Loader, "Puritans and Jews: Weber, Sombart and the Transvaluators of Modern Society," *Canadian Journal of Sociology* 26 (2001): 635–53.

28. Bodemann, "Ethnos, Race and Nation," 128–29.

29. "Die Bedeutung des Einschlages jüdischer Elemente für Deutschlands Wirtschaftsleben," *Ost und West* 4, no. 1 (January 1904): 23–32.

30. Mitchell B. Hart, *Social Science and the Politics of Modern Jewish Identity* (Stanford, Calif.: Stanford University Press, 2000), 28–55; idem, "Jews, Race and Capitalism in the German-Jewish Context," *Jewish History* 19 (2005): 49–63, esp. 53–56.

31. Sombart, *Jews*, 30.

32. Ibid. See also Jonathan Karp, "Kopf ohne Körper? Wirtschaftsgeschicte jüdische Lebenswelten," in *Kapitalismusdebatten*, ed. Berg, 64. For the history of "Jewish

contribution" discourse, see Jeremy Cohen and Richard I. Cohen, eds., *The Jewish Contribution to Civilization: Reassessing an Idea* (London: Littman, 2008).

33. Sombart, *Jews*, 235–36.

34. Hart, *Social Science*, 61.

35. Lenger, *Sombart*, 213; Hart, "Jews, Race and Capitalism," 53.

36. See Etan Bloom, "What 'The Father' Had in Mind? Arthur Ruppin (1876–1943), Cultural Identity, Weltanschauung and Action," *History of European Ideas* 33 (2007): 330–49, esp. 338–41.

37. Amos Morris-Reich, "Arthur Ruppin's Concept of Race," *Israel Studies* 11 (2006): 1–30. On the wider entwinement of Zionism and racial science, see Raphael Falk, "Zionism, Race and Eugenics," in *Jewish Tradition and the Challenge of Darwinism*, ed. Geoffrey Cantor and Marc Swetlitz (Chicago: University of Chicago Press, 2006), 137–62.

38. Penslar, *Shylock's Children*, 165–66; Lenger, *Sombart*, 208.

39. Cited in Lenger, *Sombart*, 207.

40. Ibid., 210–14; Marjorie Lamberti, "From Coexistence to Conflict: Zionism and the Jewish Community in Germany, 1897–1914," *Leo Baeck Institute Yearbook* 27 (1982): 53–86, esp. 72; Ismar Schorsch, *Jewish Reactions to German Antisemitism, 1870–1914* (New York: Columbia University Press, 1972), 195–202.

41. Sombart, *Zukunft der Juden* (Leipzig: Duncker & Humblot, 1912), 5–6.

42. Ibid., 26–27, 32.

43. Ibid., 67.

44. Ibid., 52, 89–90.

45. Artur Landsberger, ed., *Judentaufen* (Munich: Georg Müller Verlag, 1912), 3.

46. Ibid., 7–20.

47. Wolf Lepenies, *Between Literature and Science: The Rise of Sociology* (Cambridge: Cambridge University Press, 1988), 298. On the wider significance and reception of this text, see Mitzman, *Sociology and Estrangement*, 243–53.

48. Werner Sombart, *The Quintessence of Capitalism*, trans. M. Epstein (New York: Howard Fertig, 1967), 100, 210–21.

49. Ibid., 263–66, 271–72.

50. Ibid., 274–75, 357.

51. Ibid., 359.

52. Mitzman, *Sociology and Estrangement*, 264.

53. Repp, *Reformers*, 191–214; Peter Pulzer, "The First World War," in *German-Jewish History in Modern Times; Volume 3: Integration in Dispute, 1871–1918*, ed. Michael A. Meyer (New York: Columbia University Press, 1997), 361–66.

54. Werner Sombart, *Händler und Helden* (Leipzig: Duncker & Humblot, 1915).

55. Werner Sombart, *Deutscher Sozialismus* (Berlin: Buchholz & Weisswange, 1934), xii, 192–95. On this text, see Herf, *Reactionary Modernism*, 146–51; Lenger, *Sombart*, 366–77.

56. Mendes-Flohr, "Sombart," 102; Repp, *Reformers*, 201; Muller, *Capitalism*, 60.

57. See Irving Louis Horowitz, "The Jews and Modern Communism: The Sombart Thesis Reconsidered," *Modern Judaism* 6 (1986): 13–25.

58. Samuel Z. Klausner "Werner Sombart's *The Jews and Modern Capitalism*: A Methodological Introduction," in *Jews*, ed. Sombart (New Brunswick, N.J.: Transaction, 1982), xv–cvi. For a recent anthology in English of Sombart's writings on economic themes, with a useful editorial introduction, see Werner Sombart, *Economic Life in the Modern Age*, ed. Nico Stehr and Reiner Grundmann (New Brunswick, N.J.: Transaction, 2001).

59. *Jewish Chronicle*, June 23, 1911, 19. See also Tobias Metzler, "Werner Sombart im Ausland—*Die Juden und das Wirtschaftsleben* in England, Amerika und Frankreich," in *Kapitalismusdibatten*, ed. Berg, 255–92.

60. Lenger, *Sombart*, 210; Repp, *Reformers*, 205.

61. Mortin Plotnik, *Werner Sombart and His Type of Economics* (New York: Eco Press, 1937), 11–17, 43.

62. Ellis Rivkin, *The Shaping of Jewish History* (New York: Scribner, 1971), xxvi, 140–69; Freddy Raphaël, *Judaïsme et capitalisme* (Paris: PUF, 1982).

63. Sombart, *Jews*, 266, 131.

64. Ibid., 65–67; Francesca Trivellato, "Images and Self-Images of Sephardic Merchants in Early Modern Europe and the Mediterranean," in *The Self-Perception of Early Modern Capitalists*, ed. Margaret C. Jacob and Catherine Secretan (New York: Palgrave Macmillan, 2009), 49–74, esp. 55–59.

65. Werner Sombart, in Landsberger, *Judentaufen*, 20.

66. Nicolaus Sombart, *Jugend in Berlin: 1933–43, Ein Bericht* (Munich: Hanser, 1984), 16–19.

67. Heinz Ludwig, "Sombart and the Jews," in *Sombart*, ed. Backhaus, 205–10; Salo W. Baron, "Changing Patterns of Antisemitism: A Survey," *Jewish Social Studies* 37 (1976): 28.

68. Sombart, *Jews*, 13.

69. Penslar, *Shylock's Children*, 165.

70. Moses Hoffmann, *Judentum und Capitalismus: Eine Kritische Würdigung von Werner Sombarts "Die Juden und das Wirtschaftsleben"* (Berlin: Itzkowski, 1912); Penslar, *Shylock's Children*, 167–70.

71. Jacob Katz, *Tradition and Crisis: Jewish Society at the End of the Middle Ages*, trans. Bernard Dov Cooperman (New York: New York University Press, 1993), 44–51.

72. Mordechai Levin, "De'ot ve-helikhot kalkaliyot ba-masoret: Behinat torato shel Sombart le-or sifrut ha-musar ve-ha-zikhronot" [in Hebrew], *Zion* 43 (1978): 235–63.

73. See for example, Daniel Gutwein, "Ha-yichus bein ha-yehudim ve-ha-kapitalism be-tfisato shel Marx" [in Hebrew], *Zion* 55 (1990): 419–47.

74. Werner Mosse, *The Jews in the German Economy: The German-Jewish Economic Elite 1820–1935* (Oxford: Oxford University Press, 1987), 23–31; idem, *The German-Jewish Economic Elite, 1820–1935: A Socio-Cultural Profile* (Oxford: Oxford University Press, 1989); idem, "Judaism, Jews and Capitalism: Weber, Sombart and Beyond," *Leo Baeck Institute Yearbook* 24 (1979): 3–15.

75. Jonathan I. Israel, *European Jewry in the Age of Mercantilism* (Oxford: Oxford University Press, 1985); idem, "Central European Jewry During the Thirty Years' War," *Central European History* 16 (1983): 3–30.

76. Jonathan I. Israel, *Diasporas Within a Diaspora: Jews, Crypto-Jews and the World Maritime Empires (1540–1740)* (Leiden: Brill, 2002), 2–5.

77. Natalie Zemon Davis, "Religion and Capitalism Once Again? Jewish Merchant Culture in the Seventeenth Century," *Representations* 59 (1997): 75–76.

78. Ibid., 79.

79. Eli Lederhendler, *Jewish Immigrants and American Capitalism, 1880–1920* (Cambridge: Cambridge University Press, 2009), ix–xxiii, 126–31; idem, "American Jews, American Capitalism and the Politics of History," in *Text and Context: Essays in Modern Jewish History*, ed. Jack Wertheimer, Eli Lederhendler, and Ismar Schorsch (New York: Jewish Theological Seminary of America, 2005), 504–46.

80. See Artur Eisenbach, "Jewish Historiography in Interwar Poland," in *The Jews of Poland Between Two World Wars*, ed. Yisrael Gutman, Ezra Mendelsohn, Jehuda Reinharz, and Chone Shmeruk (Hanover, N.H.: University Press of New England, 1989), 453–93.

81. For a prominent recent reengagement with Weber, see Margaret C. Jacob and Matthew Kadane, "Missing, Now Found in the Eighteenth Century: Weber's Protestant Capitalist," *American Historical Review* 108 (2003): 20–49.

82. Yuri Slezkine, *The Jewish Century* (Princeton, N.J.: Princeton University Press, 2004).

Index

List of Contributors

Cornelia Aust is research associate at the Leibniz-Institute for European History in Mainz, Germany. She is currently working on a book that examines Jewish appearances and their perceptions by Jews and non-Jews in seventeenth- to early nineteenth-century central and east-central Europe.

Bernard Dov Cooperman holds the Louis L. Kaplan Chair of Jewish History and is director of the Miller Center for Historical Studies, both at the University of Maryland, College Park. His research focuses on the social and cultural history of early modern Jews in Italy. His current project is an analysis of the Jewish ghetto in the context of broader urban history.

Veerle Vanden Daelen works at the Centre for Historical Research and Documentation on War and Contemporary Society (CEGESOMA) in Brussels. Her book on the return and reconstruction of Jewish life in Antwerp after the World War II was published under the title *Laten we hun lied verder zingen: De heropbouw van de joodse gemeenschap in Antwerpen na de Tweede Wereldoorlog (1944–1960)* (2008).

Jonathan Dekel-Chen is senior lecturer in Modern History at the Hebrew University of Jerusalem. His publications include *Farming the Red Land: Jewish Agricultural Colonization and Local Power in Soviet Russia, 1924–41* (2005). He coedited (with David Gaunt, Natan Meir, and Israel Bartal) *Anti-Jewish Violence: Rethinking the Pogrom in East European History* (2010). His current project focuses on Jewish transnational philanthropy and migration.

Glenn Dynner is professor of Religion and Chair of Humanities at Sarah Lawrence College. He is author of *Men of Silk: The Hasidic Conquest of Polish*

Jewish Society (2006), and *Yankel's Tavern: Jews, Liquor and Life in the Kingdom of Poland* (2013).

Abigail Green is tutor and fellow in Modern History at Brasenose College and associate professor at the University of Oxford. She is the author of *Moses Montefiore: Jewish Liberator, Imperial Hero* (2010), and coeditor (with Vincent Viaene) of *Religious Internationals in the Modern World: Globalization and Faith Communities Since 1750* (2012). She is currently working on a general history of liberalism and the Jews.

Jonathan Karp is an associate professor in the History and Judaic Studies Departments at Binghamton University, State University of New York. He is the author of *The Politics of Jewish Commerce* (2008) and coeditor (with Adam Sutcliffe) of *Philosemitism in History* (2011) and *The Cambridge History of Judaism in the Early Modern Period* (forthcoming). A former director of the American Jewish Historical Society, he is completing a monograph entitled *Chosen Surrogates: Blacks and Jews in American Culture.*

Rebecca Kobrin is the Russell and Bettina Knapp Associate Professor of American Jewish History at Columbia University. She has written *Jewish Bialystok and Its Diaspora* (2010), which was awarded the Jordan Schnitzer Prize in modern Jewish history, and is currently finishing a book entitled *A Credit to Their Nation: Immigrant Jewish Bankers and American Finance, 1873–1930* (forthcoming).

Adam D. Mendelsohn is associate professor of Jewish Studies and director of the Pearlstine/Lipov Center for Southern Jewish Culture at the College of Charleston. He specializes in the history of Anglophone Jewish communities in the period prior to eastern European mass migration and is the author of *The Rag Race: How Jews Sewed Their Way to Success in America and the British Empire* (2015) and the coeditor of *Transnational Traditions: New Perspectives on American Jewish History* (2014).

Derek Penslar is the Stanley Lewis Professor of Israel Studies at the University of Oxford and the Samuel Zacks Professor of European Jewish History at the University of Toronto. His books include *Shylock's Children: Economics and Jewish Identity in Modern Europe* (2001), *Israel in History: The Jewish State in Comparative Perspective* (2006), and *Jews and the Military: A History*

(2013). He is currently writing a biography of Theodor Herzl for Yale University Press's Jewish Lives series.

Adam Sutcliffe is senior lecturer in European History at King's College, London. He is the author of *Judaism and Enlightenment* (2003), and the coeditor (with Jonathan Karp) of *Philosemitism in History* (2011). He is currently working on a study of Jews, religion, and radical politics in France and Germany in the late eighteenth and early nineteenth centuries.

Adam Teller is associate professor of History and Judaic Studies at Brown University. His books, both written in Hebrew, are *Living Together: The Jewish Quarter of Poznan and Its Inhabitants in the Seventeenth Century* (2003), and *Money, Power, and Influence: The Jews on the Radziwill Estates in Eighteenth-Century Lithuania* (2005). His current project deals with the Polish Jewish refugee crisis caused by the Chmielnicki uprising of 1648 and subsequent wars in the Polish-Lithuanian Commonwealth.

Carsten L. Wilke is associate professor of Jewish Thought and Culture at the Central European University, Budapest. His publications on transcultural aspects of European Jewish history from the Middle Ages to the nineteenth century include *Jüdisch-christliches doppelleben im barock* (1994), *Den Talmud und den Kant: Rabbinerausbildung an der schwelle zur moderne* (2003), *Histoire des juifs portugais* (2007), and *The Marrakesh Dialogues: A Gospel Critique and Jewish Apology from the Spanish Renaissance* (2014). His current research concerns the German branches of the Alliance Israélite Universelle.